RESEARCH IN THE SOCIOLOGY OF WORK

A Research Annual

PERIPHERAL WORKERS

Editors: IDA HARPER SIMPSON
Department of Sociology
Duke University

RICHARD L. SIMPSON
Department of Sociology
University of North Carolina at Chapel Hill

VOLUME 2 • 1983

JAI PRESS INC.

Greenwich, Connecticut   London, England

Copyright © 1983 JAI PRESS INC.
36 Sherwood Place
Greenwich, Connecticut 06830

JAI PRESS INC.
3 Henrietta Street
London WC2E 8LU
England

All rights reserved. No part of this publication may be reproduced, stored on a retrieval system, or transmitted in any form or by any means, electronic, mechanical, photocopying, filming, recording or otherwise without prior permission in writing from the publisher.

ISBN: 0-89232-233-0

Manufactured in the United States of America

RESEARCH IN THE SOCIOLOGY OF WORK

Volume 2 • 1983

PERIPHERAL WORKERS

CONTENTS

LIST OF CONTRIBUTORS   vii

INTRODUCTION
   Ida Harper Simpson and Richard L. Simpson   ix

FROM PERIPHERY TO PERIPHERAL: THE SOUTH ASIAN PETITE BOURGEOISIE IN ENGLAND
   Howard Aldrich, John Cater, Trevor Jones, and Dave McEvoy   1

SOME BEHAVIORAL CONSEQUENCES OF WOMEN'S LABORS: A NONRECURSIVE MODEL
   Sarah Fenstermaker Berk   33

SECTORAL INFLUENCES ON OCCUPATIONAL SEX SEGRETATION
   Kim M. Blankenship   69

OLDER WORKERS: CURRENT STATUS AND FUTURE PROSPECTS
   Zena Smith Blau, George T. Oser, and Richard C. Stephens   101

NURSING TURNOVER IN LONG-TERM CARE INSTITUTIONS
   Linda K. George   125

INTERNATIONAL STAIR-STEP MIGRATION: DOMINICAN LABOR IN THE UNITED STATES AND HAITIAN LABOR IN THE DOMINICAN REPUBLIC
   Sherri Grasmuck   149

MIAMI'S GARMENT INDUSTRY AND ITS WORKERS
   Madeline J. Haug   173

MONASTIC OCCUPATIONS: A STUDY IN VALUES
   George A. Hillery, Jr.   191

WOMEN'S PAID LABOR IN THE HOME: THE
BRITISH EXPERIENCE
    Jane Hoy and Mary Kennedy — 211

THE TOURING TENNIS PROFESSIONAL:
A MIGRATORY WORKER
    Nancy G. Kutner — 241

SELF-EMPLOYMENT AS A CYCLICAL ESCAPE FROM
UNEMPLOYMENT: A CASE STUDY OF THE
CONSTRUCTION INDUSTRY IN THE UNITED STATES
DURING THE POSTWAR PERIOD
    Marc Linder — 261

DRUGS AS WORK
    Peter K. Manning and Lawrence J. Redlinger — 275

SUCCESS, FAILURE, AND ANOMIE IN ARTS AND
CRAFTS WORK: BREAKING IN TO COMMERCIAL
COUNTRY MUSIC SONGWRITING
    Richard A. Peterson and John Ryan — 301

THE EMERGENCE OF PART-TIME FARMING AS A
SOCIAL FORM OF AGRICULTURE
    Ronald C. Wimberley — 325

CHINESE SWEATSHOPS IN THE UNITED STATES:
A LOOK AT THE GARMENT INDUSTRY
    Morrison G. Wong — 357

LIST OF CONTRIBUTORS

Howard Aldrich Department of Sociology, University of North Carolina at Chapel Hill

Sarah Fenstermaker Berk Department of Sociology, University of California, Santa Barbara

Kim M. Blankenship Department of Sociology, Duke University

Zena Smith Blau Department of Sociology, University of Houston

John Cater Edge Hill College of Further Education, Ormskirk, England

Linda K. George Departments of Psychiatry and Sociology, Duke University

Sherri Grasmuck Department of Sociology, Temple University

Madeline J. Haug Department of Sociology and Social Psychology, Florida Atlantic University

George A. Hillery, Jr. Department of Sociology, Virginia Polytechnic Institute and State University

Jane Hoy Department of Extra-Mural Studies, University of London, England

Trevor Jones Department of Social Studies, Liverpool Polytechnic, England

Mary Kennedy Department of Extra-Mural Studies, University of London, England

Nancy G. Kutner Department of Rehabilitation Medicine, Emory University School of Medicine

Marc Linder Harvard Law School

Peter K. Manning	Departments of Sociology and Psychiatry, Michigan State University
Dave McEvoy	Department of Social Studies, Liverpool Polytechnic, England
George T. Oser	Department of Community Medicine, University of Texas Medical School at Houston
Richard A. Peterson	Department of Sociology, Vanderbilt University
Lawrence J. Redlinger	Program in Political Economy, University of Texas at Dallas
John Ryan	Department of Sociology, Vanderbilt University
Richard C. Stephens	Department of Sociology, Cleveland State University
Ronald C. Wimberley	Department of Sociology and Anthropology, North Carolina State University
Morrison G. Wong	Department of Sociology, Texas Christian University

INTRODUCTION

This volume is about peripheral work and workers. We define these as (1) part-time, seasonal, and moonlighting work, (2) work peripheral to the main economy, e.g., hustling, gambling, sweatshop work, and (3) workers who are outside the normal labor force such as children, the elderly, and undocumented aliens. All authors address aspects of the topic.

Several authors integrate ideas from dual economy, world systems, and/or segmented labor force perspectives to examine minority group workers in peripheral industries. Chapters by Haug on Miami Cubans and Wong on Chinese immigrants analyze structures of sweatshop and domestic labor in garment manufacturing. In both groups, the vast majority of workers are women. As Haug observes, the availability of these secondary labor forces delays the flight of the industry to Third World countries. Wong shows how the subcontracting system perpetuates sweatshops. Grasmuck refines the world systems conceptualization of core vs. periphery in showing why a country may simultaneously have the migration patterns normally seen in both. The Dominican Republic imports Haitians while exporting its own workers to the United States. Grasmuck examines the system that makes this profitable, including formal and informal agreements of the Dominican government with Haiti and with U.S. corporations. Aldrich, Cater, Jones, and McEvoy look at South Asians in England. They analyze the opportunity structure that enables some of these migrants to become small shopkeepers, and the barriers that inhibit others from escaping manual labor. The authors assess, pessimistically, the prospects of South Asians' becoming fully integrated into the British economy.

Two chapters treat work and workers in low-wage personal service occupations. George examines causes of turnover among nursing personnel in long-term care institutions, a peripheral category within the nursing field. She finds that structural characteristics of work organizations have more impact on turnover rates than personal characteristics of workers. Hoy and Kennedy study British women who work for pay as childminders in their own homes. They argue that governmental inattention to the plight of these workers reflects traditional attitudes: to regulate homeworking conditions would intrude into the "private sphere" of the family. The formal neutrality of the state makes it, in effect, a defender of the subordination of women.

Three other chapters look at disadvantaged categories of workers. Blankenship shows that sex differences in earnings are due partly to concentration of predominantly female occupations in peripheral industries, and that the effect of occupational sex segregation is greater in the core sector than in the periphery. Her analysis is the first empirical test of some major predictions from dual economy theory. Berk summarizes research on the division of household labor and develops models to explore relations between the amounts of time women spend in household labor, market labor, alcohol and tranquilizer use, and feelings of anger. Blau, Oser, and Stephens survey literature on patterns of full-time and part-time work and retirement among elderly men and women. They report new survey data to show, among other things, that whether one's working or being retired is modal or deviant to one's age group has more effect on social activity and mental health than does working or being retired per se.

Linder's and Wimberley's chapters deal with irregular or part-time work. Linder analyzes relations between rates of unemployment and self-employment in the construction industry. He finds that self-employment often is not a step up, but a temporary stopgap during periods of unemployment. Wimberley examines trends in part-time farming. It has grown steadily for more than two decades; part-timers now are about half of all farmers. Data on off-farm occupations and total income suggest that non-farm work contributes to the survival of farming. Full-time family farmers are increasingly marginal. Part-time farming is a transitional stage in exit from farming for some workers, an entry phase for others, and a lifelong career pattern for others.

Two studies concern work that is peripheral to the mainstream in quite different ways. Hillery shows how the religious values of Trappist-Cistercian monks permeate and structure their work of running monasteries as self-supporting

Introduction xi

economic organizations. Manning and Redlinger analyze the work roles of illegal drug marketing and of attempts to control or eradicate it. They describe the complex web of social relationships that connects the police with different kinds of drug sellers.

Two chapters examine marginal or would-be workers who aspire to success but must cope with failure. Kutner analyzes the structure of contemporary regional tennis tournament circuits and the incentives and travails of run-of-the-mill professional players who must struggle to be allowed to compete in a marginal labor market. Peterson and Ryan delineate the production system of the country music industry, the barriers it erects against aspiring songwriters, and frustrated songwriters' reactions to failure. The broader significance of their analysis is its generalizability to other competitive arts and crafts where "breaking in" rather than routine vocational training or working one's way up an orderly ladder is the pattern of career entry and success.

We believe that this collection of papers contributes to the understanding of peripheral work and the structural conditions that generate and support it. Later volumes will focus on different themes.

Ida Harper Simpson
Richard L. Simpson
Series Editors

FROM PERIPHERY TO PERIPHERAL:
THE SOUTH ASIAN PETITE BOURGEOISIE IN ENGLAND

Howard Aldrich, John Cater,
Trevor Jones and Dave McEvoy

I. INTRODUCTION

England's emergence as a dominant power in the nineteenth-century capitalist world economy went hand in hand with the growth of a colonial empire. The South Asian subcontinent, the West Indies, and East Africa were incorporated into Britain's empire as sources of raw materials and as markets for finished goods. Population movement was from Great Britain to the colonies, but that pattern began to change after World War II. As the colonial system broke up, newly independent nation-states found themselves on the periphery of the world economy, cast into a subordinate role by their decades of economic and political dependence. Attracted by opportunities in Great Britain and frustrated by conditions at home, thousands of "colored" migrants poured into England's cities and towns. The jobs they found were primarily those that native whites had abandoned as they shifted vertically into better-paying jobs and horizontally into newly developed industries (Nowikowski, 1980). In short, workers found they had moved from countries on the periphery of the world economy to peripheral jobs on the fringe of the British economy.

One niche on the economic periphery is of special interest: self-employment in the distributive trades. Immigrant labor has played an important role in the post World War II growth of Western European economies, as immigrants constitute a disproportionate share of the industrial labor force of countries such as France, West Germany, and England. Small shopkeepers and other self-employed workers have been overlooked by researchers, who have focused mainly on industrial workers and their employment in poorly paid positions. Part of this neglect stemmed from the evident underrepresentation of ethnic minorities in self-employment, a situation which is now changing in those English cities with substantial concentrations of South Asian immigrants and their descendants. Recently, investigators have documented the growth of a South Asian petite bourgeoisie (Mullins, 1979; Aldrich, 1980), raising the question of whether the Asian minority in England is becoming better integrated into the economy. Alternatively, increased self-employment may merely signify Asian occupancy of yet another peripheral economic niche vacated by whites. We will consider these two hypotheses in our report on research conducted in four English cities between 1975 and 1978.

Work in the petit bourgeois sector is often taken as an indicator of the economic and social standing of an ethnic or racial minority. In the United States, for example, ownership and control of small businesses by groups such as the Chinese, Japanese, and Jews has been a vital instrument of social mobility. From this starting block, these minorities have propelled themselves toward a measure of economic parity with the majority society (Light, 1972). Conversely, the underrepresentation of American blacks in small business has been viewed as a serious obstacle to their social advancement (Foley, 1966). If business success is truly a catalyst for social advancement, then the Asian communities of Britain possess enormous potential for upward mobility (Cater and Jones, 1978). However, close examination of the conditions under which Asians have entered the petite bourgeoisie in England reveals a less sanguine picture.

II. SOUTH ASIANS IN GREAT BRITAIN

Large-scale immigration of nonwhites to Great Britain is an historically recent phenomenon, beginning after World War II and increasing significantly in the 1950s. West Indians, and Asians from Pakistan, India, and East Africa settled mainly in the urban areas of the Southeast, the West Midlands, and West Yorkshire. From the beginning, nonwhites were occupationally and residentially concentrated.

A. Immigration

The nonwhite or "New Commonwealth" population of Great Britain grew very rapidly in the late 1950s and through the 1960s. In the mid-1950s, immigration controls were not widely discussed, although apparently the Atlee government (1945-1951) was concerned about the level of immigration. Then, between 1955 and 1960, about 219,000 persons from the West Indies, Pakistan, and India emigrated to Great Britain. The first anti-immigration calls were heard in Parliament in 1958, partly as a response to racially motivated disorders during the summer of that year. By 1960, when the Indian government eliminated its voluntary controls over emigration to England, concern had mounted over the possibility of increased immigration from New Commonwealth (i.e., nonwhite) nations. Possibly in anticipation of immigration controls, immigration rose in 1961-1962 to over 130,000, and in the summer of 1962 controls were introduced via the Commonwealth Immigration Act.

Immigration controls were gradually strengthened, and by 1966 essentially the only nonwhites admitted were dependents of those already in Great Britain (39,130) and persons with special skills or prearranged jobs (5,141). Although some people continue to dispute the efficacy of immigration control, for all practical purposes the only significant source of population growth for nonwhites is natural increase—children born to parents who were immigrants. The last census of Great Britain was taken in 1971, and it estimated the "colored" population at 1,385,600 of whom 555,400 or 40% were native-born. More-recent estimates put the proportion of nonwhites in the population at approximately 4%.

Immigrants from South Asia to Great Britain can be separated into three categories (Nowikowski, 1980): (1) persons from business families, mainly in textiles, who migrated as agents for their families and firms, in response to changes in British international trade; (2) persons from the rural middle strata of the peasantry and from the urban nonagricultural, nonindustrial work force who migrated to take up vacancies in the work force as unskilled or semiskilled laborers, especially in declining traditional industries; and (3) persons from the Western-oriented educated and professional middle classes, who responded to opportunities for skilled and professional labor, especially in the medical services where they constitute a high proportion of the nurses, interns, and junior doctors in the National Health Service.

B. Residential Concentrations in Urban Areas

Nonwhites have settled overwhelmingly in the urbanized areas that have lost a large proportion of their native white residents, thus taking advantage of the job and housing opportunities opened up. Within urbanized areas, Asians and other nonwhites have tended to settle in highly concentrated districts, partly out of choice and partly because of several constraining forces.

1. Housing and Employment Patterns

Population statistics indicate that a suburban shift of the white population is occurring in England, just as it has in the United States. The inner-city population of London, for example, decreased from 5 million to 3 million between 1921 and 1971, while the population of the outer areas increased from 2.4 million to 4.4 million. These net changes masked an absolute decrease in the size of the native white population and an absolute increase in the size of the immigrant population. The total population of London decreased by 4% from 1951 and 1961, whereas the immigrant population increased by 44% (Davison, 1966). Indeed, the largest single grouping of nonwhites is in the Greater London conurbation: as of 1970, 34% of the Indians, 21% of the Pakistanis, and 56% of the West Indians lived there, compared to only 15% of the total population of Great Britain.

The settlement pattern of nonwhites is an example of ecological succession (Aldrich, 1975) on a national scale, as decreases in cities' indigenous populations were followed by increases in their nonwhite populations. Almost two-thirds of the New Commonwealth immigrants settled in the major conurbations, where the decline in the indigenous population was about 618,000 by 1970. Few nonwhites are found in towns with expanding white populations, and they are almost completely absent from the "new" towns (Jones and Smith, 1970).

Regions attracting nonwhites have been those unable to attract or hold a sufficiently large white labor force for their needs. The increased share of the work force represented by nonwhites, especially in semiskilled manual labor (Smith, 1974), reflected, in part, the absence of white competition (Peach, 1968). Tilly et al. (1965) described a similar process of white-to-black occupational succession in the United States.

2. Choice and Constraint

Within urbanized areas, Asians and other nonwhites are residentially clustered, with concentrations quite high in many cities. Precise comparisons with figures on racial residential segregation in the United States are difficult to make, because British Census data are collected on a different spatial scale than United States data. Some investigators have used "wards," which are 10 to 20 times larger than United States Census tracts, as their units of analysis, thus missing the street-by-street pattern of residential segregation. At the other extreme, the British Census collects data at the Enumeration District level, which are one-tenth to one-twentieth the size of United States Census tracts and which provide rather unstable percentage figures. Nonetheless, the available comparisons are rather illuminating.

Lomas and Monck (1975) studied residential segregation in Bradford, Leicester, Manchester, and Wolverhamton, using ward-level data. Using the index of dissimilarity as a segregation index, they found coefficients of between .38 and .55, in contrast to typical figures for United States cities of .80 or higher (Taeuber and Taeuber, 1965). In all four cities, New Commonwealth-origin residents were concentrated at the core, with three of the four having one central ward more than 40% New Commonwealth, with proportions falling off rapidly away from the city center. Ethnic distributions by wards closely resembled the pattern for United States cities prior to World War I and the great northward migration of southern blacks.

Blackburn is a city losing some of its white population. Asians have replaced many of these former residents, and Robinson found the index of dissimilarity for Asians in Blackburn had actually increased from 1968 to 1977, from .50 to .55, using ward-level data. He noted that when the index was calculated at the street level, it increased to .75, "demonstrating very marked spatial segregation" (Robinson, 1979:395). The extent of bias introduced by using wards as units of analysis was noted in research conducted by two of the authors (McEvoy and Jones, 1978) in Huddersfield, near Bradford. Using streets and blocks as units of analysis, they found an index of dissimilarity of about .80 between the residential distribution of Asians and whites.

These results, and observations made during fieldwork for this study, confirm that the Asian and West Indian populations are rather highly segregated from the white population, although not to the degree found in the United States. Explanations for this pattern stress two types of factors—those concerning "choice" and "constraint" (Mullins, 1979; Lee, 1977). Constraints on the intraurban settlement of Asians and West Indians are similar to those faced by blacks in the United States: white hostility and discrimination, low economic standing in the labor market, reliance on immigrants for knowledge of housing opportunities, and generally an inability to gain access to most parts of the housing market (Rex and Tomlinson, 1979). Estate agents play the same sort of brokerage role in England as in the United States, guided by a conception of the "proper use" of an area and thus systematically referring nonwhites to "immigrant" areas (Karn, 1978; Cater, 1981). Choice factors revolve around the positive force of voluntary association with cultural peers. Concentrated minority communities develop mutually reinforcing and supporting economic and social networks, and thus tend to attract persons unwilling to live as isolated "pioneers" in nearly all-white neighborhoods.

3. Employment Consequences of Concentration

Whatever the balance between choice and constraint in the formation of ethnically concentrated settlements, the employment consequences are clear enough—job opportunites are restricted to sites accessible from residential locations. In the United States, research has shown that residential segregation systematically limits black employment opportunities, especially in view of the massive suburbanization of economic activity since World War II (Aldrich, 1975). In Great Britain, research on the disadvantaged position of ethnic minorities has focused more on the characteristics of minority workers and employers than on spatial considerations, but work by Peach (1968), Rex and Tomlinson (1979) and others lends indirect support to this argument. For example, Rex and Tomlinson (1979:115) found that West Indian and Asian workers commuted much farther to their jobs than whites.

Our interest lies not with the average worker, but rather in a special subcategory: the self-employed. To what extent have the developments discussed above facilitated the growth of a South Asian petite bourgeoisie, by limiting other employment opportunities for Asians and by providing opportunities to serve a concentrated population?

III. SOUTH ASIANS IN THE ENGLISH PETITE BOURGEOISIE

As mature industrial economies, those of England and the United States present a different set of opportunities to potential small-business persons than the economics of developing nations on the periphery of the world capitalist system. The interorganizational division of labor is quite complex, a factor creating numerous opportunities for innovative business persons, but barriers to entry have closed off many business possibilities still available in less complex economies. We will review the trends affecting the petite bourgeoisie in England and then focus on the situation of Indians and Pakistanis.

A. The Petite Bourgeoisie in England

The category of "petite bourgeoisie" includes small shopkeepers, artisans, and others who work on their own account. We examine small shopkeepers because they are the most visible component of the petite bourgeoisie and are the group traditionally thought of as the backbone of this class. Small shopkeepers are a "transitional form" in the transformation from simple commodity production to monopolistic competition under advanced capitalism (Brenner, 1977). They exploit themselves by working long hours so as to hold on to their property, whereas they could probably earn more for their labor by selling it to an employer. Similarly, they are undercapitalized and resist investing in modern labor-saving (capital-intensive) equipment because it would increase the size of their fixed investment and render them more vulnerable to market fluctuations.

As Asians have tended to settle in the inner areas of declining industrial cities, we turn our attention to the situation of small shopkeepers in the inner city. Major factors affecting the viability of small shopkeeping include the secular trend of increasing concentration of economic activity in larger units, especially in retailing, and the decentralization of economic activity to the suburbs. Retailing in Great Britain is highly centralized, as compared to that in Western Europe and the United States, due to a high degree of urbanization and the weakness of voluntary associations of small shopkeepers, especially relative to Italy or France (Smith, 1971; Piore and Berger, 1980). The number of small shopkeepers has followed a trend similar to that of the self-employed sectors as a whole. From 1921 to 1939 there was a rapid expansion of small shops, followed by a rapid decline until 1951, and a more modest decline thereafter. By 1966 the number of small shops was down to about a half-million, after a brief increase in the late 1950s (Bechhofer et al., 1971).

After World War II, demographic changes involving population redistribution from city cores to suburban areas may have had the effect of creating new outlets for retailers. However, many suburban sites were in high-rent shopping centers, favoring the larger over the smaller shops, paralleling similar developments in the United States (Zimmer, 1964). Small shops were hurt by municipal parking regulations designed to cope with increasing traffic congestion, and municipal housing programs destroyed some neighborhood markets and rearranged others. Since 1950, chain stores have accounted for an increasing proportion of retail establishments and gross receipts.

A number of factors thus make the establishment of a small shop in the inner city rather difficult. Economic concentration has erected high barriers to entry in many industries, and a high rate of inflation has made it difficult for workers to save the necessary capital for a new business. Manufacturers and wholesalers are interested in high turnover outlets and consequently their policies favor large over small businesses. Population redistribution has cost older small businesses parts of their traditional central city neighborhoods, in spite of attempts by city planners to preserve the inner city.

B. Asian Entry into Small Shopkeeping

Problems facing small shopkeepers in advanced industrial societies were presented in some detail in Section III. A, because we want to emphasize the difference between Asians' entry into shopkeeping in England versus developing societies. Asian business persons have been labeled "middleman minority" shopkeepers because of their position in developing economies in East Africa, the Caribbean, Malaysia, and elsewhere (Bonacich, 1973). They confront fundamentally different conditions in England (and the rest of the United Kingdom), and their situation is best described by the phrase "occupational succession," as they enter niches whites have vacated.

1. Extent of Asian Self-Employment

Two characteristics of South Asians' self-employment must be noted so that our research is seen in its proper context: (1) proportionately fewer Asians than native whites are self-employed; and (2) the Asian petite bourgeoisie is quite distinct from an extremely small, but highly visible, number of Asian "big bourgeoisie."

First, contrary to the popular stereotype in England, the level of self-employment for South Asian males is only about 8%, in contrast to 12% for native white males (Smith, 1976), as of 1975. The Political and Economic Planning (PEP) survey also found that 64% of the self-employed Asians were in the distributive trades, and that most had no nonfamily employees. The 1966 British Census for the Greater London conurbation found that about 4% of Indian males and 6% of Pakistani males were self-employed, while in the West Midlands conurbation about 3% of Indian males and 2% of Pakistani males were self-employed. Rex and Tomlinson (1979:111), in their study of the Handsworth area of Birmingham, found only 2% the Asians were self-employed (as unskilled workers, not business owners), compared to 4% of the whites (most of whom were also unskilled "own account" workers). As is the case in the white population, the vast majority of South Asians are employees, rather than self-employed.

Second, most Asian shopkeepers become business persons on the basis of capital accumulated in England. These persons must be distinguished from the small number of established bourgeois entrepreneurs that migrated "to the West in connection with trade and business activities rooted in the developing world" (Nowikowski, 1980:225). In Manchester, Leeds, London, and other textile centers, small numbers of Asian import-export merchants and industrialists have been economically active for decades. Our research was not designed to study these persons, whose wealth and business connections qualify them as part of the bourgeoisie proper. Clearly, however, they constitute an insignificant (but highly visible) proportion of the Asian employed population.

2. *Explaining Asian Entry into Small Shopkeeping*

Two sets of factors should be distinguished in models designed to explain Asian entry into shopkeeping—those concerning forces opening up *opportunities* for Asians to enter business and those predisposing factors making it possible for Asians to *take advantage of* the opportunities as they arise. Given space and data limitations, our analysis in the results section will focus mainly on the former, although we will present some information on the latter.

a. Predisposing Factors. Occupational closure, immigrant status, and the organizing capacity of the South Asian population could potentially predispose Asians to take advantage of opportunities to enter business for themselves. Occupational closure, because of native whites' prejudice and hostility, closes off some job opportunities, forcing Asians to seek employment below their skill level or else create their own employment opportunity by forming a small business. Lawrence (1974), Hiro (1973), Smith (1976), and others have documented the extent of employment discrimination against nonwhites in England, showing that "color" is more important that immigrant status in accounting for the relatively poor occupational position of nonwhites. Bonacich (1973:583) argued that some ethnic minorities respond to discrimination with "a closing of ranks, the formation of solidary communities with considerable pride in group membership, and a special exertion to overcome handicaps."

Immigrant status might be indirectly related to business creation insofar as it gives a "sojourner orientation" to Asians' stay in England. Immigrants with a short-term outlook ultimately intend to return to their country of origin, and thus are oriented towards making the most of their short stay. A short time perspective gives immigrants a preference for acquiring easily liquidated assets, and small shops fulfull this preference. This hypothesis has been used to explain Asian predominance in shopkeeping in East Africa and the Caribbean (Dotson and Dotson, 1968; Niehoff and Niehoff, 1960). Lawrence (1974) conducted the only systematic study of this phenomenon in England, and his results confirm the results of two participant observations studies that documented the existence of a sojourner orientation among a large proportion of Asian immigrants (Hiro, 1971; Dahya, 1974). Given developments in the past decade, including the high proportion of the current nonwhite population born in the United Kingdom, the concept of a "sojourner orientation" may increasingly be of historical relevance only (Cater, 1981).

The organizing capacity of an ethnic group refers to values and orientations, family organization, and other group attributes affecting their ability to concentrate resources on projects such as forming businesses. Kinship ties have been an important instrument in the creation and survival of small businesses for many ethnic groups. Such ties permit a more rapid and efficient accumulation of capital than an isolated individual could achieve. Kinship-based organizations are a means for developing entrepreneurial talent, through apprenticeship systems and socialization into business skills. In tightly knit ethnic communities, these functions often extend beyond the bounds of kinship.

b. Opportunity Structure. Sociocultural factors help explain why a minority group is quick to seize business opportunities, but such models often overlook the crucial structural conditions that logically precede business ownership. In a mature industrial economy, with population concentrated in heavily built-up urban areas, and with economic growth proceeding slowly or not at all, would-be shopkeepers must wait for vacancies to open up before they can establish themselves. Such conditions prevail in most English industrial cities, where very little new retail development is occurring. New development is either in downtown or suburban shopping malls, both of which attract regional or national chain store operations rather than locally owned shops. Local owners simply cannot meet the credit rating requirements of new developments.

Two processess thus account for most of the opportunities open to Asians desiring to establish themselves in shopkeeping: occupational and residential succession. Occupation succession was briefly described in Section II.B.1, as we pointed out that nonwhite immigrants to Great Britain since World War II have taken jobs abandoned by whites as they moved into better-paying positions or better working conditions. As we noted in Section III.A, small shopkeepers are highly vulnerable to economic misfortune, and survive only by working long hours and underpaying themselves and their families. Our impression is that many white shopkeepers have abandoned their shops in the 1970s, as evidenced by the high proportion of vacancies in inner-city areas as well as the high proportion of aged whites in our sample surveys. We are currently conducting a longitudinal study to determine the attrition rate among white shopkeepers, and the 1981 British Census will provide information on changes in the average age of the self-employed since 1971.

Residential (or ecological) succession refers to the process by which one ethnic or racial group leaves an area and is replaced by another (Aldrich, 1975). The precondition for succession is set when the established residential group in an area no longer replaces itself, whether because of upward mobility into "better" areas, stage in the life cycle, or other factors. Withdrawal of the established group opens up opportunities for expansion into the area by a new group seeking housing because of upward mobility, crowding in their previous area, or perhaps the conversion of their old area to a new use, as in urban renewal. All three of these conditions characterize the South Asian population in British cities.

Just as residential succession opens up housing opportunities for Asians, as whites leave inner-city areas for the suburbs business opportunities are also made available. Thus a tendency develops for areas with high proportions of Asian residents to have high proportions of Asian shops. The association between residential composition and Asian shop ownership does *not* result from white owners leaving racially changing areas at an increased rate but rather from the failure of whites to buy into the area. As an area's white residential population declines, shops left vacant through the normal process of business turnover—at least one in ten per year—are not occupied by new white owners. Potential white owners define the racially changing area as undesirable, and consequently the market for vacant shops is made up almost entirely of Asians.

Changes in the ethnic residential composition of areas are typically also accompanied by some deterioration in economic status. Asians tend to have jobs not paying as well as whites', and religious strictures against working wives in the Muslim community also reduce family income. Consequently, racially changing areas become less economically attractive for white owners searching for new sites.

For their part, potential Asian shopkeepers, economizing on search costs, tend to look for business opportunities near where they live. Mullins (1979:404), in his study of Croydon, found that "Most Asian businesses occupy relatively small, old, low-rent premises and these premises are concentrated in the same areas as Asian residents, areas where the urban fabric developed at an earlier date." Obviously, not all Asians seek sites near their residences, given their economic aspirations, and not all persons seeking nearby sites can be accommodated. Thus, the association between residential and business composition is not perfect. Mullins, for example, found that about one-quarter of Croydon's Asian shops are located in areas with few local Asians.

c. *Summary.* Through occupational succession, whites moving on to more desirable jobs have opened up slots (in the petite bourgeoisie) to Asians. Because of residential succession, a high proportion of these jobs are located in areas of high minority concentration. Our research design focused on these opportunity structure propositions, or the "demand side" of the issue, because we felt that "supply side" propositions overestimated the number of projected Asian shopkeepers. Occupational closure, immigrant status, and a high potential organizing capacity characterize the situation of many South Asians in England, and yet only a small fraction have become shopkeepers. We believe the structural factors of occupational and residential succession account for this, and accordingly the remainder of this chapter focuses mainly on these processes.

IV. STUDY DESIGN

Our research was conducted in two stages: (1) an initial pilot study in 1975-1976 in the borough of Wandsworth, London, and (2) a larger follow-up study in three new areas in 1978.

A. The Wandsworth Study

The borough of Wandsworth, London, has a population of about 300,000 and lies just south of the river Thames, below Westminster and Chelsea. It was chosen because its twenty wards varied from 2% to 21% in New Commonwealth-origin population, it contained a large number of Asian-owned shops, and a large number of Asians had settled there after their expulsion from Uganda in 1971-1972. In December 1975, a complete enumeration of all 2,590 businesses in Wandsworth was made, based on direct observation of the commercial activity on each street. In the spring of 1976, a target sampling list of 132 Asian businesses was drawn up, including all known Asian shops in the borough. Interviews were obtained at 74 for a completion rate of 56%, with all interviewing conducted by Asian interviewers.

A white-owned sample was drawn from the 1975 business census list in a way that maximized its comparability with the Asian sample. All chain-owned shops with more than 5 sites were excluded. As Asians were concentrated in a few lines of trade, the white sample was limited to the following industries: grocery and food sales, newsagents, confectioners, and tobacconists; restaurants; clothing shops; chemists; and consumer household durables. A systematic sample was drawn, yielding 105 businesses. White interviewers obtained interviews at 47 sites, for a completion rate of 45%. As with the Asian sampling list, a few shops had changed hands or been misclassified, and thus some of these interviews were with nonwhites. (Another 100 interviews were obtained in the spring of 1977 from whites and Asians, but that information is not used in this report.)

B. The Three-City Study

Three urban areas were selected for the follow-up study: the cities of Bradford and Leicester and the borough of Ealing, in greater London, each with a 1971 population of about 300,000. All three areas were distinguished by relatively high proportions of Asian immigrants, with Indians outnumbering Pakistanis in Earling and Leicester, including a sizable number of Asians born in East Africa. In Bradford, Pakistanis outnumbered Indians. Within each area, the 5 wards with the highest proportion of New Commonwealth-origin immigrants were selected (out of a total of 19 wards in Bradford, 16 in Leicester, and 20 in Ealing). There was substantial within-ward variation between neighborhoods in the proportion of Asians. In practice, large parts of most wards were virtually devoid of Asians (Cater and Jones, 1979), and thus it was possible for us to relate variations in Asian population level to the level of Asian business activity, using 500-m^2 areas.

As in Wandsworth, a complete business census of each ward was prepared, using city tax lists. Chain-owned shops and cooperatives were dropped from the study. Through field observation, the ethnicity of business owners was identified. In each of the three urban areas, 100 Asian and 100 white shops were randomly selected for interviews, with the number drawn in each ward proportional to the total number of Asian (or white) shops in the ward. Reserve samples were also selected in anticipation of completion problems (see Aldrich et al., 1979, for details).

The white sample for each area was subject to two quota requirements: (1) as in Wandsworth, business types were drawn from the same categories as in the Asian business population, and (2) the number of white shops sampled in a ward was proportional to the total number of white shops in the ward. Interviews were conducted in the summer of 1978, with the ethnicity of interviewers matched to that of the shopkeepers (Asian or white) in nearly all cases. A total of 580 interviews out of the target of 600 were completed.

C. Population Estimates

Both studies required that we collect estimates of the Asian residential population of an area so that our hypothesis about residential succession could be tested. In Wandsworth, information on the population composition of the 19 wards was obtained from the 1971 census. Determining the ethnic or racial composition of the British population is difficult, as only birthplace, not "race," is recorded by the census. We calculated the nonwhite population in two ways: (1) the percentage of the population in a ward with both parents born in the New Commonwealth; and (2) the percentage of children under 14 whose parents were born in the New Commonwealth. The latter indicator was used because it is the best predictor of the school population's composition, which in turn is an important determinant of potential white residents' feelings about moving into an area.

The range of the first indicator was 2% to 21%, with a mean of 11.4% and standard deviation of 5.8%, whereas the range of the second indicator was 5% to 35%, with a mean of 19.8% and standard deviation of 10.0%. Because of resource limitations, we were forced to conduct the analysis of population data at the ward level, which have average populations of 15,000. These large areas mask a great deal of geographical variation, as some small neighborhoods had very high concentrations of Asians and others had almost none.

In the three-city follow-up study, we dealt with the geographical aggregation problem by dividing each of the 15 wards into 100-m^2 grids. The Asian and white population for each square was obtained from the names and addresses given in each city's Electoral Register. Electoral Registers are within a year of being up to date, and "Asians" were counted by identifying "Asian" names. Shops were also assigned to these squares, using the business census and address list for each ward, with the number of all shops and Asian shops recorded for each square.

For purposes of analysis, the 100-m^2 grids were aggregated into blocks of 500 m^2. These 211 blocks in the 15 wards each contained an average of 735 residents, of whom 227 were Asian, and 16 shops, of which 5 were Asian.

Table 1 presents information on the relationship between ward population and business composition for the three-city study. In the first column we give the Asian population figure, as estimated from the 1971 census, so that it may be contrasted with the estimates based on the Electoral Registers. We will analyze this information at the 500-m^2 level later, but note now that the figures in columns 2 and 4 tend to covary. Clearly, even at this aggregate level, the opportunity structure hypothesis has some merit.

V. PREDISPOSING SOCIOCULTURAL FACTORS

Before considering the results for our opportunity structure hypothesis, we will consider the three factors that may predispose South Asians to enter shopkeeping: occupational closure against them, a sojourner orientation, and the organizing capacity of family and friendship networks. Ideally, these factors should be studied by drawing a random sample of the Asian and white populations and then following this sample over time to see which persons enter self-employment. Without such a study design, we are limited to examining those persons who have already entered self-employment. Whether such people are a select group, or whether they are just like those who have not become self-employed, is thus

Table 1. Ethnic Structure of Population and Retail Establishments

Ward	Asian Percent of Population, 1971	Asian Percent of Electorate, 1977	Number of Shops 1978	Asian Percent of Shops, 1978
Bradford				
Bradford Moor	11.18	19.96	188	23.40
Laisterdyke	12.78	16.25	211	19.43
Little Horton	9.92	14.82	197	19.28
Manningham	24.82	33.94	481	35.76
University	26.38	45.92	387	31.78
Leicester				
Charnwood	8.97	26.74	259	21.62
Latimer	8.81	32.28	172	37.80
St. Margaret's	7.32	22.13	276	18.84
Spinney Hills	14.45	41.37	279	36.20
Wycliffe	18.18	41.91	172	41.86
Ealing				
Dormers Wells	6.39	22.05	132	34.85
Glebe	21.59	53.55	196	46.43
Northcote	35.74	65.63	172	55.13
Springfield	2.92	8.08	110	20.00
Walpole	4.86	10.81	289	7.61

Source: 1971 population: percent of population born in India and Pakistan, 1971 Census.
1977 electorate: percent of electorate with Asian names, 1978 Electoral Registers.
1978 shops: field work by authors.

difficult to judge. Bearing this restriction in mind, we examine the characteristics of the small shopkeepers in our sample.

A. Occupational Closure

If ambitious Asians face barriers to advancement in the white-dominated occupational structure, Asian shopkeepers ought to be recruited from (relatively) higher socioeconomic and educational backgrounds than local white shopkeepers. White shopkeeepers would be like local white small-business persons in the United States: aged, of relatively low education, and recruited from previous blue-collar employment.

As shown in Table 2, Asian shopkeepers were from 5 to 11 years younger than white shopkeepers in the four cities, a gap that undoubtedly reflects the declining attractiveness of shop ownership to native whites. More to the point is the finding that a higher proportion of Asians than whites have a polytechnic, college, or university degree, though the difference is sizable only in the two London boroughs, Wandsworth and Ealing. Here is some evidence for the blocked-upward-mobility thesis—barriers to entry into managerial jobs in white-owned firms

Table 2. Socioeconomic Background of Owners/Managers, by Ethnicity

	City and Ethnicity of Owner/Manager							
	Wandsworth		Bradford		Leicester		Ealing	
	Asian	White	Asian	White	Asian	White	Asian	White
Average age (years)	39	44**	39	47**	38	49**	38	48**
College graduate (percent)	22	3**	12	0**	10	4**	39	4**
Father self-employed (percent)	44	34	21	29	75	29**	58	28**
Inherited Business (percent)	(NA)	(NA)	1	8+	1	8+	2	8+
Self-employed in last job (percent)	25	11	8	18	20	7*	14	23
Own another business or rental property (percent)	19	17	10	12	19	17	34	26

Note: Note on significance of differences between whites and Asians in each city: significance was tested by an analysis of variance on interval variables and chi-square on other variables. Significance levels are noted by the following symbols: **.01; *.05; +.10. No symbol next to the figure for whites in a city means the difference was not statistically significant. "NA" means the information was not collected for the Wandsworth study.

have apparently pushed some Asians into self-employment. Two caveats, however, blunt the significance of this result: almost all of the Asians were educated overseas, and degree equivalence is difficult to establish; and, the great majority of Asians are not college graduates.

The proportion of self-employed fathers is quite high for both groups, providing strong evidence for the importance of occupational inheritance in the small business sector. In Wandsworth and Bradford, differences between Asians and whites are not significant, whereas they are significant for the two areas which have a large East African Asian population—Leicester and Ealing. Note that even though more than one in four whites had self-employed fathers, only about one in twelve actually inherited the business. In the Asian community, the tradition of small shopkeeping must have been transmitted between generations indirectly, such as through childhood socialization, working in the father's shop, and so forth.

In three of the four localities the proportion self-employed in the last job does not differ significantly between the two groups. The proportion currently owning another business or rental property does not differ significantly between Asians and whites in *any* area. We consider this finding particularly noteworthy, as it suggests that people with fairly similar economic ambitions have been recruited to shopkeeping in each city, regardless of their ethnicity.

Our conclusions about the occupational closure hypothesis are somewhat mixed, but they certainly do *not* allow us to characterize Asian and white shopkeepers as radically different in their socioeconomic careers or achievements. Asian shopkeepers are younger, and only a small minority (except in Ealing) have degrees, but sizable proportions of both groups come from families with a business tradition. Most significant, similar proportions of both appear to be taking advantage of the investment opportunities offered in their areas.

B. Sojourner Orientation

Bonacich (1973) and others have argued that a "sojourner orientation" gives immigrants a preference for acquiring highly liquid assets, with small shops an ideal investment. Lawrence (1974) reviewed several studies of West Indians and South Asians, all with the same result—most persons interviewed said they did *not* intend to settle in England. In Nottingham, for example, only 14% of the Pakistanis and 33% of the Indians interviewed said they intended to settle in England, with the rest either intending to return to their home country or not sure. In spite of this "sojourner orientation," the great majority were not self-employed.

In the pilot study of Wandsworth, shopkeepers were asked, "Do you intend to return to (your country of origin) just for a visit, to settle there, or not at all?" Among the shop owners, 50% said they intended to return for a visit, 34% to settle, and only 16% had no intention of making a return visit. To determine whether the strength of a shopkeeper's sojourner orientation affected business practices, this question was correlated with a series of questions about hours of operation, competitive activities, and so forth. No association was uncovered between sojourner orientation and business practices. Responses in the three-city study were similar to those in Wandsworth: 52% said they intended to return for a visit, 26% to settle, and only 22% had no intention of making a return visit. Once again, sojourner orientation failed to differentiate between shopkeepers engaged in highly competitive practices and others.

Failure to find significant differences caused by sojourner orientation in all four locales puts to rest any notion that such an orientation makes Asian shopkeepers more competitive. We could *not* test the hypothesis that a sojourner orientation leads Asians into shopkeeping, as such a test requires a comparable sample of non-shopkeepers. However, comparison of our results with earlier studies shows that the shopkeepers we studied have *less* of a sojourner orientation than the typical nonwhite in England.

C. Organizing Capacity

Even though many members of the petite bourgeoisie in the United States and Western Europe are the children of self-employed parents, they are typically fiercely individualistic (Bechhofer et al., 1974). They capitalize their businesses out of their own personal savings, they resist joining economic or political associations (except under extreme circumstances), and they operate their businesses as an extension of the family unit. Some theorists argue that the fairly rapid growth of the Asian petite bourgeoisie is partially a reflection of differences between Asians and native whites in the role of family labor and in the degree of support from kinsmen and friends in raising funds. Implicitly, the argument is that white shopkeepers' success depends on individual rather than collective achievement, in contrast to Asians' reliance on ethnic organizing capacity. Our findings, however, do not support such an extreme interpretation.

As shown in Table 3, the role of family and group resources—the contribution of spouses and children, and of kin business networks—is very similar among Asian and white shopkeepers. The proportion of shopkeepers whose extended kinship network includes other business owners is substantially the same for Asians and whites in all four localities. We suspect that these proportions are higher than for a random cross-section of the English or Asian populations, but no comparative data exist to test this speculation. While Asians may indeed

Table 3. Organizing Capacity and Ethnicity

	City and Ethnicity of Owner/Manager							
	Wandsworth		Bradford		Leicester		Ealing	
	Asian	White	Asian	White	Asian	White	Asian	White
Percent with family members owning shops	32	31	26	33	22	34	44	40
Percent who raised capital through:								
(1) family	(NA)	(NA)	33	10**	21	16	27	16
(2) friends	(NA)	(NA)	49	3**	16	9	26	5**
Average percent of total capital raised through:								
(1) family	(NA)	(NA)	7	5	7	5	7	7
(2) friends	(NA)	(NA)	11	2	3	2	7	2
Percent married	83	88	88	91	96	73**	91	81
Married owners:								
(1) Percent with spouse working in business	58	58	48	54	52	58	55	54
(2) Percent with children working in business	22	14	37	21	25	19	22	25
Average number of employees	2.4	2.1	1.7	1.6	1.9	2.0	2.6	2.5
Average number of family and relatives employed	1.2	0.9*	1.2	0.5**	1.3	0.6**	1.5	0.7**

Note: Note on significance of differences between whites and Asians in each city: Significance levels are noted by the following symbols: **.01; *05; +.10. No symbol next to the figure for whites in a city means the difference was not statistically significant. "NA" means the information was not collected for the Wandsworth study.

benefit by drawing on knowledgeable kin for information and business assistance, they apparently do not enjoy a comparative advantage over whites.

Similarly, the proportion of business capital raised via family and friends is much the same in the two groups. Although Asians in Bradford report a higher proportion of family and friends contributing, the amounts are relatively insignificant. Most capital is raised through personal savings and bank loans.

Family structures differ slightly, as almost all Asian shopkeepers are married males, while over one-fourth of white shopkeepers are women (not shown in Table 3). Nonetheless, within the traditional family unit—husband, wife, children—patterns of economic behavior are very much alike. The proportion of spouses working in the shop is nearly identical for the two groups, and the proportion with family children working in the shop is also similar. The only significant difference is greater Asian use of the extended family as shop workers, as shown in the last row of Table 3. Additional analysis indicates that the larger average number of family members and relatives employed is not due to the larger average number of children in Asian families, but rather greater employment of brothers, sisters, cousins, and so forth.

Our results reveal few significant differences in the contributions of kin and friendship networks of those Asians and whites who have entered the small shopkeeping niche. (The sample is, of course, biased against finding failures in organizing capacity.) To survive on the periphery of an advanced industrial economy, small shopkeepers rely heavily on the exploitation of family labor: spouses and children. Capital is raised not through family and friends, most of whom have precious little to spare in any case, but rather through personal savings and occasional bank loans. These findings suggest that the petite bourgeoisie niche is quite constraining, and we turn now to an examination of opportunity structures.

VI. OPPORTUNITY STRUCTURES: OCCUPATIONAL AND RESIDENTIAL SUCCESSION

Research on U.S. cities has shown that the ecological succession model of residential population change fits fairly well changes observed in the business population of racially changing areas (Aldrich and Reiss, 1976). Our research extended this model to four English cities in an attempt to test its generalizability.

A. Residential Succession

We predicted that a high proportion of Asian-owned shops would be found in areas with a high concentration of Asian residents on the basis of three propositions. First, when shops in such areas become vacant because of white owners leaving, few whites seek to take over the shop. Many Asians thus obtain shops because they have no white competitors. Second, some potential Asian shopkeepers search for business sites in the immediate vicinity of their residence, and thus business concentrations spring up around population concentrations. Third, some Asian shops offer goods or services appealing mainly to Asians, and thus they must locate in Asian areas. (This proposition is examined in Section VI.C.)

1. Wandsworth

For the Wandsworth pilot study, information on population composition was only available at the ward level (about 15,000 residents), and thus the succession hypothesis could not be rigorously tested. Using the 20 wards as units of analysis, the correlation between the percentage of New Commonwealth-origin population and the percentage of Asian-owned shops was .38. If children under 14 only are included in the population count, the correlation increases to .48.

Our hypothesis that potential white owners define racially changing areas as undesirable was tested in a 1977 follow-up of a subsample of the 1975 business census list. Of the 29 previously white-owned shops sold to new owners in wards where 15% or more of the population was nonwhite, 48% were sold to Asians. In wards where less than 15% of the population was nonwhite, only one of the nine available shops was sold to an Asian.

The occupational succession hypothesis posits that white owners leave shops in the inner city because economic decline reduces their income so much that other employment opportunities become more attractive. We used the proportion of all white-owned shops that were chain-owned as an indicator of a locality's economic potential and attractiveness, reasoning that large chain operators are more demanding in their site selection than local owners. (A part-whole correlational confounding was avoided by using the percentage of *white-owned* shops that were chain-owned, rather that the percentage of *all* shops.) The correlation between this positive indicator of economic viability and the proportion of Asian-owned shops was $-.37$.

Taken together, the relative size of the New Commonwealth-origin population and the indicator of economic viability accounted for about one-quarter of the variation in the proportion of Asian-owned shops (corrected R^2 equaled .24). This result encouraged us to collect population information for smaller geographical units in the three-city study.

2. Three-City Study

In the follow-up study, we used 500-m^2 areas as units of analysis (Section IV.C). At this level, the correlation between the proportion of Asian-owned shops and the proportion of Asian residents is .61, significant at the .01 level: the higher the proportion of Asians in an area, the larger the proportion of shops owned by Asians.

Using regression analysis, we investigated whether the form of the association between these two variables was the same in each. The effect of Asian population concentration on the proportion of shops owned by Asians is roughly the

Table 4. Regression of "Percent Asian-Owned Shops" on "Percent Asian Population," for Three Cities, 500-m² Areas

City	b	b*	Regression Coefficient for Percent Asian Population Adjusted R^2	N
Bradford	.604	.56	.31**	85
Leicester	.766	.68	.46**	61
Ealing	.635	.67	.44**	65

Notes: b = unstandardized regression coefficient
b* = standardized regression coefficient
** = all R^2's significant at .001 level

same in each locality, as shown in Table 4: .604, .766, and .635. Every one percent increase in a locality's percentage of Asian residents is associated with an increase in the percentage of Asian shops of about three-fifths to three-quarters of one percent. For all three cities combined, the full regression equation is

$$\text{percentage of Asian shops} = .032 + .654 \text{ (percentage of Asian residents)}, \quad (1)$$

where R^2 is .39, significant at the .001 level.

The remarkable similarity of the three unstandardized regression coefficients gives us confidence in our assertion that Asians in all three communities have responded to residential concentration with a high degree of business population concentration. In short, the Asian business population is *not* randomly distributed over the wards in which Asians live. This finding confirms that of an earlier study in the United States which also showed a high correlation between residential and business concentration (Aldrich and Reiss, 1976).

We could not test the hypothesis about economic viability at the 500-m² level because there was an average of less than one multiple per such area, as multiples are highly concentrated in a few main shopping districts. Thus we examined the hypothesis at the ward level, where there was an average of 13 multiples. In a regression of the proportion of Asian shops on the proportion of multiples in a ward, the unstandardized regression coefficient is -.919, indicating that a 1% increase in the proportion of multiples is associated with almost a 1% decrease in the proportion of Asian shops. Combining the two independent variables—proportion of Asian residents and proportion of multiples—results in an R^2 of .84. Because this result was obtained at the ward level of analysis, we are inclined to treat it as merely suggestive of the importance of economic deterioration in making niches available for Asian shopkeepers.

B. Market Orientation

Our finding that Asian shopkeepers tend to operate from business sites in heavily Asian neighborhoods supports the residential succession model, but it does not necessarily imply that the market actually served by such shopkeepers is mostly Asian. All the wards we surveyed had sizable white populations, and they are certainly accessible to Asian shopkeepers. An alternative hypothesis is that the processes reviewed in Section II.B, concerning the formation of segregated ethnic communities, have resulted in the creation of *protected markets* for Asian shopkeepers.

A protected market could result from three interrelated factors. First, many consumers' items are "convenience goods" for which people are not willing to travel great distances, e.g., food, candy, cigarettes, and newspapers. Even though consumers may be indifferent to the ethnicity of the shopkeeper who serves them, the discussion in Section VI.A suggests that many Asians cannot avoid patronizing Asian shopkeepers when they shop locally. Second, white shopkeepers may lack knowledge of the special needs or tastes of Asians (and West Indians) or may recognize the tastes but lack access to distribution channels for acquiring the preferred goods. Indian and Pakistani consumers have food and clothing requirements that differ from the native white population's, e.g., for special vegetables, spices, and saris. To the extent such needs are not met by white shopkeepers, Asian shopkeepers are left with a market they alone serve. Third, white shopkeepers may disdain serving a minority group in order to maintain social distance from it. Conversely, white customers may refuse to patronize Asian shops because of a desire to maintain social distance.

Asian shopkeepers' experiences in societies where South Asians are a small minority of the population, e.g.,in East Africa or the Caribbean, indicate that a protected market has *not* been a necessary condition for their success in business. Whether it is a sufficient condition can be determined by examining the ability of Asian shopkeepers to survive without significant white patronage. Note that dependence on their own ethnic group as customers severely restricts the growth potential of the Asian petite bourgeoisie.

We tested the protected market hypothesis by examining the ethnic composition of the customers served by Asian and white shops. We asked respondents to estimate customers' ethnicities, and then asked open-ended questions about how they accounted for their customer mix.

Results for Wandsworth do *not* support the protected market hypothesis, as seen in Table 5. Asian shopkeepers in Wandsworth serve about the same proportion of white customers as their white competitors, and a high proportion of Asian shops were oriented toward an exclusively white market. In the food sales sector, where we might expect the most likely existence of protected markets, the difference is still not large—58% white patronage for Asians versus 68% for

Table 5. Ethnicity of Customers, by Ethnicity of Owner

Business Type and Customer Ethnicity	Wandsworth		Bradford		Leicester		Ealing	
	Asian	White	Asian	White	Asian	White	Asian	White
All Shops: Percent Customers who are:								
White	60	65	29	70**	33	71**	28	68**
Asian	19	17	67	27	58	22	66	23
West Indian	21	18	3	2	5	5	4	6
Grocery Businesses								
White	58	68	38	76**	49	72**	36	87**
Asian	16	14	57	22	41	19	57	8
West Indian	26	18	5	1	6	6	6	3
Clothing Shops								
White	(NA)	(NA)	10	69**	19	75**	17	64**
Asian	(NA)	(NA)	84	30	71	20	74	24
West Indian	(NA)	(NA)	0	1	4	3	2	7
Restaurants								
White	61	87	31	94**	27	96**	30	83**
Asian	17	7	67	1	72	2	67	12
West Indian	23	6	1	4	2	1	2	6
Confectioners, Newsagent, Tobacconists								
White	(NA)	(NA)	61	67	44	69	58	60
Asian	(NA)	(NA)	38	28	53	26	33	30
West Indian	(NA)	(NA)	7	3	2	3	6	6

Note: Note on significance of differences between whites and Asians in each city: Significance levels are noted by the following symbols: **.01; *05; +.10. No symbol next to the figure for whites in a city means the difference was not statistically significant. "NA" means the information was not collected for the Wandsworth study.

whites. Only in the restaurant sector is there a hint of a divergence, but only four white-owned and seven Asian-owned restaurants were available for analysis.

A more sophisticated version of the protected market hypothesis would be that Asian shopkeepers benefit from serving a market that whites will not serve—West Indians. However, this hypothesis was not supported either, as the difference for all types of shops averages only 3% (21% versus 18%).

These results are very similar to Mullins' (1979:404) findings in Croydon: "Only 5% of businesses were mainly dependent on Asian customers, and in only 15% of cases were more than a quarter of the customers Asian. Only 18% provided any goods or services exclusively to meet the needs of local Asians...." Croydon is also similar to Wandsworth in one very crucial respect—only about 20% of its population is Asian (Wandsworth's wards vary from 2% to 21%), and thus the great majority of local customers are white. Opportunities for Asians to serve mostly Asians would be very limited. (Unfortunately, although Mullins notes that Asians own 34% of the grocery stores, he does not present customer figures by type of business.)

Asian population concentration is much higher in Bradford, Leicester, and Ealing, and in the follow-up study the Wandsworth results were not replicated, as shown in Table 5. Only about 30% of Asian shopkeepers' customers are white, with 64% Asian. Among the white-owned shops, about 70% of the customers are white, with only 24% Asian.

Ethnic segmentation is most complete for clothing shops and restaurants, with almost no Asians patronizing white restaurants. Ethnic segmentation is least marked among grocery stores and newsagents, confectioners, and tobacconists. Asian groceries draw more than 40% of their trade from the white community, and among newsagents, confectioners, and tobacconists differences in ethnic patronage are insignificant in all three communities. We might speculate that these types of shops are least threatening to whites in terms of maintaining social distance, as no special products are involved and little interpersonal contact occurs.

C. Explaining Market Orientations

Which of the three factors mentioned above accounts for ethnic customer segmentation—residential concentration, special consumer tastes, or communal norms of social distance? We used two approaches in examining these interrelated propositions. First, we asked shopkeepers for *their* explanations. Second, we used regression analysis to test the effect of population composition on customer composition.

1. Shopkeepers' Perceptions of Their Customers

Shopkeepers were asked how they explained the pattern of ethnic segmentation revealed in the customer mix information. Specifically, respondents were asked why their proportion of white patronage was so high or low. Answers to each question grouped rather easily into two categories (plus "other"), as shown in Table 6. Responses in Wandsworth, interestingly, were very similar to those in the other three communities.

Among those with less than 50% white trade, almost all of the white shopkeepers attributed the low proportion to their neighborhood's population composition. They said that few whites lived or worked in the areas they served, and consequently most of their customers were nonwhites. Many Asians also gave this response (about 44% in the three-city survey), but a slightly larger proportion responded that they carried special products that appealed mainly to Asian customers. Some phrased their answer in terms of carrying goods that whites did not use or offering services whites did not need.

Table 6. Explanations for Ethnic Composition of Customers

	City and Ethnicity of Owner							
	Wandsworth		Bradford		Leicester		Ealing	
	Asian	White	Asian	White	Asian	White	Asian	White
White Customer Percent is Under 50: Why?								
1. Area population composition (percent)	24	75**	42	92*	46	100**	45	100**
2. Special products for Asians (percent)	41	25	52	0	50	0	43	0
3. Other (percent)	35	0	6	8	4	0	12	0
Total (percent)	100	100	100	100	100	100	100	100
N	17	8	66	12	56	14	49	17
White Customer Percent is 50 or More: Why?								
1. Area population composition	39	56	33	54	22	37	35	41
2. Special products for Whites (percent)	29	24	44	30	52	25	30	34
3. Other (percent)	32	20	23	16	26	38	35	25
Total (percent)	100	100	100	100	100	100	100	100
N	49	34	27	56	40	68	23	70

Notes: N for each column is the total number of responses given for each question by Asians and whites in each city.
**Difference between Asian and white responses is significant at the .01 level.
* Difference is significant at the .05 level.

Among shops with 50% or more in white trade, the modal white shopkeepers' explanation was, once again, the area's population conposition. About one-third of the Asian shopkeepers gave a similar response, except in Leicester. Between one-quarter and one-third of the whites in all four communities responded that they carried products that appealed mainly to whites, e.g., women's clothing. Curiously enough, a higher proportion of Asians than whites give this same explanation, except in Ealing. Another response, given by 17% of the Asians but only 3% of the whites in the three-city study, was that they offered good prices or services that whites appreciated. By implication, the Asians were offering something that white shopkeepers didn't match.

Three generalizations can be derived from these findings. First, a large proportion of both groups cite area population composition as the reason for the ethnic mix of their customers—38% of the Asians and 54% of the white shopkeepers mentioned "the people who live and work in the area" as the explanation for their patronage. Second, a significant proportion of both groups perceive that part of their trade results from offering products or services appealing to their own ethnic group—28% of the Asians and 24% of the whites. For Asians and whites, the proportion claiming a protected market is very similar in all four communities.

Third, whereas only two white shopkeepers in the entire survey felt they carried products appealing only to Asians, 16% of the Asian shopkeepers felt they *lost* Asian customers because their products appealed mainly to whites. If we add to this figure the 9% who felt whites came to them because of their lower prices, longer hours, or better service, then 25% of the Asian shops with a majority of white customers are mainly oriented toward the *white* market.

Only a few shopkeepers cited hostility by customers of opposite ethnicity as an important factor. Other evidence from our survey supports the argument that overt acts of hostility are extremely rare.

2. Ecological Analysis of Customer Composition

As a more rigorous way of testing the hypothesis that residential succession has created a de facto protected market for Asian shops, we employed correlation and regression analysis. Shopkeepers themselves perceive that an area's population composition heavily influences their ability to draw customers of diverse ethnicities, and this factor may explain the results reported in Table 5. The Wandsworth study, using wards as units of analysis, found a $-.34$ correlation between the percentage of New Commonwealth-origin population and the proportion of a shop's customers who are white.

For the regression analysis of the three-city data, we used the business sites as units of analysis, making a total of 543 cases after those with incomplete data were excluded. The dependent variable is the proportion of a shop's customers who are Asian. (Results are unchanged if the proportion of white customers is used, instead.) The three independent variables were as follows: (1) the proportion of Asian residents in the 500-m^2 square within which the business is located; (2) the ethnicity of the owner, coded one for whites and zero for Asians; and (3) a multiplicative interaction term to test for possible differences between groups in the effect of population composition on customer composition (this variable was constructed by multiplying the percentage of Asian residents by one if an owner was white; otherwise, it was left at zero).

The resulting regression equations are shown in Table 7. The first two independent variables account for 44% of the variation in a business's customer composition. In equation 2, the unstandardized coefficient of .58 for the proportion of Asian residents indicates that for every increase of 1% in locality's proportion of Asians, the proportion of a shop's customers who are Asian increases by nearly three-fifths of 1%.

The $-.29$ coeffiecient for an owner's ethnicity indicates the difference in intercepts for the point at which the slopes for the two groups would, if extrapolated, cross the point of 0% Asian in a given area. Net of the proportion of Asian residents in an area, which is controlled for by the first independent variable,

Table 7. Regression of Customer Ethnicity on Area
Population Composition and Owner's Ethnicity
(Dependent Variable = Proportion of Asian Customers)

	\multicolumn{5}{c}{Independent Variables}				
Equation	Constant Term	Percent of Asian Residents	Owner's Ethnicity[a]	Interaction Term	Adjusted R^2	N
2:	.36	.58 (.38)[b]	−.29 (−.41)	—	.44	543
3:	.33	.63 (.42)	−.25 (−.35)	−.10 (−.06)	.44	543

Notes: a) Owner's ethnicity is coded 1 for whites and 0 otherwise.
b) Figures in parentheses denote standardized regression coefficients. All are significant at the .001 level except for the interaction term.

white shopkeepers attract, on average, about 29% fewer Asian customers than Asian shopkeepers. The interaction term's coefficient, shown in Equation 3, is *not* significant, indicating that the relationship between a community's population composition and a shopkeeper's customer composition is not significantly different between Asians and whites. This finding indicates that an Asian shopkeeper, in the same 500-m^2 area as a white shopkeeper, facing the same demographic environment, will draw a significantly higher proportion of Asian customers.

For example, in an area that is 50% Asian, 65% of an Asian shopkeeper's customers, on average, compared to 36% of a white shopkeeper's customers, will be Asians. This 29% difference could reflect white customers' unwillingness to shop in Asian businesses, a similar reluctance on the part of Asian customers vis-à-vis white shops, the effect of special products for one ethnic group, or any combination of these factors.

The standardized coefficients for the two significant variables are essentially the same, .38 and -.41, meaning that both contribute about equally toward explaining 44% of the variance in customer ethnicity. Interpreted simply, these results show ecological and sociocultural factors as equally powerful. Indeed, the regression analysis complements very well our analysis of shopkeepers' perceptions, reported in Section VI.C.1, while leaving quite a bit of variation unaccounted for. For both white and Asian owners, the higher the proportion of Asians in an area, the higher the proportion of customers who are Asian. However, regardless of an area's population composition, white shopkeepers lose Asian customers to Asian shopkeepers (and vice versa).

D. Summary: Opportunity Structures

The ecological model of residential succession, with the accompanying hypothesis of occupational succession, does very well in accounting for the proportion of Asian-owned shops and such shops' share of the Asian trade in the four communities studied. We are not arguing from an environmental determinist position, however, as the Asian petite bourgeoisie is not limited to ethnically segregated neighborhoods. Our position is that the rapid growth of this segment of the employed Asian populated has been enormously facilitated by the changes occurring in English cities during the past three decades. Changes in opportunity structures have allowed the recruitment of thousands of South Asians into the English petite bourgeoisie without changing the fundamentally peripheral nature of the niche.

VII. CONCLUSIONS

We have characterized the petite bourgeoisie as a peripheral niche in advanced industrial economies and have noted that Asians are entering this niche in English cities, though not yet in proportion to their share of the population. In this concluding section we will discuss the market constraints on the petite bourgeoisie that make that class marginal economically and will show that Asians have not escaped these constraints. We conclude with some speculations about the petite bourgeoisie as an avenue of upward mobility for Asians in England.

A. Market Constraints on the Petite Bourgeoisie

Survival in the petite bourgeoisie is a risky proposition, at best. Irrespective of ethnicity, small retail business is characterized by high rates of turnover, partially as a result of increased competition from regional and national chains that are taking over an increasing proportion of retail activity. High failure rates of small shops are particularly pronounced in inner-city areas, where low incomes, rapid population turnover, and environmental and social decay add up to an insecure business environment. Asians in Bradford and Leicester, in particular, are by their very location destined to suffer disproportionately. Many are located in high business vacancy areas such as Manningham in Bradford, which has 17% of its shop premises vacant, compared with a city-wide average of 11%.

As we noted in Section III.A, petit bourgeois owners work long hours to survive, and the data in Table 8 confirm this view. Contrast the work schedule of these small shopkeepers with the typical industrial worker's 5-day, 40-hour workweek. Asians and whites are indistinguishable in the hours they report working per week. However, in every city, Asian shops are open about one-half day more per week, and are open more hours per day. Their workweek is lengthened because 41% or more are open on Sundays (usually a half-day), in comparison to 26% or less of the white shopkeepers. Given similar numbers of employees, Asians can only manage these longer hours by asking workers—typically family members—to put in more time. (An alternative possibility is that white owners operate their shops with fewer staff on duty at any one time.)

In spite of intense competitive pressures, few small shopkeepers use coopera-

Table 8. Ethnicity and Competitive Economic Behavior

	City and Ethnicity of Owner							
	Wandsworth		Bradford		Leicester		Ealing	
Economic Behavior	Asian	White	Asian	White	Asian	White	Asian	White
Days Open per Week	6.3	5.8**	6.4	5.8**	6.1	5.6**	6.2	5.6**
Hours Open per Day	10.4	9.2**	11.1	9.6**	9.2	8.8	9.9	8.6**
Open Sundays (percent)	48	26**	66	22**	41	19	48	11**
Hours Worked per Week	64	64	68	61*	60	56	54	54
Belong to Merchants' Cooperative (percent)	(NA)	(NA)	22	31	10	2	10	7
Percent with Savings from Business	(NA)	(NA)	26	60**	21	46**	27	44**
Want Children to Take Over Business (percent)	(NA)	(NA)	30	18	61	27**	38	31
Why *Not* Want Children to Take Over? (percent)								
(1) Work hard, income low	(NA)	(NA)	69	40	44	46	*	38
(2) Child uninterested	(NA)	(NA)	14	29	32	24	*	40
(3) Other	(NA)	(NA)	17	32	24	29	*	23
Total (percent)			100	101	100	99	*	101

Note: Note on significance of differences between whites and Asians in each city: Significance levels are noted by the following symbols: **.01; *.05; +.10. No symbol next to the figure for whites in a city means the difference was not statistically significant. "NA" means the information was not collected for the Wandsworth study.

tive strategies to cut costs. Only in Bradford do more than 10% of either Asians or whites belong to merchants' buying cooperatives.

Shopkeepers were asked whether they had managed to save any money from their business operations; we assumed that few could do so. Surprisingly, a high proportion of white shopkeepers reported they had saved money, albeit not much. By contrast, only about one-quarter of the Asians responded affirmatively. We are not inclined to make too much of this finding, as definitions of what constitutes "saving" (versus investment) vary greatly. Nevertheless, most Asian shopkeepers believe that they are unable to save.

What of the future—do these members of the petite bourgeoisie wish to pass their business on to the next generation? We asked shopkeepers who had children whether they wanted one of their children to take over the business when they retired. About 44% of the Asians and 26% of the whites said yes, but the figure for the Asians was inflated by the large proportion of East African Asians in Leicester who said yes. (Most of them had self-employed fathers.)

The majority of both groups said no, and their reasons for not wishing to pass the business on are very revealing, as shown in the last rows of Table 8. (Ealing

Asians were omitted because too few answered the question.) As expected, many said the work was too hard and the economic return was too low. Many respondents stressed that their children were not interested in taking over the business, with some adding that they wanted their children to obtain a good education as a route to white-collar employment.

Small shopkeeping requires a great deal of its incumbents: generally, long hours for a very low economic return, compared to many other jobs. In an earlier age, prior to the rapid increase in market concentration, shopkeepers' children may have seen carrying on the family business as a viable employment alternative. We have found that many shopkeepers had self-employed fathers, but we have also found that a new era has arrived. Few of today's shop owners seek to pass them on to their children. Undoubtedly the reluctance of white shopkeepers' children to take over shops has accelerated occupational succession, supplying the niches now filled by Asians.

B. From Periphery to Peripheral

A unique historical conjuncture brought economically ambitious South Asians to Great Britain during a period when its economic and social structures were undergoing substantial transformation. As white workers moved vertically and horizontally into better occupational positions, abandoning jobs in relatively declining industries, white residents were leaving the inner city. These two processes were, of course, interrelated. South Asians and West Indians succeeded whites in these positions, with succession in the 1970s extending to openings in the petite bourgeoisie. Although they had immigrated from peripheral nations to a core economic power, nonwhites still found themselves on the periphery. Our research has examined the ecological and structural dimensions of this movement.

An Asian bourgeoisie proper does exist, involved mainly in import-export commerce commerce and textile manufacture, but the great majority of self-employed Asians are in the petite bourgeoisie, where they are more preoccupied with survival than expansion or personal enrichment. Asian shopkeepers may have exchanged the status of second-class worker for that of second-class proprietor, with the visible gloss of self-employment simply concealing the continuing presence of racial disadvantage. Growth in self-employment has generally absorbed surplus labor (fairly abundant in Great Britain currently) rather than increased the collective economic well-being of Asians.

Some may object that, rather than suffering from constraints imposed by racial disadvantage, the Asian petite bourgeoisie is simply facing the problems inherent in any form of emergent capitalism. Current disadvantages may stem from internal weaknesses related to commercial infancy rather than from externally imposed barriers. The situation of South Asian business persons may well be comparable to the American experience of Chinese or Japanese entrepreneurs in the 1920s, when a solid foundation was being laid at the cost of short-term sacrifice, leading eventually to real economic progress.

We cannot settle this question on the basis of our empirical evidence. Perhaps Asian capitalism in Britain is about to flourish well enough to provide all aspiring entrepreneurs with viable businesses of their own. Such projections can neither be justified nor refuted, but Britain's current economic difficulties are not grounds for optimism. Moreover, we know not how many aspiring entrepreneurs live in the Asian communities studied, nor can this be easily ascertained. We do know, however, that commercial self-employment is one of the few options open to an ambitious Asian and that, because of market size, it is open to only a small fraction of the Asian population.

REFERENCES

Aldrich, Howard
    1975 "Ecological succession in racially changing neighborhoods: a review of the literature." Urban Affairs Quarterly 10: 327-348.
    1980 "Asian shopkeepers as a middleman minority: a study of small businesses in Wandsworth." Pp. 389-407 in Alan Evans and David Eversley (eds.), The Inner City: Employment and Industry. London: Heinemann.

Aldrich, Howard and Albert J. Reiss, Jr.
    1976 "Continuities in the study of ecological succession: changes in the race composition of neighborhoods and their businesses." American Journal of Sociology 81: 846-866.

Aldrich, Howard, John Cater, and Dave McEvoy
    1979 "Retail and Service Businesses and the Immigrant Community." Final Report submitted to the Social Science Research Council in fulfill of Grant H.R. 5520. Liverpool, November.

Bechhofer, Frank, Brian Elliott, and M. Rushforth
    1971 "The market situation of small shopkeepers." Scottish Journal of Political Economy 18: 161-180.

Bechhofer, Frank, Brian Elliott, M. Rushforth, and R. Bland
    1974 "The petite bourgeoisie in the class structure: the case of the small shopkeeper." In Frank Parkin (ed.), The Social Analysis of Class Structure. London: Tavistock.

Bonacich, Edna
    1973 "A theory of middleman minorities." American Sociological Review 38: 583-594.

Brenner, Robert
    1977 "The origins of capitalist development: a critique of Neo-Smithian Marxism." New Left Review 104: 25-92.

Cater, John
    1981 "Asian and white estate agents in Bradford." In P. Jackson and S.E. Smith (eds.), Social Interaction and Ethnic Groups. London: Academic Press.

Cater, John C. and Trevor P. Jones
    1978 "Asians in Bradford." New Society (April 13): 81-82.
    1979 "Ethnic residential space: the case of Asians in Bradford." Tijdschrift voor Economische en Sociale Geografie 70 (2): 86-97.

Dhaya, Badr
    1974 "The nature of Pakistani ethnicity in industrial cities in Britain." Pp. 77-118 in A. Cohen (ed.), Urban Ethnicity. London: Tavistock.

Davison, R.B.
    1966 Black British. Oxford: Oxford University Press.

Dotson, Floyd and Lillian Dotson
   1968   The Indian Minority of Zambia, Rhodesia, and Malawi. New Haven: Yale University Press.
Foley, E.P.
   1968   The Achieving Ghetto. Washington, D.C.: Washington National Press.
Hiro, Dilip
   1971   Black British, White British. Bristol: Eyre and Spotiswoods.
Jones, Kit and A.D. Smith
   1970   The Economic Impact of New Commonwealth Immigration. Cambridge: Cambridge University Press.
Karn, Valerie
   1978   "The financing of owner occupation and its impact on ethnic minorities." New Community 6.
Lawrence, Daniel
   1974   Black Migrants, White Natives: A Study of Race Relations in Nottingham. Cambridge: Cambridge University Press.
Lee, Trevor
   1977   Race and Residence. London: Oxford University Press.
McEvoy, Dave and Trevor P. Jones
   1978   "Race and space in cloud-cuckoo land." Area 10(3): 162-166.
Light, Ivan
   1972   Ethnic Enterprise in America. Los Angeles: University of California Press.
Lomas, G.B. and Elizabeth Monck
   1975   The Coloured Population of Great Britain. London: Runnymede Trust.
Mullins, David
   1979   "Asian retailing in Croydon." New Community 7: 403-405.
Niehoff, Arthur and Juanita Niehoff
   1960   East Indians in the West Indies. Milwaukee: Milwaukee Public Museum.
Nowikowski, Susan
   1980   "The social stituation of an Asian community in Manchester." Ph.D. Thesis, University of Manchester.
Peach, Ceri
   1968   West Indian Migration to Britain. London: Oxford University Press.
Piore, Michael and Suzanne Berger
   1980   Dualism and Discontinuity in Industrial Societies. Cambridge: Cambridge University Press.
Rex, John and Sally Tomlinson
   1979   Colonial Immigrants in a British City: A Class Analysis. London: Routledge.
Robinson, Vaughan
   1979   "Choice and constraint in Asian housing in Blackburn." New Community 7: 390-396.
Smith, A.D.
   1971   Small Retailers: Prospects and Policies Committee of Inquiry on Small Firms. London: HMSO.
Smith, David
   1974   Racial Disadvantage in Employment. London: PEP.
   1976   The Facts of Racial Disadvantage. London: PEP.
Taeuber, Karl and Alma Taeuber
   1965   Negroes in Cities. Chicago: Aldine.
Tilly, Charles, Wagner Jackson, and Barry Kay
   1965   Race and Residence in Wilmington, Delaware. New York: Teachers College, Columbia University.

Zimmer, Basil
   1964   Rebuilding Cities: The Effects of Displacement and Relocation on Small Business. Chicago: Quadrangle.

SOME BEHAVIORAL CONSEQUENCES OF WOMEN'S LABORS:
A NONRECURSIVE MODEL

Sarah Fenstermaker Berk

I. INTRODUCTION

The nonmarket productive activities that Americans undertake in their homes have not been of critical concern to mainstream social science. Since household work has not been considered "real" work, it has rarely fallen within the purview of traditional research on labor. Situated outside the large high-technology institutions which characterize Western society, household labor has been neglected by students of industrial organization. Its routine quality has also made it too easily overlooked in research on the family. Perhaps most important, as "woman's work" it has rarely sparked the interest of social science researchers. Indeed, the categorization of household labor as "peripheral work" is less a commentary on the nature of the work itself than a reflection of attitudes toward it.

However, an important reorientation seems to be underway. Social scientists are turning theoretical and empirical attention to the social organization of unpaid domestic labor, its implications for and responses to social change (e.g., Oakley, 1974; Himmelweit and Mohun, 1977; Robinson, 1977; Gronau, 1977; Vanek, 1977; Berk and Berk, 1979; Berk, 1980). Numerous policy concerns have also surfaced in the context of the contribution of this work both to particular households (e.g., Becker, 1974) and to the economy as a whole (e.g., Galbraith, 1973; Kreps and Leaper, 1974). Finally, scholars have apparently recognized that, besides structural and economic concerns, the production of household commodities and the general maintenance of household well-being have important implications for the psychic welfare of the individuals who labor toward those ends (e.g., Berheide et al., 1976; Cannon, 1978). In short, the social science community has slowly begun to focus an array of technical resources on the routine productive activities that constitute household work and child care.

Yet one must guard against "force-fitting" the household work experience of women into sociological frameworks derived from the market experiences of men. On one hand, household labor exhibits some qualities of market labor, regardless of the setting or the absence of monetary remuneration. On the other hand, the standard sociological concepts employed to apprehend the social organization of market work are probably deficient to understand labor inextricably tied to family relations. As Dorothy Smith (1977:22) remarks:

> If we started with housework as a basis, the categories of "work" and "leisure" would never emerge.... The social organization of the role of housewife, mother and wife does not conform to the divisions between being at work and not being at work. Even the concept of housework as work leaves what we do as mothers without a conceptual home.

Briefly put, it is the combination of the household labor experience as work and the household labor experience as family life which defies routine conceptualization. Consequently, if we are interested in charting some features of the experience as it directly influences mental health, we must be open to an exploration of a *unique* work site, inhabited primarily by women, which may generate special configurations of attitudinal and behavioral responses. (For further discussion see Berk, 1980.)

This paper represents an initial development of some strategies for the study of household labor and its links to mental health. To provide a general context for the later statistical analysis, the first part of the paper summarizes some of the relevant research on the characteristics and social organization of household labor. For this brief summary I will draw on my own prior research, citing findings from a study undertaken in 1974-1975 in Evanston, Illinois, as well as more recent findings from a national study of household labor initiated by R. A. Berk and myself in 1975-1976. The second part of the paper draws on results solely from the national survey of household labor and explores some nonrecursive models of the relationships between time women spend on household labor, market work, women's alcohol use, one form of drug use, and their feelings of anger.

II. THE JOB OF HOUSEHOLD LABOR

A. The Data and Samples

In the earlier Evanston study, three data-gathering procedures were used. Participant observation and interviewing were undertaken in over 40 households (for discussion see Berk and Berheide, 1977), a 40-minute telephone survey was administered to a simple random sample of 309 married women from intact households, and finally a 24-hour diary was collected from a self-selected subset of 159 survey respondents. For the more comprehensive national survey, a probability sample of 758 intact households in moderate to large urban areas generated the data analyzed here. For the national survey, the wife in each household was interviewed twice, about a week apart. In addition, 748 wives kept a 24-hour diary or log for one random weekday between interviews, in which all their household activities were recorded as well as answers to questions about each. Finally, for a random sample of 350 households, an interview was conducted with husbands. For purposes of this analysis and discussion, data from husbands will largely be ignored, although such data are obviously critical to a full understanding of the social relations surrounding household labor. (For further discussion see Berk, 1979; Berk and Berk, 1979).

Since results from the study of women's household labor undertaken in Evanston will be briefly discussed, some description of that sample's characteristics is appropriate. The Evanston sample had an obvious upper-middle-class character, with over 60% of the husbands holding high-status jobs (professional/technical/managerial). Sixty-four percent of the husbands and 50% of the wives held college degrees. Almost 40% of the husbands earned over $20,000 per year, with 43% of the female respondents employed full-time. Forty percent of the sample had no children living at home, and 88% were white.

The characteristics of the national sample of households are more crucial to the statistical analysis employed here. At the time data were collected, the respondent's mean age was 39, and her husband's 42. Twenty-seven percent of the families had no children living at home, and 16% had an infant child (i.e., less than two years of age). At the time of data collection, only about 17% of the wives were employed full-time, with another 18% employed part-time. They were found primarily in clerical and retail sales jobs as well as lower-level professional and technical occupations. Eighty-two percent of the husbands were employed full-time, with about 30% at relatively high-prestige jobs. The mean yearly income for husbands was about $15,000, while employed wives earned an average of about $6,000. About 35% of the wives and 43% of the husbands held a college degree. Lastly, 86% of the families were white.

These summary statistics suggest a good cross-section of married households in urban areas, with the exception of the relatively low proportion of wives who were employed full-time. It is important to note, however, that over one-third of the national sample of wives were employed in some capacity at the time data were collected. The lower proportion of full-time employed wives suggests a sampling bias in which we received greater numbers of refusals from employed women. They were likely to be unavailable during the day and too busy at other times to complete the relatively involved survey procedures. (Of course, this is itself a finding.)

Despite the differences in the characteristics of the two samples, the information provided by women on their experience with and reactions to household labor was strikingly similar. Therefore, in this initial discussion, the two samples of women will be discussed together. I will turn first to a review of the overall conclusions about the division of household labor and then cite some selected results concerning respondents' assessments of and reactions to the job of household labor. This will provide a grounded context in which to consider a presentation of the marginals of the variables developed from the national survey and the statistical models intended to reveal the relationships between women's household labor time, employment time, alcohol use, drug use, and anger.

B. The Division of Household Labor

Past research into women's roles (e.g., Lopata, 1971; Glazer-Malbin, 1976) and women's work (e.g., Myrdal and Klein, 1956; Smuts, 1959; Holmstrom, 1972; Oakley, 1974; Sokoloff, 1980) has underscored the fact that the household remains a significant environment for the productive activities of women. Nevertheless, many observers of the family, women, and work life in general have offered sweeping predictions that change within the household is imminent. With the massive influx of women into the labor force, heightened consciousness of sex discrimination, and a general movement away from traditionally defined roles, a fundamental reordering of household and family relations has been heralded (e.g., Young and Wilmott, 1973).

Focusing on the division of household labor, the preponderance of evidence, marshalled from a variety of methodological approaches, clearly contradicts a "new family equality" (see Vanek, 1977, for further discussion). Whether measured by total time spent on household labor (e.g., Cowles and Dietz, 1956; Morgan et al., 1966; Walker, 1973; Chapin, 1974; Walker and Woods, 1976; Robinson, 1977), "dollar-value" contributions of family members (e.g., Gauger, 1973; Walker and Gauger, 1973), or ordinal or proportional contributions (e.g., Oakley, 1974; Berk and Berk, 1978), the routine allocation of household task responsibility and effort clearly falls to women. The minimal task "division" which does appear seems firmly constrained by sex-stereotyped distinctions (e.g., yard work vs. infant care) and relatively traditional rationales for allocation among members (for discussion see Berk and Shih, 1980).

My own work on the division of household labor has focused on the proportion of household activities undertaken by various family members (Berk and Berk, 1978) and from diary data, a quantitative processual analysis of the structure of husbands' and wives' household activities over the course of a typical weekday (Berk, 1979; Berk and Berk, 1979). Despite stark differences in data and methods, the findings confirm that age and gender are critical factors in the allocation of household labor *over and above* measures of household and market marginal productivity. That is, households seem to be doing far more than simply maximizing the production of household commodities. Moreover, in the face of significant and comparable market commitments from both husbands and wives, husbands rarely make large investments in household labor and child care. Finally, activities associated with child care take on a preemptive quality which, when coupled with the almost random moments when childrens' needs surface, can turn even the most thoroughly planned sequence of activities into total chaos. Employed wives are particularly vulnerable while their husbands seem impervious to the ongoing disruptions children manage to create. In short, despite claims that "the times, they are a-changing," women remain the primary contributors to household labor and the primary recipients of both its satisfactions and frustrations.

C. Worker Assessments and Reactions

In both the Evanston and national survey interviews, wives were asked a variety of questions which tapped their descriptions of and reactions to household labor. The picture that emerges is complicated and not sufficiently conveyed through traditional stereotypes.

To begin, a group of questions on both surveys and some features of the diaries were designed to measure the pressures, isolation, lack of discretion, and repetitiveness which have been said to mark household labor (e.g., Gavron, 1966; Oakley, 1974). In both the local and national studies, respondents were asked when they do household work, how frequently they have to work "very quickly" (operationalized as "like the speed of a busy supermarket check-out clerk"). Approximately 36% of the Evanston respondents and 43% of the national survey respondents reported that they had to work "very quickly" at least a few times each day.[1] Further, both the local and national respondents were asked how often they felt that there were not enough hours in the day to get their household work done. Approximately 46% of the Evanston respondents and 67% of the national survey respondents said they felt that way at least some of the time. By the same token, the Evanston respondents were also asked how much pressure they felt from family or friends to do more household work, or to do it in different ways. Seventy-five percent said they never felt such pressure. Finally, the national survey respondents were asked how often they felt they have to be "on call" almost 24 hours a day. Over 60% of the respondents reported feeling this way at least some of the time.

To get some sense of the repetitive nature of household labor, the Evanston respondents were asked, for each activity listed in their diaries, when they would do the task again. For the total of over 8,500 activities listed, 65% were designated as those which would be repeated the following day, with 98% designated as those which would be repeated within a month. Two diary respondents' comments summed up the general feeling about the repetitiveness of household labor:

> Most tasks are simply repetitive and not necessarily frustrating by themselves, but frustrating by the nature of their need to be done over and over. By the same token, I don't find most of my work difficult *to do*, but difficult to *face* on a daily basis.

> Housework is not too unpleasant to me unless it is never-ending, like 'picking up' or 'cleaning up' [after meals]—tasks which I seem to be doing and re-doing constantly, yet never finishing or never being able to see an end accomplished.

A less than idyllic picture emerges on the issue of isolation. Of the Evanston diary activities listed, 50% were designated as being done alone, with an additional 25% being done only in the presence of children (and/or pets). And, if we assume that the daydreaming "on the job" represents some measure of how much the work at hand actually engages the mind, household labor is less than engaging. Forty-eight percent of the Evanston respondents and 53% of the national survey respondents reported that while doing household work they "thought about other things they have done or could be doing" at least some of the time.[2] A comment by one respondent is typical of what was heard more generally in interviews:

> It doesn't bother me that it's mindless. I think about other things. I work my tail off and no one notices. It just has to be done all over again. There isn't anything else I can do to have someone say I keep a good house. I never make progress. I have to work so hard to keep even.

The question of how much discretion is available to women doing household labor is a difficult one to address sensitively. On one hand, it has been pointed out that the job of household labor seems relatively unconstrained by work schedules, set hours, and external supervision. Moreover, some women report the autonomous character of household work to be satisfying (e.g., Lopata, 1971; Arvey and Gross, 1977; Wright, 1978). On the other hand, an analysis of respondents' diaries suggests that while all these "freedoms" are theoretically inherent in the arrangement of household labor, the degree of discretion actually available on a routine basis is quite limited. The demands of family members, extra-household commitments (e.g., employment of adult members, chauffeuring children, etc.), the sequential constraints imposed by household tasks themselves (e.g., dusting before vacuuming), and the potential for unexpected disruption which children (and others) cause—all these actually leave little room for discretion and autonomy. This is not to deny that the *idea* of labor without constant supervision or fixed task assignments could well be satisfying. However, once the organization of household labor is empirically examined, it no longer seems the bastion of worker control that some have claimed (for further discussion see Berk and Berk, 1979).

For both survey samples, respondents were asked to attach a "feeling" to each activity they listed in their diaries. They were asked to note whether the activity listed was pleasant, tiring, boring, satisfying, difficult, unpleasant, frustrating, and/or neutral (i.e., with no feeling attached). The reason for including such detailed measurement of affective reaction to specific tasks came from insights gained from the qualitative component of the study. Feelings about specific tasks are not accurately tapped through broadly defined assessments of the roles of mother, wife, and housewife. Diary findings proved provocative not only because there was considerable variance in reactions but also because (with the exception of child-care tasks) a large proportion of the activities were designated "neutral." Open-ended comments from diary respondents helped put such a finding in perspective:

> I'm not sure your categories of 'feelings' describe exactly how I felt performing tasks—neutral or numb would best describe how I operate generally. No strong feelings—just rather doing things because they must be done and I happen to be there to do them.

> Some things are done so many times a day and for so many years that it is difficult to assess my true reaction to having to do them. They are taken for granted and done without thinking about them.

And one respondent in Evanston summed up a number of comments quite lucidly:

> Fortunately, but almost unexplicably, the myriad of small unenjoyable tasks performed each day in the line of 'child care' somehow add up to fulfilling, enjoyable work (also quoted in Berheide et al., 1976).

A more recent analysis of the diarists' designations of task affect from the national survey sample reveals one additional finding of note. Those tasks which respondents designated as "leisure" were not necessarily accompanied by positive affect. Likewise, those activities they more commonly labeled "work" were not necessarily accompanied by negative affect. In particular, the designation of a task as "satisfying" was most often accompanied by recognition that the task in question was "work", also entailing negative affect (e.g., "frustrating," "difficult"). One can make sense of this pattern by recognizing that, while the *doing* of tasks may engender negative reactions, the *completion* of such tasks may be all the more satisfying (Cannon, 1978).

Thus, arguments that the "work" of household labor is isolating, demeaning, repetitive, and ultimately damaging to the worker may have some merit. Yet such arguments also miss some of the qualities of household labor which make it so compelling and resistant to change (e.g., Bernard, 1972). By the same token, to engage in endless debates over "how satisfied" housewives really are (versus employed women or other workers) is to focus solely on the broad social roles embedded in this work life (e.g., Ferree, 1976 and 1980; Arvey and Gross, 1977; Wright, 1978). In either case, the complex nature of the phenomenon is sacrificed and the experience of women is lost.

It is both the "job" of household labor and the social roles of wife, mother, and housewife which combine to shape the mental and physical health of women. Given that, very little evidence exists which helps us capture the interaction of factors affecting women's responses to household labor. In the section to follow, and through a quantitative analysis of national survey data, three nonrecursive models of the reciprocal effects of household labor, labor force participation, and the three "responses" of women's alcohol use, one form of drug use, and anger will be explored.

II. DEVELOPING THE MODELS

A. The Endogenous Variables

As a first attempt to model the possible reciprocal effects among wives' labor force participation, household labor time, and health, the three models discussed below are substantively simple. In each, the first two equations are structurally identical; based on self-reported estimates, they predict hours per week spent on outside employment and hours per day spent on household labor. Across the three models the third equation differs only in the variable predicted. In the first model the third equation predicts the frequency of alcohol use among respondents. In the second model the third equation predicts the frequency with which respondents take "pills to relax." In the final model the third equation predicts the frequency with which respondents reported being "angry about the way life has been going." The three sets of nonrecursive equations represent an initial attempt to examine the two spheres of work which women encounter, how they affect each other, and to include their causal effects on three possible "responses" to work. Table 1 presents the means, standard deviations, and distributions of those variables treated as endogenous in the models analyzed.

To begin, the three models (each consisting of three equations) rest on considerable evidence suggesting that labor force participation has a direct causal effect on the time invested in household labor (e.g., Vanek, 1974, 1977; Berk and Berk, 1978). Attention either to hours spent in each sphere or some version of "commodity production" in each (e.g., Becker, 1974) leads to the conclusion that there are often nontrivial trade-offs involved between these competing spheres. It is important to reiterate, however, that this does not necessarily imply full

Table 1. Distributions, Means, and Standard Deviations for Endogenous Variables

Variable	$\bar{X}$	S.D.	N
Wives' Hours/Day Household Labor	4.46	3.07	736
Wives' Hours/Week Employment	29.06	13.72	232

Variable	Percent	N
Frequency of Wives' Alcohol Use		710
Don't Drink	32.2	
Less than Once a Month	16.1	
About Once a Month	13.1	
Several Times a Month	11.3	
About Once a Week	13.9	
Several Times a Week	9.0	
About Once a Day	3.7	
Several Times a Day	0.7	
Frequency of Wives' Tranquilizer Use (excludes sleeping pills)		740
Never Take Them	81.3	
Less Than Once a Month	5.3	
About Once a Month	2.8	
Several Times a Month	2.2	
About Once a Week	0.5	
Several Times a Week	2.2	
About Once a Day	3.2	
Several Times a Day	2.4	
Frequency of Wives' Anger About "The Way Life is Going"		747
Never	21.0	
Rarely	37.7	
Occasionally	32.9	
Frequently	6.4	
All of the Time	1.9	

substantial *substitutability* among the efforts of household members. While from Table 1 we see that, on the average, wives spend over four hours per day on household labor, prior research (e.g., Berk and Berk, 1978; Pleck, 1979) would caution against the assumption that wives' employment necessarily generates heightened household efforts by other members.

In all three models there is a direct causal link posited from hours of wives' employment to hours spent by wives on household labor. In contrast, there appears little theoretical or empirical justification for assuming a *direct* causal link in the opposite direction. It is assumed here that, in general, households *first* allocate their labor in response to market opportunities and *second* adjust their contributions to household labor. The former precedes the latter. Of course, particular characteristics of households may profoundly affect both the levels of wives' labor force participation *and* their hours of household work. The presence of young children, for example, can transform the nature of and demand for household labor, and likewise require a redistribution of a mother's time from market to household work. Nevertheless, in each model a *direct* causal relationship of hours employed predicting hours spent on household labor is posited, but the *direct* reciprocal relation is not.

Turning to the three remaining endogenous variables, the first of the three models contains a measure of drinking behavior which serves as an endogenous predictor in the first two equations and an outcome variable in the third equation. As presented in Table 1, this variable is based on an eight-point frequency scale ranging from "don't drink" to "drink several times a day." Obviously, this measure is insufficiently precise to conclude that it has tapped the complex issues associated with alcohol use among women. It does not, for example, chart the quantity or type of alcohol consumed. Indeed, there are good reasons to suspect that there is systematic underreporting of alcohol use, especially at the more "frequent" end of the scale. Despite these problems of measurement, this variable is perhaps still effective for use in this analysis, since the intent is not to estimate the *precise* amounts of alcohol consumed by women but to capture covariation between alcohol consumption and women's work lives.[3]

Alcohol use was chosen as one aspect of women's response to work which would prove central in any study of mental health. A great deal of literature exists on the lack of concern with female alcohol use and treatment for female alcoholics (e.g. Curlee, 1968; Fraser, 1973; Beckman, 1976). Some empirical research has been conducted on women alcoholics, much of it consisting of unfocused discussion and simplistic empirical analysis of the "hidden drinker" (e.g. Curlee, 1968, 1969; Gomberg, 1974), the increasing number of female alcoholics, the differential motivations or "profiles" of male and female drinkers (e.g., Edward et al, 1973), and the underlying etiology of female alcoholism (e.g., Lisansky, 1957; Johnson, 1965; Schuckit, 1972). Very seldom are such studies based on nontreatment populations (for exceptions see Cahalan et al., 1969; Edward et al., 1973), nor do they control for the essential features of women's work and family roles.

If we are cognizant of the kinds of household labor experiences faced by women on a routine basis, and we borrow Roman and Trice's (1970) notion of occupational "risk" factors as they would apply to household labor, we would conclude that alcohol use among women may be reciprocally related to household labor. To varying degrees, household work is characterized by the absence of supervision, relatively undefined work standards, little sense of closure, and strong normative pressures to place work demands above personal needs. Thus, one might posit that the time invested in household labor is simultaneously affected by, and affects, alcohol consumption. At the same time, it is difficult to anticipate the signs (let alone the magnitudes) of the relevant regression coefficients.

An argument can also be made for the reciprocal relationship between alcohol use and hours spent in outside employment. For example, if we take a somewhat simplistic view of alcohol use as one "leisure" activity in which time can be invested, one can easily posit that alcohol use may demand certain trade-offs with employment. Yet, perhaps demanding employment is a cause of increased drinking. Consequently, these variables are posited as causally related, perhaps in a complicated fashion.

In the second set of three equations the use of tranquilizers and like substances is inserted as a replacement for alcohol use. In lieu of compelling theoretical or empirical work which specifies the relationships among the variables of drug use, household labor, and employment for women, the second model is especially exploratory. The use of tranquilizers is taken to be yet another response which may simultaneously affect and be affected by the work experiences of women. This variable was measured by asking respondents the following question: "Excluding sleeping pills, how often do you take pills to relax you, such as tranquilizers, or other medication?" As illustrated in Table 1, the eight response categories ranged from "never take them" to "several times a day." The precise way in which this variable affects and is affected by the other endogenous variables was difficult to anticipate, although it was thought that perhaps different effects would surface from those found for alcohol use. Obviously, the social and medical contexts in which these substances are used may be quite different, as well as the motivations for their use (e.g., Brahen, 1973; Badiet, 1976). However, this does not change the fact that an examination of the reciprocal effects between this form of drug use, employment, and household labor may be fruitful.

In the final set of three equations, a less precisely measured variable was used as an endogenous predictor of hours spent in household labor and in the labor force, as well as itself being predicted by participation in these spheres. Women were asked, "How often are you angry about the way your life has been going?" Respondents were presented with a five-point scale ranging from "all of the time" to "never." Table 1 presents the distribution of responses on this variable. While hardly an innovative or exciting item, it was deemed a reasonable first approximation to general dissatisfaction and was included as one mental health outcome responding to stress, unhappiness, or disaffection with work and social expectations (e.g., Bedell, 1973; Badiet, 1976). It was thus posited as potentially related in reciprocal fashion to the time invested in women's work spheres within and outside the household.

Figure 1 illustrates the reciprocal relationships posited among the five endogenous variables. One might wonder why a single model with five equations was not specified. Perhaps most important, the exploratory nature of the models specified argued for initial simplicity rather than the complexity of a five-equation model.

Figure 1. Anticipated Causal Relations Among Endogenous Variables.

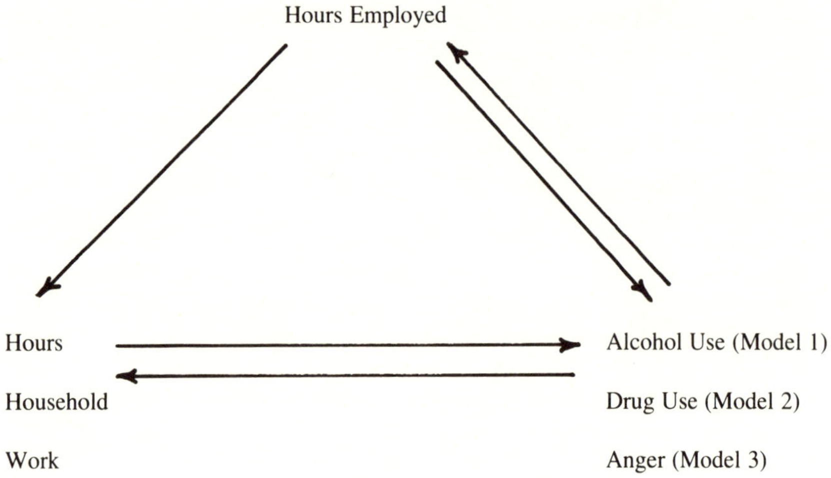

```
                      Hours Employed
                         ↗  ↘↖
                        ↙      ↘
                       ↙        ↘
Hours                              Alcohol Use (Model 1)
              ──────────────────→
Household     ←──────────────────
                                   Drug Use (Model 2)
Work
                                   Anger (Model 3)
```

B. The Exogenous Variables

The exogenous variables are identical for all three models, and so the three equations appearing in each can be discussed together. The means, standard deviations, or percentage distributions for the exogenous variables are presented in Table 2.

In all three models, the first equation predicts wives' hours of employment per week, with the variables tapping the frequency of alcohol use, use of tranquilizers, or anger serving as endogenous predictors. The exogenous predictors used in each of the first equations begin with two dummy variables for the presence of small children in the household. The variables described households with children less than two years of age, and children of preschool age (two to five). These variables are present to tap normative and practical (e.g., breast feeding) commitments that have been consistently shown to affect wives' time spent in the labor force.

The second set of exogenous variables in the first equation of all three models describes the status of the wives' employment. The level of the respondents' current employment (unemployed, employed part-time, employed full-time) is included as an exogenous predictor primarily to facilitate the interpretation of occupational effects. These effects are captured through the inclusion of the next two exogenous variables. They represent interaction terms and are the products of the wives' level of employment and either the occupation of professional/technical worker or the occupation of manager/proprietor. Rather than simply including

Table 2. Distributions, Means, and Standard Deviations for Exogenous Variables

Variable	Percent	N
Child Less Than 2 Years in Household	15.6	758
Child 2-5 Years in Household	29.0	758
Boy 11-15 Years in Household	16.9	758
Girl 11-15 Years in Household	15.2	758
Boy 16-20 Years in Household	11.7	758
Girl 16-20 Years in Household	13.7	758
Wives' Current Employment		739
No Current Employment	64.8	
Part-time Employment	13.7	
Full-time Employment	17.9	
Wives Unemployed		758
Currently and in Last 5 Years	33.5	
Wives' Occupation		758
Professional/Technical	9.1	
Manager/Proprietor	2.4	
Clerical/Sales	11.6	
Crafts/Laborer/Operative	3.3	
Service	6.6	
Housewife/Unemployed	64.8	
Missing	2.2	
Husbands Currently Employed	81.8	758
Husbands' Occupation		758
Professional/Technical	18.7	
Manager/Proprietor	13.2	
Clerical/Sales	11.9	
Crafts/Operative	35.1	
Laborer	2.9	
Unemployed	18.3	
Missing	1.1	
Wives' Prior Divorce	12.0	758
Frequency of Wives' Feeling "on call"		742
Never	19.3	
Rarely	19.1	
Some of the Time	33.5	
All of the Time	28.0	
Frequency of Interruption When Wife Does Things "just for herself"		732
Never	4.1	
Rarely	15.3	
Occasionally	35.0	
Frequently	45.6	
Frequency of Keeping Disagreement With Husband to Self		746
Never	11.7	
Rarely	30.0	
Occasionally	40.3	
Frequently	18.0	

(*Continued*)

(*Table 2.* Continued)

Variable	$\bar{X}$	S.D.	N
Employed Wives' Earnings from Previous Year	$ 5,984.23	$4,781.77	163
Employed Husbands' Earnings from Previous Year	$15,628.42	$8,708.60	420
Wives' Year Married	1959.54	12.15	734
Wives' Age	39.26	14.13	745
Number of Days Wives Ill in Bed	7.06	14.51	734

dummy variables for wives' occupations, the interaction terms tap the effects of the type of occupation held, over and above the effect of employment.[4]

The third group of variables in the first equations describes features of husbands' employment. The first is a dummy variable which simply measures whether or not the husband is currently employed. The second measures husbands' income (dollars earned), in 1975, with the mean for employed husbands' income inserted for missing data. To correct for the bias in the variance of income that this procedure introduces, a dummy variable is included for whether or not the husband's income is unreported.[5] The last two variables relevant to husbands' employment are similar to those capturing the effects of wives' occupations. The two occupational categories of professional/technical worker and manager/proprietor are put in interaction with the variable for whether or not the husband is employed to capture the effects of occupation over and above the effect of simply being employed.

The final variable in the first equation for all three models is included to capture at least roughly the effect of physical health on the number of hours wives spend in the labor force. Respondents were asked, "Last year, about how many days were you ill and went to bed?" with the resulting variable a measure of a potentially important determinant of wives' allocation of time to the labor force.

Taken together, the variables treated as exogenous in the first equations were based on prior empirical work (e.g., Gronau, 1977; Berk and Berk, 1978) and, in the case of the variable measuring wives' illness, simple curiosity informed the incorporation of the variable into the model. In sum, the exogenous predictors in the first equation of all three models tap the effect of young children (who are thought to heighten the "costs" of women's employment), the resources which husbands bring to the household that may determine the time wives spend in the labor force, and, finally, wives' physical health.

The second equation in all three models predicts the hours per day spent by wives on *household labor*. The hours of wife employment per week and one of the three "output" variables of alcohol use, tranquilizer use, or anger serve as endogenous predictors. In addition to the two variables describing the presence of young children in the household, several other exogenous variables describing family composition were included. Four variables center on the presence of teenagers in the household, who have been shown to provide significant contributions to household labor and can significantly reduce wives' work efforts in the home. In particular, teenage girls have been shown to "reward" households for their early training in domestic skills (for discussion see Berk and Berk, 1978). Thus, four dummy variables reflecting the presence of boys and girls of various age ranges are included in the second equation of all three models.

As in the first equation, the two variables for husbands' yearly income are included in the second equation. When predicting wives' hours of household labor, one could expect among other things that (a) greater income from husbands increases the demand for household commodities and (b) when husbands command higher market income, substitution of the wives' household efforts for husbands' is likely. As a rather rough proxy for marginal household productivity, an exogenous variable for wives' year of marriage is included. In the absence of better indicators, length of marriage (in various forms) has been a common way to measure "on-the-job" experience and, consequently, marginal productivity. In this specification the relationship between wives' year of marriage and hours spent at household work should be positive, since (given the typical division of labor) the wife's experience and productivity will increase faster than her husband's. Consequently, the household will tend to substitute her more productive labor for his. Finally, the number of days wives spent ill and in bed is included once again, since illness may in the short run reduce the time spent on household work.[6] Thus, the second equation for all three models centers primarily on the demands placed on women when young children are present in the home, the potential labor supplied to the household by older children, the marginal productivity of wives (relatively to their husbands'), and wives' physical health.

Somewhat different variables appear in the third equation for all three models. These equations take the endogenous variables of wives' alcohol use (first model), tranquilizer use (second model), or anger (third model) and regress them on a variety of behavioral and "feeling state" variables. In contrast to the earlier equations, the inclusion of exogenous predictors for the third equations was informed much more by hunches and much less by theory and past research.

First, a number of dummy variables for the age of respondents are used to predict alcohol use, tranquilizer use, and anger. There have been strong arguments made that alcohol or drug dependence among women may be particularly problematic during middle age. However, the precise functional form for the relationship between drug use and women's age is unclear (e.g., Curlee, 1968, 1969; Badiet, 1976). In order to allow for a nonlinear relationship between age and alcohol use, tranquilizer use, or anger, four dummy variables describing four age ranges (26-35, 36-45, 46-55, 56 and older) were employed in the third equation of all three models. The dummy variable for the 18-25 age range was dropped and became the reference point for each effect.

Four of the exogenous variables included in the third equations describe wives' employment status, occupation, and income. "Wives unemployed" is a dummy variable describing those women who were neither currently employed nor employed in the preceding five years. This variable was included to tap the effects of long-term separation from the labor force and to explore whether such women are more likely to exhibit higher levels of alcohol or tranquilizer use, or more likely to report frequent feelings of anger. Three other exogenous variables are the two interaction terms for wives' employment level × occupation discussed earlier[7] and a variable measuring husbands' income. The variables for both wives' and husbands' income are inserted primarily to control for the effects of financial resources which may permit more frequent consumption of alcohol and tranquilizers, and also to address broader class effects not tapped by measures of occupational status.

The final biographic variable included in the third equation of each model measures whether respondents had a prior marriage which ended in divorce. This variable was intended to measure the effects of past stress, and perhaps a predisposition to marital discord and internalized anger. The third equations also include the measure of wives' illness previously discussed. Frequent illness may well heighten the use of alcohol or tranquilizers, and may have a direct effect on feelings of anger.

Three exogenous variables appear only in the third equations and tap "feeling states" relevant to women's work experiences. First, women were asked, "How often do you feel that in doing household work you have to be on call almost 24 hours a day?" Responses were coded in four levels of frequency, ranging from "all the time" to "never" (see Table 2 for percentage distributions). Second, respondents were asked how many times per week they do things at home just for themselves, like "reading, working on a hobby, or simply relaxing." They were then asked, "When you do these things, how often are you interrupted before you finish?" The measure of interruption is reflected in a four-point scale ranging from "frequently" to "never." With this measure of interruption as with the prior variable of feeling "on call," feelings of pressure or stress were expected to predict greater levels of the three outcome variables of alcohol use, use of tranquilizers, and anger. Finally, in an attempt to measure uncommunicated hostility, respondents were asked, "How often do you disagree with your husband, but keep it to yourself?" There is some evidence (e.g. Berheide et al., 1976; Berk and Berheide, 1977) to suggest that, while a large proportion of wives report satisfaction with their marriages, and specifically the division of labor within them, they also avoid bringing perceived inequity to the attention of their husbands. Consequently, this variable was included as a rough indicator of dissatisfaction turned inward and a potential predictor of the three endogenous variables of interest.

With detailed discussion of the models behind us, some general comments are in order. First and most obviously, a few variables deemed exogenous in the models may in fact be endogenous. In particular, the three variables tapping feelings of being "on call," interruptions of leisure time, and unexpressed disagreements are perhaps most suspect. For instance, the models require that "hidden" disagreements are unaffected by the amount of time wives invest in the labor force, household work, and the degree to which they use alcohol or tranquilizers. While one could perhaps live with these assumptions, the case for the endogenous variable of anger is much harder to make. That is, feelings of anger may indeed affect reports of how often one perceives disagreements but allows them to remain unexpressed. Nevertheless, in the short run at least, the vast majority of the other variables can probably be treated as exogenous without serious distortion.[8]

In addition, there were some variables of interest which were not included. For example, one could argue that the levels of wives' and husbands' education could prove critical to prediction of the endogenous variables. However, severe problems of multicollinearity prohibited the inclusion of such variables.

Finally, it should be reiterated that complicated sets of causal equations can rapidly become intractable for identification, estimation, and interpretation. Hence, it is usually a wise strategy to start simply and include only those variables for which relatively strong justification can be provided. Similarly, one is usually on surer footing, at least initially, if the number of equations (and hence the number of endogenous variables) is minimized. Of course, one does not want to consciously distort one's theory in the service of simplicity. Nevertheless, ambiguous specification decisions should be resolved in favor of fewer variables and fewer equations. These concerns informed the models estimated here.

Table 3 displays the identification restrictions for the three models analyzed. The table makes clear that identification is not problematic; the models meet the order condition (Kmenta, 1971:541-543) and in fact, each equation is overidentified. For the rank condition, each equation has a rank of 2, based on an examination of the matrix of coefficients (fixed or to be estimated) for variables excluded from the equation (Kmenta, 1971:543-545; Maddala, 1977:223-225). This is a sufficient condition for identification of the models.

III. RESULTS

Three-stage least-squares was used to obtain parameter estimates for the models. Alternatively, two-stage least-squares analysis also produces consistent estimates, although they are less efficient. In essence, three-stage least-squares techniques enable one to take advantage of information contained in the correlated residuals across equations. While both forms of analysis were applied to these data, only the three-stage results are reported, since (a) results proved highly stable across techniques and (b) the statistical efficiency gained from estimation through three-stage least-squares techniques was helpful (Kmenta, 1971:573-579).

Table 3. Identification Restrictions for Three Equation, Nonrecursive Models*

Variable	Equation 1	Equation 2	Equation 3
Wives' Hours/Week Employed	1	X	X
Wives' Hours/Day Household Labor	0	1	X
Frequency of Wives' Alcohol/ Tranquilizers/Anger	X	X	1
Child Less Than 2 Years	X	X	0
Child 2-5 Years	X	X	0
Boy 11-15 Years	0	X	0
Girl 11-15 Years	0	X	0
Boy 16-20 Years	0	X	0
Girl 16-20 Years	0	X	0
Wives Age 26-35 Years	0	0	X
Wives Age 36-45 Years	0	0	X
Wives Age 46-55 Years	0	0	X
Wives Age 56 Years or Older	0	0	X
Wives Unemployed (Current and Past)	0	0	X
Wives' Current Employment Level	X	0	0
Wives' Employment X Professional/ Technical	X	0	X
Wives' Employment X Managerial/ Proprietor	X	0	X
Wives' Earnings Previous Year	0	0	X
Husbands Employed	X	0	0
Husbands' Earnings Previous Year	X	X	X
Husbands' Income Missing	X	X	X
Husbands Employed X Professional/ Technical	X	0	0
Husbands Employed X Managerial/ Proprietor	X	0	0
Wives' Prior Divorce	0	0	X
Wives' Year Married	0	X	0
Frequency of Wives Feeling "on call"	0	0	X
Frequency of Wives' Interrupted Leisure	0	0	X
Frequency of Wives' Unexpressed Disagreement with Husbands	0	0	X
Wives' Days/Year Ill in Bed	X	X	X

Note: * X denotes structural coefficient must be estimated.

A. Model 1: Wives' Hours Employed, Hours of Household Labor, and Alcohol Use

Table 4 presents the three-stage least-squares estimates of the parameters of the first structural model in metric (natural) form. Reduced-form equations are not shown, although 86% of the variance in wives' hours of employment, 19% of the variance in wives' hours of household labor, and 11% of the variance in alcohol use are accounted for by the exogenous variables.

The strongest determinants of wives' hours of employment are the level at which the wives are currently employed, husbands' income, a high occupational level for husbands, and the frequency with which respondents use alcohol. As expected, husbands' employment and income have negative effects on wives' hours employed. Over and above whether or not the husband is employed, a high-status occupation for the husband will decrease the wife's hours employed per week by almost nine hours. Moreover, for every $10,000 increment in husband's yearly income, wife's time in the labor market will decrease by well over one hour. Startingly precise is the effect of the level of wives' employment on the number of hours spent in the labor force. The impact of a wife's holding a part-time job is an increase of about 18 hours of employment per week. A full-time job increases her time spent in the market by about 36 hours. Lastly, we see the effect of the endogenous predictor of alcohol use on wives' hours of employment. Here, the coefficient implies that, based on the eight-point scale, for every unit increase in the frequency of alcohol use by the wife, her employment time increases by 2.16 hours per week. For this finding, it is important to remember that we are discussing *direct* effects from frequency of alcohol consumption to employment, so (however tempting it may be) an explanation based on an associative rather than a causal relationship is wholly inappropriate. Thus, this finding may represent a specification error or some chance pattern.[9] In any case, the finding is a puzzling one, and not one easily reconciled with a grounded sense of women's lives.

Three exogenous and one endogenous predictor have significant impact on the number of hours wives spend doing household labor each day. The presence of small children increases the time spent in household labor by over one hour per day. The presence of a child less than two years of age increases wives' household work time by a little over one hour; a child two to five years of age increases it by about 1¼ hours. Along with the effects of small children, we also see that the presence of a male child 16-20 years of age in the household generates a significant *increase* in the amount of time spent on household labor (about 45 minutes per day).[10] The endogenous predictor of hours employed in the labor force generated the expected negative effect, although it is quite small. The coefficient indicates that the approximate difference between part-time employment and full-time employment (20 hours × .05) effects a decrease of about one hour in household labor time. These findings are wholly consistent with prior

Table 4. Metric Parameter Estimates and Standard Errors for Structural Model 1 (N = 644)

Variable	Equation 1	Equation 2	Equation 3
Wives' Hours/Week Employed	—	−.05(.009)*	−.03(.011)*
Wives' Hours/Day Household Labor	—	—	.22(.107)*
Frequency of Wives' Alcohol Use (8 levels)	2.29(.655)*	−.08(.325)	—
Child Less than 2 Years (dummy)	.27(.725)	1.14(.331)*	—
Child 2-5 Years (dummy)	.67(.617)	1.29(.288)*	—
Boy 11-15 Years (dummy)	—	.53(.288)	—
Girl 11-15 Years (dummy)	—	.49(.300)	—
Boy 16-20 Years (dummy)	—	.80(.345)*	—
Girl 16-20 Years (dummy)	—	.40(.339)	—
Wives' Age 26-35 Years (dummy)	—	—	.03(.194)
Wives' Age 36-45 Years (dummy)	—	—	.33(.228)
Wives' Age 46-55 Years (dummy)	—	—	−.08(.234)
Wives' Age 56 Years or Older (dummy)	—	—	−.27(.253)
Wives Unemployed (Current and Past) (dummy)	—	—	−.32(.174)
Wives' Current Employment Level (3 levels)	18.19(.463)*	—	—
Wives' Employment X Professional/Technical	.30(.682)	—	−.22(.184)
Wives' Employment X Managerial/Proprietor	−1.04(1.022)	—	−.30(.269)
Wives' Earnings Previous Year (units = $1,000s/year)	—	—	.17(.041)*
Husband Employed (dummy)	.49(.911)	—	—
Husbands' Earnings Previous Year (units = $10,000s/year)	−1.45(.544)*	−.08(.207)	.41(.103)*
Husbands' Income Missing (dummy)	.14(.645)	.23(.246)	.07(.178)
Husbands Employed X Professional/Technical	−8.63(3.187)*	—	—
Husbands Employed X Managerial/Proprietor	2.26(4.472)	—	—

(*Continued*)

(Table 4. Continued)

Variable	Equation 1	Equation 2	Equation 3
Wives' Prior Divorce (dummy)	—	—	.50(.203)*
Wives' Year Married	—	.01(.010)	—
Frequency of Wives' Feeling "on call" (4 levels)	—	—	− .08(.075)
Frequency of Wives' Interrupted Leisure (4 levels)	—	—	− .05(.090)
Frequency of Wives' Unexpressed Disagreement with Husbands (3 levels)	—	—	.03(.070)
Wives' Days Ill in Bed (units - X 7/year)	—	—	− .03(.037)

	Correlation of Disturbances		
	Hours/Week Employed	Hours/Day Household Labor	Alcohol Use
Hours/Week Employed	—		
Hours/Day Household Labor	− .011	—	
Alcohol Use	− .461	.379	—

Note: * p < .05

research examining the division of household labor among family members using the proportion of tasks undertaken as endogenous predictors. Factors affecting the time spent in employment and household labor here are virtual replications of results from nonrecursive models based on another data set, using somewhat different measures (e.g., Berk and Berk, 1978).

The final equation in Model 1 shows three exogenous and both endogenous predictors exerting significant impact on wives' alcohol use. Both the income variables for wives and husbands generate positive effects on wives' alcohol use. Moreover, wives' prior divorce has a strong positive effect on alcohol use. Finally, both endogenous predictors generate *negative* effects on wives' alcohol use. An increase in either hours employed or hours spent on household labor decreases the likelihood of alcohol use. A more complete consideration of the substantive findings of each model will be postponed until the entire set of nine equations is presented.

B. Model 2: Wives' Hours Employed, Hours of Household Labor and Tranquilizer Use

Table 5 presents the metric parameter estimates for the second structural model. Again, reduced-form equations are not presented, but 86%, 19% and

Table 5. Metric Parameter Estimates and Standard Errors for Structural Model 2 (N = 692)

Variable	Equation 1	Equation 2	Equation 3
Wives' Hours/Week Employed	—	−.05(.007)*	−.01(.010)
Wives' Hours/Day Household Labor	—	—	−.15(.100)
Frequency of Wives' Tranquilizer Use (8 levels)	.30(.607)	.32(.349)	—
Child Less Than 2 Years (dummy)	−.03(.672)	1.10(.313)*	—
Child 2-5 Years (dummy)	.10(.536)	1.16(.259)*	—
Boy 11-15 Years (dummy)	—	.30(.327)	—
Girl 11-15 Years (dummy)	—	.48(.315)	—
Boy 16-20 Years (dummy)	—	.91(.376)*	—
Girl 16-20 Years (dummy)	—	.61(.337)	—
Wives' Age 26-35 Years (dummy)	—	—	.08(.192)
Wives' Age 36-45 Years (dummy)	—	—	.25(.214)
Wives' Age 46-55 Years (dummy)	—	—	.55(.228)*
Wives' Age 56 Years or Older	—	—	.50(.237)*
Wives Unemployed (Current and Past) (dummy)	—	—	.10(.166)
Wives' Current Employment Level (3 levels)	18.94(.369)*	—	—
Wives' Employment X Professional/Technical	.40(.590)	—	.07(.166)
Wives' Employment X Managerial/Proprietor	−1.44(.888)	—	.19(.241)
Wives' Earnings Previous Year (units = $1,000s/year)	—	—	−.02(.040)
Husbands Employed (dummy)	.32(.953)	—	—
Husbands' Earnings Previous Year (units = $10,000s/year)	−.19(.387)	−.10(.140)	−.12(.086)
Husbands' Income Missing (dummy)	.26(.559)	.27(.253)	−.21(.145)
Husbands Employed X Professional/Technical	−9.32(3.137)*	—	—
Husbands Employed X Managerial/Proprietor	2.37(4.424)	—	—

(Continued)

(Table 5. Continued)

Variable	Equation 1	Equation 2	Equation 3
Wives' Prior Divorce (dummy)	—	—	.65(.198)*
Wives Year Married	—	.02(.013)	—
Frequency of Wives' Feeling "on call" (4 levels)	—	—	.00+(.075)
Frequency of Wives' Interrupted Leisure (4 levels)	—	—	.11(.090)
Frequency of Wives' Unexpressed Disagreement with Husbands (3 levels)	—	—	.13(.070)
Wives' Days Ill in Bed (units = X 7/year)	—	—	.12(.031)*

	Correlation of Disturbances		
	Hours/Week Employed	Hours/Day Household Labor	Tranquilizer Use
Hours/Week Employed	—		
Hours/Day Household Labor	.029	—	
Tranquilizer Use	−.113	.039	—

Note: *p < .05

12% of the variance is explained by the exogenous variables for wives' hours of employment, wives' hours of household labor, and tranquilizer use, respectively.

While the coefficients for the first two equations of the second model are presented in Table 5, as one would expect, the substantive findings are nearly identical to those of the first model. However, there are slight differences in the first equation which deserve mention. Unlike the prediction of wives' hours of employment in the first model, Table 5 indicates that there is no significant relationship between the use of tranquilizers and hours of employment. Thus, the perplexing finding from the last model has disappeared with the substitution of tranquilizer use as an edogenous predictor. In addition, while the impact of wives' employment level exerts an effect identical to that of the previous model, the negative effect of husbands' income has dropped away. What remains, however, is an identical effect for husbands' high occupation. Over and above the impact of husbands' employment, a high-status occupation (i.e., professional/ technical) for husbands decreases the time wives spend in the labor force by about nine hours. In the second equation, where wives' hours of household labor are predicted, all effects are virtually identical to the first model.

For the third equation, in which the use of "pills to relax" is predicted, effects appear somewhat different from those for the prediction of alcohol use. To begin, neither endogenous predictor exerted significant effects on the prediction of this form of drug use. On the other hand, just as in the first model, the signs are negative. Perhaps something of interest is represented here as well. Second, two age variables emerge as statistically significant in predicting the use of tranquilizers and like substances. Compared to those in the 18-25 age range, the effect of being either 46-55 years or over 55 years of age increases the likelihood of this type of drug use by about one-half unit in the eight-point scale. In addition, while none of the prior income effects surfaced as significant, previous divorce exerts a positive effect, as does the number of days one is ill in bed. Thus, we see that for the explanation of this form of drug use, income and the allocation of time in work spheres has little effect. In contrast, age, past marital difficulty, and illness exert positive effects.

C. Model 3: Wives' Hours Employed, Hours of Household Labor and Anger

Table 6 presents the metric parameter estimates for the third and final structural model. Eighty-six percent, 19%, and 15% of the variance is explained in the reduced form for hours employed, hours spent on household labor, and frequency of anger, respectively.

The significant determinants of wives' employment hours are identical to those of the second model. Level of current employment and husbands' high-status occupation exert the same positive effects as those of the first and second models. Moreover, as with alcohol use, we see that the endogenous predictor of anger has a positive effect on women's work hours (in this instance, household labor). While the practical effect is quite minimal, the finding nonetheless argues for further work to specify more clearly relationships between work and intrapsychic states. Some speculations on the implications of this finding are offered in the next section.

The second equation is nearly identical to its counterpart in the second model. Small children and male teenagers produce positive effects on the numbers of hours spent on household labor. Moreover, hours employed exerts the familiar negative effect. However, an unanticipated effect is produced by the endogenous predictor of anger. Based on the five-point frequency-of-anger scale, for every unit increase in anger reported by respondents there is a corresponding increase of about one hour in the amount of time they spend on household labor. This finding may result from chance. However, it may also reflect women's efforts to control the household work environment more completely by increasing the time spent doing housework. Regardless, any such interpretation must be treated with caution. This finding will be discussed more fully in the next section.

The third equation reveals the greatest number of departures from those examined thus far. Unexpectedly, neither of the endogenous variables of hours employed or hours of household labor emerges as a significant predictor of anger (although, once again, the signs are negative). In addition, only one of the dummy variables for age (46-55) decreases the frequency of anger by a signifi-

Table 6. Metric Parameter Estimates and Standard Errors for Structural Model 3 (N = 699)

Variable	Equation 1	Equation 2	Equation 3
Wives' Hours/Week Employed	—	−.05(.008)*	.01(.005)
Wives Hours/Day Household Labor	—	—	−.01(.051)
Frequency of Wives' Feelings of Anger (5 levels)	−.28(.713)	.94(.377)*	—
Child Less Than 2 Years (dummy)	−.07(.651)	.96(.311)*	—
Child 2-5 Years (dummy)	.02(.552)	1.09(.264)*	—
Boy 11-15 Years (dummy)	—	.31(.307)	—
Girl 11-15 Years (dummy)	—	.30(.311)	—
Boy 16-20 Years (dummy)	—	.79(.364)*	—
Girl 16-20 Years (dummy)	—	.59(.338)	—
Wives' Age 26-35 Years (dummy)	—	—	.05(.099)
Wives' Age 36-45 Years (dummy)	—	—	.02(.111)
Wives' Age 46-55 Years (dummy)	—	—	−.29(.118)*
Wives' Age 56 years or Older	—	—	−.19(.124)
Wives Unemployed (Current and and Past) (dummy)	—	—	−.13(.084)
Wives' Current Employment Level (3 levels)	18.89(.361)*	—	—
Wives' Employment X Professional/ Technical	.42(.585)	—	−.05(.085)
Wives' Employment X Managerial/ Proprietor	−1.37(.880)	—	−.03(.123)
Wives' Earnings Previous Year (units = $1,000s/year)	—	—	−.02(.020)
Husbands Employed (dummy)	.32(.872)	—	—
Husbands' Earnings Previous Year (units = $10,000s/year)	−.25(.386)	−.07(.141)	−.04(.046)
Husbands' Income Missing (dummy)	.19(.548)	.25(.250)	−.03(.077)
Husbands Employed X Professional/ Technical	−9.16(3.135)*	—	—
Husbands Employed X Managerial/ Proprietor	2.38(4.459)	—	—

(*Continued*)

(Table 6. Continued)

Variable	Equation 1	Equation 2	Equation 3
Wives' Prior Divorce (dummy)	—	—	.01(.101)
Wives' Year Married	—	.00 + (.010)	—
Frequency of Wives Feeling "on call" (4 levels)	—	—	.15(.039)*
Frequency of Wives' Interrupted Leisure (4 levels)	—	—	.10(.046)*
Frequency of Wives' Unexpressed Disagreement with Husband (3 levels)	—	—	.20(.037)*
Wives' Days Ill in Bed (units = X 7/Year)	—	—	.02(.017)

	Correlation of Disturbances		
	Hours/Week Employed	Hours/Day Household Labor	Feelings of Anger
Hours/Week Employed	—		
Hours/Day Household Labor	.004	—	
Feelings of Anger	.005	−.284	—

Note: *p < .05

cant margin, and prior divorce exerts no significant effect. Not in common with the two previous models, husbands' occupation categories produce no significant effects. However, the three variables which serve as proxies for the kinds of pressures inherent in women's work, and uncommunicated disagreements with husbands, do show significant effects. Increases in any of these three variables—feeling "on call" when doing household labor, being interrupted during leisure moments, or keeping disagreements with husband to oneself—generate increased anger about life. Since these predictors may not be fully exogenous, such findings should not be uncritically accepted. Nevertheless, some internal processes which describe the causes of anger in women are perhaps being tapped.

IV. DISCUSSION

Table 7 presents a summary of the significant causal variables for the three models analyzed. The variables affecting time spent in employment and household labor are in large part stable across all models and consistent with past research (e.g., Berk and Berk, 1978.) Across all three models, the primary determinants of hours spent in the labor force were the level at which wives had earlier decided to participate (i.e., part-time or full-time) and whether husbands had a high-status occupation, which consistently reduced wives' time in the labor force. Hours of employment as an endogenous predictor always exerted a negative effect on hours spent on household labor, while the presence of small

Table 7. Significant Determinants of Endogenous Variables in Three Structural Equation Models

MODEL 1

Hours/Week Employed	Hours/Day Household Labor	Alcohol Use
(+) Alcohol Use*	(−) Hours/Week Employed*	(−) Hours/Week Employed*
(+) Current Employment Level	(+) Child Less Than 2 Years	(−) Hours/Day Household Labor*
(−) Husbands Employed X Professional/Technical	(+) Child 2-5 Years	(+) Wives' Earnings
(−) Husbands' Income	(+) Boy 16-20 Years	(+) Husbands' Earnings
		(+) Wives' Prior Divorce

MODEL 2

Hours/Week Employed	Hours/Day Household Labor	Tranquilizer Use
(+) Current Employment Level	(−) Hours/Week Employed*	(+) Wives Age 46-55
(−) Husbands Employed X Professional/Technical	(+) Child Less Than 2 Years	(+) Wives Age 56 or >
	(+) Child 2-5 Years	(+) Wives' Prior Divorce
	(+) Boy 16-20 Years	(+) Wives' Days Ill

MODEL 3

Hours/Week Employed	Hours/Day Household Labor	Anger
(+) Current Employment Level	(−) Hours/Week Employed*	(+) Wives Age 46-55
	(+) Anger*	(+) Wives' Feeling "on call"
(−) Husbands Employed X Professional/Technical	(+) Child Less than 2 Years	
	(+) Child 2 - 5 Years	(+) Wives' Interrupted Leisure
		(+) Wives' Unexpressed Disagreement
	(+) Boy 16-20 Years	

Note: *Endogenous predictors

children and male teenagers always increased time spent. In the first model the puzzling finding of alcohol use "causing" employment was perhaps a chance result. Likewise, in the third model we see anger increasing household labor time, which may or may not be a result of chance. We will return to a discussion of the latter finding shortly.

The novel results in these analyses centered on the equations which predicted alcohol use, the use of tranquilizers, and anger. In each instance they provide some insight into which relationships are likely to be reciprocal and which experiences of women's work lives have causal implications. For alcohol use Table 7 recapitulates the findings that the yearly incomes of husbands and wives, as well as prior divorce, are positively associated with wives' alcohol use. In the first instance, an income effect is suggested where perhaps the consumption of alcohol depends fundamentally on the resources needed to buy such commodities. The impact of prior divorce is somewhat consistent with past studies of female alcoholics (e.g., Badiet, 1976), although it primarily suggests that marital history should be explored further in studies of drinking populations. The most provocative findings are those showing that alcohol use is negatively related to time spent in *either* household labor or employment. One might argue that extensive time investments in either of these work spheres may simply leave little remaining time for the "leisure" activity of alcohol use. At least for household labor, we see in addition that, since the presence of small children consistently increases household labor time commitment, mothers with young children may be less likely to use alcohol frequently. This lends indirect corroboration to arguments that the "empty nest" is a strong stimulus to the increased use of alcohol (e.g., Curlee, 1969). Lastly, this finding raises important questions about the presumed debilitating effects of employment on women. While zero-order associations may suggest that one response to the pressure of two "jobs" may be increased alcohol use, these nonrecursive models counsel some caution.

While somewhat different findings were expected for the use of tranquilizers, the specific differences found were not anticipated a priori. In the third equation of the second model, there is a strong and significant age effect leading to heightened use of tranquilizers and like substances. Coupled with the positive effect for illness, these causal variables may be tapping the experiences of some middle-aged women with ready access to prescribed drugs. In addition, we may be seeing some consequences of the cycle of "overprescription" that has been partially documented in the literature and popular press (e.g., Ashby, 1974; Badiet, 1976). Lastly, the meaning of the positive effect which prior divorce has on drug use will not be elaborated here, except to suggest that further research be focused on marital history and related variables.

The final equation in the third model predicted anger. Prior discussion of this equation included a caveat concerning the difficulty of firmly establishing the exogeneity of some of the variables which predict it. However, a negative effect on anger is produced by the age variable of 46-55 years. This negative effect is found for precisely that age group which is most likely to take tranquilizers or other such medication. Perhaps it is depression rather than verbalized (and reported) anger which is the more salient feeling state for some women in mid-life.

The variables that describe feelings of constantly being "on call," being frequently interrupted during leisure time, and keeping disagreements with husband to oneself all produce positive effects on anger. Admittedly, it is difficult to argue unequivocally that these factors produce anger and are not produced by it. However, their presence in the equation suggests something further about the previous finding that anger leads to increased time investments in household labor. To again engage in some speculation, if feelings of pressure, vulnerability to interruption, and unresolved disagreement make a woman report anger, then perhaps one response to that anger would be to invest more time in household labor. That is, such feelings may well be perceived by the "worker" as a result of the inability to control her work environment. Increased attention and time devoted to household labor may reflect an effort to get a "jump" on the taxing features of the job itself. Indeed, while not significant, the relationship between the endogenous predictor of time spent in household labor and anger is negative (see Table 6). Consequently, we may be seeing a rough (yet perhaps partially misspecified) reflection of a cycle whereby the job of household labor may create feelings of pressure, lack of control, and unresolved conflict. The resulting feelings of anger may be reduced by increased time invested in household work. While not necessarily typical of the general attitude of our sample, the remarks from two respondents suggest that both the characteristics of household labor and the social context in which it occurs can generate strong behavioral and psychic consequences for women:

> My household tasks keep me busy, but I wish to do it my own way, so that I can be satisfied with my way of doing things. Taking short cuts, or leaving something out might give me some time to do other things, or take some time off and do nothing. But, if the work is not done in the way I like to do it, I feel very uncomfortable. That is the reason I have to sweep the kitchen floor two or three times a day, when once a day would be okay.

> The only thing I can be certain of on any given day is that the husband and children will be fed, the children diapered and given attention and 30 diapers will be washed and dried. On some days that's all I can handle.

V. CONCLUSIONS

This paper began with the observation that the household labor experiences of women have been treated primarily as a peculiar subtype of the market work experiences of males, or have been lost completely in the morass of research questions surrounding family life. Providing some context in which to view women's household work and their reactions to it, I then presented some preliminary models for the specification of the nonrecursive relationships between women's domestic and market work lives and their responses to them. The analysis was intended to draw attention to the fact that the social relationships surrounding women's work interact one with another to produce a unique configuration of life experiences and problems.

Specifically, the paper presented some empirical results that represent a "mixed bag" of substantively interesting observations about women and their work. The paper has also argued that there is some advantage in modeling a set of structural relationships surrounding the work experiences of women and responses to them.

Yet, this paper must also contain a critique of its own approach. The analyses offered examined the effect of "productive" activities on a variety of mental health outcomes. The degree to which women engaged in such activities was measured through reports of total time invested in them. As a consequence, there is nothing which would suggest that the *social reality* of time spent in employment is any different from time spent in household labor. The analysis does not allow for any qualitative experiential differences between the way in which the two clusters of activities are characterized. In short, household labor has by default been cast as just another "job" (e.g., Vanek, 1977; Berk and Berk, 1978). This perspective is not necessarily harmful (and certainly represents an improvement over total neglect), but it may also ignore the essence of the *social* organization of household labor by simply "adding" it to the age-old traditions in the study of wage labor. In fact, perhaps the work life of the employed woman is better characterized as a market job plus an as yet unapprehended activity which demands effort (both psychic and physical) but only partly shares the characteristics of market labor.

Perhaps we must begin by reconceptualizing our notions about the measurement of human productivity with time as the metric. Perhaps the currency of time is different depending upon where it is invested. The social context in which time is spent may alter both the meaning of the activity itself *and* the social meaning of the investment. At this point, there are very few answers to these questions. The study of household labor and, more importantly, the study of women who engage in it demand that we take account of the complex meaning of their experiences and that we develop new concepts to generate generalizable conclusions about them. Without this effort, we fundamentally limit our abilities to apprehend the work experiences of women or to understand the social responses which result from them.

ACKNOWLEDGMENTS

A preliminary version of this article was presented at the NIAAA Intramural Research Workshop on Occupational Conditions and Alcohol Consumption, Smithsonian Conference Center at Belmont, 1978. Thanks to Richard A. Berk, David Rauma, and Joan Huber for helpful comments. Additional thanks to Trina Marks Miller for typing the manuscript. The research was supported in part by a grant from the NIMH Center for the Study of Metropolitan Problems (#MH 27340-01).

NOTES

1. Interestingly enough, an identical question was asked of respondents in a study of clerical workers from banks and insurance companies. Forty percent of those workers responded in the same manner about their responses on the job (Bridges and Berk, 1974).

2. An identical question was put to clerical workers about their jobs, and this same answer was given by only 21% of the respondents (Bridges and Berk, 1974).

3. A bit more formally, I am assuming that, while the mean may systematically underestimate the actual amount of alcohol consumption, there are no systematic patterns in the covariation of the measurement error with the observed or true scores of the exogenous variables used in the equations. If this is correct, the measurement error produces a biased and inconsistent estimate of the intercept when alcohol use is predicted (which has little substantive meaning here in any case) and an inflated

(i.e., biased and inconsistent) estimate of the amount of variance which may be attributed to stochastic factors (which is also not of central interest). More important, the existence of such measurement error produces biased and inconsistent estimates of the regression coefficients when alcohol use is inserted as a predictor. However, this is a problem in virtually all social science research, and the concern then becomes one of the relative seriousness of the distortions. There is no simple response to this in the context of a single study, and without multiple indicators of alcohol use the application of adjustments based on models with unmeasured variables is not feasible. Hence, for this analysis the best gauge may be simply whether the results seem sensible. (For a further consideration of these kinds of issues see Kmenta, 1971:307-322.)

4. This model assumes that at some prior moment in time a decision has been made about whether or not to take a job, and at what level (i.e., full-time, part-time). Here the relevant question is: *conditional upon that decision*, how can one explain variation in hours employed? *Why* a job is taken initially is another question.

5. In essence, this approach to missing data prevents one from losing cases while at the same time adjusting for the somewhat arbitrary values inserted in the substantive variable of interest. The dummy variable removes the impact of the values inserted for missing data. In addition, since its regression coefficient is dependent in part on those values, it should not be interpreted substantively (Fuller and Battese, 1974).

6. In the long run, one might react to short-term illnesses by doing *more* household work, to "catch up."

7. These are still interpreted as effects over and above employment per se, since the number of hours employed is included as an endogenous predictor. However, with that said, it is difficult to predict their likely impact. On one hand, people in higher-status jobs may gain considerable satisfaction from their achievements and be less vulnerable.

8. I would be the last to claim that on a priori grounds alone the models' specifications are fully satisfactory. However, it is not at all clear what genuine alternatives are available. First, in the absence of controlled experiments and/or longitudinal data, model specifications rest almost entirely on prior theory and empirical generalizations. Particularly for the third equations in the three models, compelling guidelines for thorough specification are difficult to find. Second, dropping the idea of employing formal multiple-equation causal models is hardly a solution. Single-equation regression approaches are also causal models, although this is sometimes not fully acknowledged; that is, there is nothing less "causal" about single-equation strategies unless prediction without regard to substantive mechanisms is the sole aim. Some might try to justify the use of single-equation models alone by arguing that they represent reduced-form equations resting on underlying structural equations. However, this can make sense *only* if the structural equations are shown, their merits argued, and then the reduced-form equations are formally derived. In short, single-equation models are subject to the very same sorts of challenges one may raise for multiple-equation models. Finally, resorting to the use of sets of zero-order correlations is perhaps even less justified. Zero-order correlations are, of course, simply standardized regression coefficients for bivariate (single-equation) regression models that are almost certainly misspecified. Hence, the correlations are almost necessarily biased and inconsistent estimates of the real relationship in question.

9. To explore the implications for the whole set of equations, several related strategies were employed. First, the set was re-estimated using the *observed* alcohol use variables rather than its instrument. While the resulting sign was negative, the coefficient was easily attributed to chance. In any case, the results for all of the other variables in the same equation and in different equations were virtually unchanged. Second, the set was re-estimated several additional times with the effect of alcohol use on employment constrained to equal a range of plausible values (both positive and negative). The point was to determine if the results for *other* variables changed depending on the value of the constrained parameter. By and large the same story consistently emerged. This means that, even if the reported coefficient is in error, the other coefficients are probably sound.

10. The increase appears to result from the fact that teenaged boys create work for others in the

household (as do all family members) but are less likely to carry their share of the family chores. Thus, viewed solely in terms of their net contribution to household production, teenaged boys may well be debtors (Berk and Berk, 1978).

REFERENCES

Arvey, Richard D., and Ronald H. Gross
    1977 "Satisfaction levels and correlates of satisfaction in the homemaker job." Journal of Vocational Behavior 10: 13-24.

Ashby, B.
    1974 "Overcoming depression." Family Circle Magazine (June): 74.

Badiet, P.
    1976 "Women and legal drugs: a review." Pp. 57-81 in A. MacLennan (ed.), Women: Their Use of Alcohol and Other Legal Drugs. Toronto: Addiction Research Foundation of Ontario.

Becker, Gary S.
    1974 "A theory of marriage." Pp.229-344 in T. W. Schultz (ed.), Economics of the Family. Chicago: University of Chicago Press.

Beckman, Linda J.
    1976 "Alcoholism problems and women: an overview." Pp. 65-96 in M. Greenblatt and M. Schuckit (eds.), Alcoholism Problems in Women and Children. New York: Grune and Stratton.

Bedell, J.W.
    1973 "The alcoholic housewife in the American culture." Fullerton, California: California State University.

Berheide, Catherine W., Sarah Fenstermaker Berk, and Richard A. Berk
    1976 "Household work in the suburbs: the job and its participants." Pacific Sociological Review 19: 491-517.

Berk, Richard A., and Sarah Fenstermaker Berk
    1978 "A simultaneous equation model for the division of household labor." Sociological Methods and Research 6: 431-468.
    1979 Labor and Leisure at Home: Content and Organization of the Household Day. Beverly Hills: Sage.

Berk, Sarah Fenstermaker
    1979 "Husbands at home: the organization of the husband's household day." Pp. 125-158 in K.W. Feinstein (ed.), Working Women and Families. Beverly Hills: Sage.

Berk, Sarah Fenstermaker (ed.)
    1980 Women and Household Labor. Beverly Hills: Sage.

Berk, Sarah F., and Catherine W. Berheide
    1977 "Going backstage: gaining access to observe household work." The Sociology of Work and Occupations 4: 27-48.

Berk, Sarah F., and Anthony Shih
    1980 "Contributions to household labor: comparing wives' and husbands' reports." Pp. 191-227 in S.F. Berk (ed.), Women and Household Labor. Beverly Hills: Sage.

Bernard, Jessie
    1972 The Future of Marriage. New York: Bantam.

Brahen, S.L.
    1973 "Housewife drug addiction." Journal of Drug Education 3: 13-24.

Bridges, William P., and Richard A. Berk
    1974 "Determinants of white collar income: an evaluation of equal pay for equal work." Social Science Research 3: 211-233.

Cahalan, D., I. H. Cisin, and H. Crossley
   1969   American Drinking Practices: A National Study of Drinking and Attitudes. New Haven: College and University Press.

Cannon, Rebecca L.
   1978   The Private Sphere: How Women Feel About the Work They Do. M.A. thesis, Department of Sociology, University of California at Santa Barbara.

Chapin, F. Stuart
   1974   Human Activity Patterns in the City: Things People Do in Time and Space. New York: John Wiley.

Cowles, May L. and Ruth P. Dietz
   1956   "Time spent in homemaking activities by a selected group of Wisconsin farm homemakers." Journal of Home Economics 48: 29-35.

Curlee, J.
   1968   "Women alcoholics." Federal Probation 32: 16-20.
   1969   "Alcoholism and the empty nest." Bulletin of the Menninger Clinic 33: 165-171.

Edward, G., C. Hensman, and J. Peto
   1973   "A comparison of female and male motivations for drinking." International Journal of Addictions 8: 577-587.

Ferree, Myra Marx
   1976   "Working-class jobs: housework and paid work as sources of satisfaction." Social Problems 23: 431-441.
   1980   "Satisfaction with housework: the social context." Pp.89-112 in S. F. Berk (ed.), Women and Household Labor. Beverly Hills: Sage.

Fraser, J.
   1973   "The female alcoholic." Addictions 20: 64-80.

Fuller, Wayne, and George E. Battese
   1974   "Estimation of linear models with crossed-error structure." Journal of Econometrics 2: 67-78.

Galbraith, John K.
   1973   Economics and the Public Purpose. Boston: Houghton Mifflin.

Gauger, William
   1973   "Household work: can we add it to the GNP?" Journal of Home Economics 65: 12-15.

Gavron, Hannah
   1966   Captive Wife. Harmondsworth, England: Penguin.

Glazer-Malbin, Nona
   1976   "Housework." Signs 1: 905-922.

Gomberg, E. S.
   1974   "Women and alcoholism." Pp. 169-190 in V. Franks and V. Burtle (eds.), Women in Therapy: New Psychotherapies for a Changing Society. New York: Burnner/Mazel

Gronau, Reuben
   1977   "Leisure, home production and work: the theory of the allocation of time revisited." Journal of Political Economy 85: 1099-1124.

Himmelweit, Susan, and Simon Mohun
   1977   "Domestic labour and capital." Cambridge Journal of Economics 1: 15-31.

Holmstrom, Lynda L.
   1972   The Two Career Family. Cambridge, Mass. Schenckman.

Johnson, M. W.
   1965   "Physicians' views on alcoholism: with special reference to alcoholism in women." The Nebraska State Medical Journal 50: 378-384.

Kmenta, J.
   1971   Elements of Econometrics. New York: Macmillan.

Kreps, Juanita M., and R. John Leaper
- 1976 "Home work, market work and the allocation of time." Pp. 61-81 in J. M. Kreps (ed.), Women and the American Economy: A Look to the 1980's. Englewood Cliffs, N.J.: Prentice-Hall.

Lisansky, E.S.
- 1957 "Alcoholism in women: social and psychological concomitants. I. Social history data." Quarterly Journal of Studies on Alcohol 18: 588-623.

Lopata, Helena Z.
- 1971 Occupation: Housewife. London: Oxford University Press.

Maddala, G. S.
- 1977 Econometrics. New York: McGraw-Hill.

Morgon, James N., Ismail A. Sirageldin, and Nancy Baerwaldt
- 1966 Productive Americans. Ann Arbor: Institute for Social Research, University of Michigan.

Myrdal, Alva, and Viola Klein
- 1956 Women's Two Roles: Home and Work. London: Routledge and Kegan Paul.

Oakley, Ann
- 1974 The Sociology of Housework. New York: Pantheon.

Pleck, Joseph
- 1979 "Men's family work: three perspectives and some new data." The Family Coordinator 28: 481-488.

Robinson, John P.
- 1977 How Americans Use Time: A Social-Psychological Analysis of Everyday Behavior. New York: Praeger.

Roman, Paul M., and H. M. Trice
- 1970 "The development of deviant drinking behavior: occupational risk factors." Archives of Environmental Health 20: 424-435.

Schuckit, M.
- 1972 "The women alcoholic: a literature review." Psychiatry in Medicine 3: 37-42.

Smith Dorothy E.
- 1977 "A sociology for women." Paper presented at the Women's Research Institute of Wisconsin, Inc.

Smuts, Robert W.
- 1959 Women and Work in America. New York: Columbia University Press.

Sokoloff, Natalie J.
- 1980 Between Money and Love: The Dialectics of Women's Home and Market Work. New York: Praeger.

Vanek, Joann
- 1974 "Time spent in housework." Scientific American 231: 116-120.
- 1977 "The new family equality: myth or reality?" Paper presented at the annual meetings of the American Sociological Association, Chicago, Illinois.

Walker, Kathryn
- 1973 "Household work time: its implications for family decisions." Journal of Home Economics 65: 7-11.

Walker, Kathryn E., and William Gauger
- 1973 "Time and its dollar value in household work." Family Economics Review 62: 8-13.

Walker, Kathryn E., and Margaret E. Woods
- 1976 Time Use: A Measure of Household Production of Family Goods and Services. Washington D.C.: Center for the Family of the Home Economics Association.

Wright, James D.
   1978 "Are working women really more satisfied? Evidence from several national surveys." Journal of Marriage and the Family 40: 301-313.

Young, Michael, and Peter Wilmott
   1973 The Symmetrical Family. New York: Pantheon.

SECTORAL INFLUENCES ON OCCUPATIONAL SEX SEGREGATION

Kim M. Blankenship

Numerous studies have shown that occupational segregation by sex is the primary structure of earnings discrimination against women. The mechanisms by which this structure operates, however, have not been clearly identified. The present study brings dual economy theory to bear on the problem. In particular, it is argued that economic sectors are relevant to the analysis of occupational sex segregation and female earnings in two ways. First, typically female occupations are located disproportionately in the periphery sector. Second, the extent to which occupational segregation accounts for low female earnings varies by sector. This study, then, will examine both the between- and the within-sector effects of occupational sex segregation on male-female earnings disparities.

The dual economy approach provides an alternative to more conventional explanations of the earnings determination process offered by classical human capital and status attainment theories. Classical theories assume that workers earn the value of their marginal products and therefore that pay differentials reflect quality differentials among workers. In the conventional view, earnings disparities between men and women are frequently attributed to quality differences rooted in the sexes' differing patterns of labor force participation. This has clear implications for interpretations of occupational segregation by sex and its relationship to earnings (Blau and Jusenius, 1976: 185-188; England, 1980: 9-14).

According to the classical approach, women anticipate discontinuous employment and therefore choose occupations in which temporary withdrawal from the labor force will not make their skills obsolete (Polachek, 1976). At the same time, however, continuous employment in these occupations does not enhance skill development (Oppenheimer, 1970). The earnings levels of these occupations merely reflect this tendency. Consequently, it is argued, not only do women workers tend to be less qualified than male workers but also predominantly female occupations tend to receive lower pay than other occupations. In this view, occupational segregation and the low earnings of typically female occupations are explained in terms of the characteristics of occupational incumbents. What cannot be accounted for in these terms is often attributed to employer discrimination.

In contrast to this individualistic perspective and in line with the dual economy approach, the present study locates the source of earnings differences between the sexes in the productive structure of advanced capitalist society. Specifically, it is argued that the industrial structure is partitioned into distinct sectors which operate according to fundamentally different rules. The structural characteristics of these sectors generate divergent labor supply requirements, such that worker productivity differs by sector not because of the characteristics of individuals but rather as a result of the structural characteristics of the sectors (Gordon, 1972; Doeringer and Piore, 1971; Beck et al., 1980b). Hence, it is argued, earnings are structurally determined. Similarly, it is the requirements of the advanced capitalist industrial structure that determine the occupational distribution of workers. This has at least two implications for the relationship between occupational sex segregation and earnings. To some extent the skill requirements and low pay of typically female occupations may reflect their disproportionate location in the periphery sector. In addition, occupational segregation can be viewed as a primary mechanism for maintaining a cheap supply of labor in the core sector.

From this perspective it is the characteristics of typically female occupations themselves, in part as they are determined by sectoral location, that are the source of low earnings. The differential work qualifications of men and women may reinforce the process, but these differentials are largely a reflection, not the cause, of the placement of men and women in different occupations and/or sectors. For this reason the present study uses descriptive statistics and regression analyses of occupations to demonstrate the way in which economic sectors relate to segregation and male/female earnings differences.

The study is divided into four sections. The first elaborates the empirical and theoretical concerns from which the present analysis emerges. This is followed by a section on data and variables as well as a section in which the findings are discussed. Finally, the study concludes with some comments on the implications of the present research for an understanding of the relationship between occupational segregation and the earnings determination process as well as for the development of dual economy research in general.

I. PERSPECTIVES ON OCCUPATIONAL SEGREGATION AND EARNINGS DETERMINATION

Numerous studies have noted that, in spite of recent increases in the rates of female labor force participation, sex segregation among occupations persists (Blau and Jusenius, 1976; Ferber and Lowry, 1976; Gordon, 1976; Oppenheimer, 1970, 1973; Stevenson, 1975; Whitehurst, 1977:Chapter 4; Spaeth, 1979; England, 1980), as does the earnings gap between the sexes (Sanborn, 1964; Fuchs, 1971; England, 1979; Bridges and Berk, 1974; 1978; Wolf and Fligstein, 1979; Griffiths, 1976; Kohen et al., 1977). Although this research reflects a diversity of perspectives, most of the empirical evidence demonstrates that sex discrimination in the form of unequal pay for equal work is of minor, if any, importance. Instead, earnings disparities result form the concentration of women in low-paying occupations. The sources of occupational differentiation and the way in which segregation operates to produce observed earnings discrepancies are not as clear.

A. Classical Approach

In an effort to comprehend these relationships, much of the current research is primarily concerned with specifying the appropriate dimensions along which to conceptualize occupations (Stevenson, 1975; England and Mclaughlin, 1979; Wolf and Fligstein, 1979). For more than a decade the most frequently used measure of occupation has been that associated with the classic status attainment model of American social stratification and earnings determination, namely, the Duncan SEI score (Blau and Duncan, 1967; Sewell and Hauser, 1975; Hauser and Featherman, 1977; Featherman and Hauser, 1978; McClendon, 1976; Treiman and Terrell, 1975; Suter and Miller, 1973; Sewell et al., 1980). Recently, however, the ability of this metric to reflect important aspects of sexual inequalities in labor market processes has been called into question. While sexual differentials are well documented, differences in levels of occupational status either in terms of prestige ratings or SEI scores between the sexes are minimal (Featherman and Hauser, 1976; England, 1979; Suter and Miller, 1973; Treiman and Terrell, 1975; Fligstein and Wolf, 1978), and there is little evidence that women are concentrated in jobs with less status or prestige than men (Treiman and Terrell, 1975; England, 1979). In addition, a number of studies have noted the similarity between the sexes with respect to the status attainment process (England, 1979;

McClendon, 1976), and, even where differential rates of monetary returns to occupational prestige between men and women have been observed, occupational prestige accounts for a relatively small share of the earnings gap between the sexes (Suter and Miller, 1973). These and related findings have led both supporters and critics of the status attainment tradition to question the adequacy of prestige and SEI measures of occupations for explaining earnings differences across groups of workers and occupations (Spaeth, 1979; Stevenson, 1975; Wolf and Fligstein, 1979; Beck et al., 1978; Campbell and Parker, n.d.; Kalleberg and Sorenson, 1979; Scoville, 1969; England, 1981).

In a recently published article Sewell et al. (1980) confront these criticisms by elaborating the process of occupational achievement among men and women from labor market entry to mid-life. Operating from within a status attainment framework, Sewell et al. argue that the earlier findings of similarity between the sexes in the effects of socioeconomic background and in the total effect of education on occupational status at mid-life are deceptive because they fail to differentiate between status of first and current jobs. By including the status of first job in their model Sewell et al. (1980:578) "reveal striking sex differences in the occupational attainment process." These are presumably the consequence of sex differences in reliance on educational qualifications, which in turn result primarily from sex differences in patterns of labor force participation. While it remains implicit in their argument, these findings suggest that it is the skill levels of individuals which are most important in determining the outcome of the socioeconomic achievement process.[1]

Rather than elaborating the process of status attainment, critics of conventional SEI or prestige measures of occupations have identified a number of occupational characteristics that are more meaningful dimensions along which to compare the sexes. One of the most significant of these is the amount of power or authority an individual has in an occupation. Not only has authority been shown to be an occupational characteristic distinct from prestige (Spaeth, 1979) but also sex differences in authority in the workplace have been documented (Wolf and Fligstein, 1979). Similarly, substantial sex differences have been found along a number of other dimensions of occupations, including industrial location (Oppenheimer, 1970; Blau, 1975; Bridges, 1980), the nature of work experience and task requirements (Spaeth, 1979; Gordon, 1976; Stevenson, 1975), and career affiliations (Spilerman, 1977; Grimm and Stern, 1974). Assuming that these occupational characteristics at least partly determine earnings, then sex differences along these dimensions may anticipate earnings differences between the sexes.

While many of these studies have not directly examined the extent to which such occupational attributes explain the earnings gap between men and women, they have implications for such an explanation. In particular, if these attributes are income-producing characteristics—for instance, if location in a position of authority, or in a particular industrial group, or in occupations that require certain skills affects earnings—then occupational segregation may influence earnings in at least two ways. First, predominantly female occupations may be lower in these "income-producing" attributes than other occupations. Indeed, some studies suggest this to be the case (Wolf and Fligstein, 1979; Stevenson, 1975). More importantly, these and other studies (England, 1979; England and McLaughlin, 1979; Bridges and Berk, 1978; Ferber and Lowry, 1976; Wolf and Rosenfeld, 1978) have demonstrated the independent influence of sex composition on earnings levels such that differences between the earnings of predominantly female occupations, on the one hand, and sexually mixed and predominantly male occupations, on the other hand, persist regardless of their differences along these dimensions. This may partly be explained by a failure to control for sex differences in other significant income-producing attributes. In addition, it indicates a second way in which occupational segregation influences the earnings determination process, namely, through the tendency for predominantly female occupations to receive less than other occupations for comparable attributes. Apparently this occurs through the differential translation of various kinds of worker qualifications and performances into earnings according to the sex label of jobs.

These studies represent an advance over the classical approach insofar as they suggest that structural considerations mediate, even determine, the effect of individual qualifications on earnings. Nevertheless, they leave the question of why this occurs unanswered. A dual economy approach can advance the literature on segregation and earnings in two ways. First, sectoral location is an attribute of occupations which has not been examined in this context. It may be that differences in earnings of sex-labeled jobs result partly from differences between them with respect to sectoral location. It may also be that advantageous sectoral location is less likely to be translated into high earnings in predominantly female occupations than it is in other sex-labeled occupations. Second, a dual economy approach advances understanding of how and why these processes occur.[2] In order to show this it is necessary to elaborate on dual economy theory more systematically.

B. Dual Economy Approach

Throughout the present discussion the "dual economy" rubric has been used to refer to the general body of literature that has emerged as a reaction against the failure of human capital and status attainment theories to specify societal constraints on an individual's work choices and possibilities for socioeconomic achievement (Beck et al., 1978; Tolbert et al., 1980; Doeringer and Piore, 1971; Gordon, 1972; Wachtel, 1975; Baron, 1975; Blau and Jusenius, 1976; Horan, 1978). In particular, this approach is a response to the assumption that informs the classical status attainment tradition to the effect that income differences among workers which persist after differences in human capital investments are accounted for merely reflect imperfections in an otherwise perfectly competitive market. Instead, a dual economy approach suggests that these "imperfections" are fundamentally rooted in the structure of advanced capitalist society and thereby systematically affect certain groups of workers. These theorists identify economic sectors as the primary structures that mediate, or determine, the relationship between human capital investments and socioeconomic achievement.

The most recent empirical and theoretical advances in this literature have been made by those who locate the source of economic segmentation in the industrial organization of production.[3] It is this school of thought which provides the theoretical rationale for the present analysis. In particular this study draws upon the work of Tolbert et al. (1980), who have derived a strategy whereby industries are assigned to either the core or the periphery sector depending on their position along a continuum of industrial diversification ranging from competitive to monopolistic.

In using this core-periphery scheme, a number of theoretical debates have been subsumed. For example, dual economy theorists with an industrial structure orientation do not agree over what precisely the historical origins of the industrial structure are (Edwards et al., 1975; Gordon, 1972; Kalleberg and Sorenson, 1979; Doeringer and Piore, 1971; Piore, 1975). Nevertheless, they do agree on one fundamental issue: there are critical differences in the kinds of labor power demanded by each sector, and these in turn have significant implications for the outcome of the socioeconomic achievement process. These differences are captured by the Tolbert el al. scheme.

The core sector is composed of monopolistic and oligopolistic firms characterized by heavy investment in technology and a complex production process. Hence, jobs in the core require fairly high levels of education and training. Furthermore, because much of this training is job-specific, it demands heavy investment on the part of the firm itself. Worker stability in this context is a particularly important consideration, as the costs to the firm of retraining are large. One of the primary structural manifestations of this requirement is the presence of well-developed internal labor markets which essentially represent permanent employment relationships (Doeringer and Piore, 1971; Piore, 1975; Gordon, 1972). In this structure, the wages paid for specific jobs are not necessarily commensurate with the marginal productivity of labor (Doeringer and Piore, 1971: 77-78). Moreover, insofar as wages may be used as incentives to encourage stability, they tend to be relatively high. High wages also result from the tendency on the part of specialized laborers to unionize. For all of these reasons, the core sector generally depends on a costly supply of labor.

The periphery, on the other hand, is composed of firms organized on the basis of competitive capitalism. The lack of investment in technology as well as the relative simplicity and instability of production in this sector mean that worker productivity is low. Whatever growth occurs in industries in this sector depends on keeping labor costs minimal. In this context, investment in training is low and worker stability relatively unimportant. Indeed, the structure of the periphery is such that it tends to encourage unstable employment; for, high rates of turnover maintain low labor costs by hindering unionization efforts and justifying low wages. Job differentiation in the periphery is minimal, and the primary requirement is that labor be cheap. (Bonacich and Hirata, 1981:52-54)

From this perspective it is clear that sectoral location should have consequences for earnings such that the low earnings of typically female occupations may be more a reflection of their sectoral location than of their sex composition per se. Consequently, if predominantly female occupations are disproportionately located in the periphery sector, this may account for both the low wages paid to these occupations and the low earnings of women in general. If this were the only way in which economic sectors related to occupational segregation and earnings disparities between the sexes, however, the sex label of occupations would coincide with sectoral boundaries. Not only is this unlikely, but more importantly a dual economy approach implies that the segregation of women in low-paying occupations is a predictable outcome of the operation of core industries.

Beck et al. (1980b) suggest, although they do not rigorously demonstrate, that occupational segregation in the core may result from the way in which worker credentials are evaluated in this sector. They argue that, because of the importance of on-the-job training and worker stability, these evaluations are a much more important part of employment decisions in the core than they are in the periphery. However, evaluations and subsequent employment decisions tend to be based on group rather than individual characteristics. Consequently, because employers view women in general as stability risks regardless of their individual attributes, they become segregated in certain occupations. Moreover, these occupations are accorded the low wages commensurate with their location in the hierarchically arranged job structure of the core. Essentially, this argument attributes occupational segregation to employer discrimination, although the bases for these discriminatory practices are located in the structure of the core sector.

Occupational segregation may also be viewed more generally as a way in which employers in the core can make direct use of a cheap labor supply and thereby lower their costs of production. In a sense occupational segregation in the core is analogous to segmentation in the economy as a whole. Whereas in the periphery direct use of cheap labor is one of the primary ways in which production costs are kept low, the organization of the core, to some degree, precludes this possibility (Bonacich and Hirata, 1981:52-55). Nevertheless, monopolistic firms do develop a need for large staffs of clerical workers as well as for workers to handle the more basic aspects of machine operations. The labor supply requirements of these occupations are similar to those of peripheral work in general, although they tend to emphasize higher levels of minimum training and stability. Not only does occupational segregation in the core reflect these needs but also it helps keep the cost of labor relatively low in at least part of the sector.

Whatever the source of occupational segregation, this general line of reasoning suggests two hypotheses about within-sector variations in the relationship between occupational segregation and earnings. Not only is occupational segregation less likely to occur in the periphery than it is in the core but also it is likely to account for more of the earnings differences between the sexes in the core than it is in the periphery. This would, in turn, explain why location in the core might be less likely to be translated into high earnings in predominantly female occupations than it would be in sexually mixed or predominantly male occupations.

II. DATA AND VARIABLES

In order to test these hypotheses, data from the 1/10,000 neighborhood sample tapes of the 1970 census were used (Bureau of the Census, 1972). For each individual, earnings data and information on weeks worked refer to the year prior to the interview, 1969, while data on all other characteristics were recorded in April 1970. From this overall sample, a sample of civilian workers, either part-time or full-time, who in 1970 were sixteen years or older and who reported earnings for the previous year was selected. This procedure yielded a sample of 8883 workers: 5282 males, 3601 females; 4085 workers in the core, 4798 workers in the periphery sector.

While information on the variables was collected at the individual level, the unit of analysis in the present study is the occupation. Occupational level data were generated by a summary subroutine available in the statistical analysis system packaged program (SAS Institute Inc., 1979). This procedure resulted in a data set containing the averages on each of the relevant variables for all workers in each of the detailed census occupational categories, of which there are 388. In addition, two other similar data sets were created, one for detailed occupational categories in the core and one for occupations in the periphery, of which there are 297 and 292, respectively. In all of the subsequent analyses, occupations are weighted by the number of individuals within each category so as to prevent any atypical cases from exerting an unwarranted impact on the results.[4]

The principal dependent variable is based upon the natural log of weekly earnings, where earnings refers to individual money receipts from wages, salaries, and both farm and nonfarm self-employment. The other dependent variable is based upon sectoral location. This is defined by assigning the industry of the job held during the week of the interview to either the core or the periphery sector, using the dichotomous classification scheme derived by Tolbert et al. (1980). This operationalization of economic sectors has been criticized on a number of statistical grounds (Hauser, 1980; Hodson and Kaufman, 1981). However, the scheme has been convincingly defended (Beck et al., 1980a; Beck et al., 1980b; Horan et al., 1981) and seems to represent the best available measure of sectoral location.

Two variables based on the human capital characteristics of workers in each occupation, average years of schooling completed and average experience, are included in the occupational earnings determination model. Unfortunately, it is difficult to measure directly either work experience or on-the-job training with the public use data. Instead, experience is approximated by subtracting from each individual's age the number of years of schooling completed plus five. This assumes that individuals who are not in school are working. While this may be true for males, female labor force participation patterns tend to be less continuous than those implied by this measure of experience. Consequently, this study defines work experience for females on the basis of a set of analyses of 30- to 44-year-old women performed by Beck et al. (1980b:117) in which the number of years worked since completion of schooling was regressed on the conventional experience measure separately by race and marital status.[5] By using this refined measure, the bias inherent in describing female work experience in terms of the typical male experience is reduced.

Three other independent variables are also included in the analyses that follow. The percentage of the work force in an occupation whose spouse was enumerated as living in the same household and the percentage of the occupation-specific work force who reported having at least one child under the age of eighteen living at home were used as measures of worker stability in an occupation, it being reasoned that workers with family commitments would be more likely to remain with a job. Finally, the percentage of the work force in an occupation who reported being self-employed in 1970 was included as a very rough estimate of the amount of control associated with an occupation, which is demonstrated to be of such importance by Wolf and Fligstein (1979) and Spaeth (1979).

The sex composition of an occupation has been defined in a number of ways (Wolf and Rosenfeld, 1978; England, 1980; Bridges, 1980; Oppenheimer, 1970). However, the present analysis relies on the method employed by Jusenius (1975). Any occupation in which the proportion of women is ten percentage points higher than that which would be expected on the basis of their presence in the labor force in general constitutes a predominantly female occupation. Conversely, any occupation in which the proportion of women is more than ten percentage points lower than that which would be expected given their level in the labor force as a whole is defined as a predominantly male occupation. On the basis of this strategy and because 40% of the labor force defined in this sample consists of women, predominantly female occupations are those in which more than 50% of the work force is female, and predominantly male occupations are those in which less than 30% of the work force is female.

The sex label of an occupation is redefined for each sector in order to control for the distribution of workers within sectors by sex. Consequently, in the core, where only 28% of the work force is female, predominantly female occupations are those with more than 38% female workers and predominantly male are those in which women are less than 18% of the work force. The cutoff points for predominantly female and predominantly male occupations in the periphery are 61% and 41%, respectively.

III. RESULTS

Essentially two sets of hypotheses are to be examined. The first set directly addresses much of the recent research into occupational segregation and earnings discrimination against women by examining the between-sector effects of occupational segregation on earnings. Specifically, the sectoral location of an occupation is defined as an important structural source of earnings, and the concern is with considering how differences in the sectoral location of occupations may anticipate income inequalities between the sexes. The second set of hypotheses elaborates within-sector variations in the relationship between occupational segregation and earnings. In particular, it is argued that variations occur along quantitative a well as qualitative dimensions.

A. Between-Sector Effects of Occupational Segregation on Earnings

The first hypothesis to be tested is that sex differences in earnings partly result from the tendency for women to be concentrated in occupations with fewer income-producing attributes than those in which men are more commonly found. This involves demonstrating, first, that predominantly female occupations are disproportionately located in the periphery and, second, that sectoral location accounts for a substantial part of the earnings gap between predominantly female occupations and other sex-typed occupations.

In order to determine whether predominantly female occupations are more likely to be located in the periphery than the core, the sectoral location of detailed occupational categories was regressed on their sex composition. Table 1 presents the results of this regression equation. As the unstandardized coefficient of $-.373$ in the first equation indicates, each percentage point increment in the percentage female in an occupation results in a .37 percentage point decrease in the probability that an occupation is located in the core. This supports the hypothesis that predominantly female occupations are disproportionately located in the periphery.

It might be argued that this negative relationship results from the tendency for occupations in which women are frequently located to be characterized by low levels of education and training, which in turn accounts for their disproportionate location in the periphery, where jobs are generally characterized in this way. To test this contention, sectoral location was regressed on sex composition, average education, and average experience levels of workers in each of the detailed occupations. The second equation in Table 1, then, presents the unstandardized regression coefficients for sectoral location regressed on sex composition controlling for education and experience levels of occupations. While the addition of these two independent variables significantly increases the variance explained in the dependent variable, the negative effects of sex composition on sectoral location remain substantial and significant. Indeed, controlling for education and

Table 1. Coefficients of Reduced-Form Equations in the
Average Sector Location Model for all Occupations
($N^* = 388$)

Predetermined Variable	Unstandardized Regression Coefficients (S.E.) Dependent Variable = AVGSEC70	
AVGSEX	−0.373 (.010)	−0.440 (.014)
AVGED		0.009 (.002)
AVGEXPER		−0.004 (.001)
Constant	0.610	0.614
R^2	0.141	0.150

Note: *Reported N's are unweighted, coefficients are based on weighted N's.

experience levels increases the effects of sex composition, which suggests that part of the relationship between sex composition and sectoral location is hidden by the relationship among the independent variables. (This will be explored further later.) Not only, then, are the occupations in which women are typically located more likely to be located in the periphery sector but also this occurs independent of the skill levels associated with these occupations.

To discern whether their disproportionate location in the periphery helps account for the low earnings of predominantly female occupations, two regression equations were estimated. Table 2 presents the unstandardized results of these regression analyses. In the first equation the natural log of average weekly earnings for occupations was regressed on the sex composition of these occupations. The unstandardized coefficient confirms that predominantly female occupations pay less than other occupations. A one-percentage-point increase in the percentage female in an occupation is reflected in a 48% reduction in the earnings of occupations.[6] The introduction of sectoral location into the equation significantly increases the amount of variation in occupational earnings explained and reduces the negative effects of sex composition on earnings. This testifies to the significance of sectoral location in explaining part of the earnings gap between predominantly female and other occupations.

On the basis of these analyses it appears that there are "between-sector effects" of occupational segregation on occupational earnings. This finding, in turn, has implications for explanations of individual earnings differences between the sexes. It suggests (although this remains untested here) that part of the reason women have lower earnings than men is that they are concentrated in occupations which are disproportionately located in the periphery sector of the economy. Nevertheless, as the regression coefficients in the second equation in Table 2

Table 2. Coefficients of Reduced-Form Equations in the
Earnings Determination Model for all Occupations
(N* = 388)

Predetermined Variable	Unstandardized Regression Coefficients (S.E.) Dependent Variable = LNEARNS	
AVGSEX	−0.656 (.011)	−0.536 (.012)
AVGSEC70		0.320 (.012)
Constant	5.121	4.926
R^2	0.270	0.325

Note: *Reported N's are unweighted, coefficients are based on weighted N's.

demonstrate, the low earnings of predominantly female occupations cannot be completely accounted for in this way. Sex composition continues to impact earnings negatively even after controlling for sectoral location. This finding is relevant for the second set of hypotheses to be tested, for it implies the presence of "within-sector effects" of occupational segregation on earnings disparities as well.

B. Within-Sector Effects of Occupational Segregation on Earnings

It has been argued that predominantly female occupations receive less for income-producing attributes than do other occupations and that this may be accounted for by within-sector variations in the relationship between occupational sex segregation and earnings. This contention is addressed here in two ways: first, the occupational earnings determination process is examined in each sector, and, second, the characteristics of occupational sex segregation are examined in each sector.

1. Earnings Determination Within Sectors

The coefficients in Table 2 suggest that predominantly female occupations are not rewarded as highly as other occupations for location in the core. To document this tendency more carefully, separate earnings determination models were estimated for each sector. Table 3 presents the unstandardized coefficients of the reduced-form equations in the model for the core (on the left) and the periphery (on the right). Focusing on the first four equations for each sector, and leaving the interaction terms for later discussion, several tendencies warrant attention.

These coefficients illustrate the negative effect of sex composition on occupational earnings. Furthermore, as expected the magnitude of this effect is larger in the core than in the periphery, although in both cases the effect is significant. Thus, in the core a one-percentage-point increase in the percentage female in an occupation results in a 48% reduction in weekly earnings. In the periphery, on the other hand, the associated reduction in earnings is 37%. These findings demonstrate that, within sectors, female crowding in an occupation continues to have a detrimental effect on earnings.

Part of the negative effects of sex composition may result from characteristics of occupations in which women are frequently located which are not wholly accounted for by specifying their sectoral location. In other words, sectoral location is only one of several income-producing attributes of an occupation, and some of the positive effect on income of core location per se may be undermined by the tendency for typically female occupations to have lower levels of these other income-producing attributes. To test this argument, four independent variables defined as having an effect on income were introduced into the equation. The first set of variables, average education and average experience, are measures of skill-related characteristics. The second set of independent variables—percentage of the occupation-specific work force that is married with the spouse living at home and percentage of the work force with own children under 18 living at home—broadly speaking, are estimates of work force stability. The third variable, percentage of the work force that is self-employed, is an estimate of authority structured into the occupation. As the unstandardized results of the regression equations presented in the fourth column and the twelfth column of Table 3 indicate, all of the variables except the percentage of the work force with children under 18 in the periphery explain a significant portion of the variance in the sector-specific earnings levels of occupations. Consequently, it could be argued that in each sector one of the reasons the occupations into which women are concentrated tend to generate low earnings is that they tend to be characterized by low skill levels, an unstable work force, and low levels of authority. Yet this does not entirely account for the impact of sex composition on earnings, which remains negative and significant. This, in turn, confirms the hypothesis that part of the earnings differential between predominantly female and other occupations occurs because "women's occupations" tend to receive lower returns in earnings, relative to "men's occupations," for comparable income-producing attributes. While it remains untested here, this also suggests that individual earnings disparities between the sexes may result from women's concentration in these kinds of occupations.

The next task is to examine sex-labeled occupations to determine whether there are systematic characteristics of these occupations, resulting from their sectoral location, which structure their impact on earnings. For these purposes an examination of within-sector variations in the nature of occupational sex segregation is particularly informative.

Table 3. Coefficients of Reduced-Form Equations in the Occupational Earnings Determination Model For Each Sector

Unstandardized Regression Coefficients (S.E.)
Dependent Variable = LNEARNS

Core (N* = 297)

Predetermined Variable[a]	(1)	(2)	(3)	(4)	(5)	(6)	(7)	(8)
AVGSEX	−.661 (.017)	−.438 (.018)	−.252 (.020)	−.244 (.020)	−.244 (.020)	−.823 (.135)	−.713 (.168)	−2.038 (.341)
AVGED		.145 (.002)	.143 (.003)	.134 (.003)	.144 (.008)	.124 (.009)	.124 (.009)	.111 (.010)
AVGEXPER		.002 (.0009)	.024 (.001)	.021 (.001)	.026 (.004)	.020 (.004)	.020 (.004)	.013 (.005)
AVGKIDS			−.450 (.032)	−.438 (.032)	−.444 (.032)	−.472 (.033)	−.469 (.033)	−.482 (.033)

Periphery (N* = 292)

Predetermined Variable[a]	(1)	(2)	(3)	(4)	(5)	(6)	(7)	(8)
AVGSEX	−.456 (.017)	−.269 (.016)	−.293 (.016)	−.293 (.016)	−.290 (.016)	−.751 (.073)	−.676 (.101)	−.001 (.197)
AVGED		.148 (.002)	.131 (.002)	.130 (.002)	.104 (.006)	.070 (.008)	.071 (.008)	.095 (.010)
AVGEXPER		.026 (.001)	.018 (.001)	.017 (.001)	.0005 (.003)	−.009 (.004)	−.008 (.004)	.006 (.005)
AVGKIDS			−.084 (.035)	−.068 (.036)	−.036 (.036)	−.043 (.036)	−.039 (.036)	−.044 (.036)

	(1)	(2)	(3)	(4)	(5)	(6)	(7)	(8)	(9)	(10)	(11)	(12)	(13)	(14)	(15)	(16)
AVGSPPRS			.323 (.035)	.353 (.035)	.350 (.035)	.343 (.035)	.341 (.035)	.354 (.035)			.546 (.030)	.540 (.030)	.549 (.030)	.534 (.030)	.530 (.030)	.518 (.030)
AVGSLF7C				.309 (.035)	.318 (.036)	.310 (.036)	.303 (.037)	.297 (.037)				.070 (.024)	.078 (.024)	.070 (.024)	.063 (.024)	.050 (.024)
EDEXP					−.0004 (.0003)	.0002 (.0004)	.0002 (.0003)	.0008 (.0004)					.001 (.0003)	.002 (.0003)	.002 (.0003)	.001 (.0004)
SEXED						.050 (.011)	.043 (.013)	.154 (.028)						.042 (.006)	.038 (.007)	−.023 (.017)
SEXEXPER							−.003 (.002)	.071 (.017)							−.002 (.002)	−.041 (.010)
SEXEDEXP								−.006 (.001)								.004 (.001)
Constant	5.228	3.040	2.948	3.052	2.938	3.188	3.170	3.326	4.909	2.671	2.727	2.749	3.021	3.405	3.372	3.103
R^2	.265	.592	.629	.635	.635	.637	.637	.638	.127	.547	.585	.586	.588	.591	.591	.593

Note: *Reported N's are unweighted, coefficients are based on weighted N's.

2. Within-Sector Variations in Occupational Sex Segregation

It has been argued that, in the core sector, occupational sex segregation is a mechanism for directly employing and maintaining a cheap labor supply. In the periphery, however, production in general is dependent on the direct use of cheap labor, and the structure of the sector itself virtually guarantees that the low cost of this supply is maintained. Occupational segregation is not likely to occur in this structure, at least not for the same reasons that it appears in the core. Furthermore, because the characteristics of "women's occupations" are likely to reflect this tendency, it is reasonable to assume that the differences between predominantly female occupations and other occupations will vary by sector.

a. Quantitative differences. The first sectoral difference in occupational sex segregation anticipated is a quantitative one. Specifically, it is argued that occupational sex segregation per se is a more likely outcome of the productive process in the core than it is in the periphery. The hypothesis can be tested through a comparison of the occupational distribution of workers by sex within each sector. Table 4 presents this distribution for Duncan's 17 occupational categories, modified so as to distinguish between durable and nondurable manufacturing industries. The first two columns represent the percentage of the total male and female work force in occupations in the core, respectively. These are followed by the equivalent sex distributions for the periphery and for the work force as a whole.

In the core almost 55% of all females are concentrated in the clerical occupations (clerks), and over three-fourths of all female workers are concentrated in three occupations—clerks, and operatives in durable and nondurable manufacturing. In the periphery, on the other hand, no occupational category accounts for more than 27% of the female work force, and only two-thirds of women workers in the periphery are located in three occupations—service work, clerical work, and salaried professionals. Not only is occupational sex segregation somewhat more prevalent in the core than it is in the periphery, but also it is more pronounced in the core than in the occupational structure as a whole. Almost 53% of the female workers in the core would have to change occupations with men to be equally distributed as compared to about 43% in the periphery and 48% in the work force as a whole. This is evidence that, while occupational sex segregation is an important form of discrimination against women, economic sectors are particularly important to an understanding of the way in which this discrimination occurs and its subsequent impact on socioeconomic outcomes.

b. Qualitative differences. The second hypothesis concerning intrasectoral differences in the nature of occupational sex segregation and earnings is a qualitative one. Two such "qualitative" differences are investigated here: occupational earnings levels, on the one hand, and the way in which occupational characteristics are translated into occupational earnings, on the other. Furthermore, two occupational attributes are identified as particularly relevant to the present purposes, namely, experience and educational characteristics. Not only does focusing on these help clarify the way in which sex and sectoral location operate to determine occupational earnings, but also it is a useful way of empirically comparing classical and dual economy approaches to the socioeconomic achievement process.

The classical literature defines these variables as human capital investments. Classical theorists, either directly or by implication, emphasize differences in education and experience levels of individuals in explaining the earnings differences between predominantly male and predominantly female occupations (Sewell et al., 1980; Polachek, 1976). Their reasoning suggests that, whenever earnings differences persist in the face of controls for differences in experience and education, they are primarily a consequence of employer "tastes" and discrimination. However, in the classical framework there is no reason to expect systematic differences in the way in which these characteristics are rewarded.

In contrast, the dual economy literature implies that occupational earnings differences cannot be explained by reference to the characteristics of the individuals within them. Furthermore, discrimination in this view is embedded in the structure of production and as a result has systematic consequences for certain groups of workers. In particular, dual economy theorists emphasize the effects of economic sectors in conditioning and constraining the socioeconomic achievement process. In this framework there is good reason to expect systematic sectoral differences in the returns to such "productivity components" as education and experience. Furthermore, because it is argued here that occupational sex segregation is similarly embedded in the structure of production, there are also likely to be systematic differences in the way in which these characteristics are rewarded depending on the sex composition of occupations.[7]

To determine how variations in the sex composition of occupations are related to variations in returns to average education and experience, a number of interaction terms were introduced in the occupational earnings determination models presented in Table 3. Columns 5 through 8 and 13 through 16 show the results of these regression equations for the core and the periphery, respectively.

The first interaction term of interest is that of education and experience. In the core, as column 5 indicates, the effects on earnings of education and experience are contingent on one another such that education has less of an income-generating effect at high levels of experience. Conversely, the effects of experience on earnings are reduced at high levels of education. Essentially this suggests that, in the core sector, jobs are structured in such a way that education and experience are substitutable. In the periphery, on the other hand, experience is not translated into earnings and education is an income-generating attribute of occupations only at high levels of experience. These findings document important differences in the way in which the occupational characteristics of experience and education are

Table 4. Occupational Distribution of Workers by Sex

	Core				Periphery				Population			
	Males		Females		Males		Females		Males		Females	
	number	percent	number	percent	number	percent	number	percent	number	percent	number	percent
Self-Employed Professionals	52	1.8%	7	0.6%	21	0.9%	13	0.5%	73	1.4%	20	0.6%
Salaried Professionals	338	11.5	77	6.7	256	10.9	405	16.5	594	11.2	482	13.4
Managers	212	7.2	27	2.4	168	7.2	59	2.4	380	7.2	86	2.4
Proprietors	44	1.5	5	0.4	96	4.1	24	1.0	140	2.7	29	0.8
Other Salespeople	145	4.9	11	1.0	71	3.0	44	1.8	216	4.1	55	1.5
Retail Salespeople	—	—	—	—	159	6.8	237	9.7	159	3.0	237	6.6
Clerks	289	9.9	626	54.6	124	5.3	616	25.1	413	7.9	1242	34.5
Craftspeople (durable manufacturing)	229	7.8	7	0.6	58	2.5	5	0.2	287	5.4	12	0.3
Craftspeople (nondurable manufacturing)	118	4.0	10	0.9	31	1.3	6	0.2	149	2.8	16	0.5
Craftspeople (construction)	338	11.5	5	0.4	—	—	—	—	338	6.4	5	0.1
Craftspeople (other)	179	6.1	3	0.3	239	10.2	23	0.9	418	7.9	26	0.7

Service Workers	150	5.1	72	6.3	321	13.7	660	26.9	471	8.9	732	20.3
Operatives (durable manufacturing)	310	10.6	133	11.6	77	3.3	37	1.5	387	7.3	170	4.7
Operatives (nondurable manufacturing)	136	4.6	120	10.4	47	2.0	161	6.6	183	3.5	281	7.8
Operatives (other)	200	6.8	23	2.0	244	10.4	101	4.1	444	8.4	124	3.4
Laborers (durable manufacturing)	35	1.2	8	0.7	23	1.0	3	0.1	58	1.1	11	0.3
Laborers (nondurable manufacturing)	—	—	—	—	3	0.1	1	0.04	33	0.6	9	0.3
Laborers (other)	30	1.0	8	0.7	144	6.1	18	0.7	277	5.2	23	0.6
Farmers	—	—	—	—	152	6.5	7	0.3	152	2.9	7	0.2
Farm Laborers	—	—	—	—	110	4.7	34	1.4	110	2.1	34	1.0
TOTAL	2938	100.0	1147	100.0	2344	100.0	2454	100.0	5282	100.0	3601	100.0

Index of Dissimilarity—52.7   Index of Dissimilarity—43.1   Index of Dissimilarity—48.1

translated into occupational earnings depending on the sectoral location of the occupation.

The second interaction term of interest is that of sex and education. The unstandardized regression coefficients in columns 6 and 14 represent the effects of the independent variables on occupational earnings after the addition of the interaction term. In both the core and the periphery the negative impact of sex composition on occupational earnings increases once the sex-education interaction is controlled for. This suggests that some of the negative effects of sex composition on occupational earnings in both sectors are hidden by the tendency for these effects to be less in occupations characterized by high levels of education. Nevertheless, there are differences between the sectors in the way in which the sex composition of an occupation affects the earnings determination process. In particular, sex composition appears to have varying effects on the ways in which education and experience interact to determine earnings. In order to specify the nature of these, occupational earnings determination models were estimated separately for each sector and within sector, for predominantly female as well as predominantly male occupations. Table 5 presents the unstandardized results of these regression equations for the core (on the left) and the periphery (on the right).

Looking first at the core and comparing the coefficients in the first and third columns, all of the effects of the independent variables are significant and positive with the exception of the percentage of the work force with children under 18. The addition of the education-experience interaction term introduces multicollinearity into the equation for predominantly female occupations and thereby makes the coefficients somewhat difficult to interpret. To the extent that they are interpretable, it is apparent that the positive effects on earnings of average education are greatest where experience is minimal and lowest where experience is high. In predominantly male occupations, on the other hand, the education-experience interaction is insignificant: both independent variables have positive, linear effects on earnings.

Turning next to the periphery, comparing the coefficients in the fifth and seventh columns reveals some important sectoral differences in the process of occupational earnings determination. In the periphery, neither percentage of workers with children under 18 nor percentage of workers who are self-employed affects average earnings. Furthermore, average experience is just barely a significant predictor of earnings in predominantly female occupations in the periphery, and it is an insignificant predictor in predominantly male occupations. Apparently experience is of minor consequence in determining occupational earnings in the periphery, a finding which is reaffirmed by the introduction of the education–experience interaction term.

As the sixth and eighth columns in Table 5 illustrate, the education-experience interaction is significant in both predominantly female and predominantly male occupations in the periphery. In addition, in both occupational groups this effect

Table 5. Coefficients of Reduced-Form Equations in the Occupational Earnings Determination Model for Sectors, By Sex Label of Occupations

Unstandardized Regression Coefficients (S.E.)
Dependent Variable = LNEARNS

Predetermined Variable	Core			Periphery		
	Predominantly Female (N* = 71)	Predominantly Male (N* = 179)	Predominantly Male (N* = 179)	Predominantly Female (N* = 83)	Predominantly Female (N* = 83)	Predominantly Male (N* = 169)
AVGED	.151 (.008)	.268 (.018)	.124 (.004)	.112 (.011)	.124 (.004)	.034 (.011)	.125 (.004)	.082 (.012)
AVGEXPER	.024 (.002)	.105 (.011)	.020 (.001)	.014 (.005)	.005 (.002)	−.062 (.008)	.016 (.002)	−.005 (.006)
AVGSPPRS	.209 (.050)	.231 (.049)	.655 (.055)	.665 (.056)	.340 (.052)	.318 (.051)	.691 (.045)	.728 (.046)
AVGKIDS	−.537 (.052)	−.613 (.052)	−.409 (.050)	−.404 (.050)	.021 (.069)	.119 (.069)	−.075 (.048)	−.038 (.049)
AVGSLF70	1.381 (.142)	1.460 (.139)	.289 (.042)	.279 (.042)	.023 (.060)	−.093 (.061)	.054 (.028)	.073 (.028)
EDEXP		−.007 (.001)		.0005 (.0004)		.006 (.0007)		.002 (.0005)
Constant	2.759	1.384	2.939	3.078	2.792	3.709	2.670	3.119
R²	.407	.433	.545	.545	.456	.476	.605	.608

Note: *Reported N's are unweighted, coefficients based on weighted N's

is such that rewards to education are contingent on high levels of experience. Indeed, this tendency is magnified in predominantly female occupations, as evidenced by the change in direction of influence of experience on earnings.

These findings might be interpreted as confirming the classical prediction that women are concentrated in occupations which do not penalize their labor force experience patterns; yet, they suggest that this is less a consequence of the sex, and subsequently the characteristics of the occupational incumbents, and more the result of the sectoral location of occupations. In the periphery, experience and stability characteristics are not income-generating attributes of either predominantly female or predominantly male jobs. This relationship does not hold across sector, however. Indeed, in the core there are important differences in the ways in which education and experience are translated into earnings, depending on the sex label of the occupation. Hence, it is incorrect to characterize all predominantly female occupations in the same way.

It has also been hypothesized that, because of the processes which give rise to occupational sex segregation in the core and the subsequent role it plays in combating the high costs of production in this sector, the earnings gap between predominantly female and predominantly male occupations will be greater in the core than it is in the periphery. To test this hypothesis, expected earnings were estimated for each sex label occupation group by sector. This was accomplished using a technique employed by Beck et al. (1980b), whereby specific regression equations were estimated at the mean level of the relevant variables for the appropriate universe. For example, the cost of being located in predominantly female occupations in the core was calculated first by taking the mean levels of the independent variables for predominantly female occupations in the core (see Table 6) and substituting them into the regression equations predicting earnings in predominantly male occupations in the core [see Stolzenberg (1979) for a discussion of how to handle interaction terms in this procedure]. The antilog of the estimate obtained in this way represents the expected earnings associated with location in predominantly male occupations in the core. Similarly, an estimate of the expected earnings associated with locations in predominantly female occupations in the core was also calculated. The difference between these two earnings estimates is then an indication of the cost of being located in female occupations in the core, and is presented in the first column and first row of Table 7. In an analogous fashion, the benefits of location in predominantly male occupations were estimated by substituting into the respective regression equations the mean levels on the independent variables for predominantly male occupations in the core. The results of this procedure are presented in the first column, second row, of Table 7. These two figures reflecting the costs/benefits of occupational location were then averaged to estimate the overall effects of occupational segregation on earnings in the core. This, in turn, appears in the first column, third row, of Table 7. Finally, the entire procedure was repeated for the periphery, and the results are recorded in the second column of Table 7.

Table 6. Means and Standard Deviations of Variables in the Occupational Earnings Determination Equation By Sector and Sex Label of Occupation

	CORE		PERIPHERY	
	Mean	(S.D.)	Mean	(S.D.)
Population				
LNEARNS	5.04	(0.42)	4.68	(0.44)
AVGED	11.49	(1.70)	11.33	(2.10)
AVGEXPER	20.53	(6.73)	18.00	(7.50)
AVGSPPRS	0.74	(0.16)	0.61	(0.18)
AVGKIDS	0.46	(0.15)	0.52	(0.14)
AVGSLF70	0.06	(0.13)	0.10	(0.21)
(N)*	(297)		(292)	
Predominantly Female				
LNEARNS	4.73	(0.27)	4.51	(0.35)
AVGED	11.81	(1.09)	11.57	(1.88)
AVGEXPER	13.46	(4.54)	13.80	(4.29)
AVGSPPRS	.60	(0.14)	0.57	(0.12)
AVGKIDS	.54	(0.14)	0.51	(0.11)
AVGSLF70	.01	(0.05)	0.04	(0.09)
(N)*	(83)		(71)	
Predominantly Male				
LNEARNS	5.22	(0.41)	4.82	(0.46)
AVGED	11.42	(1.88)	10.81	(2.05)
AVGEXPER	24.07	(5.37)	22.98	(7.73)
AVGSPPRS	0.81	(0.13)	0.66	(0.22)
AVGKIDS	0.42	(0.14)	0.51	(0.17)
AVGSLF70	0.09	(0.16)	0.19	(0.29)
(N)*	(169)		(179)	

Note: *Reported N's are unweighted, coefficients are based on weighted N's.

As the estimates in Table 7 demonstrate, there is a greater cost in terms of earnings associated with location in predominantly female occupations in the core than there is in the periphery. In the core predominantly female occupations pay on average of $146.34 less in weekly earnings than predominantly male occupations pay for the same levels of income-producing attributes. In the periphery, on the other hand, location in predominantly female occupations is itself an income-producing attribute insofar as it implies $107.54 more in average weekly earnings than men's occupations for the same characteristics. While it is best to interpret these figures relatively, rather than absolutely, in either case they lend support to the hypothesis. Furthermore, these findings suggest that at the individual level occupational sex segregation may be a more important source of the earnings gap between the sexes in the core than in the periphery.

Table 7. Earnings Advantage/Disadvantage of Occupational Location By Sector

Advantage/Disadvantage	Core	Periphery
Cost of being in predominantly female occupation	$103.49	-$67.79
Benefit of being in predominantly male occupation	$189.20	-$147.30
Average cost of occupational segregation by sex	$146.34	-$107.54

IV. SUMMARY AND CONCLUSIONS

The present analysis uses a dual economy approach to elaborate the way in which occupational sex segregation structures the earnings determination process. It is argued that classical theories cannot adequately account for sex differences in occupational location and earnings because of their reliance on prestige or status measures of occupations as well as their individualistic explanations of the earnings determination process. On the other hand, studies that have attempted to identify the structural characteristics of occupations that mediate the earnings determination process have not considered economic sectors in this context.

In this study sectoral location has been defined as a structural attribute of occupations that has income-producing effects; and it has been shown to anticipate sex differences in occupational location and occupational earnings in a number of ways. First, between-sector effects of occupational segregation on earnings have been documented. Not only are predominantly female occupations disproportionately located in the periphery, but also this accounts for a significant portion of the earnings gap between predominantly female and other occupations. In addition, within-sector differences in occupational segregation and their relation to earnings have been identified. Occupational sex segregation is more prevalent in the core than it is in the periphery. Furthermore, sectoral location has implications for the way in which occupational segregation structures the earnings determination process. In particular, it helps determine how experience and educational levels of occupations are translated into occupational earnings.

Not only do these results indicate that sectoral location is an important dimension along which to classify occupations, but also they call into question individualistic interpretations of the earnings determination process. Clearly there are systematic variations both in the way the "human capital" characteristics are translated into earnings and in the amount of earnings they receive. While there is little basis in classical theory either for predicting or for explaining these findings, they are anticipated by a dual economy approach as the outcome of the operation of advanced capitalist society. In this framework the between-sector differences in occupational location and occupational earnings are attributed to the industrial organization of production particular to each sector, and its subsequent impact on labor supply requirements. Similarly, within-sector differences in the characteristics of sex-labeled occupations arise from the particular way in which occupational segregation operates to lower production costs in the core.

While the present study helps advance the understanding of the socioeconomic achievement process beyond that offered by classical approaches, it still leaves two particularly important questions unanswered. First, it is not clear theoretically why in the periphery predominantly female occupations receive higher earnings than predominantly male occupations. These findings may simply reflect the way in which the dual economy approach has been operationalized here. For instance, it may be that a measure of economic sectors other than that of Tolbert et al. (1980) would yield different results. A more detailed examination of occupations that specified their location in a hierarchical job structure, or an analysis at the firm level, might also help explain this apparent anomaly. On the other hand, this finding might indicate the need to draw out more carefully the implications of a dual economy approach for an explanation of the nature of occupational sex segregation in the periphery. This in turn could involve an elaboration of the historical origins of the economic structure, or a demonstration of the articulation between class structure and economic sectors.

A second question left unanswered in the present analysis concerns the specification of the ways in which these findings at the occupational level anticipate individual earnings inequalities between the sexes. It has been suggested that these occupational characteristics have a direct bearing on the individual earnings determination process. However, substantiation of this argument is in order.

In spite of these problems, the findings here testify to the importance of considering the role of economic sectors in influencing the relationship between occupational sex segregation and earnings. By stressing the structural foundations of this relationship, the study contributes to an understanding of the way in which inequalities are embedded in contemporary American society. It is this structural feature of inequality that future research must continue to address.

ACKNOWLEDGMENTS

A previous version of this paper was presented at the conference on "New Directions in Theory and Methods of Immigration and Ethnicity Research" at Duke University in May 1981. The paper has benefited from the comments and advice of Richard T. Campbell, Angela O'Rand, Patrick Horan, Charles Hirschman, and Paula England, as well as from the careful scrutiny of the editors. I am grateful to Robert Jackson and Richard Landerman for computational assistance. Finally, a warm thank-you to Morrison Wong, Jan Colbert, Janine Dewitt-Heffner, and Suan Pow Yeoh for their invaluable help in getting the tables and manuscript ready for publication. Responsibility for the analysis and interpretations is entirely my own.

NOTES

1. Sewell et al. (1980) acknowledge the role of occupational segregation in this process in two ways. First, they demonstrate the tendency for women to be concentrated in occupations of middle-level status. Second, they argue that occupational segregation partly accounts for women's failure to gain higher levels of occupational status over the course of their work lives. Nevertheless, they assert that occupational segregation stems from and is perpetuated by differences between the sexes with respect to sex role socialization, on the one hand, and labor force experience based on differing family obligations, on the other hand.

2. Radical theory supplies more structurally oriented research on these questions. Essentially, radical theories of women's role and subsequent inferior position in the economy are of two varieties. Marxist theories argue that capitalist society uses gender to restrict the number of persons able to participate legitimately in the competitive process. Consequently, women constitute a reserve army of unemployed workers who can be easily circulated in and out of the paid labor force (Saffioti, 1978; Whitehurst, 1977). Radical feminists, on the other hand, view economic inequalities between the sexes as inherent in the structure of patriarchal society (England, 1980:24-25; Weinbaum, 1977; Quick, 1977). They contend that earnings differences between the sexes result from the dependence of women on men, which itself reflects conscious efforts by men to maintain their position of dominance in society. While these theories are gaining support among researchers, they have not yet been empirically tested. Consequently, they will not be emphasized in the present study.

3. Some argue that the sexual division of labor is the principal source of labor market segmentation (e.g., Harris-Kessler, 1975). In this view relations of dependence between the sexes constrain individuals' work choices. Others perceive labor markets to be differentiated on the basis of social relations and hence contend that differences between groups in social and power relations determine worker opportunities (Wright, 1978; Wright, 1980; Bonacich, 1976; Marks, n.d.; Markusen, 1977; Bonacich, 1972; Bonacich, 1973).

4. This procedure has both statistical and theoretical consequences. Aggregating and weighting the data in this way reduces the amount of variance on each of the variables and thereby increases the amount of variance explained by the regression equations. To some extent, then, the high R^2 coefficients in the regression equations are statistical artifacts. Nevertheless, changes in these coefficients are interpretable. Furthermore, in the analyses that follow the data are interpreted as reflecting occupational characteristics, although they are fundamentally derived from the characteristics of the individuals in those occupations. The degree to which one is willing to accept this assumption will undoubtedly influence one's acceptance of the present research and interpretation of the findings.

5. This procedure yielded four equations which were subsequently used to define female work experience.

White Ever-Married Females:
EXPERIENCE = .5483 (AGE-YRSED-5)

White Never-Married Females:
EXPERIENCE = .8757 (AGE-YRSED-5)

Nonwhite Ever-Married Females:
EXPERIENCE = .6164 (AGE-YRSED-5)

Nonwhite Never-Married Females:
EXPERIENCE = .7731 (AGE-YEARS-5)

6. In a regression equation in which the dependent variable has been logged, the antilog of the regression coefficient is interpreted as the percentage incremented in the dependent variable per each

one-unit increase in the independent variable. However, when the regression coefficient is negative, the antilogged coefficient represents a decrement, and the percentage reduced in the dependent variable with a one-unit increase in the independent is one minus the antilog of the coefficient. In this case, the antilog of −.656 is .518. This means that for each percentage point increment in the percentage female in an occupation earnings are 52% of their previous level. Presumably, workers in an occupation in which 33% of the work force is female can expect 52% of the earnings they would receive in an occupation in which 32% of the work force was female. This represents a 48% reduction in earnings (see Henretta and Campbell, 1978).

Clearly this is a sizeable reduction in earnings. The magnitude of this reduction testifies to the non-linearity of the relationship as a whole. It is the decomposition of this effect into its specific components with which much of the subsequent analysis is concerned.

7. Beck et al. (1980b) note important sectoral variations in the returns to education and experience for women and minorities at the individual level. They suggest that this partly results from differences between the sexes and between races with respect to occupational location. The present analysis is thus concerned with elaborating these relationships at the occupational level.

REFERENCES

Baron, Harold M.
    1975 "Racial domination in advanced capitalism: a theory of nationalism and divisions in the labor market." Pp. 173-216 in Richard C. Edwards, Michael Reich, and David M. Gordon (eds.), Labor Market Segmentation. Lexington, Mass.: D.C. Heath and Company.

Beck, E.M., Patrick M. Horan, and Charles M. Tolbert II
    1978 "Stratification in a dual economy: a sectoral model of earnings determination." American Sociological Review 43: 704-720.
    1980a "Social stratification in industrial society: further evidence for a structural alternative." American Sociological Review 45: 712-719.
    1980b "Industrial segmentation and labor market discrimination." Social Problems 28: 113-130.

Blau, Francine D.
    1975 "Sex segregation of workers by enterprise in clerical occupations." Pp. 257-278 in Richard C. Edwards, Michael Reich, and David M. Gordon (eds.), Labor Market Segmentation. Lexington, Mass.: D.C. Heath and Company.

Blau, Francine D., and Carol L. Jusenius
    1976 "Economists' approaches to sex segregation in the labor market: an appraisal." Pp. 181-199 in Martha Blaxall and Barbara Reagan (eds.), Women and the Workplace: The Implications of Occupational Segregation. Chicago: The University of Chicago Press.

Blau, Peter M., and Otis Dudley Duncan
    1967 The American Occupational Structure. New York: Wiley.

Blaxall, Martha, and Barbara Reagan (eds.)
    1976 Women and the Workplace: The Implications of Occupational Segregation. Chicago: The University of Chicago Press.

Bonacich, Edna
    1972 "A theory of ethnic antagonism: the split labor market." American Sociological Review 37: 547-559.
    1973 "A theory of middleman minorities." American Sociological Review 38:583-594.
    1976 "Advanced capitalism and black/white relations in the United States: a split labor market interpretation." American Sociological Review 41: 34-51.

Bonacich, Edna, and Lucie Cheng Hirata
    1981 "International labor migration: a theoretical orientation." Paper presented at conference on "New Directions in Theory and Methods of Immigration and Ethnicity Research," Duke University.

Bridges, William P.
  1980 "Industry marginality and female employment: a new appraisal." American Sociological Review 45:58-75.
Bridges, William P., and Richard A. Berk
  1974 "Determinants of white collar income: an evaluation of equal pay for equal work." Social Science Research 3:211-233.
  1978 "Sex, earnings, and the nature of work: a job level analysis of male-female income differences." Social Science Quarterly 58:553-365.
Campbell, Richard T., and Robert Nash Parker n.d.
  n.d. "Substantive and statistical considerations in the interpretation of multiple measure of SES." Unpublished manuscript, Duke University.
Doeringer, Peter B., and Michael J. Piore
  1971 Internal Labor Markets and Manpower Analysis. Lexington, Mass.: D.C. Heath and Company.
Edwards, Richard C., Michael Reich, and David M. Gordon
  1975 Labor Market Segmentation. Lexington, Mass.: D.C. Heath and Company.
England, Paula
  1979 "Women and occupational prestige: a case of vacuous sex equality." Signs: Journal of Women in Culture and Society 5:252-265.
  1980 "Explanations of occupational sex segregation: a review." Duke University and University of Texas at Dallas. Unpublished manuscript.
  1981 "The failure of human capital theory to explain occupational sex segregation." Forthcoming, Journal of Human Resources.
England, Paula, and Steven D. McLaughlin
  1979 "Sex segregation of jobs and male-female income differentials." Pp. 189-213 in Rodolfo Alvarez, Kenneth Lutterman, and Associates (eds.), Discrimination in Organizations. San Francisco: Jossey-Bass.
Featherman, David L., and Robert M. Hauser
  1976 "Sexual inequalities and socioeconomic achievement in the U.S., 1962-1973." American Sociological Review 41:464-483.
  1978 Opportunity and Change, New York: Academic Press.
Ferber, Marianne A., and Helen M. Lowry
  1976 "Women: the new reserve army of the unemployed." Pp. 213-232 in Martha Blaxall and Barbara Reagan (eds.), Women and the Workplace: The Implicatons of Occupational Segregation. Chicago: The University of Chicago Press.
Fligstein, Neil, and Wendy Wolf
  1978 "Sex similarities in occupational status attainment: are the results due to the restriction of the sample to employed women?" Social Science Research 7:197-212.
Fuchs, Victor
  1971 "Differences in hourly earnings between men and women." Monthly Labor Review 94:9-15.
Gordon, David M.
  1972 Theories of Poverty and Underemployment: Orthodox, Radical, and Dual Labor Market Perspectives. Lexington, Mass.: D.C. Heath and Company.
  1976 "Comment ii." Pp. 238-44 in Martha Blaxall and Barbara Regean (eds.), Women and the Workplace: The Implications of Occupational Segregation. Chicago: The University of Chicago Press.
Griffiths, Martha W.
  1976 "Can we still afford occupational segregation? Some remarks." Pp. 7-14 in Martha Blaxall and Barbara Reagan (eds.), Women and the Workplace: The Implications of Occupational Segregation. Chicago: The University of Chicago Press.
Grimm, James, and Robert Stern
  1974 "Sex roles and internal labor market structures: the female semiprofessions." Social Problems 21:690-705.

Harris-Kessler, Alice
   1975   "Stratifying by sex: understanding the history of working women." Pp. 217-242 in Richard C. Edwards, Michael Reich, and David M. Gordon (eds.), Labor Market Segmentation. Lexington, Mass.: D.C. Heath and Company.

Hauser, Robert M.
   1980   "On stratification in a dual economy (comment on Beck et al., American Sociological Review, October 1978)." American Sociological Review 45:702-712.

Hauser, Robert M., and David L. Featherman
   1977   The Process of Stratification: Trends and Analyses. New York: Academic Press.

Henretta, John C., and Richard T. Campbell
   1978   "Net worth as an aspect of status." American Journal of Sociology 83:1204-1223.

Hodson, Randy D., and Robert L. Kaufman
   1981   "Circularity in the dual economy: comment on Tolbert, Horan, and Beck." American Journal of Sociology 86:881-887.

Horan, Patrick M.
   1978   "Is status attainment research atheoretical?" American Sociological Review 43:534-541.

Horan, Patrick M., Charles M. Tolbert, and E.M. Beck
   1981   "The circle has no close." American Journal of Sociology 86:887-894.

Jusenius, Carol L.
   1975   "Occupational change, 1967-1971." Chapter 2 in U.S. Department of Labor, Dual Careers. Washington, D.C.: U.S. Government Printing Office.

Kalleberg, Arne L., and Aage B. Sorenson
   1979   "The sociology of labor markets." Annual Review of Sociology 5:351-379.

Kohen, Andrew I., Susan C. Breinich, and Patricia M. Shields
   1977   "Women and the economy: a bibliography and a review of the literature on sex differentiation in the labor market." Working paper, Center for Human Resource Research, Ohio State University.

Marks, Carole
   n.d.   "Split labor markets and black-white relations, 1865-1910." Comparative Studies of Immigration and Ethnicity, Occasional Paper Series. Center for International Studies, Duke University.

Markusen, Ann
   1977   "Feminist notes on introductory economics." Pp. 1-6 in the Review of Radical Political Economics—3rd Special Issue on the Political Economy of Women. Vol. 9 No 3. Women, Class and the Family.

McClendon, McKee J.
   1976   "The occupational status attainment process of males and females." American Sociological Review 41:52:64.

Oppenheimer, Valerie Kincade
   1970   "The female labor force in the United States: demographic and economic factors governing its growth and changing composition." Population Monograph Series, No. 5. Berkeley: University of California.
   1973   "Demographic influence on female employment and the status of women." American Journal of Sociology 78:946-961.

Piore, Michael J.
   1975   "Notes for a theory of labor market stratification." Pp. 125-150 in Richard C. Edwards, Michael Reich, and David M. Gordon (eds.), Labor Market Segmentation. Lexington, Mass.: D.C. Heath and Company.

Polachek, Solomon
   1976   "Occupational segregation: an alternative hypothesis." Journal of Contemporary Business 5:1-12.

Quick, Paddy
    1977   "The class nature of women's oppression." pp. 42-53 in the Review of Radical Political Economics—3rd Special Issue on the Political Economy of Women. Vol. 9, No 3. Women, Class and the Family.

Saffioti, Heleieth I.B.
    1978   Women in Class Society. Trans. by Michael Vale. New York: Monthly Review Press.

Sanborn, Henry
    1964   "Pay differences between men and women." Industrial and Labor Relations Review 17:534-550.

SAS Institute Inc.
    1979   SAS User's Guide: 1979 Edition. Raleigh, N. C.: SAS Institute Inc.

Scoville, James G.
    1969   The Job Content of the U.S. Economy: 1940-1970. New York: McGraw-Hill.

Sewell, William H., and Robert M. Hauser
    1975   Education, Occupation and Earnings: Achievement in the Early Career. New York: Academic.

Sewell, William H., Robert M. Hauser, and Wendy C. Wolf
    1980   "Sex, schooling, and occupational status." American Journal of Sociology 86:551-583.

Spaeth, Joe L.
    1979   "Vertical differentiation among occupations." American Sociological Review 44:746-762.

Spilerman, Seymour
    1977   "Careers, labor market structure, and socioeconomic achievement." American Journal of Sociology 83:551-593.

Stevenson, Mary
    1975   "Women's wages and job segregation." Pp. 243-255 in Richard C. Edwards, Michael Reich, and David M. Gordon (eds.), Labor Market Segmentation. Lexington, Mass.: D.C. Heath and Company.

Stolzenberg, Ross
    1979   "The measurement and decomposition of causal effects in nonlinear and nonadditive models." Pp. 459-488 in Karl F. Schuessler (ed.), Sociological Methodology 1980. San Francisco: Jossey-Bass.

Suter, Larry E., and Herman P. Miller
    1973   "Income differences between men and career women." American Journal of Sociology 78:962-974.

Tolbert, Charles, Patrick M. Horan, and E.M. Beck
    1980   "The structure of economic segmentation: a dual economy approach." American Journal of Sociology 85:1095-1116.

Treiman, Donald J., and Kermitt Terrell
    1975   "Sex and the process of status attainment: a comparison of working women and men." American Sociological Review 40:174-200.

U.S. Bureau of the Census
    1972   "Public use samples of basic records." From the 1970 Census: Description and Technical Documentation. Washington, D.C.: U.S. Bureau of the Census.

Wachtel, Howard M.
    1975   "Class consciousness and stratification in the labor process." Pp. 95-115 in Richard C. Edwards, Michael Reich, and David M. Gordon (eds.), Labor Market Segmentation. Lexington, Mass.: D.C. Heath and Company.

Weinbaum, Batya
    1977   "Redefining the question of revolution." Pp. 54-78 in The Review of Radical Political Economics—3rd Special Issue on the Political Economy of Women. Vol. 9, No 3. Women, Class and the Family.

Whitehurst, Carol A.
    1977   Women in America: The Oppressed Majority. Pacific Palisades, Cal.: The Goodyear Publishing Co., Inc.

Wolf, Wendy C, and Neil D. Fligstein
 1979 "Sex and authority in the workplace: the causes of sexual inequality." American Sociological Review 44:235-252.
Wolf, Wendy C., and Rachel Rosenfeld
 1978 "Sex structure of occupations and job mobility." Social Forces 56:823-844.
Wright, Erik Olin
 1978 "Race, class, and income inequality." American Journal of Sociology 83:6 :1368-1397.
 1980 "Class and occupation." Theory and Society 9:177-214.

OLDER WORKERS:
CURRENT STATUS AND FUTURE PROSPECTS

Zena Smith Blau, George T. Oser, and
Richard C. Stephens

I. INTRODUCTION

Retirement from the labor force at some arbitrarily fixed age is a *social* invention, not a biological imperative, and is a relatively recent phenomenon that has become predominant only among industrialized nations. In semi-industrialized nations a majority of males 65 and older work, and that majority is even larger in agricultural nations (Riley and Rones, 1968). The process by which older workers increasingly have become marginal to the regular labor force with industrialization and the growth of corporate enterprise is exemplified in the history of decline in labor force participation of older male workers in the United States.

In 1900 68% of men 65 and older were gainfully employed. By 1940, on the eve of this country's entry into World War II, only 45% of older men were still working. The proportion of older male workers rose to 52% in 1944 during wartime, with an accompanying increase in the percentage of older women working from 7.4% to 9.8% and increases also in the proportions of both male and female workers in the 55-64 age group. In short, older workers along with women and newly urbanized ethnic minorities served as a reserve labor supply that was recruited to replace the millions of men in the armed forces during the war years.

By 1950 less than half of American males 65 and older were gainfully employed (45.8% among whites and 45.4% among blacks and others). By 1960 only 33.3% of whites and 31.2% of black and other males 65 and older were in the labor force, and this proportion continued to decline so that by 1978 only 20.5% of white and 21.3% of black and other men in this age group were gainfully employed. Over the same period a decline also occurred in the labor force participation of men in the 60-64 age group: in 1950 87.3% of white and 81.9% of black and other men in this category were employed, versus 73.9% and 69.1%, respectively, in 1978.

The labor force participation of white women 65 and older increased from 9.2% to 10.6% during the period 1950-1960, while that of black and other women decreased from 16.5 to 12.8%. From 1965 to 1978 the proportion of white women workers declined from 9.7% to 8.1%; over the same period the labor participation of black and other women declined from 12.9% to 10.7%. Among 55- to 64-year-old white women the proportion of workers rose from 26% in 1950 to a peak of 42.5% in 1971, followed by a slow decline to 40.8% by 1977 and a rise to 41.2% in 1978. The proportion of black and other women workers in this age group peaked at 48.9% in 1965, declined to 42.7% by 1977 but also increase in 1978, to 43.6% (Rosenfeld and Brown, 1979).

These figures simply document the fact that occupational retirement at an arbitrarily fixed age, which became institutionalized over a relatively short span of time in the United States, has materially altered the status and prospects of the older worker. In contrast to other adult workers currently, to be a worker 65 or older is to be deviant relative to the preponderantly younger people who constitute the bulk of the work force and also to be deviant relative to one's own age peers, who for the most part have ceased to work.

A considerable body of literature has accumulated that details the reasons people give for retiring and their modes of adaptation in retirement. By comparison, studies to date of older workers have been relatively sparse. However, certain trends and issues have begun to dominate public discussion sufficiently to stimulate new interest in that deviant minority of older people who have remained in the labor force or, having once retired, have returned to work. While there is no immediate prospect of any large increment of older workers in the labor force, there is some reason to expect that over the long term recent shifts in public policy, which will be discussed presently, may serve to delay the age at which older workers retire and thus may well result in an increased representation of older workers in the labor force.

The enactment of the Social Security Act in 1935, making 65 the age of entitlement to Social Security benefits, and the establishment of ceilings on earnings of workers and of penalties for exceeding these limits until age 72, were the first major mechanism to promote the institutionalization of compulsory retirement in industry at an arbitrarily fixed age. Amendments to the Social Security Act that extended coverage to additional classes of workers contributed to the decline of gainful employment of older workers. Additional amendments that created eligibility for actuarially reduced benefits at age 62 to women in 1956 and to men in 1961 coupled with the indexing of Social Security benefits to the ever-rising cost of living over the past decade have resulted in higher-than-anticipated rates of early retirement among workers aged 62-64. The growth of disability payments has further enhanced the financial ability of older workers and even workers under 62 with demonstrable work handicaps to withdraw from the labor force.

The proliferation of private pensions, which in 1972 covered about 52% and 31% respectively, of male workers and female workers, created a further financial incentive for retirement (Schulz, 1978). Finally, the spread of pensions based on years of service rather than on age per se makes it possible for millions of workers still in middle age either to retire from the labor force or to pursue second careers in different occupations.

The evolution of the aforementioned forms of replacement income was prompted by but also has contributed to the spread of discriminatory practices respecting the employment and retention of aging workers and to their increasingly marginal position in the American economy. Indeed, one of the notable ironies of American society since World War II is that, during the same period when employment discrimination on the basis of ascriptive criteria such as race, ethnicity, and sex diminished, age discrimination increased (Wilensky and Lawrence, 1979).

II. REPRESENTATION OF OLDER WORKERS IN INDUSTRY AND OCCUPATIONS

The distribution of male workers 60-64 in various industries is much the same as that of workers aged 25-59. But there are marked differences in the distribution of workers 65 years and older in various industries. For example, the proportion of workers who are in manufacturing drops from 30% among younger workers to 13% among workers 65 and older. In contrast, workers in trade comprise 17% of workers below 65 and 26% of older workers, and in miscellaneous services 21% and 35%, respectively. There is a smaller increase in the representation of older male workers in finance, insurance, and real estate, from 5% of workers under 60, to 6% of those 60-64, to 9% of workers 65 and older.

Philip Rones (1978) has calculated an index of representation of workers aged 60-64 and of those 65 and older in various industries which reveals that an underrepresentation of workers 60-64 occurs primarily in construction, transportation other than railroads and railway express, utilities, retail trade, hospitals, and among other professional workers. Workers 65 and older are underrepresented in mining, construction, manufacturing, transportation, and public administration and are overrepresented in trade, finance, insurance and real estate, and in most service settings other than hospitals and educational institutions.

Several factors help account for variations in work opportunities for older workers in various industries. Workers 65 and older are markedly underrepresented in industries with the greatest incidence of pension coverage such as mining, manufacturing, transportation, and public utilities. These industries as a rule have compulsory retirement policies. Finance, insurance, and real estate also have widespread pension coverage, but because jobs in these industries often permit flexible work schedules, such as part-time work, work opportunities are numerous and attractive to older workers who choose to remain in the labor force.

Another factor that influences the proportion of older workers is the growth rate of industries. Slow-growing or declining industries that employ relatively few new, younger workers, such as railroads and manufacturing, exhibit an overrepresentation of workers in their early sixties whereas industries that have grown rapidly are likely to have an underrepresentation of older workers. Industries with high rates of self-employment are more likely to have higher proportions of older workers, since self-employment allows more flexible work schedules and the self-employed worker is not subject to compulsory retirement policies.

The representation of older workers varies according to occupation as well as according to industry. The overrepresentation of workers 60 and over is most marked among farmers and farm managers. Farming has been a declining occupation for some years, and the average age of farmers has been rising. Moreover, self-employment, which is more characteristic in farming than in other industries, affords the aging farmer a good deal more flexibility with respect to work schedules and the amount of time worked. Farmers are not covered by pensions and often have had lower incomes over their work careers. These factors provide incentives to prolong work which is physically demanding but has been made easier by mechanization.

Managers and administrators have an overrepresentation of older workers, which becomes less marked in the 65-and-over age group. In sales and service occupations, workers 65 and older are more overrepresented than those who are 60-64 years old, probably because these occupations are less likely than others to be covered by pensions. The most marked underrepresentation of workers 65 and older, as might be expected, is among operatives who are usually in unionized industries with good pensions. Such workers are also underrepresented in the 60-64 age group. Blue-collar workers, of course, perform more physically demanding work, and the work of operatives, in particular, is likely to be less satisfying than white-collar work. Professional and technical workers are somewhat less represented in the younger than in the older group. The proportion of professionals who are employees rather than self-employed has been rising, and as a rule they are covered by pensions with good income replacement ratios; hence, we expect their representation in younger groups to increase over time.

III. FULL-TIME AND PART-TIME OLDER WORKERS

With rising age, the proportion of men still in the labor force who work part-time increases. For example, in 1977, among working men 25-59 only 2% worked part-time, and among workers aged 60 less than 4% worked part-time, but among working men aged 65 and 70 the proportions of part-time workers are markedly higher, 28% and 53%, respectively (Rones, 1978).

Self-employed men 60-64 work part-time more than twice as often as wage and salaried employees, which, of course, reflects the greater discretion they can exercise over the extent of their labor force participation. This factor also helps to account for the considerably higher proportions of self-employed among workers 65 and over (25%) than of workers aged 60-64 (13%).

The availability of the option to work part-time instead of full-time is conditioned by the occupation and also by the industry in which wage and salaried workers are located. For example, sales and service occupations afford more part-time opportunities than do managerial or operative jobs. Industries in the core sector are less likely to provide part-time work opportunities generally than industries in the peripheral sector (Beck, Horan, Tolbert, 1978).

Aggregate Social Security data based on new beneficiaries indicate that low-income older workers are more apt to need part-time work to supplement Social Security benefits. Persons who are partly retired have lower Social Security benefit levels than either retired or nonretired older workers, and the partly retired are rarely eligible for private pensions. In addition, the ceiling on the amount Social Security beneficiaries may earn without penalty is less likely to affect beneficiaries who had low monthly earnings over their working lives (Rones, 1978).

The reasons that older workers give for part-time work change according to their age. Unemployment (or lay-off) and illness or disability are the most frequently reported reasons for working part-time by workers aged 60 to 64, and this pattern is rather similar for men and women (when cases of women taking care of the home are excluded).[1] Among part-time workers 65 and over, particularly among men, retirement becomes the most frequent reason given for working part-time and the frequency of unemployment and illness as reasons declines (Rones, 1978; Thompson, 1974).

The pattern of reasons for part-time work among women is more complex than among men. "Taking care of home" is the most frequent reason women 60 and over give for working part-time. This response does not vary with age among the married but increases with age among the nonmarried (widowed, divorced/separated, and never-married). The frequency of illness or disability does not vary with age among married women. Unemployment as a reason for part-time work is also less age-dependent among married than among nonmarried women. Finally, retirement as a reason for part-time work is much more frequent among nonmarried than among married women (Thompson, 1974).

Earnings and total money income of workers 50 and over vary by extent of work and by marital status (Thompson, 1974). Gainful employment and extent of work both decline with age among married and nonmarried people. However, within each age group married couples are more likely to have worked and to have done so full-time. But the proportion of two-worker units drops with age and the proportion of working couples in which the wife is the sole worker increases, a reflection of the widespread marital pattern in which husbands are somewhat older than their wives. The proportion of part-time workers rises with age among both married and nonmarried, and in both groups earnings decline but the amount of work performed annually does not fully account for the higher earnings of younger and of married workers. A strong relationship is found between work status, extent of work, median total money income, and poverty rates among the married and nonmarried. Poverty rates are highest among nonmarried, nonworking older people, a considerably larger proportion of whom are women. Since women during their entire working lives average lower earnings than men, these sex differences are likely to be reflected in differences in their social security benefits and in other pension coverage and benefits. Finally, the pattern of intermittent and part-time labor force participation, which is more prevalent among adult women than men, reduces the likelihood of public and private pension coverage and thus contributes to women's higher rates of poverty in later life.

IV. AGING TEXANS: A COMPARATIVE ANALYSIS OF PART-TIME AND FULL-TIME WORKERS

In 1977 we carried out a statewide study of Texans 55 years and older for the Texas Department of Human Resources. Data obtained through telephone interviews with a probability sample of 2672 men and women yielded data on an extended range of variables. What follows is a report of selected findings based on a comparison of full-time and part-time workers, who together constitute 36% of the sample, broken down into three age groups: 55-59, 60-64, and 65 and older.

In our sample of male and female workers, among the youngest group 88% and 12%, respectively, are employed full-time and part-time; the corresponding proportions in the middle group are 73% and 27%, respectively, and in the oldest group 41% and 59%, respectively.

With respect to marital status, most full-time workers under 65 in our sample are still married and living with their spouses, but those 65 and older, as a rule, are not. This holds true as well for part-time workers of comparable age.

The full-time workers in our sample have higher educational attainment; as a rule they are high school graduates. The youngest part-time workers as a rule have slightly less education, whereas those 60 and over average still fewer years of schooling.

Blacks and Mexican-Americans are about equally represented among full- and part-time workers in the three age groups. In both categories of workers, there is a decline in ethnic workers among those who are 65 years or older and a relatively higher presence of Anglos for several reasons. These minorities have a shorter life expectancy; they are less educated and more likely to have worked in less skilled occupations; and they have more health problems that prevent them from working at jobs for which their experience would otherwise qualify them. Both full-time and part-time workers 65 and over reside in somewhat smaller communities than their younger counterparts, and part-time workers aged 55-64 reside in somewhat smaller communities than their age peers who work full-time.

The mean occupational level of part-time workers' current jobs is lower than that of full-time workers (3.0 vs. 3.7). This pattern of differences is most pronounced among workers aged 60-64 (2.7 vs. 3.6), less pronounced among younger workers (3.1 vs. 3.8), and least pronounced among workers 65 and older (3.2 vs. 3.5).[2]

A large majority of older workers are doing the same kind of work in their current job (69%) as in their longest-held job. Among the 31% of workers doing different work currently than in their longest-held job, the mean prestige level of their longest-held job is lower among part-time than full-time workers (3.2 vs. 3.5), but this pattern of differences is more marked among workers in the youngest age group (3.1 vs. 3.6) than in the 60-64 year group (3.0 vs. 3.4), and in the 65-and-older age group this difference disappears.

The mean annual household income among full-time and part-time workers declines with age, but at each age level, as might be expected, the mean income of part-time workers is lower than that of those employed full-time. Thus, the means in the youngest age group are 3.2 and 2.6, respectively, for full-time and part-time workers; in the middle group the corresponding figures are 2.9 and 2.1, and in the oldest group 2.6 and 2.1, respectively. Stated in terms of dollars, the above figures signify that only full-time workers under 65 have average household incomes within the $10,000-$15,999 range; full-time workers 65 and older and part-time workers under 60 are apt to have somewhat lower incomes, and part-time workers 60 and over have mean income within the $4,000-$9,000 range.

Part-time workers report more health problems than full-time workers in each of the three age groups, but the mean difference between them declines with age. In the youngest group the General Health Status (GHS) mean scores are 3.5 vs. 2.4, respectively, for part-time and full-time workers; in the middle group the respective scores are 3.9 vs. 3.0, and in the oldest group 4.1 vs. 3.7. There is a sharper increment in reported health problems with age among full-time than among part-time workers. Notwithstanding these differences, these older workers, whether part-time or full-time and regardless of age, as a rule assess their health as good.

On a measure of daily leisure activity level, mean number of activities rises with age among part-time workers from 9.4 to 9.5 to 9.8, but among full-time workers no linear relationship with age is observed. The youngest and oldest age groups' mean score (9.5) is slightly lower than that of the middle age group (9.7). Moreover, while in the groups under 65 full-time workers average somewhat higher scores than part-time workers, this pattern becomes reversed in the oldest group; part-time elderly workers' mean score (9.8) is higher than that of full-time elderly workers (9.5).

A somewhat similar pattern of difference is observed on a measure of extent of friendship interaction. There is no difference between the mean scores of part-time and full-time workers under 60 (4.2). But among workers in their sixties, scores of part-time workers rise (4.4) and their mean scores are higher than those of their full-time counterparts aged 60-64 (4.2) and 65 and older (4.1).

That leisure activities and interaction with friends decline among full-time older workers 65 and over and increase among part-time workers suggests that opportunities to engage in leisure activities become curtailed for full-time workers in a context where the large majority of their age peers are likely to be retired and therefore to have leisure time during the day to engage in such activities. Part-time workers, in contrast, have some free time during the day to devote to leisure activities and friendship association.

On zestful engagement, a positive indicator of mental health, full-time workers' mean score is slightly higher (14.4) than that of part-time workers (14.3) in the 55-59 age group; that difference is more pronounced among workers 60-64 (14.5 vs. 14.0), but in the 65-and-older group the mean scores of the two groups are identical (14.3). No linear relationship with age is observed in either group.

On depression, a negative indicator of mental health, full-time workers' mean scores are lower than those of part-time workers in all three age groups, but the difference is most pronounced in the youngest groups (8.6 vs. 9.2); in the two older groups the mean scores of full-time workers are only slightly lower. Thus, among those 60-64 the mean scores of full-time and part-time workers are 8.6 and 8.7, respectively, and the corresponding figures in the oldest group are 8.5 and 8.6.

With respect to alienation, another negative mental health indicator which is quite a strong correlate of depression, a similar pattern of differences is observed between the two groups of workers. In the youngest group, under 60, full-time workers' mean score (6.9) is considerably lower than that of part-time workers (7.7). In the 60-64 age group the difference, while in the same direction, declines (6.9 vs. 7.2) and in the 65-and-older group it declines still further (7.1 vs. 7.2).

That part-time workers under 60 report more health problems, average a somewhat lower level of daily leisure activities, score lower on zestful engagement, and score higher on the depression and alienation measures than their age peers working full-time or older part-time workers suggests that reduction in work activity at an age when most of one's age peers are likely to still be working full-time may have demoralizing effects for several reasons. Workers in this age group may or may not be eligible for private pensions, but are not yet eligible to receive social security benefits that would offset to some extent the reduction in earnings that accompanies a shift from full-time to part-time employment. Reduced income relative to their previous income level and relative to the large majority of age peers still working full-time is likely to be experienced as a greater deprivation and as more stressful than in older age groups where many more of one's age peers are likely to be retired and living on a reduced income. In such a context part-time work serves to augment income and, relative to his or her retired peers, the part-time worker is advantaged, although not to the same degree as the full-time worker. Moreover, part-time work prior to age 60 is probably more likely to have been involuntary, occasioned either by health problems or by unemployment. Indeed, more workers in this group have been operatives in their longest-held jobs than in any of the other groups, and more of them are working at jobs different from their longest-held jobs than in any of the other groups. It was reported earlier that work opportunities for older operatives in industry are more limited than for those in sales and service occupations, and the pressures for retirement before age 60 are probably greater for such workers than for workers in professional, sales, and service occupations.

Just as the part-time worker is in a deviant position relative to the large majority of his or her age peers under 60, so the full-time worker is in a deviant position relative to age peers who as a rule are either retired or, if employed, working part-time. Workers 65 and older are also likely to be a small minority relative to their considerably younger co-workers. As already noted, therefore, full-time employment appears to curtail opportunities for friendship participation with age peers in the oldest group, and the considerable age gap between such workers and their younger co-workers may also constitute an impediment to informal relations on and off the job. Thus, while their work role provides the oldest group of workers with income and lends structure to their daily existence, it also appears to have some isolating and alienating effects. This is reflected in the fact that they average lower friendship participation scores and lower scores on zestful engagement than any other group of workers, and their mean score on alienation is higher than those of the two younger groups of full-time workers (7.1 vs. 6.9), although lower than part-time workers in the three age groups. On the other hand, the oldest workers average lower scores on the depression measure than *any* of the other groups of workers being compared, and they register less depression and alienation than the majority of retirees in our study.

V. RETURN TO THE LABOR FORCE

A significant proportion of retirees return to the labor force, and two recent studies provide some information about such workers. One study of 1,000 middle-level managers, professional and technical workers in three companies engaged in manufacturing, utilities, and retailing who had retired and subsequently re-entered the work force is worth summarizing because it sheds light on a wide range of experiences and attitudes of retirees who returned to the work force (Gray and Morse, 1980). Two out of five respondents in this sample returned to paid work, one-third to salaried positions, the rest to consulting, self-employment, or some combination of the latter. Those who returned to salaried employment usually found new jobs without delay, generally through personal contacts developed before their retirement. Although they had been employed in large corporations before retirement, the majority returned to jobs in *small* firms with fewer than 100 employees. Two-thirds of the sample had been managers before retirement, but, as returnees, three-quarters of them were engaged in technical or professional work. Small companies seemed less interested in their managerial skills than in their accumulated professional and technical experience. The overwhelming majority of the respondents who had been technical or professional workers returned to the same kind of work. The majority of returnees were at least as satisfied with their current jobs as with those they had before retirement, and a third were more satisfied. Most returnees preferred part-time work and were working part-time, but a significant minority were working full-time.

Reasons given for returning to the work force were more often of a noneconomic than an economic nature: the most often mentioned reason (3 out of 5) was that respondents "like working"; half gave as a reason the desire for more income; 2 out of 5 mentioned inflation; one-third wanted the contact with people a job affords, and one-quarter were concerned that their health would suffer if they did not work. Returnees exhibited considerable continuity in their postretirement careers and as a rule had worked for only one employer.

Before their retirement returnees indicated that their work had been an important source of satisfaction and pride, and many of their comments centered around work-related achievements and unusual qualifications. Most of the returnees had been subject to mandatory retirement. Nevertheless, they experienced their employers' decision as an invidious reflection on their past achievements and qualifications.

The authors identified three major mobility paths found among returnees. Some moved to higher levels of managerial control and compensation and in quite different types of companies than in their preretirement positions. Others, primarily consulting and self-employed workers, enhanced previously developed skills and interests and were working in new settings offering them more control and flexibility. Such workers expressed, according to the authors, "intense satisfaction" with radically different work roles. Two out of five self-employed or consultant returnees reported that they had always wanted to do the type of work they were now doing (which was "extremely diverse"), and the most frequently mentioned satisfaction in such work (3 out of 5) was that their work schedule was more flexible and their opportunities to work were indefinite. A third pattern spelled downward mobility. Financial pressures or "intolerable" boredom led some returnees to jobs they regarded as demeaning, undemanding, and unrewarding. Unfortunately, the authors do not report the proportional distribution of these patterns in their sample.

The major reasons given by retirees who had not re-entered the work force were, first, an unwillingness to work any longer and, second, that after taxes and other deductions working was not worthwhile. The authors observe that "many respondents will not consider even lucrative positions" because the social security earned-income limitations and the resulting heavy marginal tax rates are such an irritant and disincentive. They conclude from their findings that if the government were to decrease or even abolish these disincentives to work more retirees, at least at the occupational levels represented in their study, would return to the labor force.

In a subsample of 1189 respondents who were interviewed twice in our Texas study, among the 508 respondents who had ever retired 11.4% had returned to the labor force and were employed at the time of the study. Among the other retirees 13.4% exhibited keen interest and 12% some interest in five hypothetical work options they were asked about and 63.2% would not consider resuming work. Elsewhere we have compared these groups of retirees in some detail (Blau, Oser, Stephens, 1981). In the present chapter we will summarize our findings with respect to the group of retirees who returned to the labor force.

The returnees were, on the average, younger when they retired than other retirees; the median retirement age of males and females, respectively was 58 and 61, and they were as a rule younger (64) by three or four years than other retirees at the time of the study.

Twice as many returnees as other retirees (20%) had been retired less than two years, and fewer of them (40%) had been retired six or more years.

Returnees had higher educational attainment than other retirees; 18% had attended college or were college graduates and only 36% had not completed high school compared to well over half of other retirees. The average prestige of their longest-held job was also somewhat higher (44) than that of other retirees, and the proportion among them who had had supervisory responsibilities (63%) and authority to hire and fire employees was higher than among others. One of several indications that returnees were better off financially than other retirees is that the proportion who reported their income as "very adequate" (38%) was considerably higher than among other retirees.

Of all retirees, a majority reported that they had not looked forward to retirement, but the largest majority (70%) is found among returnees. Indeed, the pattern of our findings suggests that there is a monotonic relationship between workers' attitudes toward retirement and their disposition to return to the labor force after retirement, which is consistent with the evidence from an early longitudinal study of workers before and after retirement (Streib and Schneider, 1971).

A considerably higher proportion of returnees and of retirees who exhibited the greatest interest in returning to the labor force than of other groups reported that they had retired when all their friends were still employed (37% and 34%, respectively). This finding suggests that the work status of friends conditions workers' attitudes toward retirement and also their readiness to return to the work force after retirement.

Returnees were less likely to mention health as a reason for their first retirement than were other retirees (23% of returnees); less often reported that retirement had affected their health (18%); reported fewer health problems currently; more frequently rated their health as excellent or good (72%) and reported fewer symptomatic complaints (1.0). They averaged a higher mean score on a measure of zestful engagement, a positive indicator of mental health (14.9), and a lower mean score (8.2) on a measure of extent of worrying. They also scored lower than most retirees on a measure of alienation (7.3).

Returnees scored higher on a measure of preretirement planning for new activities and roles and more frequently preferred "being busy and active" (88% to "just relax[ing] and tak[ing] it easy." On a measure of optional roles that respondents had engaged in at age 45 and currently, returnees' mean scores were higher than nonreturnees' at both periods (3.5 and 2.9, respectively).

Finally, returnees averaged a considerably higher score (8.5) on a measure of weekly contact with relatives than other groups of retirees. The only measures on which they did not exhibit higher mean scores were the extent of weekly contact with friends and of daily leisure time activities. Thus, it appears that the time spent at work curtailed somewhat the time they could devote to such pursuits. But even on these two measures they ranked above retirees irrevocably committed to retirement.

The picture that emerges from our study of returnees is consistent with the results of the study of returnees discussed earlier, and both are quite uniformly positive. Returnees appear to be a well-educated, healthy, energetic, active group who exhibit a high sense of well-being and have sustained a relatively high level of optional role activity since mid-life. They appear to be aging more successfully than that majority of retirees who are irrevocably committed to retirement. Aging least successfully are retirees who evidence interest in working again but who apparently lack opportunities to return to gainful employment.

VI. LABOR FORCE PARTICIPATION AFTER AGE 71

At age 72 and beyond, workers covered by Social Security are no longer subject to the work-income limitation imposed on workers in their sixties. It is therefore of considerable interest to compare the labor force participation of older workers in this age group with that of younger beneficiaries. If, as is generally reported, health is a major reason for retirement among older workers, one would expect an even lower labor force participation rate at more advanced ages. On the other hand, if the work-income test is a significant influence on the decision of older workers to retire or to limit their work, then labor force participation should rise when the ceiling on earnings is lifted (Campbell & Campbell, 1976).

Several studies show an increase in the proportion of employed male beneficiaries at age 72 or older. Galloway (1965) reports a rise in the proportion of employed men entitled to social security benefits from 25.4% at age 71 to 27.2% at age 72. Epstein and Murray (1967) report that in the 1963 Survey of the Aged 6% of men aged 65-72 entitled to benefits were full-time workers compared to 7% among men 73 and older. Bowen and Finegan (1969) analyzed a 1/1000 sample of the 1960 census for all persons 65 an over and found, adjusting for certain variables, that for men 65-71 the labor force participation rate declined but then increased from 31.5% at age 71 to 34.4% and 35.2% at ages 72 and 73, respectively. Finally, Viscuse and Zechenhauser (1975) performed a multivariate analysis of the labor force participation of men and women 60-74, based on 1960 census data, using three independent variables—age, a 65-and-older dummy and a 72-and-older dummy. Their findings revealed a significant positive effect of the 72-and-older dummy variable and a retardation in the decline of labor force participation for people 72 and older. Thus, the weight of the evidence supports the hypothesis that the work limitation provision of Social Security is indeed a significant deterrent to the labor force participation of older workers in those age groups subject to the penalties.

VII. REASONS FOR RETIREMENT

The sharp rise in the proportion of workers taking early retirement with reduced benefits is a phenomenon that has elicited mounting comment and concern because of the heavy drain it is imposing on Social Security funds, particularly in view of the fact that older people are living considerably longer than in former decades.

Sheppard (1970) a decade ago reported that unemployed workers whose unemployment compensation benefits run out are disproportionately found among people in their sixties. No longer eligible for this form of income replacement, such workers are in effect forced into retirement. Sheppard (1970:73) further observes:

> The longer an unemployed worker is unsuccessful in finding re-employment, the lower his active efforts to search effectively for a job. Once he stops his search, he is then no longer defined officially as among the unemployed.

This discouragement process merits more study than it has as yet received. It is not known how widespread this phenomenon is among older workers, but there is evidence it has contributed to the surge of early retirees. For example, Barfield and Morgan (1978) report that the Social Security Administration's Survey and its Retirement History Study suggest that significant numbers seem to have been driven to retirement by a history of prior unemployment or by health problems.

An extensive study of newly entitled workers in 1968-1970 (HEW, Social Security Administration, 1976) which asked new beneficiaries "the most important reason for leaving your last job" reveals that 14% aged 62, 12% aged 63-64, and 6% aged 65 gave as the major reason loss of job due to lay-off, plant closings, cutbacks in the work force, automation, or being forced out of business.[2] Only small proportions of workers under 65 gave compulsory retirement as their major reason for retirement (1% at age 62 and 7% at 63-64), but at 65 that proportion increased to 36 percent. Similarly, the proportion of workers who gave as their major reason that they had reached retirement age was small among workers under 65 (2% and 4%, respectively, at age 62 and ages 63-64), but at age 65 this proportion increased to 13 percent.

One of the most consistent findings in studies carried out under the auspices of the Social Security Administration (SSA) is that older workers very rarely mention eligibility for Social Security or a pension as a reason for leaving the labor force. For example, in the SSA study discussed above, only 2% of newly eligible beneficiaries under 65 and 1% of those aged 65 mentioned this as the major reason for leaving the work force.

Health, in sharp contrast, was mentioned by 57% and 48% of new beneficiaries aged 62 and 63-64, respectively, but that proportion dropped to 23% among those 65 years and older.

Until recent years few researchers voiced skepticism that health was actually the major factor that prompted the sharp rise in retirement rates among older workers (Sheppard, 1970; Blau, 1973) despite evidence from U.S. Public Health Service reports (1973) of a decline between 1959 and 1972 in inactivity due to poor health among older men. Moreover, workers covered by Social Security who are actually disabled are entitled to disability benefits under SSA. But entitlement to such benefits requires objective medical verification. Entitlement to Social Security benefits, in contrast, simply requires authentication of age eligibility and coverage.

This is not to deny that many older workers have at least one chronic health problem, but so do a large majority of middle-aged workers (Blau, 1973). Nevertheless, an overwhelming majority of men and a majority of women without spouses under 62 are gainfully employed. Beyond that age a precipitous decline in labor force participation occurs, but only a small net decline in people's self-assessment of health, as SSA's longitudinal Retirement History Study shows (Bond, 1976). In that study 11,153 respondents aged 58-63 were interviewed in 1969, and there were follow-up interviews in 1973 with 8928 of the original respondents (Bond, 1976).

Among men, 84% had been in the labor force in 1969; in 1973 this proportion had declined to 49%, and the corresponding decline among women was from 58% to 33%. Health, as usual, was reported most often by both sexes as the reason for leaving their last jobs. Among the men who worked both in 1969 and 1973, 15% shifted from full-time to part-time work, and 19% of the women did so. A third of the men who worked part-time in 1969 were full-time workers in 1973; this pattern was less common among women.

It is noteworthy that in 1973 the proportion of the sample that reported a work-limiting health condition (25%) was the same as in 1969. In 1973, 26% of the men's self-assessments of their health had declined and 17% had raised their self ratings, a net decline of only 9%. A similar pattern was found among women. Finally, very few respondents spent a night in the hospital either in 1969 or 1973, but the number who did so was somewhat greater in 1973.

Thus, despite the fact that health was the most frequent reason given for retirement, there is nothing in the above data to suggest that any marked decline in the health status of most respondents had occurred over the four-year interim that might account for the marked decline in their labor force participation.

A further basis for disbelief that poor health is the principal determinant of retirement is that, even among early retirees in the 1969 study who reported *no* health limitation on the kind or amount of work they could do and who perceived their health as *better* than that of their peers, 10% of the men and 13% of the women still claimed health as their reason for retirement, and another 13% of the men and 22% of the women who perceived their health being the same as their peers' claimed health as the principal reason for their retirement (Quinn, 1977).

Since the mid-1970s, research employing multivariate strategies that analyze health status in the context of economic measures provides strong evidence that the replacement income available to older workers in the form of SSA benefits and public and private pensions, on the one hand, and work disincentive features of SSA and often in other pension systems as well are more powerful factors in the escalation of retirement among older workers over the past few decades than changes in their health status. Researchers now generally hold the view that health is perceived by Americans as a more legitimate and socially acceptable reason for withdrawal from the labor force than the desire to stop working when another source of income is available (Campbell and Campbell, 1976; Quinn, 1977; Boskin, 1977, Burkhauser and Tolley, 1978). Furthermore, early retirees are more apt to need legitimation than workers who retire at 65, which has been the normal retirement age.

Boskin (1977), using a subset of data from an ongoing panel study of income dynamics, follows a cohort of white married males through their sixties. His regression analyses indicate that the income guarantee in Social Security has a large positive effect on the probability of retirement, far larger than the positive effect of income from assets. Boskin attributes the larger effect of Social Security to the facts that it is guaranteed for life, that it is indexed against inflation, and that it cannot be transferred to heirs as assets can. Net earnings (after tax and SS earnings test effects are taken into account) have a large negative effect on retirement. According to Boskin's estimate, a reduction of the penalty imposed by Social Security on earnings from one-half to one-third would cut the annual probability of retirement in half for the average worker. Using hours ill as the health measure, instead of the more conventional self-assessment of health measure, Boskin finds the health effect to be far smaller and in a direction opposite to that indicated in SSA studies. While Boskin does not rule out health as a motive, he finds no evidence that it is the prime determinant of retirement. Inclusion of age 65 as a dummy variable in his equation reveals, not surprisingly, that there is a large increase in the probability of retirement at age 65 independent of other variables measured, which reflects the facts that this has been until very recently the most commonly designated age for compulsory retirement and that at that age workers become eligible for full Social Security benefits.

VIII. EARLY RETIREMENT

Enactment of amendments to the Social Security Act in 1956 permitting women workers to retire at age 62 with reduced benefits and in 1961 extending that option to men as well has resulted in a dramatic increase in the proportion of workers leaving the labor force before the normal retirement age. The proportion of early retirees among women rose from 16% in 1957 to 54% in 1974; among men, the proportion increased from 20% in 1962 to 44% in 1974 (Campbell and Campbell, 1976.379).

Joseph Quinn (1977) performed a number of multivariate analyses based on the initial 1969 data set from the Social Security Retirement History Study to determine what factors differentiate early retirees from workers of the same age who continue gainful employment. In one analysis he separated white married men who reported a health limitation from the others (and excluded those eligible for disability benefits) and performed separate analyses of the two groups. The analysis reveals a significant relationship between health status and eligibility for Social Security and/or other pension benefits. The probability of remaining in the labor force was markedly reduced by Social Security pension eligibility among workers who reported a health limitation. Eligibility also significantly, but more moderately, reduced the participation of healthy men. Eligibility for other pension benefits had similar effects, though smaller. According to Quinn's estimates, for a man who perceives himself as healthy the probability of labor force participation "is almost 21 percentage points lower if he is eligible for both Social Security *and* a pension than if he is eligible for neither." For men with a health limitation there was no significant interaction between eligibility for Social Security and another pension.

The effect of income from other assets on labor force participation was also negative, though far more modest than the effect of Social Security and pensions, but it decreased participation of those with a health limitation more than it did that of healthy men. Labor force participation was significantly higher for healthy men in low unemployment areas and also higher, but not significantly, for men with a health limitation.

Quinn's study provides the strongest evidence to date that, while health is a factor in the early retirement decision of older workers, far more influential factors promoting early retirement have been the lowered age of eligibility for Social Security benefits and the spread of coverage by other pension systems, particularly in the case of healthy older workers and to a lesser degree in the case of workers who report health problems.

IX. SHIFTS IN PUBLIC POLICY AND FUTURE PROSPECTS

The enactment of the Age Discrimination in Employment Act (ADEA) in 1967 represents an important turning point in American public policy with respect to aging workers and employment. It signified public acknowledgment that age discrimination in employment had become a significant threat to the job security and work prospects of workers aged 40-65, the very cohorts which since the end of World War II had been the first beneficiaries of a policy to encourage the withdrawal of older workers from the labor force.

This legislation denies employers the right to use age as a basis for hiring, firing, or promoting workers in this age range and, in effect, places the burden of proof on employers charged with discriminatory practices to demonstrate that age bears a significant relationship to job performance. Evidence has been gradually accumulating that in many types of work there is no significant correlation between age and job performance. For example, no relationship between age and accidents was found in a study of bus and train drivers in Helsinki, Finland. In a study of London bus drivers, those between 60 and 64 had the fewest accidents. Data on airline pilots, who are subjected to exacting examination twice a year, reveals that the average age of pilots forced to retire on medical grounds was 40-45, not older as might be expected. In a review of commercial airline accidents that occurred between 1956 and 1959 in which the commanding pilot was found responsible, the highest rate of such accidents occurred with pilots in their thirties and forties; only one pilot was in his twenties and one was fifty (Sheppard and Rix, 1977).

The findings cited pertain to a limited number of occupations, and it would be unwarranted to generalize these results to all types of work tasks. But they do serve to cast doubt on the monotonic decline-with-age model and will serve to stimulate the development and use of functional measures of job performance. Moreover, there is a growing body of evidence that indicates a variable relationship of age to performance; on some measures younger subjects perform better, for example, reaction speed; on some measures no difference by age is found, and on still others older subjects perform better (Horn and Donaldson, 1980).

In this context an observation by Ross McFarland is pertinent, namely, that "compensation takes place for every decline, and if certain capacities diminish, others are enhanced" (Sheppard and Rix, 1977:74). A great deal more research is needed on the nature and extent of such compensatory processes, in relation to which skills, under what conditions. Such research will help advance our understanding of the *sources* of variability in the work performance of aging individuals within and between occupational groups.

In 1978 an amendment to ADEA was enacted by Congress that became effective in 1979 extending protection against discrimination to most classes of workers until the age of seventy, thereby outlawing compulsory retirement at an earlier age.

In addition SSA raised the ceiling on allowable earnings for Social Security beneficiaries, which in 1977 was $3,000, to $4,000 in 1979 with the further proviso that the ceiling would rise an additional $500 annually until 1982 after which it will rise automatically in proportion to average wages nationally. This liberalization with respect to the work option is expected to stem, somewhat at least, the tide of older workers' full withdrawal from the labor force and to create an incentive for more Social Security beneficiaries to engage in at least part-time work.

Several factors precipitated these changes in public policy. Demographic trends, such as lengthening life expectancy, even more marked for women than for men, combined with a trend toward earlier exit from the work force that has taken place over the past twenty years, and inflationary pressures requiring substantial increases in Social Security benefits are imposing heavy strains on the Social Security system. The drain on the system is currently being alleviated by raising payroll taxes paid by workers and employers, with the prospect of further increases in future years. Additional burdens will be imposed on the system when baby boom cohorts begin to retire in the early decades of the twenty-first century, especially since the decline in the birth rate that began in 1960 will gradually raise the dependency ratio in the meantime, there being relatively fewer workers to support substantially increased numbers of retirees.

It is still too early to predict what impact recent legislation will have on retirement decisions of older workers and on company policies, but there are some indications that a rising number of older workers plan to prolong their work lives or to return to the work force after retirement, at least in some industries. For example, in a recent survey Traveler's Insurance Companies of Hartford found that 43% of their employees aged 62-65 planned to continue working past 65. But among employees 61-62 about 74% planned to retire between ages 62 and 65 and 22% planned to continue working past 65. An overwhelming majority of the employees surveyed indicated that they wanted to work part-time after retirement. As a result, the company has altered its pension plan. Retired employees may register at the company's new job bank for temporary jobs to work up to 960 hours a year, the equivalent of about one-half-year's work, without losing any pension benefits. Retirees will be used for such jobs instead of hiring outside temporaries. The chairman of this company (who also chaired a committee for the 1981 White House Conference on Aging) believes that "requiring people to retire at age 65 has been a great waste of a national resource," and he predicts that the trend toward remaining in the labor force past 65 will gain momentum (Houston *Chronicle*, March 15, 1981).

Such innovative programs constitute a new and interesting area for research of various kinds. For example, studies of how and to what extent such programs for the utilization of older workers become diffused in various industries, studies assessing the impact of such innovations on productivity and costs, and studies of the effects on older workers of participation in such programs, we believe, would be challenging and fruitful not only for researchers in the field of aging but also for researchers working in the areas of occupations and professions.

APPENDIX
DESCRIPTION OF MEASURES
IN THE ANALYSIS

Scale Name	First, Second and Third Quartile Scores*		Scale Items
Zestfull Engagement	$P_{25}^1 = 12.0$ $P_{50}^1 = 14.1$ $P_{75}^1 = 16.1$	$P_{25}^2 = 12.0$ $P_{50}^2 = 14.0$ $P_{75}^2 = 16.0$	How often in the last few weeks did you feel: On top of the world? Pleased about having accomplished something? Proud because someone complimented you on something you had done? That things were going your way?
Depression	$P_{25}^1 = 6.7$ $P_{50}^1 = 8.6$ $P_{75}^1 = 10.3$		How often in the last few weeks did you feel: Depressed or very unhappy? Very lonely or remote from other people? Bored? Upset because someone has criticized you? So restless you couldn't sit long in a chair?
Alienation	$P_{25}^1 = 5.5$ $P_{50}^1 = 7.3$ $P_{75}^1 = 9.2$	$P_{25}^2 = 5.4$ $P_{50}^2 = 7.4$ $P_{75}^2 = 9.4$	How often do you find yourself: Feeling your life today isn't very useful? Feeling things keep getting worse and worse for you as you get older? Regretting chances you missed during your life to do a better job of living? Feeling there's just no point to living?

(Continued)

(Appendix. Continued)

Scale Name	First, Second and Third Quartile Scores*	Scale Items
Friendship Interaction	$P^1_{25} = 3.8$ $P^1_{50} = 4.8$ $P^1_{75} = 5.6$	How many close friends do you have here in this community? How often do you see a close friend? Do you have a circle (group) of friends with whom you visit back and forth? Have you made any new friends in recent years? Some people go out of their way to make friends and others don't. Would you say you are more like the people who go out of their way to make friends, or more like those who don't?
Daily Leisure	$P^1_{25} = 8.0$ $P^1_{50} = 9.8$ $P^1_{75} = 11.4$	How often these days do you find yourself doing the following things: Work at a hobby you enjoy? Read books or magazines? Take walks or get other exercise?
Worrying	$P^2_{25} = 6.3$ $P^2_{50} = 7.4$ $P^2_{75} = 9.0$	Can you tell me if you find yourself thinking about these things: Becoming financially dependent? So forgetful others will need to look out for you? Being alone? Having to live in a nursing home? Becoming so ill or feeble that you can't care for yourself? Death and dying?
Optional Roles Currently	$P^2_{25} = 7.0$ $P^2_{50} = 8.5$ $P^2_{75} = 8.8$	Do you engage in any of the following activities: Volunteer work? Church work? Enroll in class? Hobbies? Group of friends seen regularly? Belong to club or organization?
Optional Roles at Age 45	$P^2_{25} = 7.6$ $P^2_{50} = 8.5$ $P^2_{75} = 10.5$	Did you engage in any of the following activities at age 45? (See list directly above).

(*Continued*)

(Appendix. Continued)

Scale Name	First, Second and Third Quartile Scores*	Scale Items
Weekly Contact with Relatives	$P^2_{25} = 1.9$ $P^2_{50} = 6.4$ $P^2_{75} = 12.7$	Number of individual contacts with relatives in one week.
Annual Household Income	$P^1_{25} = 1.4$ $P^1_{50} = 2.1 \sim \$7,700.$ $P^1_{75} = 3.3$	
General Health Problems	$P^1_{25} = 1.2$ $P^1_{50} = 3.4$ $P^1_{75} = 7.1$	Do you have trouble: Getting up stairs? Making the bed? Getting out of a chair? Putting out the trash? Standing for more than 10 to 15 minutes? Buttoning clothes or closing zippers? Remembering little things? Walking more than a block or so? Bathing? Preparing meals? Which of these health problems bothered you last month: Can't sleep through the night? Keeping warm or cool enough? Trouble seeing even with glasses? Trouble hearing? Headaches? Irregularity or Constipation or Diarrhea? Trouble starting or stopping urine? Getting up at night to use the toilet? Getting up at night because of difficulty breathing? Feeling faint or weak or dizzy after slight effort? Swollen feet and hands? Heartburn? Shortness of breath after slight exertion? Stiffness or soreness in joints? Any burning or itching?
Symtomatic Complaints	$P^1_{25} = 4.1$ $P^1_{50} = 5.0$ $P^1_{75} = 6.1$	Do you have trouble remembering little things? Have you in the last month: Been bothered by headaches? Can't sleep through the night? Heartburn?

Note: *The percentile scores P refer to the entire sample of 2,672 respondents; P refers to the subsample of 1,189 respondents to an additional questionnaire.

Respondents Having Ever Retired
(Retirees)
N = 508

Retirees		Percent
Returned to work (Returnee)		11.4%
Interested in	Keenly	13.4%
(returning to work)	Somewhat	12.0%
Not interested in (returning to work)		63.2%

NOTES

1. Older black men much more often give unemployment or layoff as the reason for part-year work (Rones, 1978).

2. The prestige level of occupations is a truncated version of the NORC Prestige Scale, where the larger-scale values correspond to higher-prestige occupations. In the Texas study, for the currently held job, the median value, P_{50}, of the prestige level was 3.5 and the 25th, P_{25}, and 75th, P_{75}, percentiles scores were 2.5 and 4.5, respectively. For the longest-held job, the correspondent scores were $P_{25} = 2.2$, $p_{50} = 3.4$, $P_{75} = 4.3$. For information on the scales referred to subsequently, the appendix provides the scale items and the first, second, and third quartile scores. All scales are directed so that higher values of the score indicate an increase in the trait. The values reported in the text are mean values for the referenced subsample.

REFERENCES

Barfield, Richard E. and James N. Morgan
   1978 "Trends in planned early retirement." Gerontologist 18: 13-18.
Beck, E.M., Patrick M. Horan, and Charles Tolbert
   1978 "Stratification in a dual economy." American Sociological Review 43: 704-720.
Blau, Zena Smith
   1973 Old age in a changing society. New York: Franklin Watts.
Blau, Zena S., George T. Oser, and Richard C. Stephens
   1982 "Patterns of adaptation in retirement." In Eliza Kolker and George Ahmed (eds.), Aging. New York: Elsevier.
Bond, Kathleen
   1976 "Retirement history study's first four years: work, health and living arrangements." Social Security Bulletin 39: 3-14.
Boskin, Michael J.
   1977 "Social security and retirement decisions." Economic Inquiry 15: 1-25.
Bowen, W.G., and T.A. Finegan
   1969 The Economics of Labor Force Participation. Princeton: Princeton University Press.
Burkhauser, Richard V., and G.S. Tolley.
   1978 "Older Americans and market work." Gerontologist 18: 449-453.

Campbell, Colin D., and Rosemary G. Campbell
  1976 "Conflicting views on the effect of old-age and survivors insurance on retirement." Economic Inquiry 14: 369-388.
Epstein, L.A., and J. H. Murray
  1967 The Aged Population of the United States. The 1963 Social Security Survey of the Aged, Social Security Administration Office of Research and Statistics, Report No. 19, Washington.
Galloway, L.E.
  1965 The Retirement Decision, an Exploratory Essay. Social Security Administration, Division of Research and Statistics, Report No. 9. Washington, D.C.
Gray, Susan, and Dean Morse
  1980 "Retirement and re-engagement: changing work options for older workers." Aging and Work 3: 103-112.
Harris, Louis, and Associates
  1975 The Myth and Reality of Aging in America: A Study for the National Council on the Aging, Inc., Washington.
Horn, Johnson, and Gary Donaldson
  1980 "Cognitive development in adulthood." In Orville G. Brim and Jerome Kagan (eds.), Constancy and Change in Human Development. Cambridge: Harvard University Press.
Kreps, Juanita M. (ed.)
  1963 Employment, Income and Retirement Problems of the Aged. Durham, N.C.: Duke University Press.
Lynd, Robert S., and Helen Merrell Lynd
  1929 Middletown: A Study in American Culture. New York: Harcourt, Brace.
Quinn, Joseph F.
  1977 The Early Retirement Decision: Evidence from the 1969 Retirement History Study. HEW, Social Security Administration, Administrative Staff Paper, No. 29.
Riley, Matilda White, and Anne Foner
  1968 Aging and Society. New York: Russell Sage Foundation.
Rones, Philip L.
  1978 "Older men—the choice between work and retirement." Monthly Labor Review. U.S. Department of Labor, Bureau of Labor Statistics, November.
Rosenfeld, Carl, and Scott Campbell Brown
  1979 "The labor force status of older workers." Monthly Labor Review. U.S. Dept. of Labor, Bureau of Labor Statistics, November: 12:18.
Schulz, James. H.
  1978 "Private pensions and women." In Women in Midlife—Security and Fulfillment (Part I). A Compendium of Papers Submitted to the Select Committee on Aging and the Sub-Committee on Retirement Income and Employment, U.S. House of Representatives. Washington: U.S. Government Printing Office.
Sheppard, Harold L.
  1970 "The potential role of behavioral science in the solution of the older worker problem." In Ethel Shanas (ed.), Aging in Contemporary Society. Beverly Hills: Sage.
Sheppard, Harold L., and Sara E. Rix.
  1977 The Graying of Working America: The Coming Crisis in Retirement Age Policy. New York: Free Press.
Smelser, Neil J., and Sydney Halpern
  1978 "The historical triangulation of family, economy, and education." In John Demos and Sarane S. Boocock (eds.), Turning Points. Chicago: University of Chicago Press.
Streib, Gordon F., and Clement J. Schneider
  1971 Retirement in American Society. New York: Basic Books.

Thompson, Gayle B.
  1971 "Work experience and income of the population aged 60 and older." Social Security Bulletin 27: 3-20.
Viscusi, W.K., and R. Zeakhauser
  1975 Welfare of the Elderly. Unpublished manuscript. Cambridge, Mass.: Harvard University.
Wilensky, Harold L., and Anne T. Lawrence
  1980 Job Assignment in Modern Societies: A Re-examination of the Ascription-Achievement Hypothesis. Reprint No. 429. Institute of Industrial Relations, Berkeley: University of California.
U.S. Dept. of Health, Education and Welfare, Social Security Administration
  1976 Reaching Retirement Age: Findings from a Survey of Newly Entitled Workers 1968-70, Research Report No. 47.
U.S. Public Health Service
  1962 Chronic Conditions Causing Limitation of Activities, U.S., July 1959-June 1961 Health Statistics, Series B, No. 36, October.
U.S. Public Health Service
  1973 Current Estimates from Health Interview Survey, U.S., 1972, Vital and Health Statistics, Series 10, No. 85, September.

NURSING TURNOVER IN LONG-TERM CARE INSTITUTIONS

Linda K. George

Nursing personnel employed by long-term care institutions may be considered peripheral workers for four reasons. First, the nursing profession itself tends to view employment at long-term care facilities as lying outside the mainstream of the profession. Few nurses express the desire to work in nursing or rest homes (American Nurses' Association, 1976; NCHS, 1979), and those who are employed in such facilities are significantly less active in professional organizations and networks (Levine, 1975). Second, the nursing personnel employed by long-term care institutions are almost exclusively women, many of whom work part-time or arrange their work hours to meet competing family demands. Third, the majority of nursing personnel at long-term care institutions are nurses aides, who typically have low educational attainments, uneven work histories, and low incomes. Finally, long-term care administrators often report turnover rates (i.e., rates of voluntary quits) in excess of 100% per year (cf. NCHS, 1979; Pecarchik and Nelson, 1973). If these turnover rates are even approximately true for long-term care institutions in general, it appears that nursing staff at long-term care facilities have peripheral attachments to their jobs.

Although a considerable body of sociological research addresses employee turnover, staff turnover in long-term care institutions has not received systematic sociological scrutiny. This neglect of long-term care facilities appears to be in part a failure to examine human service organizations more generally. In spite of the labor-intensive character of human service organizations, the vast majority of previous studies of employee turnover have focused upon technologically based work environments, especially manufacturing firms. There have been a few studies of turnover among nursing personnel, but these studies focused on hospital-based nurses rather than staff members at nursing homes (cf. Archibald, 1971; Price and Mueller, 1981; Wieland, 1969).

The purpose of this chapter is to examine voluntary turnover among the three types of nursing personnel employed in long-term care institutions: (1) registered nurses (RNs), (2) licensed practical nurses (LPNs), and (3) nurses aides, orderlies, attendants, and patient care assistants. (The job title for the last category varies among institutions—for reasons of convenience this job category subsequently will be referred to simply as nurses aides.) More specifically, two broad categories of independent variables are used to predict voluntary turnover among a sample of 469 nursing personnel from long-term care institutions. The two categories of predictors represent differing theoretical perspectives about the primary factors that facilitate or impede worker retention. The first category of independent variables consists of organizational characteristics hypothesized to influence turnover via their impact upon worker involvement and attachment. In essence, this perspective suggests that organizational inputs into the work environment largely account for variation in employee turnover. The second category of independent variables consists of social characteristics of workers (e.g., age, marital status) hypothesized to distinguish among "quitters" and "stayers." From this perspective, employee inputs are viewed as the primary determinants of turnover. Predictors derived from both of these theoretical perspectives are examined in this chapter. We do not argue that either perspective should be the exclusive focus of empirical study; rather, we wish to determine the relative explanatory power of the independent variables derived from each theoretical perspective.

I. ORGANIZATIONAL CHARACTERISTICS

A large body of literature testifies that the characteristics of organizations affect their ability to recruit and retain members (cf. Blau and Schoenherr, 1971; Etzioni, 1964; 1975; Meyer, 1978). The organizational characteristics of the workplace are ubiquitous, including the design of the physical environment; the configuration of statuses and roles that comprise the staff structure; administrative policies that define work loads, criteria for performance, and distribution of rewards; and so forth. Employee retention is enhanced to the degree that organizational characteristics facilitate employee involvement, commitment, and attachment to the workplace. Consequently, the organizational characteristics described in this chapter are those (1) suggested in previous literature as relevant to employee turnover and (2) that are especially relevant to long-term care institutions.

For purposes of measurement and analysis, it is essential to distinguish two general types of organizational characteristics: those that vary across institutions or organizations and those that are differentially distributed within institutions. Although previously recognized, this distinction has received insufficient attention in existing research. In most previous research addressing employee turnover, the work organization is the unit of analysis, the independent variables are organizational characteristics that vary across work organizations, and the dependent variable is rate of turnover. In order to examine the impact of characteristics that vary both across and within organizations, the unit of analysis must be individual workers and the dependent variable is the behavioral outcome of quitting or staying on the job. The research reported in this chapter includes examination of organizational characteristics of long-term facilities that vary both across and within long-term care institutions. As will be demonstrated, our findings suggest that it is important to examine the impact of both categories of organizational characteristics.

A. Structural Characteristics of Long-Term Care Institutions

As defined here structural characteristics refer to those aspect of long-term care institutions that vary only across institutions and are assumed to impact equally upon all workers in a given organization. Structural characteristics potentially useful for an examination of employee turnover in long-term care facilities are ownership, size, and differentiation.

Two aspects of ownership have been suggested as relevant to employee turnover: (1) who owns the facility (i.e., corporate versus noncorporate) and (2) the degree to which owners are directly involved in organizational management. Corporate ownership and/or ownership that is external to management limits organizational control over members and workers' access to decision-making processes (McEachern, 1975; Zeitlin, 1974) and thus is hypothesized to increase the likelihood of employee turnover. Although the literature suggests that these two aspect of ownership are conceptually distinct, in reality they typically are confounded: corporate-owned institutions are characterized by nonowner management and noncorporate facilities are managed by owners. In this study ownership is measured simply in terms of corporate versus noncorporate ownership, with the assumption that corporate ownership serves as a proxy for the degree to which owners are directly involved in the management of the long-term care facility.

Size refers to the scale of operations and, depending upon the organization under examination, has been measured in terms of either number of workers or quantity of output (e.g., production in manufacturing firms). There is no general consensus about the relationship between an organization's size and worker turnover. Some studies suggest that large size is associated with increased turnover; others indicate that turnover is greater in small organizations. Kimberly (1976), in an effort to synthesize this contradictory evidence, suggested that size has a differential effect on distinct dimensions of organizational life. Large size, for example, may increase communication problems and perceptions of impersonality, thus increasing the likelihood of employee turnover. But large size also may be associated with increased resources (e.g., equipment) which facilitate worker retention. In previous studies of long-term care institutions, size has been measured either as number of personnel or as number of beds (an indicator of production capacity). Although number of employees is an intuitively attractive indicator of size, it is not clear precisely what categories of employees should be counted—should size refer to the total the number of all employees working at the home, the total number of nursing personnel, or what? Because of these problems in defining the appropriate employee base, size is measured in this study as number of beds, which appears to represent a relatively straightforward indicator of production capacity.

Differentiation refers to the degree of specialization of functions or tasks within an organization (Blau, 1970). Some differentiation of staff appears desirable in that work loads are more manageable and tasks are better matched to the skills and training of personnel. Extreme differentiation, however, can have negative effects on personnel retention as a result of task routinization and lack of autonomy. Nursing homes vary in degree of differentiation. Skilled and intermediate homes are required, for licensing purposes, to have some staff differentiation. This is especially true of homes licensed for Medicare and Medicaid reimbursement. Rest homes, on the other hand, typically exhibit little staff differentiation. This study includes a number of indicators of differentiation, including licensure for Medicare and Medicaid (which is simply a proxy for defined kinds of differentiation), and the presence of certain specialized employees, including social workers and physical therapists.

B. Differentially Distributed Organizational Characteristics

There are two theoretically distinct types of organizational characteristics that are differentially distributed to employees within the same work organization (although they also can vary across institutions): (1) control mechanisms used to regulate the behavior of workers and increase commitment to the job and (2) organization-determined characteristics of particular jobs within the workplace.

The two primary control mechanisms used by work organizations to regulate worker performance and increase employee commitment are socialization processes and rewards. Socialization processes refer to mechanisms that help a status occupant to master a corresponding role. Although much socialization occurs in informal and unplanned ways, many work organizations also provide formal training programs intended to develop, refresh, or expand job skills and to develop, maintain, or increase the worker's commitment to the organization. In this study employee participation in job orientation programs and in-service training programs is measured. Admittedly, these training programs constitute only limited aspects of socialization to the work role. Nonetheless, they are included as indicators of organization-initiated efforts to provide socialization experiences to workers. There is wide variation in the use of orientation and in-service training programs by long-term care institutions: some facilities offer such programs while others do not; some homes offer such programs to some employees (e.g., RNs) but not to others; the frequency, content, length, and quality of such programs vary among facilities. Thus, participation in specialized training programs will vary both across and within long-term care facilities.

Material rewards refer primarily to wages and fringe benefits (e.g., sick leave, vacation, insurance, pension) and are the most obvious mechanisms that work organizations use to commit workers to continued employment. Existent descriptions of long-term care institutions suggest that nursing personnel do not fare well in terms of material rewards. National data describe nursing personnel at all levels (i.e., RNs, LPNs, nurses aides) employed at long-term care facilities as receiving low wages and meager fringe benefits compared with nursing personnel employed at hospitals and other health care settings (NCHS, 1979). In this study, wages and a variety of fringe benefits are examined as indicators of material rewards. We hypothesize that higher wages and increased fringe benefits will be associated with lower likelihood of staff turnover. Material rewards must be measured for individual employees since rewards may be provided to some workers and not others (e.g., fringe benefits often vary by full-time versus part-time work status) and the amount or value of some rewards (e.g., wages) varies across employees at the same institution.

Specific job characteristics—that is, the specific tasks and characteristics assigned to a particular job by the work organization—also are hypothesized to influence employee turnover (cf. Meyer, 1978). Although there is considerable evidence concerning the significance of specific job characteristics for work-related behavior, there is not, at this point, any fail-safe method for identifying those characteristics that are most salient. Precisely because job characteristics vary so widely both within and across work organizations, there are myriad potential variables to be examined. In long-term care institutions, five variables appear particularly relevant: shift, hours, amount of direct patient contact, number of patients, and specific job category.

Shift refers to the specific hours worked by an employee in a specific job. Long-term care facilities provide 24-hour-per-day patient care and typically have three formal shifts (although the exact hours may differ across institutions): day, evening, and night. Additionally, many homes use part-time or "on-call" employees to work a rotating shift, with work hours varying from day to day or week to week. The nature of work in long-term care facilities varies by shift, even across individuals with the same job title. The day shift is characterized by the largest nursing staff/patient ratio; increased availability and presence of administrative, supervisory, and specialized (e.g., social worker, recreation worker) personnel; greatest levels of direct patient contact; and increased participation in staff meetings and in-service training programs. The night shift is characterized by the smallest nursing staff/patient ratio; the lowest availability and presence of administrative, supervisory, and specialized personnel; and lowest levels of direct patient contact. The evening shift lies between the day and night shifts in terms of the ratio of nursing staff to patients; amount of time spent in direct patient care; and the presence and availability of administrative supervisory, and specialized personnel. Additionally, however, nursing staff who work the evening shift have the greatest contact with family and friends who visit patients—which may be viewed negatively by nursing staff (York and Calsyn, 1977). Finally, persons who work rotating shifts face a set of relatively unique demands that do not bode well for the development of job commitment. Working a rotating shift requires mastering the unique requirements of all three standard shifts and also decreases the likelihood of developing stable relationships with fellow workers.

"Hours" refers simply to the amount of time spent on the job during a typical workweek, and may be measured either in continuous form as number of hours worked or in dichotomous form as part-time versus full-time. The results of this study suggest that the distinction between part-time and full-time workers is sufficient for detecting dramatic differences in attachment to the workplace. Theoretically, the increased attachment of full-time workers may reflect either the fact that attachment increases as a function of time invested in an organization or the impact of other variables associated with full-time status (e.g., increased opportunities for promotion, better fringe benefits).

The amount of time spent in direct patient care and the number of patients for whom the worker has direct responsibility are expected to affect employee retention. Attitudinal surveys suggest that nursing personnel prefer direct patient care to clerical or housekeeping duties (e.g., charts, medication records, cleaning of equipment) and that this is especially true for LPNs and nurses aides (Schwartz, 1974). Consequently, other things being equal, we expect that time spent in direct patient care will be positively associated with commitment to and retention by the nursing home. This hypothesized relationship, however, may be mediated by the number of patients for whom the nursing staff member has direct responsibility. Responsibility for too many patients may render nursing personnel incapable of providing their preferred quantity or quality of care. Indeed, excessive patient load is reported to be a primary complaint of nursing personnel (Winn and McCaffree, 1976). Thus, we hypothesize that excessive patient load will be negatively associated with worker satisfaction and retention of nursing personnel in long-term care institutions.

Finally, the rights and duties associated with specific job categories or positions may affect employee turnover. This study includes three categories of nursing personnel at long-term care institutions: RNS, LPNs, and nurses aides. These three job categories vary widely in terms of amount of autonomy, specific job duties, and relations with management (as well as differing on a number of the variables previously discussed such as wages and amount of time spent in direct patient care). These job categories also form a status hierarchy within long-term care institutions, with RNs highest, nurses aides lowest, and LPNs intermediate in status. We hypothesize that the higher the occupational status within the institution, the greater the likelihood of employee retention. Consequently, we expect RNs to have the lowest rates of turnover, nurses aides the highest turnover rates, and LPNs to be intermediate.

C. Characteristics of Employees

Thus far, discussion has focused upon those variables hypothesized to affect employee turnover that either are characteristics of or are distributed by the work organization. An alternative theoretical perspective suggests that employee inputs, especially the social and demographic characteristics of personnel, account for variations in employee turnover. From this perspective, the central issue in the study of turnover is identification of those characteristics that best distinguish "quitters" from "stayers." Once these characteristics are identified, work organizations can hire those workers who are most likely to stay on the job. From the employee input perspective, problems of excessive turnover can best be solved by appropriate screening of job applicants. This position is considerably different from the organizational perspective, which suggests that problems of excessive turnover can best be addressed by restructuring the workplace or specific jobs within the workplace to enhance worker attachment and commitment.

A broad body of literature testifies to the relationships between demographic variables and employee turnover (e.g., Price, 1977; Van der Mewre and Miller, 1976). In general, being young, being female, being nonwhite, low education, low income, and low occupational status are related to high job turnover. With the exception of gender, nursing personnel in long-term care facilities exhibit wide variation in these demographic variables.

Nursing personnel at long-term care institutions are almost exclusively women. In addition to precluding an examination of the relationship between gender and turnover, a female labor pool suggests that other demographic variables may impact upon employee retention. It now is widely recognized that women's employment patterns are related to a number of family variables including marital status, family income (in addition to the woman's own earnings). the husband's occupation, and child-care responsibilities. This study includes these family characteristics as well as the more conventional demographic variables noted above.

Employees also bring different work histories to their jobs. In the context of nursing personnel at long-term care institutions, three aspects of the work history appear especially relevant for understanding turnover. First, both time on the current job and total time in the current occupation may affect turnover. Presumably, time in the current job is related to employee commitment to the work organization, although it is unclear whether time in the current job is simply a proxy indicator of commitment or whether increased exposure to the work organization facilitates commitment.[1] To the extent that total time in current occupation (e.g., as an RN, LPN, or nurses aid) differs from time on the current job (and our data suggest that these two variables often *are* different), it can be hypothesized that commitment to the occupation (although not necessarily to the specific work organization) is more likely. The third work history variable included in this study is presence or absence of special training in geriatrics (exclusive of any orientation or in-service training programs provided by the work organization). Those workers who seek out specialized training in geriatrics are expected to enter the work setting with increased commitment to the goals of the organization and the duties of their jobs.

In summary, this study examines the explanatory power of variables derived from two theoretical perspectives for predicting turnover among nursing personnel at long-term care institutions: (1) organizational inputs, including structural characteristics of the institution, control mechanisms employed by the institution, and the characteristics of specific jobs within the institution; and (2) employee inputs, which consist of the social and demographic characteristics of workers. As well as describing the theoretical basis for examining each class of variables, discussion focused upon the particular variables included in this study.

We recognized that factors that lie outside the purview of this chapter affect turnover. For example, the larger labor market in which the care facility competes and local unemployment rates might also influence employee turnover. Although such factors undoubtedly affect the ability of long-term care institutions to recruit and retain employees, such factors are outside the scope of this study. Our focus in on organizational variables that can help to explain variations in turnover across and within long-term care institutions in the same economic market. As described below, the data for this study were gathered at long-term care facilities within a relatively restricted geographical area (see Section III). Consequently, although factors such as the unemployment rate and the presence of competing employment settings may influence employee turnover, these factors will be relatively constant across the sample institutions and should not account for variations among and within those institutions.

II. RESEARCH DESIGN

The research design involved two units of analysis: long-term care institutions and staff members at the institutions. A questionnaire designed to gather information about structural characteristics and personnel policies was completed by administrators of the long-term care facilities. The staff questionnaire, which was administered to RNs, LPNs, and nurses aides, was designed to gather data about staff members' specific job characteristics, control mechanisms, and social and demographic characteristics.[2]

One year after administration of the questionnaires, the names of staff members who participated in the study were sent to the administrators of the long-term care facilities. The administrators indicated whether each employee on the list was still employed at the institution, had been terminated by the institution, or had voluntarily left the institution's employ. The follow-up information was used to classify staff members into groups of "quitters" and "stayers." (The very small number of employees who had been terminated by the institutions were excluded from further analysis.) Data from the original administrator and staff questionnaires were used to operationalize the antecedents of employee turnover. Clearly this research design does not represent a conventional longitudinal study (i.e., a panel study). This research is longitudinal, however, in the sense that characteristics and behavior at one point in time are used to predict behavioral patterns exhibited at a later point in time.

III. SAMPLE

The institutional sample consisted of 15 long-term care facilities in central North Carolina. The long-term care institutions offered a variety of levels of care to residents. There are three levels of care recognized by official certification agencies. The least medically complex level is rest home care, in which residents receive basic custodial and self-care services. The next level is intermediate care, in which residents receive some medical services as well as custodial care. The most complex medical services are offered in skilled nursing care. Institutions may be—and typically are—certified to provide more than one level of care. In this sample, five homes provided either rest home or intermediate care only. Three homes provided only skilled nursing care. Five homes provided both skilled and intermediate care. Finally, two facilities provided skilled, intermediate, and rest home care. These long-term care institutions represent nearly the entire universe of such facilities in a three-county area. Indeed, only one nursing home in the three countries declined to participate in the study. Consequently, the institutional response rate was 93.3%.

According to administrative records at the 15 long-term care facilities, 609 nursing personnel were eligible for participation in the study. Completed and usable questionnaires, as well as follow-up data, were obtained from 469 nursing personnel.[3] Thus, the total response rate for staff members was 77%—a very adequate figure by conventional social science standards (cf. Dillman, 1978). In subsequent sections of this study we demonstrate that it is essential to distinguish between part-time and full-time employees as well as among categories of nursing personnel. Therefore, Table 1 presents a description of the response rates for part-time and full-time nursing personnel.

As Table 1 indicates, the response rate was somewhat higher for full-time than part-time employees—a factor attributable simply to accessibility (e.g., some part-time employees work very few hours or on an "on-call" basis). In addition, the higher the level of nursing personnel, the higher the response rate (i.e., RNs had a higher response rate than LPNs, and LPNs had a higher response rate than nurses aides). This variation in response rate, reflecting differences in levels of education, is commonly observed in survey research (cf. Dillman, 1978).

IV. INDEPENDENT VARIABLES

As noted above, independent variables derived from two theoretical perspectives addressing the causes of employee turnover are examined as predictors of turnover among nursing personnel. In this section the operational definitions and descriptive statistics for the predictors are presented. For ease of interpretation the independent variables are grouped according to the theoretical perspective from which they are derived: (1) organizational characteristics (with further distinctions among structural variables, control mechanisms employed by the institution, and specific characteristics of various jobs within the institution) and (2) social and demographic characteristics of the nursing personnel. The distributions and means for each independent variable are provided in Table 2. For convenience, discussion is limited to those predictors that were significantly correlated with nursing staff turnover.

Table 1. Response Rate by Type of Personnel and Part-time vs. Full-time Work Status

Job Category and Work Status	Number of Eligible Personnel	Number of Completed Questionnaires	Response Rate
Part-time RNs	25	19	76
Full-time RNs	57	52	91
Part-time LPNs	37	24	65
Full-time LPNs	68	60	88
Part-time Nurses Aides	69	47	68
Full-time Nurses Aides	353	267	76

Table 2. Descriptive Statistics for Predictors of Nursing Turnover

	Potential Range	Actual Range	Mean
Structural Characteristics			
Ownership	0-1	0-1	.67
Size	NA	20-360	104.33
Licensed for Medicare	0-1	0-1	.67
Licensed for Medicaid	0-1	0-1	.73
Social Worker	0-1	0-1	.67
Physical Therapist	0-1	0-1	.47
Proportion Nursing to Total Staff	0-1	.24-.87	.52
Control Mechanisms			
Job Orientation Program	0-1	0-1	.565
Inservice Training Programs	0-1	0-1	.551
Wages	NA	$2.75-$8.00	$3.73
Sick Leave	NA	0-10	6.46
Vacation	NA	0-10	6.67
Private Pension	0-1	0-1	.16
Life Insurance	0-1	0-1	.609
Health Insurance	0-1	0-1	.876
Job Characteristics			
Part-time vs. Full-time	0-1	0-1	.808
Day Shift	0-1	0-1	.474
Evening Shift	0-1	0-1	.279
Night Shift	0-1	0-1	.187
Rotating Shift	0-1	0-1	.060
Time in Direct Patient Care	1-5	1-5	4.067
Patients Per Day	1-4	1-4	3.673
RN	0-1	0-1	.151
LPN	0-1	0-1	.179
Nurses Aide	0-1	0-1	.670
Social and Demographic Characteristics			
Age	NA	17-74	35.56
Education	1-9	2-9	5.26
Race	0-1	0-1	.560
Married	0-1	0-1	.488
Never Married	0-1	0-1	.205
Widowed	0-1	0-1	.058
Divorced/Separated	0-1	0-1	.249
Family Income	1-8	1-8	4.46
Husbands' Occupation	1-9	1-9	5.09
Number of Children	NA	0-9	1.19
Months in Current Job	NA	1-443	31.20
Total Months in Occupation	NA	1-489	60.04
Geriatrics Training	0-1	0-1	.237

A. Organizational Characteristics: Structural Variables

Ownership refers to whether the institution was corporate-owned, and was coded as a dummy variable with zero representing noncorporate and 1 indicating corporate ownership. One-third of the long-term care facilities in this sample were noncorporate and two-thirds were corporate-owned.

Size of institution was operationalized as number of beds, as previously described. The 15 long-term institutions in the sample ranged in size from 20 to 360 beds, with an average size of about 104 beds.

As noted above, long-term care facilities licensed for Medicare and Medicaid must meet a number of criteria—some of which (e.g., staff qualifications and patterns) are indicators of differentiation. In this sample, two-thirds of the homes were licensed for Medicare reimbursement; 73% were licensed for Medicaid reimbursement.

Specialized personnel also increase the differentiation within an organization. Social workers and physical therapists are specialized personnel sometimes found in long-term care institutions. In this sample, two-thirds of the institutions employed a staff social worker and 47% employed a physical therapist.

We should recall that the structural characteristics of the long-term care institutions apply to all personnel employed at each facility. Thus, structural variables cannot account for variations in staff turnover within institutions. Instead, the effects of structural characteristics upon staff turnover can be identified only by comparing personnel from institutions with differing structural characteristics. Each staff member from a given institution was assigned the same values on the structural variables. The remaining independent variables were measured at the individual level and varied both within and across facilities. This procedure of including both organizational and individual variables in a single analysis is the crux of what some sociologists term "contextual effects analysis."

B. Organizational Characteristics: Control Mechanisms

We examined two types of organizational control mechanisms: training programs, which are indicators of organization-initiated socialization programs, and material rewards.

Participation in organization-initiated training programs was measured in terms of job orientation and in-service training programs. Respondents simply indicated whether or not they had participated in either type of program in their current jobs. Each variable was coded in dummy form, with zero representing no participation and 1 representing participation in such a program. In this sample, about 57% of the nursing personnel had participated in job orientation programs and 55% had participated in in-service training programs.

Material rewards were measured in terms of wages and a variety of fringe benefits. Wages were measured simply as pay per hour. Hourly wages among the nursing personnel ranged from $2.75 to $8.00 per hour, with an average hourly rate of $3.73. As expected, wages varied significantly by job category: the average hourly rates were $5.97, $4.27, and $3.08 for RNs, LPNs, and nurses aides, respectively.

Five types of fringe benefits were examined. Sick leave and vacation were measured in days per year. Private pension coverage, life insurance, and health insurance were measured simply in terms of absence (a value of zero) or presence (a value of 1). As Table 2 indicates, the nursing personnel in this sample averaged about 6½ days per year of sick leave and vacation. The long-term care institutions provided about 88% of the nursing personnel with health insurance, 61% with life insurance, and 16% with private pensions. Closer examination of the data revealed that the receipt of fringe benefits was strongly related to both job category and full-time versus part-time employment status. RNs received considerably greater fringe benefits than LPNs, and LPNs were significantly more likely than nurses aides to receive each type of fringe benefit. Even more dramatic were the differences between full-time and part-time employees. Regardless of job category, full-time employees were far more likely than part-time employees to receive each type of fringe benefit.

C. Organizational Characteristics: Specific Job Characteristics

The primary job characteristics examined in this study were part-time versus full-time employment status, shift, time spent in direct patient care, number of patients, and job category.

Nursing personnel who worked 35 or fewer hours a week were considered part-time employees (a value of zero); those who worked 36 or more hours a week were considered full-time employees (a value of 1). Nearly 81% of the study participants were employed full-time.

Respondents were asked to report their usual work shift. Each shift was coded as a dichotomous dummy variable (a code of 1 for the shift reported and a code of zero on all other shifts). In this sample, 47.4% of the respondents worked days, 27.9% worked evenings, 18.7% worked nights, and 6% worked rotating shifts.

Time spent in direct patient care was measured by a single item, requiring respondents to choose the alternative that best described their job duties. The potential and observed range was 1-5, with a mean of 4.07 indicating very high amounts of direct patient care responsibility. More specifically, less than 1% of the respondents reported that they spent no time in direct patient care, while approximately 11%, 13%, 39%, and 43% spent, respectively, 1%-25%, 26%-50%, 51%-75%, and 75%-plus of their time in direct patient care.

A single item with ordinal response categories also was used to measure the number of patients typically worked with each day. Both the potential and observed ranges on this variable were 1-4, with a mean of 3.63 representing high patient loads, on the average. More specifically, 1% of the respondents worked with no patients per day, 3% worked with 1-5 patients, nearly 24% worked with 6-10 patients, and 72% worked with more than 10 patients per day.

As noted earlier, three categories of nursing personnel were included in the study. For purposes of analysis each job category was coded as a dummy variable (with the respondent coded as 1 for her job category and zero for the remaining categories). Among the respondents, 15% were RNs, 18% were LPNs and 67% were nurses aides.

D. Social and Demographic Characteristics of Nursing Personnel

The questionnaire measured a number of standard social and demographic variables. The nursing personnel ranged in age from 17 to 74, with an average age of 35.6. Education varied widely, with nurses aides averaging less than a high school education and, on the other end of the continuum, RNs averaging four years of college. The sample also was racially diverse—56% of the respondents were black (a value of 1) and 44% were white (a value of zero). Marital status was coded as a series of dummy variables: 48.8% of the respondents were married, 20.5% had never married, 5.8% were widowed, and 24.9% were divorced or separated.

Family variables examined include family income, husband's occupational status, and number of children. The average family income in this sample fell in the interval of $7,000-$9,999. Using the census bureau first-digit occupational codes, which range from 1 (unskilled labor) to 9 (professionals, proprietors, and managers), the average in this sample was 5.09. The median and mode also fell in the 5 interval, which represents craftsmen and foremen. The nursing personnel averaged 1.19 children at home, although there was a wide range on this variable. This variable was restricted to number of children in the respondent's home in order to tap child-care responsibilities.

Three aspects of the respondent's work history were included in the analysis: length of time in current job, total time in occupation, and special training in geriatrics. In this sample, the number of months in current job ranged from 1 to 443, with an average of 31.20 months. Total time in current occupation (i.e., as RN, LPN, or nurses aide) ranged from 1 to 489 months, with an average of 60 months. In light of the reports of excessive turnover among such personnel, these averages appear quite high. As important as the mean values, however, is the wide variation for both variables—in fact, the distributions for both variables were bimodal, indicating significant numbers of both very short-term and very long-term employees. Training in geriatrics was coded as a dummy variable, with zero representing no training and 1 indicating geriatric training. Nearly 24% of the respondents reported that they had received geriatric training (exclusive of employer-provided training programs).

V. DEPENDENT VARIABLE: NURSING STAFF TURNOVER

The dependent variable in this analysis is turnover among nursing personnel at long-term care institutions. The measurement of turnover is somewhat controversial (cf. Price, 1977; Van der Mewre and Miller, 1976). Two definitions are reported in this study, although only one definition is used in subsequent data analysis. Table 3 presents two sets of turnover rates relevant to this study. Because the effects of job category and employment status are very significant, turnover rates are separately presented for part-time and full-time employees in each job category.

The top of Table 3 presents the turnover rates among the nursing personnel who participated in the initial survey and whose employment status was determined one year later. This method of defining and measuring turnover is referred to as the "quit rate" exhibited by a group of employees (Price, 1977). The quit rates exhibit three significant patterns. First, the turnover rates are quite high (for five of the six groups, more than half of the employees quit during a one-year interval), as expected given previous reports of staff turnover in long-term care institutions. Second, turnover rates vary significantly by job category. RNs consistently exhibit the lowest turnover rates, nurses aides exhibit the highest turnover rates, and LPNs are intermediate. Third, turnover rates differ significantly for full-time and part-time employees. Regardless of job category, part-time employees exhibit significantly higher turnover rates than full-time employees. In the subsequent multivariate data analysis, the independent variables are used to predict quitting versus staying on the job (see Section VI).

Table 3. Two Sets of Turnover Rates

Job Category	Sample Turnover Number Eligible	Number Quit	Percent Quit
Part-time RNs	19	10	52.6
Full-time RNs	52	25	48.1
Part-time LPNs	24	13	54.2
Full-time LPNs	60	31	51.7
Part-time Nurses Aides	47	27	57.4
Full-time Nurses Aides	267	158	59.2

Job Category	Institutional Turnover (in percents)	
	Range	Mean
Part-time RNs	0-333.3	67.3
Full-time RNs	0-200	55.3
Part-time LPNs	0-366.7	74.3
Full-time LPNs	0-300	61.1
Part-time Nurses Aides	0-750	145.1
Full-time Nurses Aides	20-188.5	65.2

The bottom of Table 3 presents the institutional turnover rates for the 15 long-term care facilities. For the institutions, turnover is reported as *separation rates*—that is, the proportion of employees in a particular job category who voluntarily quit during a specified time period (in this case, one year). The institutional separation rates exhibit patterns similar to those observed for the employee quit rates: separation rates were very high (ranging from 55% to 145%); turnover was lowest for RNs, highest for nurses aides, and intermediate for LPNs; and turnover rates were considerably higher among part-time than full-time employees. Additionally, turnover rates varied widely among the sample institutions, as evidenced by the large ranges observed.

The major differences between the quit rates and the separation rates is that the latter were considerably higher—quit rates ranged from 48% to 59% and separation rates ranged from 55% to 145%. There are two reasons for this. First, participation in the study may be related to turnover. That is, those nursing personnel who agreed to participate in the study may have been less likely to quit than those who refused to participate. Second, and more important, the differences in turnover rates reflect differences in the definition of turnover and the unit of analysis—quit rates measure turnover among a group of employees and are measured at the individual level; separation rates measure turnover in a set of organizational slots and apply to the institution as a unit of analysis. For quit rates, the highest possible turnover rate is 100% (i.e., every employee quits). For separation rates, organizational slots may be held by numerous employees over a specified time period and turnover rates in excess of 100% are possible (and, in the present case, observed).

VI. DATA ANALYSIS

Multiple regression was used to examine the impact of the independent variables upon employee turnover. Using multiple regression, it was possible to determine the effect of each independent variable upon employee turnover, net of intercorrelation among the other independent variables in the equation.

Before turning to the results of the regression analysis, a note about the use of ordinary least squares (OLS) regression with a dichotomous dependent variable is prudent. As several authors note, using OLS regression to predict a dichotomous dependent variable can be problematic (Duncan, 1975; Kerlinger and Pedhazur, 1973). It also is generally recognized, however, that if the split on the dependent variable is 40-60 or better (i.e., more even), OLS regression is sufficiently robust to generate an accurate and meaningful solution (Bohrnstedt and Carter, 1971; Cohen and Cohen, 1975). The dependent variable used in this study has a 44/56 split (i.e., over the one-year interval, 44% of the sample members remained on the job and 56% quit). Thus, use of OLS regression was appropriate.

Table 4 presents the regression equation predicting employee turnover. The

Table 4. Regression Equation: Significant Predictors of Employee Turnover

Independent Variable	b	β
Structural Characteristics		
Size	.08	.10
Ownership	.07	.26
Licensed for Medicare	.04	.09
Physical Therapist	.10	.17
Control Mechanisms		
Wages	−.02	−.39
Sick Leave	−.09	−.07
Vacation	−.07	−.05
Pension	−.16	−.17
Inservice Training	−.04	−.09
Specific Job Characteristics		
Part-time versus Full-time	−.26	−.48
Evening Shift	.11	.15
Night Shift	.02	.02
Rotating Shift	.15	.21
Patients per Day	.05	.02
LPN	.19	.24
Nurses Aide	.28	.36
Social/Demographic Characteristics		
Age	−.06	−.42
Education	.02	.04
Married	.13	.16
Children	.07	.08
Months in Current Job	.04	.31
Geriatrics Training	.05	.05
Constant	.06	
Total R^2		.41
Net R^2 Organizational Characteristics		.19
Net R^2 Employee Characteristics		.09

unstandardized regression coefficients (b) indicate the predicted increase in the dependent variable for a one-unit increase in the independent variable, net of all the other independent variables in the equation. The standardized regression coefficients (ß) can be used to determine the relative strength of each predictor. Only independent variables that were statistically significant predictors of employee turnover ($p \leq .05$) are presented. The regression analysis first was performed using the set of independent variables included in Table 2. The complete set of independent variables explained 42.4% of the variance in the dependent variable, but included a number of nonsignificant regression coefficients. The regression analysis was repeated restricting the set of independent variables to those predictors that were statistically significant in the first regression analysis. This second equation, presented in Table 4, explained 41.4% of the variance in the dependent variable, and the values of the regression coefficients were highly stable across the two equations. Because of the similarities in explained variance and the magnitudes of the regression coefficients, the shorter, more easily interpreted equation is presented.

As noted above, the statistically significant independent variables explain 41% of the variance in employee turnover in this sample. This proportion of explained variance is both statistically and substantively significant. Overall, the results suggest that the independent variables comprise a useful model for understanding staff turnover in long-term institutions. In the following paragraphs, each class of independent variables is discussed in terms of (1) that class's contribution to the prediction of employee turnover and (2) the degree to which the specific independent variables operated as hypothesized.

A. Organizational Characteristics: Structural Variables

Four of the seven hypothesized predictors of employee turnover were statistically significant, net of the other independent variables. Size was positively related to turnover: the larger the long-term care facility, the greater the rate of turnover. As noted earlier, the expected effect of size is ambiguous because of contradictory findings in previous studies. The results of this study are compatible with previous findings which suggest that increased organizational size may hinder the development of commitment by members. As expected, corporate ownership was related to increased turnover among the nursing personnel. Two indicators of organizational differentiation—licensure for Medicare reimbursement and presence of a staff physical therapist—were significant predictors of employee turnover. Contrary to our hypothesis, however, both differentiation measures were positively related to employee turnover. As noted previously, extreme differentiation is expected to increase turnover as result of routinization and lack of autonomy; moderate differentiation is expected to decrease turnover as a result of optimizing the relationship between job duties and employee skills. It may be that the differentiation represented by Medicare licensure and the presence of a staff physical therapist is sufficient to increase turnover—these measures may tap excessive differentiation in the context of long-term care institutions.

B. Organizational Characteristics: Control Mechanisms

Five of the eight control mechanisms investigated in this study were statistically significant predictors of employee turnover, and all operated in the hypothesized direction. Although its impact is relatively weak, participation in in-service training programs was associated with decreased employee turnover. In terms of material rewards, both higher wages and increased fringe benefits fostered employee retention. More specifically, higher wages, greater sick leave and vacation benefits, and employer-provided private pension coverage decreased the likelihood of turnover among the nursing personnel in this sample.

C. Organizational Characteristics: Specific Job Characteristics

A number of specific job characteristics were statistically significant predictors of employee turnover. The most powerful single predictor of turnover was part-time versus full-time employment status. As expected, part-time employees were more likely to quit their jobs than full-time employees. Shift was operationalized as a set of four dummy variables, with day shift serving as the omitted variable. The results indicate that employees who worked nights were slightly more likely to quit, employees who worked evenings were considerably more likely to quit, and those who worked rotating shifts were much more likely to quit than those employees who worked days. The increased turnover among the evening and rotating shifts was hypothesized. Also, as expected, patient load was positively related to increased turnover, although this relationship was quite weak. Finally, as expected, turnover was related to job category. LPNs and, especially, nurses aides were significantly more likely to quit than RNs.[4]

D. Employee Characteristics: Social and Demographic Variables

Several social and demographic characteristics of employees were significant predictors of turnover. There was a relatively strong negative relationship between age and likelihood of turnover. The older the nursing staff member, the less likely she was to quit her job. Somewhat surprisingly, in light of previous research, education was positively related to turnover. It should be noted, however, that the zero-order correlation between education and turnover was negative. It appears that job category, which was highly correlated with education, accounts for the reversal in direction between the correlation coefficient and the regression coefficient. RNs had the highest level of educational attainment and also were least likely to quit their jobs. With the effects of job category controlled, education had a weak but significant positive impact upon turnover. Thus, within job categories, those with the highest educational attainment were more likely to quit—which may reflect increased job alternatives for the better-educated.

Two family variables also were significant predictors of employee turnover. Married nursing personnel were significantly more likely than nonmarried employees to quit their jobs.[5] The number of children in the respondent's home also was positively related to likelihood of turnover. These findings suggest that family responsibilities and also family resources (i.e., income from the husband) increased the likelihood of turnover among nursing personnel.

Two work history variables also had a significant impact upon the likelihood of employee turnover. The longer the respondent had held her current job prior to the initial survey, the less likely she was to quit during the subsequent year. As expected, time in current job indexes, to some extent, commitment to the current job. Also, as expected, respondents who had participated in training programs with an emphasis on geriatrics were less likely to quit their jobs.

Table 4 also presents the net R^2 values for the two theoretically derived sets of independent variables: organizational characteristics and characteristics of employees. Net R^2 refers to the amount of variance explained by a set of independent variables, controlling for the other predictors in the regression analysis. Net R^2 is a conservative estimate of the explanatory power of a set of independent variables (since all intercorrelation with other predictors is attributed to those other predictors), but is the best estimate available of the unique effects of a set of independent variables. In this study the net R^2 was .19 for organizational characteristics and .09 for employee characteristics. These results suggest that both organizational and employee characteristics predict nursing staff turnover, but organizational characteristics are more important.

Before turning to a broader discussion of the findings, a note is merited about those hypothesized variables that did *not* appear in the final regression equations as significant predictors of employee turnover. Such variables form two general categories: variables with restricted variances and variables that were highly intercorrelated with one or more other predictors. Using multiple regression analysis, both of these categories of independent variables were unlikely to emerge as significant predictors of employee turnover, net of other independent variables included in the analysis. This does not mean that those variables were unrelated to turnover—as stated earlier, all the variables in Table 2 were statistically significant correlates of turnover. Thus, the failure of some hypothesized variables to appear in the regression equation does not mean that the theoretically based hypothesis of a relationship was wrong, but only that the relationship was not statistically significant net of the effects of other independent variables in the analysis.

VII. DISCUSSION AND IMPLICATIONS

The purpose of this study was to compare the relative power of organizational characteristics and employee characteristics to predict turnover among nursing personnel employed at long-term care institutions. The expectation that organizational characteristics are important in predicting turnover is based on the sociological perspective that organizational inputs determine, in large measure, worker commitment and retention. The employee input perspective, in contrast, posits that certain social and demographic characteristics distinguish between "quitters" and "stayers." The results of this study, especially the multiple regression analysis, provided an empirical test of the relative explanatory power of independent variables derived from each perspective.

The results of this study document in a compelling manner the degree to which structural characteristics of the work organization, the control mechanisms employed by the organization, and the characteristics of specific jobs within the organization impact upon turnover among nursing personnel. In this study, most of the significant predictors of employee turnover are either characteristics of or factors determined by the work organization. These results suggest that problems of excessive turnover may be amenable to administrative intervention.

Our results further suggest that those organizational characteristics differentially distributed within long-term care institutions are important predictors of nursing staff turnover. In these data both control mechanisms employed by the institution and specific job characteristics varied as greatly within institutions as across them, and both categories of variables proved to be significant predictors of employee turnover. The theoretical significance of organizational variables that vary within work organizations has been noted in previous research. Nonetheless, much, if not most, previous sociological research has been based upon a comparison across organizations (in such cases, the dependent variable is turnover rates rather than individual-based measures of turnover), with the independent variables consisting of characteristics that are constant within organizations. This study suggests that it is useful to predict individual employment outcomes, using organizational characteristics that are differentially distributed with organizations as well as those that differ only across organizations. The importance of organizational characteristics differentially distributed within institutions also has implications for interventions designed to alleviate turnover problems. In terms of increasing worker commitment, it appears that each organizational slot or job can, and perhaps should, be separately examined, and interventions may need to be focused on the characteristics of specific jobs rather than across-the-board changes in administrative policies.

Administrators of the long-term care institutions in this study typically subscribed to the employee input perspective. Although such data were not an explicit goal of the study, most administrators volunteered their theories about the causes of high turnover, placing much of the responsibility squarely upon the personal characteristics of nursing personnel. Young employees are reported to be unreliable and to quit more often and with less notice than older workers. A number of administrators also mentioned issues of social class. They pointed out that nurses aides have the highest turnover rates and suggested that persons in lower-status occupations feel little sense of job commitment or responsibility.

The results of this study offer some support to the administrators' theories and to the employee input perspective more generally. A number of social and demographic variables distinguished between quitters and stayers. These relationships do not necessarily imply, however, that quitters and stayers are social "types" in the sense that administrators often refer to them. Given the evidence that organizational characteristics are the primary predictors of nursing staff turnover, we might argue that many nursing jobs in long-term care institutions are unattractive in the sense that they are associated with low wages, little status, and lack of autonomy. Indeed, quitting such jobs may be as understandable as staying. We also might predict that those nursing home employees who quit their jobs are those who can afford to quit—those who possess sufficient social and economic resources to relinquish the job or secure a more attractive job. The social and demographic variables that predict turnover in this study support such an interpretation. Of special interest is the finding that higher educational attainment is associated with increased turnover, net of job category. Within each job category, those workers with the highest levels of education may be better able to secure alternatives to continued employment in long-term care institutions. The relationship between age and likelihood of turnover also may reflect the fact that younger workers are better able than older employees to secure more attractive alternatives to continued employment—either other jobs or resumption of education. Being married also may be a resource—the presence of an employed spouse may enable married women in unrewarding jobs to quit at higher rates than are possible for unmarried women. Obviously the meaning attached to the relationships between demographic variables and turnover is a matter of interpretation. But we would argue that the interpretation that demographic variables represent resources which distinguish among persons who can and cannot afford to quit unrewarding jobs in long-term care facilities is at least as plausible as the position that such variables index a personal propensity to avoid occupational commitment.

Finally, the results of this study indicate that long-term care institutions are a strategic site for the sociological study of employee turnover. On the basis of our results, we echo the recommendations of Hage (1980) and Price (1977) that sociologists broaden the scope of their research on employee turnover to include human service organizations. Such organizations are characterized by both high turnover rates and labor-intensive organizational structures, making such sites attractive for further research.

ACKNOWLEDGMENTS

The author would like to thank Richard Landerman and Bernice Halbur for their contributions to this project. The research reported in this chapter was funded by a grant from the Andrus Foundation of NRTA-AARP.

NOTES

1. It also might be argued, on the intuitive grounds, that time on the job is a measure of turnover—and that using time on the job to predict turnover confounds the independent and dependent variables. We argue that this is not the case. Although a relatively long period of time in the current job may represent employee retention, the reverse cannot be argued. That is, short-term employment need not indicate lack of retention—some short-term employees are recently hired

workers who eventually stay for long periods of time. In this study length of time on the job is included to compare nursing personnel employed varying lengths of time in terms of likelihood of quitting over a one-year period.

2. All of the administrators permitted the staff questionnaires to be distributed and completed on staff time. These were generous offers, indeed, and we are confident that this method of data collection increased the response rate achieved. In a few cases the questionnaires were completed during staff meetings. More frequently, and for all the employees who worked evenings and nights, staff members came to a specified location (e.g., the dining room) in groups of two or three to complete the questionnaire. At all times, a member of the research team administered the questionnaires and was available for questions.

3. The 469 staff members who comprise the sample all are female. Excluded from analysis are two questionnaires completed by men employed as patient care assistants. It is interesting to note that both male staff members quit their jobs over the course of the study.

4. Job category also was operationalized as a set of dummy variables, with RNs serving as the excluded category in the regression analysis.

5. Examination of the data indicated that the critical aspect of marital status was the distinction between married and nonmarried respondents. Thus, for the regression analysis (Table 4) marital status was dichotomized. The four dummy variables are presented in Table 2 for the purposes of description.

REFERENCES

American Nurses' Association.
    1976 Facts About Nursing, 1974-75. Kansas City, MO: American Nurses' Association.

Archibald, K.A.
    1971 The Supply of Professional Nurses and Their Recruitment and Retention by Hospitals. New York: Rand.

Barney, J.
    1974 "Nursing directors in nursing homes," Nursing Outlook 22: 434-440.

Blau, P.M.
    1970 "A formal theory of differentiation in organizations." American Sociological Review 35: 201-218.

Blau, P.M., and R.A. Schoenherr
    1971 The Structure of Organizations. New York: Basic Books.

Bohrnstedt, G.W., and T.M. Carter
    1971 "Robustness in regression analysis." Pp. 118-146 in H.L. Costner (ed.), Sociological Methodology, 1971. San Francisco: Jossey-Bass.

Cohen, J., and P. Cohen
    1975 Applied Multiple Regression/Correlation Analysis for the Behavioral Sciences. Hillsdale, N.J: Lawrence Erlbaum.

Dillman, D.A.
    1978 Mail and Telephone Surveys: The Total Design Method. New York: Wiley.

Duncan, O.D.
    1975 Introduction to Structural Equation Models. New York: Academic Press

Etzioni, A.
    1964 Modern Organization. Englewood Cliffs, NJ: Prentice-Hall
    1975 A Comparative Analysis of Complex Organizations. New York: Free Press.

Friedsam, H.J.
    1974 "Some issues in manpower for parallel services." Gerontologist 14: 19-26.

Gow, J.S., A.W. Clark, and G.S. Dossett
    1974 "A path analysis of variables influencing labor turnover." Human Relations 27: 703-719.

Gubrium, J.F.
  1975 Living and Dying at Murray Manor. New York: St. Martin Press.
Hage, J.
  1980 Theories of Organizations: Form, Processes, and Transformation. New York: Wiley.
Kerlinger, F.N., and E.J. Pedhazur
  1973 Multiple Regression in Behavioral Research. New York: Holt, Rinehart, and Winston.
Kimberly, J.R.
  1976 "Organizational size and the structuralist perspective: a review, critique, and proposal." Administrative Science Quarterly 21: 571-597.
Levine, D.M.
  1975 "Staffing patterns and professional profiles of health care." Gerontologist 13: 314-316.
McEachern, W.A.
  1975 Managerial Control and Performance. Lexington, MA: D.C. Heath.
Meyer, M.M.
  1978 Environments and Organizations. San Francisco: Jossey-Bass.
National Center for Health Statistics
  1979 The National Nursing Home Survey: 1977 Summary for the United States. Washington, D.C.: Public Health Service.
Pecarchik,R., and B. Nelson
  1973 "Employee turnover in nursing homes." American Journal of Nursing 72: 289-290.
Pettman, B.O.
  1973 "Some factors influencing labor turnover: a review of research literature." Industrial Relations 4: 43-61.
Price J.L.
  1977 The Study of Turnover. Ames: Iowa State University Press.
Price, J.L. and C.W. Mueller
  1981 Professional Turnover: The Cases of Nurses. Jamaica, NY: SP Medical and Scientific Books.
Schwartz, A.N.
  1974 "Staff development and morale building in nursing homes." Gerontologist 14: 50-53.
Van der Mewre, R., and S. Miller
  1976 Measuring Absence and Labor Turnover. Johannesburg: McGraw Hill.
Wieland, G.F.
  1969 "Studying and measuring nursing turnover." International Journal of Nursing Studies 6: 61-70.
Winn, S. and K.M. McCaffree
  1976 "Characteristics of nursing homes perceived to be effective and efficient." Gerontologist 16: 415-419.
York, J.L., and R.J. Calsyn
  1977 "Family involvement in nursing homes." Gerontologist 17: 500-505.
Zeitlin, M.
  1974 "Corporate ownership and control: the large corporation and the capitalist class." American Sociological Review 79: 1073-1119.

INTERNATIONAL STAIR-STEP MIGRATION:
DOMINICAN LABOR IN THE UNITED STATES AND HAITIAN LABOR IN THE DOMINICAN REPUBLIC

Sherri Grasmuck

I. INTRODUCTION

A recent spate of literature has suggested that present patterns of international labor imports and exports may contribute to the reproduction of existing development inequalities between nations (Sassen-Koob, 1978; Portes, 1978a; Alba, 1978). These studies have emphasized the structural "determinants" of international labor migration in terms of both the domestic division of labor through which social class relations are produced and the international division among national units which specialize in the production of unequally rewarded commodities (Castells, 1975; Castles and Kosack, 1973; Bach, 1978). It is only by focusing on the labor functions of these movements for both the sending and receiving countries that the process can be fully understood. The focus in this literature has been on a general movement of labor from "peripheral" areas of the international capitalist economy to the more developed "core" areas. In the attempt to analyze the nature of international labor circulation, emphasis has been placed on two phenomena: (1) labor scarcity—the demand for labor in core societies—and (2) labor "surplus"—the abundance of labor in peripheral societies. Most frequently labor scarcity and surplus, or demand and supply, are viewed as processes physically separated by national borders, the former typifying developed capitalist nations and the latter, peripheral or underdeveloped countries.

The argument presented here is that the "enclave" pattern of development typical of many Latin American societies (Cardoso and Faletto, 1979) may be a much more heterogeneous process than suggested by this dichotomized approach to the study of international migration. Specifically, the nature of dependent development in certain cases produces simultaneously a relative labor surplus, resulting in the exportation of native workers, and a relative labor scarcity, marked by a significant importation of foreign labor. The object of this paper is to analyze the nature and functions of international labor transfers using the case of the Dominican Republic to illustrate the interrelationship between conditions of labor scarcity and labor surplus.

II. LABOR SCARCITY

Recent research on illegal immigration has pointed to the existence within advanced capitalist societies of a scarcity of labor, meaning either an absolute scarcity in terms of depleting the domestic labor supply or a relative scarcity of those prepared to work for low wages. In capitalist economic production the labor supply must be made to fit the needs of capital accumulation and not the latter to the existing labor supply. Thus, a labor shortage need not be objective but may merely reflect the need of sectors of the economy which, for example, unable to rely on productivity increases, seek to maintain profit levels by reliance on a continous cheap source of labor. This type of relative labor scarcity especially characterizes those agricultural and nonmonopoly sectors of the economy in developed societies which are unable to rely on costly methods for augmenting labor productivity available to the "oligopolistic" sectors (Castells, 1975; O'Connor, 1973; Leahy and Castillo, 1977). Moreover, this relative scarcity is in turn a function of the history of working class organizations and the existence of minimally acceptable working conditions and wage levels associated with the state's provision of social security and welfare payments (Bonacich, 1976; Cornelius, 1979).

The circulation of migration streams between receiving and sending countries benefits employers as a whole in the core countries by diminishing the cost of reproducing the labor force at the point of production (Burawoy, 1976). The importation of labor not only functions to increase profits but also acts as an anticyclical mechanism such that in economic down cycles migrants can be made redundant without significantly affecting total consumption (Sassen-Koob, 1978:520). Moreover, the political vulnerability of the immigrant worker, especially the undocumented alien who faces the constant threat of deportation, means that the traditional defenses of labor provided by labor unions are often inaccessible to the immigrant worker (Rosenblum, 1973; Castles and Kosack, 1973; Mohl and Betten, 1972).

III. LABOR SURPLUS AND DEPENDENT DEVELOPMENT

Labor exports not only reflect the demands of receiving societies but have important correlates in the internal structures of the sending countries. The structuralist approach to the study of international migration has emphasized the association between labor exports and the development pattern typifying many peripheral countries which have been characterized by a set of internal contradictions loosely described as "dependent development" (Portes, 1978c; Sassen-Koob, 1978; Alba, 1978; Maldonado-Dennis, 1980). In summarized form, the ingredients of the complex usually include the following. First, through the process of capitalist industrialization the agricultural sectors tend to displace formerly isolated peasants and rural proletariat and bring them into contact with modern urban environments. The resulting needs for mass employment are not typically met, and concomitant high rates of disguised unemployment and underemployment appear, especially in urban areas. Second, these societies are plagued by increasingly unequal distributions of national income even in the face of sustained economic growth. Third, partly as a reaction to the importation of technologies appropriate to production in the core regions, the modern culture of mass consumption penetrates the peripheral societies, simultaneously raising expectations for modern consumer goods and denying the mass of the population the means of obtaining even a minimal fraction of these goods. Mass communications and the parading of the "modern essentials" of urban existence through advertisements by foreign firms, coupled with a highly unequal income distribution, only reinforce this situation, described as "modernity-in-underdevelopment" (Frank, 1967; Furtado, 1964; Alba, 1978). Fourth, and finally, extreme external control of peripheral economies by foreign firms, especially in the most technologically advanced branches of industrial production, is likely to be dominated by a very few core societies—in some cases, almost exclusively by the United States (Demas, 1965:32).

This type of development often generates a large exodus of workers seeking employment outside national boundaries. Mexican immigration, the largest component of the illegal flow of labor into the United States, has been shown to reflect the contours of Mexican economic development (Alba, 1978; Portes, 1979b). Typically, this kind of population exodus has been viewed as a safety valve for governments operating in developing societies who prefer to export the physical reminders of severe unemployment and underemployment. Only in more recent times has serious attention been given to the consequences of labor exports for sending countries; given the widely held assumption that labor exports must be of benefit to societies marked by high unemployment. This assumption relies on an aggregated model of the economy, a simple comparison of overall figures of national unemployment and labor exports (Sassen-Koob, 1978:533). However, any assessment of the impact of labor exports for a developing society must take account of the internal differentiation in the composition of labor exports as well as the internal sectoral shortages of the sending economy, both in the short and long run.

Just as earlier push-pull theories of immigration overemphasized sociopsychological factors to the exclusion of others (Portes, 1979:2), the structuralist approach runs the risk of addressing only the global determinants of international migration while perhaps simplifying not only the internal differentiation of the labor surplus but also the degrees of freedom available to migrants within both the sending and receiving societies. The Dominican Republic is selected for analysis in this study because it provides a clear case of a society simultaneously marked by a number of distinct types of labor exports and labor imports, for example, which are not typically conceptualized as occurring within the same national boundary. In the Dominican case we are confronted with an instance of a peripheral society marked by trends which are associated on the one hand with conditions of labor surplus and on the other hand with conditions of labor scarcity. The apparently contradictory "social facts" are that: (1) Dominicans, to the extent of 20,000 a year, leave their homeland to find employment in the United States; (2) many more remain at home without work or are severely underemployed; and (3) every year Haitian workers are imported in order to fill jobs in strategic sectors of the Dominican economy.

A. Dominicans in the United States

Estimates of the total number of Dominicans living in the New York City area alone range from 300,000 to 500,000 (including legal migrants and undocumented migrants who possess expired tourist or student visas or who entered the United States via Puerto Rico) [Ugalde et al., 1979:235; Kayal, 1978a; Dominquez, 1978]. New York is sometimes called the second city of the Dominican Republic since the number of Dominicans residing there falls between the population size of Santo Domingo, the capital, with about one million inhabitants, and Santiago, the second largest city on the island, with over 255,000 inhabitants.

The pattern of Dominican emigration to the United States over this century falls into three well-defined periods. The first three decades of the 1900s were marked by substantial emigration, to the extent that the decline in the Dominican population between 1897 and 1928 has been estimated to have been as much as 43 percent (Patterson, 1978:119—120). Although this figure is probably an exaggerated estimate, given the fact that overall population density in the Dominican Republic was relatively low at the turn of the century (Schoenrich, 1977:146), the population exodus before the Trujillo era was dramatic. During the Trujillo dictatorship (1930–1961), emigration was severely curtailed due to a restrictive state policy. The contemporary phase of mass migration commenced a few years after Trujillo's death. The annual average number of Dominican immigrants officially admitted to the United States in the period 1966–1977 was 12,513, for a grand total of 150,155. This is a tenfold increase over any given year prior to 1960. Moreover, the number of officially admitted nonimmigrants during recent times has soared, climbing from 78,800 in 1967 to 155,900 in 1976, a total of 1,126,000 for the decade. Only Mexico (with 12,608,800) and Canada (with 1,766,810) surpass the Dominican Republic in numbers of nonimmigrants admitted to the United States over this period (INS, 1976, 1977).

B. Haitians in the Dominican Republic

It is notoriously difficult to establish reliable estimates of the number of Haitians entering the Dominican Republic over the past century because of not only the dearth of official data but also the relatively high absolute numbers involved. The Dominican censuses estimate the number of Haitians living in the country as 28,258 in 1920, 52,567 in 1935, 18,772 in 1950, and 29,350 in 1960 (Censo Nacional Población de la República Dominicana). The 1970 census does not include the required national breakdowns, but the Migration Department of the Secretary of the Interior estimated 97,142 Haitians to be living in the country in 1970—43,142 registered and some 45,000 living illegally there (Acosta, 1976:140). In 1975, the number of Haitians living permanently in the Dominican Republic was estimated at between 200,000 and 300,000 (Lundahl, 1979:626).

It is notable that this final approximation of the number of Haitians living in the Dominican Republic is strikingly close to the estimated number of Dominicans living in the United States at the same point in time. This apparent paradox of "Dominicans out, Haitians in" illustrates that the movement of labor is not as straightforward or mechanical a process as is some times implied by discussions which stress the surplus labor of sending countries and the relative labor scarcity of receiving countries. Moreover, the massive annual importation of Haitian labor into the Dominican Republic challenges the assumption that "the labor needs of capital-intensive industries in peripheral countries can be easily met by the abundant domestic labor supply" (Portes, 1978c:476). Therefore, the basic question before us becomes "What is the nature of a 'labor surplus' in a developing society which simultaneously exports a part of its domestic labor force and imports labor from a society further removed in terms of the international economic hierarchy?"

Many of the seemingly contradictory patterns of labor transfers affecting the Dominican Republic are comprehensible when related to the model of economic development characterizing the Dominican Republic. It is precisely the structural characteristics of the Dominican economy which logically relate to the expulsion of native workers and the importation of Haitians. Many of the features familiar to peripheral capitalist societies which have been associated with international migration in other contexts characterize the Dominican Republic, along with others more unique to the Dominican case.

IV. THE SUGAR ENCLAVE AND RELATIVE LABOR SCARCITY

It is impossible to understand contemporary Dominican society without taking account of the development of the modern sugar plantations in the latter part of the nineteenth century. With the technological advances at the turn of the century, a division of labor was established in the sugar economy between the industrial sectors which processed and refined sugarcane and the agricultural sectors which produced it (Corten et al., 1976:59). This marked a vast expansion of sugar production in the Dominican Republic through the establishment of modern sugar centrales in the east of the country largely stimulated by the penetration of North American capital investments (Del Castillo et al., 1974:150: Acosta, 1976:123).

The first 20 years of this century mark an important phase in the development of the Dominican sugar industry in that many of the essential characteristics of the contemporary industry were rooted in this epoch. The sugar industry, which has remained one of the pillars of the modern Dominican economy, was consolidated under foreign interests, principally North American, after the first U.S. military occupation of the island between 1916 and 1924. This occupation facilitated, among other things, the forced appropriation of land to the benefit of foreign interests (Knight, 1939) and followed an explosive growth in sugar production directed almost exclusively for export. Total production grew from 4,000 tons in 1880, to 50,000 tons in 1905, to 204,018 tons in 1919 (Del Castillo et al., 1974:150).

The characteristics associated with *plantation enclaves* (Cardoso and Faletto, 1979:71) manifested themselves during this epoch: a high degree of land concentration; a relatively high labor/capital ratio, especially in the agricultural sectors; the erosion of local forms of subsistence agriculture through the confiscation of land; and the production of a primary product which serves as the raw material for the dominant export trade. Sugar expansion destroyed the local subsistence economy in the eastern regions of the Dominican Republic (Del Castillo et al., 1974:151) and produced the classic uprooted "free labor" force, in this case dependent on the sugar centrales on a seasonal basis for employment and income (Hoetink, 1971). However there were a number of reasons why the exclusive reliance on a native labor force for the agricultural sector of this industry was not desirable from the point of view of sugar industrialists:

1. *Relative population scarcity.* Although the large sugar centrales took root in the eastern regions of the Dominican Republic, the bulk of the population at this time was located in the northern regions known as the Cibao (Hoetink, 1965:8). Moreover, given a dramatic out-migration of the Dominican population in the early 1800s (Moya-Pons, 1978:175–192) and in spite of a 2.4% annual growth in the population between 1819 and 1908 (Del Castillo, 1978:28), the overall population of the Dominican Republic at the turn of the century was low. The scarcity of population has remained a severe problem during much of Dominican history.

2. *Viable subsistence agriculture.* The low density of population meant a relative abundance of agricultural land. Such conditions favored the persistence of independent agricultural production for much of the Dominican population (Del Castillo, 1978:28). Moreover, it has been estimated that communal land tenure patterns characterized a majority of landholdings in 1907 (Lopez, 1973:129). Therefore, in order to attract a native peasant and semi-proletarianized agricultural population to the seasonal wage employment associated with the eastern sugar industry, subsistence forms of agricultural existence would have had to have been less viable, or even seriously threatened, *or* the wage levels offered by the capitalist sectors of agriculture, the sugar centrales, relatively high.

3. *Speculative nature of sugar production.* The profitability of sugar production, like much primary crop production geared for export, is completely vulnerable to fluctuations in world market prices. The speculative nature of this industry has tended to mean that a premium is placed on minimizing the cost of the labor component of production. Moreover, the timing of the creation of the labor market for the cane-cutting sectors of the sugar industry in the Dominican Republic coincided with a general depression in sugar prices in the favored North American market (Del Castillo, 1978:35). This situation provided a further incentive for the creation of a relatively low salary structure in the cane-cutting sectors of sugar production. Thus the "pull factors" were not adequate to attract a sufficiently large labor force to meet the needs of the expanding sugar market.

The combination of relative population scarcity in the Dominican Republic, independent precapitalist agricultural production, the relatively low wages offered by the emerging sugar industry, and the seasonal nature of the work, meant that an abundant local, cheap labor force was not available to the emerging sugar enclaves. The factors encouraged sugar industrialists to opt at a *strategic time* for the importation of proletarian labor consisting of former slaves from the Antilles, particularly the English, Danish, Dutch, and French possessions in the Caribbean. The drop in world sugar prices in 1920 and the subsequent 1929 depression encouraged a progressively greater reliance on cheaper Haitian labor to the exclusion of other national groups. This pattern became especially marked with the growth of American influence in the sugar industry. In the most recent decades, Haitian labor still plays a central role in sugar agriculture in the Dominican Republic. Brief consideration must be given to the importance of the Dominican state in the contemporary Dominican economy in order to address adequately the importance of Haitian migration for the contemporary sugar sectors.

V. THE DOMINICAN STATE AND HAITIAN MIGRATION

Industrialization in the Dominican Republic after World War I was not carried out by an emerging national bourgeoisie whose base rested in economic control of vital sectors of the economy. Rather, the Dominican Republic passed from a feudal economy to a stage of low-level industrialization while the economy was for all intents and purposes the property of one man, Trujillo. This one "person-state" promoted capitalist development under conditions of monopoly, political control, and an extremely small internal market, and unabashed personal whim (Bosch, 1979; Gutierrez, 1972; Vilas, 1976).

Capitalist industrialization under Trujillo took a decidedly different character than it had taken in Western Europe. For one thing, competitive conditions—which maximized revolutionary industrial techniques, rationality in production, and high levels of productivity in Europe—never existed in the Dominican Republic. Trujillo seized political control of the economy first, and subsequently used the power of the state to gain control of the economy. Thus, the economic enterprises which resulted tended to be monopolistic and backward, with relatively low levels of productivity (Vilas, 1976:175).

The relative backwardness of the Dominican internal market as compared with the international one meant that the export trade associated with the sugar industry continued to be the central pillar of the economy. The most modern capitalist techniques were introduced in the export trade, and this area remains among the most modern sectors of the economy, although these advances scarcely have compensated for the low levels of productivity and undercapitalization in agriculture as a whole, including the agricultural sectors of the sugar industry (Vilas, 1976:181).

The Trujillo economic model meant that limited industrialization was accomplished without the consolidation of a national bourgeoisie, nor did such a class benefit from it. Before the assassination of Trujillo in 1961 his control of the economy was almost absolute: almost 35% of all cultivated land was his, more than 25% of cattle livestock, the production and exportation of rice, and twelve of seventeen sugar refineries, with partial or complete control of the remaining sectors of the economy (Vilas, 1976:171; Bosch, 1979:263). The legal provisions which confiscated the Trujillo empire subsequent to his death provoked a de facto nationalization of major sectors of the economy, a step which Bosch has described as an artificial advance in the face of an atrophied bourgeoisie (Gutierrez, 1972:133).[1] In fact, the relatively high degree of economic centralization and the expansive role played by the state in contemporary Dominican economic development is a feature of the Dominican economy inherited from the military epoch of Trujillo. The strength of the state is evident in the fact that in 1962, one year after the fall of Trujillo, total capital investment in the Dominican Republic, in order of size, was as follows: state investment 51%; foreign investments, 42%; and private national investments, 7% (Bosch, 1979:269).

The predominance of the state in the contemporary sugar sector is also a carry-over from the Trujillo period. Trujillo had acquired the sugar plantations of the West Indies Sugar Company in 1953, and upon his assassination these properties were placed under state control. In more contemporary times the sugar industry has been concentrated in three groups: the Consejo Estatal de Azucar (CEA, the state corporation), Central Romana (subsidiary of the U.S.-owned Gulf & Western Corporation), and Casa Vicini (a private Dominican corporation). Of total raw sugar production in 1974–1975, 65% came from the state corporation (CEA), 28% from the U.S. owned sector, and 7% from Casa Vicini (World Bank, 1978:36). Thus, the state dominates sugar production and is responsible for employing the majority of agricultural workers in the sugar enclave (Corten et al., 1976:17).

It was during the Trujillo era that state regulation of the annual importation of Haitian labor, which coincided with the annual sugar harvest, officially began. In 1939 a presidential decree authorized sugar plantations to recruit black labor and thereby an informal state-regulated traffic of Haitian labor was stimulated, complete with military regulation of transportation (Veras, 1980:12). Between 1940 and 1952, Haitians working in the Dominican Republic did so illegally, as there was no legal agreement between the two countries covering them during this period (Veras, 1980:12). Since 1952 there has been a series of five-year agreements (1952, 1959, 1966) between the Dominican and Haitian governments which has established in effect a bracero program. These agreements, which continue to be renewed in the present, establish the number of workers that the Dominican state contracts annually for its ingenios (sugar plantations); provide for the transportation of workers to and from the cane fields by Dominican officials; provide for the immediate exportation of workers who leave the agreed-upon work site or who are generally "undesirable"; apply Dominican labor laws to Haitian workers; and provide for a forced savings plan whereby daily wage deductions are withheld and made repayable upon repatriation.[2]

The annual contracts between Haiti and the Dominican Republic since 1966 are based upon the terms of these early accords. These contracts specify the number of workers needed in a given harvest year, wages, and working conditions. For example, the stipulated price for the cutting of a ton of cane in 1978 was RD$1.35, which means probable earnings of not more than RD$3.50 daily (equivalent to about 2.80 U.S. dollars on the black market). In 1979 the price paid per ton was $1.55.[3]

In 1978 15,000 Haitian workers were contracted by the state sugar corporation. An important and rather obscure clause of the contract reveals an agreement by the Dominican government to pay $1,225,000 to the Haitian government. This exchange of money was justified on the basis of expenses incurred by the Haitian government through transportation within Haitian borders, processing fees, and so forth.

Subsequent to an international denunciation of the "purchase of foreign workers," the 1979 contract made no reference to the sum of money that the Haitian government would receive for its delivery of 14,000 workers to CEA (Ultima Hora, 1980). The dogged inquiries made by a Dominican lawyer regarding the terms of this agreement, specifically the quantity of money paid to the Haitian government, revealed the following: although the contracts between Haiti and the Dominican Republic regarding the Haitian traffic were government-to-government agreements, they were technically illegal not only because the accords upon which the contracts were based had expired but more significantly because neither of the official representative bodies (the Senate or the Chamber of Representatives) had participated in the authorization of the contracts.[4] The following year considerable fanfare was accorded the fact that the 1980 contract would not be a government-to-government agreement; instead, CEA, the state corporation, would participate directly in the negotiations. As an "autonomous" state body, CEA has the legal right to negotiate contracts without congressional approval and without necessarily revealing the terms of the contract—namely, with the legal right not to divulge the Haitian government's "fee" for the delivery of the annual crop of workers (Sierra, 1981:4).

In many ways it may be misleading to place too great an emphasis on the legality of these contracts given (1) the tremendously large inflow of "illegals" or those working without benefit of contract in both the state-owned and private agricultural sectors and (2) the considerable gap between the terms specified by the contracts and the reality of the working conditions of most Haitians. Merely reading the formal terms of the state contracts makes it apparent that the life of the contracted cane cutter is worse than grim. The reality has been an elaborate system of corruption ranging from the wholesale confiscation of all forced savings to rigged systems of weights, local usury credit institutions, backbreaking labor of up to 14 hours a day, and arbitrary wage payments, conditions popularized in the novel *Over* by Ramón Marrero Aristy.

A visit to Batey Muñoz in the Montellan sugar estate in March 1979 confirmed that in a hut of four square meters lived six persons who slept without beds and lacked both electric light and potable water. The workers were obliged to work 14 hours daily for US$2.75. There was no medical attention and the money earned permitted only the consumption of cane juice with lemon and bread. A large proportion were plagued by infectious bontoncitos over the body, and the majority suffered from dislocations of the vertebral column. Protests against working conditions were and are made extremely difficult by the presence of Haitian secret police (Tontons Macoutes) who are hired as "supervisors" and serve the dual purposes of defusing incipient protests by Haitian laborers and of spying on Haitian political exiles living in the Dominican Republic (Veras, 1980:17-19).

The situation described above is as applicable to those workers legally "covered" by the bracero contracts as it is to the undocumented Haitians who illegally reside on a permanent basis in the Dominican Republic and work in the sugar plantations owned by private domestic and foreign capital. Regardless of legal status, Haitians make a central contribution to sugar production. In 1973 it was estimated that, considering all the sugar centrales, 47–62% of all agricultural workers were of Haitian origin (Corten et al., 1976:17; Del Castillo et al., 209). (See Table 1.) It should be recalled that the bracero program covers only those Haitians working in the state sector. Thus, although an important part of the Haitian traffic is legal, it is apparent that a sizable proportion of all agricultural workers in the Dominican sugar enclave consist of Haitian laborers who illegally reside permanently or temporarily in the Dominican Republic. Although about 15,000 Haitians were officially brought into the country in 1978, the actual figure is judged to be as high as 30,000 (World Bank, 1978:37).

Table 1. Minimum and Maximum Estimate of Haitians Working in the Agricultural Sectors of the Sugar Enclave in the Dominican Republic

Corporation	Minimum Percent Haitian (residents)	Maximum Percent Haitian (residents and seasonal)	Total agricultural workers (1967)	Minimum Estimate of Haitians (n)	Maximum Estimate of Haitians (n)
Central Romana	57	72	17,228	9,757	12,578
CEA	48	64	40,220	19,305	25,740
Casa Vicini	15	20	5,500	825	1,100

Source: Corten et al., 1976:17.

The reliance on Haitian labor in the key sectors of the Dominican economy has a number of structural consequences.

VI. THE STRUCTURAL IMPACT OF HAITIAN MIGRATION

The fundamental division within the sugar enclave between the industrial sector and the agricultural sector established at the end of the nineteenth century has persisted throughout the development of this industry in the twentieth century. The industrial sectors of the sugar enclave have been the fastest-growing, most "modern" sectors of the Dominican economy, whereas the agricultural sectors which service the former have remained backward, primitive, and characterized by working conditions which parallel, down to the reliance on the single machete for cane cutting, nineteenth-century conditions of labor. Emphasis on increases in productivity in order to augment production have typified only the industrial sectors of the sugar enclave, just as they have marked the patterns of industrial growth in the Dominican Republic as a whole. On the other hand, from the outset cane agriculture persistently has been marked by extremely low levels of capital investment. Instead, reliance upon extremely cheap sources of labor and increases in the extension of land devoted to sugar cane production have been the preferred means for increasing total production. This feature of the agricultural sector of the sugar industry, namely, reliance upon *absolute exploitation* of labor, or the minimization of capital investment per worker, in order to maintain a competitive position in the international sugar export trade has necessitated the persistent reliance upon the annual importation of foreign workers willing or forced to work in the most strenuous, dehumanizing working conditions imaginable for compensation which only questionably meets basic subsistence needs.

The productivity of the agricultural sector of sugar has not only remained low but in many instances has worsened. For example, in 1957 21,000 more workers were employed than in 1956 in the agricultural sectors of sugar in order to realize the same overall production. The average level of production per worker dropped from 1.40 tons of cane daily to 1.25 tons.[5] The emphasis on new investments in the agricultural sector of sugar is placed not on augmenting the yield of individual workers but rather on increasing the *number* of workers by devoting more agricultural land to cane production. In fact, overall sugarcane yield per cultivated hectare declined by nearly 57% annually from 1963–1965 to 1973–1975 (World Bank, 1978:38). The increase in total raw sugar production during the same period (about 4.6% annually) resulted from the expansion in total cultivated area by 8.8% annually (from 89,300 to 206,600 hectares). (See Table 2.)

These low levels of investment characterize the private, foreign, and state sectors of agriculture. Most state investments, for example, are dedicated to sectors outside sugar, which means a persistently low level of mechanization in the work associated with the cutting and gathering of cane. One of the indirect advantages of this low level of mechanization made possible by the availability of cheap Haitian labor involves a relatively high yield in sugar cane processing. The World Bank estimated in 1978 that reliance upon Haitian labor produced a

Table 2. Sugar Trends

	Sugar Cane			Raw Sugar	
	Area Cultivated ('000 ha)	Production ('000 mt)	Yield[a] (mt/ha)	Production ('000 mt)	Yield[b]
Aug. 1963-65	89.3	6,909.9	77.4	738.1	0.107
Aug. 1968-70	128.6	7,557.1	58.8	855.0	0.133
Aug. 1973-75	206.6	9,853.1	47.7	1,157.7	0.117
Annual Growth Rate (percent)					
1963/65-1968/70	7.6	1.8	−5.4	3.0	4.5
1968/70-1973/75	10.0	5.5	−4.1	6.2	−2.5
1963/65-1973/75	8.8	3.6	−4.7	4.6	0.9

Notes: [a]Production per unit area cultivated
[b]Metric tons of sugar per metric ton of cane
Source: World Bank, 1978:37

distinct advantage for the Dominican Republic over other sugar-producing countries because of the resulting low proportion of waste, in terms of leaves and tops, and because in this manner the cane is unburnt. The sugar content of Dominican cane (11.7%) is among the highest in the world (World Bank, 1978:37). From this it becomes apparent that the agricultural sector indirectly subsidizes the industrial sector which refines this inexpensively produced raw material. The Haitian worker has served as the historical and contemporary foundation of this subsidy to the sugar refining sector.

The importation of Haitians not only serves to maintain profits through a low ratio of fixed to variable costs but more generally serves as an important anticyclical mechanism in two respects. For one thing, cane growing and sugar refining are intimately related since cane must be refined rapidly if it is to retain its high sugar content. The export trade associated with sugar refining is highly vulnerable to world market fluctuations. Low sugar prices can be relatively easily offset in the agricultural sector by simply reducing the number of Haitians imported in a given period. For another thing, apart from fluctuating international sugar prices, the seasonal nature of cane cutting necessitates similar anticyclical adjustments. These adjustments are possible with an imported labor force which provides no costs to employers during off-season months.

VII. MODERN DEPENDENT DEVELOPMENT AND RELATIVE LABOR SURPLUS

Thus far the focus has been specifically on the importation of foreign labor into the Dominican Republic to meet the needs of specialized sectors of the economy. The concern here is to examine a number of features of Dominican society which have produced since the early 1960s high rates of out-migration on the part of

Dominican labor. There are a number of contradictory features of the model of economic development implemented in the Dominican Republic, especially after 1961, which account for the paradoxical pattern of high out-migration of Dominicans in the face of persistent labor shortages in the sugar enclave.

A. Persistent Agricultural Stagnation and Rural–Urban Migration

Dominican agrarian structure, like that of many Latin American societies, remains characterized by a high concentration of cultivated land ownership. In 1971, for example, 77.1% of the landholdings were small parcels of 80 tareas or less, occupying only 13% of the cultivated land surface. At the other extreme, 57.2% of the land surface was held by only 2.3% of the landholdings (Oficina Nacional de Estadística, 1971). In spite of this land concentration, Dominican agriculture has remained extremely backward, with persistently low levels of agricultural production and very low levels of capital investment (Dore y Cabral, 1979:21). Since 1960 most state investments have gone into nonagricultural areas such as commerce and construction (Vilas, 1976:227; Weiskoff, 1978), and no concerted agrarian reforms have altered the traditional lati-minifundio concentration of land or the accompanying semi-feudal stagnation in agricultural production (Dore y Cabral, 1978). Although there was an increase in the amount of land dedicated to the cultivation of the four principal products of the Dominican Republic (sugar cane, cacao, coffee, and tobacco) during the period of 1960–1971, this increase did not result in an increase in the production of these commodities (Gomez, 1979:191).

As a result, the proletarian labor force has grown only slightly. The agricultural system has instead favored subsistence farming and a floating semi-proletarianized labor force. That is, in 1970 only 22% of agricultural workers were true peasants in the sense that they subsisted by working their own land or the land of their family members without resort to occasional day labor; 17% were strictly proletarizanized in the sense that they existed exclusively by selling their labor to agricultural employers; fully 61% of agricultural workers existed somewhere in between, producing directly their own consumption goods while also selling their labor (Duarte, 1979:9).

This semi-proletarization of the rural population, combined with high population growth (3% annually) (World Bank, 1978), has meant that a large part of the agricultural population has no longer been able to meet familial subsistence needs on reduced landholdings and has migrated to urban areas. During the period 1920–1970 the urban population grew at an explosive rate, increasing elevenfold. During the same period the rural population only tripled. This process has especially accelerated in more recent times; between 1960 and 1970 the annual net rate of population growth in the urban zones of the country was 5.9% versus only 1.4% in rural areas (Ramirez et al., 1977:3).

B. Enclave Industrialization

Industrial development in the Dominican Republic in recent decades has followed the familiar pattern associated with "dependent development" in other Latin American countries. Industrial growth has largely been financed by the massive importation of foreign capital, especially in sectors geared for re-export. Direct foreign investment grew from $108 million in 1962, to $120 million in 1968, accelerated to $171.7 million in 1971, and reached $233.0 million in 1974 (Gomez, 1979:185).

The influx of foreign capital was stimulated by an industrial incentives act in 1966 (Ley 299), which gives generous tax incentives to new businesses and exempts firms producing for export completely from taxes on profits, whether from imports or exports. In many cases this exemption is guaranteed for up to twenty years (World Bank, 1978:56).

The "success" of this model has been well heralded and is manifested in growth of the Gross Domestic Product, which expanded at an annual real rate of 11% in 1968-1974, one of the highest growth rates in the world. Further, GNP per capita has climbed from 269.9 pesos in 1962, to 286.2 in 1969, to 359.8 in 1971, and reached 417.1 in 1975, at constant 1962 prices (World Bank, 1978:i, 129).

The impact of this expanded industrialization has been extremely negative in two principal areas, namely, employment and income inequality. As has been the case in other countries which have relied upon the import substitution model of industrialization (Alba, 1978), expanded manufacturing activity in the Dominican Republic has not been able to absorb a fraction of the newly urbanized population. This is because a strong incentive was provided for the introduction of capital-intensive techniques of production, which has made the use of machinery cheaper than the reliance on Dominican labor (World Bank, 1978:56). Moreover, the incentive system has favored firms which process foreign inputs over those which transform local raw materials and has not tended to aid the severe balance-of-payments problem (Vega and Castillo, 1980:4-5). In social terms this has been translated into soaring urban unemployment and underemployment. Open unemployment in Santo Domingo was estimated at 20% of the labor force in 1973. A study of five proletarian neighborhoods in Santo Domingo in 1976-1977 concluded that 60% of the heads of houses fell in the category of "relative surplus population" in the sense that they were without any form of regular employment and earned less than four pesos daily in their irregular activities (Duarte, 1979:20). Underemployment in rural areas was estimated by the World Bank to be as high as 60% in 1978. Moreover, the high GNP growth experienced in the sixties and seventies has not corrected the persistently unequal distribution of income. Two studies on income distribution in the capital city, one conducted in 1969 by the Dominican Central Bank and one in 1973 by the

International Labor Organization, give an indication of the relative change in income distribution during the years of maximum GNP growth (see Table 3). The bottom fifth of the population earned relatively less in 1973 (1.4% of the total) than it had in 1969 (2.9%). On the other hand, that fifth of the population earning the highest income in 1969 maintained its position in 1973 (54.8% of the total income in 1969 and 54.4% in 1973). To the extent that the middle 30% succeeded in capturing a larger share of total income during this period (27.6% in 1969 and 30.2% in 1973), it did so at the expense of the poorest stratum of the population and not the wealthiest.

Table 3. Changes in the Distribution of Income in Santo Domingo, 1969-1973

Categories of Income *(percent of all families)*	*Percentage of All Families*	
	1969	*1973*
Bottom 20 percent	2.9	1.4
Bottom 50 percent	17.6	15.4
Middle 30 percent	27.6	30.2
Top 20 percent	54.8	54.4

Source: Oficina Nacional de Planificación, Bases para Formular una Politica de Empleo en la República Dominicana (Santo Domingo, ONAPLAN) 1974, p.41: Quoted in Cabral, 1975:7.

C. Modern Consumption Aspirations

Another consequence of industrialization and the penetration of foreign economic interests has been the widespread diffusion of aspirations for styles of consumption associated with life in developed societies. These modern consumption values are created and catered to by advertisements from foreign and local consumer and industrial firms, which parade the merits of "living modern" in a persistent campaign to expand the internal market for their products. This pattern is certainly a general one and has been noted repeatedly in other Latin American contexts.

In the Dominican Republic this aspiration takes on dramatic proportions. The situation is fueled not only by the mass media, which reach the most remote areas, but also by migration itself. It has been documented that a large proportion of Dominicans who migrate to the United States return to live in the Dominican Republic (Ugalde et al., 1979). These return migrants bring with them the consumption orientations characteristic of New York. It should be recalled that Dominicans have been migrating to New York in significant numbers since 1964. Fifteen years of exposure to waves of returning "Dominican-Yorkers," be it for visits or permanent residence, have contributed *autonomously* to the craving for foreign consumer goods and for the inaccessible life styles. The examples abound. One has only to stand at the international airport in Santo Domingo during Christmas to witness this inflow of modern consumption symbols—the ubiquitous electrical appliances, the conspicuous New York fashions, and the utterly internalized, cosmopolitan lifestyles of returning Dominicans who have paid their dues afar.

It would be difficult to exaggerate the extent to which New York life styles are highly esteemed in the Dominican Republic, especially by the aspiring middle class. It appears, in fact, that even the Dominican state has in recent times conceded the relative attractiveness of foreign symbols over national ones. In 1979 the official state tobacco corporation, La Tabacalera, launched a national campaign to promote a new cigarette designed to challenge the recent market advances made by Marlboro. The name selected for the *indigenous* attack against the cowboy symbol of Marlboro was "Hilton."

In summary, the processes set in motion by the Dominican model of industrial development, especially since World War II, have been the following: persistent agricultural stagnation combined with growing land concentration, population growth, the absence of structural agrarian reform, and high levels of farm-to-city migration. Industrialization has created a productive structure which is capital-intensive and concentrated and therefore has not been able to absorb enough of the nation's labor resources. Rather, it has merely augmented the incomes of those already employed. The result has been an expanding sector of the urban population without regular access to minimal resources for survival. Simultaneous with the production of a progressively marginalized urban population and the declining work-force absorption of the economy, there has been increased awareness of, and aspirations for, consumption standards associated with life in developed societies. The result is a significant dichotomy between what the economy is designed to produce and that to which the bulk of the population aspires. These are the principal structural factors which have combined to provide a powerful impetus to the emigration of Dominicans.

Dominican migration to the United States offers an interesting case of population displacement, or of a relative labor surplus, from an underdeveloped society which has *not* on the whole been characterized by capitalist industrialization of agriculture. In other cases of Latin American migration to the United States the industrialization of agriculture has been cited as one of the factors contributing to the displacement of agricultural workers (Portes, 1978c). However, we have seen that agricultural sectors of the Dominican economy are notoriously backward, stagnant, even less productive over time (Dore y Cabral, 1980:98). This holds true for not only the sugar plantations but Dominican agriculture as a whole. The increased land concentration combined with population growth have meant that farming families no longer able to meet subsistence needs on reduced landholdings have migrated to urban areas and contributed, directly or indirectly, to the Dominican out-migration.

It is important to note that the argument made here is not necessarily that those most marginalized by this process are the actual migrants. We are not here addressing the separate issue of the character of the migrant flow or the individual characteristics of migrants. Evidence regarding the nature of the Dominican migrant profile is contradictory. Some studies have indicated, often implicitly, that the Dominican migrant pool represents a rural hard-core surplus population (Gonzales, 1970:155; Hendricks, 1974; Sassen-Koob, 1979:317), whereas one study based on a national survey has described the migrants not only as urbanized but as middle-class (Ugalde et. al., 1979:242). A definitive analysis of the migrant flow and of the implications for future Dominican economic development should this migration persist awaits further evidence.[6] We note here rather the coincidence between these structural variables and a population displacement or what appears to be the generation of a relative labor surplus of Dominicans.

One thing, however, is clear, Dominicans in large numbers are opting to leave their country rather than fill the "open" jobs in the cane fields. The work of cutting and sorting sugar cane is considered the worst of all possible jobs in the Dominican Republic. It is the bottom rung of the survival ladder—the tropical equivalent to garbage collection. Cutting cane, moreover, is considered "Haitian work" and thereby associated with living conditions in Haiti, which are widely regarded as the worst in the western hemisphere. The exodus of so many Dominicans in search of employment in the United States dramatically underscores the *relative* nature of the labor scarcity in the sugar industry of the Dominican Republic.

VIII. CONCLUSION

The Dominican case provides an illustration of an international hierarchy of labor migration. A labor force imported from a peripheral society occupies positions in a developed society which apparently are undesirable to the native working class, whereas the same peripheral society in turn imports part of its labor force from another peripheral society further down in the international economic hierarchy. The fascinating thing about this stair-step process of labor exchange is the similarity in the economic functions, the political implications, and the ideological or cultural interpretations which accompany migrant workers imported into developed societies and "bottom-rung" peripheral workers imported into "middle-rung" underdeveloped societies. The cultural and ethnic division of the working class in the developed world between migrant and native workers is similarly reproduced within the peripheral society which imports foreign labor. All the familiar racial stereotypes which accompany Mexican, Cuban, and other minority workers in the United States are applied to Haitian workers in the Dominican Republic. If Latins are held in low regard in the United States for accepting working conditions below the level accepted by many native workers, the same holds true for Haitians in the Dominican Republic (Mejia-Ricart, 1980:15).

The cultural and social differences between Dominican and Haitian workers have reduced the possibility of organized efforts by sugar plantation workers to bargain with their employers. This inhibited class consciousness has been noted since the establishment of the sugar industry and the importation of workers from Curaçao, the British West Indies, and Haiti in the last quarter of the nineteenth century. The first strike recorded in the Dominican Republic occurred not in the sugar plantation area but on a railway project in the northern part of the country, where only native Dominican workers were employed (Hoetink, 1971). This cultural and social division is compounded by the animosity and undisguised racism toward Haitians expressed by many Dominicans, which reflect long-standing political conflicts between the Dominican Republic and Haiti and a history of brutalities suffered by both peoples at the hands of aggressors (Logan, 1968).

Third-world migrants often fill jobs in the secondary sectors in developed societies, especially those nonmonopolistic sectors which rely on a high labor/capital ratio. We have observed a related phenomenon with the importation of Haitian workers in the Dominican Republic. That is, agriculture in the Dominican Republic has suffered from notoriously low capital/labor ratios and maintains competitives prices only by reducing labor costs to the bone, to that which will barely keep its labor force alive.

The functions served by the importation of foreign labor, however, depend very much on the position of the importing country in the international division of labor. There are important differences between the role played by Haitian workers in the Dominican Republic and the role typically attributed to foreign labor in developed societies. Although Haitians are working in backward, labor-intensive sectors, these sectors are directly linked to the most modern, dynamic sectors of the economy, the sugar refining branches. Given the enclave pattern of development in the Dominican Republic, the Haitian workers serve a much more strategic economic role than is commonly assumed to be the case with the foreign workers in developed societies.

A large proportion of the Haitian traffic is "swallow migration" of workers imported and exported annually depending on the seasonal needs of the sugar industry. This implies an essential geographic division between the point of reproduction and *maintenance* of the work force (Haiti) and the sites of production (the sugar fields of the Dominican Republic). The division benefits not only the private and state sectors of the sugar industry with an immediate seasonal need for the labor but also the employing class as a whole, which is in no way burdened with the long term costs associated with the reproduction of a work force nor with the political pressure of a large group of lingering unemployed men during the long nonharvesting seasons. This advantage to the capitalist class as a whole has been noted in a variety of other contexts (Castles and Kosack, 1973; Castells, 1975, 1975; Burawoy, 1976; Sassen-Koob, 1978). However, in the Dominican case we see that there is almost a double bonanza for the foreign sectors.

For one thing, the foreign sector, it should be recalled, does not officially receive any of the annually contracted workers who enter legally from Haiti. Therefore, one can safely assume that the large number of Haitians working in the sugar fields of the U.S. sector include a high proportion of undocumented workers, the most vulnerable of the Haitian stream. The fact that as many as one-half of the Haitians working in the sugar industry as a whole may be illegals means that wages and job conditions are determined by this group. Rather than guarantee minimally acceptable wage levels and job conditions, the legal contracts merely *reflect* the existence of a large stratum of undocumented workers.

For another thing, there is the advantage the U.S. sector has had periodically over the state and Dominican private sectors in the international sugar market. The fact that U.S. sugar prices have in recent decades been on the average higher than world prices means that competition to sell in the U.S. market has been fierce. The U.S. sector, the Central Romana, has over time received a share in the distribution of sales quotas in the U.S. market disproportionate to its share of Dominican sugar production. The quotas for selling in the U.S. market by Dominican sugar producers established in the mid 1950s were still in effect in the early 1970's although the relative volume of production of the various groups had changed considerably. One economist in 1970 described the situation in the following manner: "[T]he state *ingenios* subsidize the private *ingenios* in that the former have increased their production in the last 15 years, without a proportional increase in their share of the U.S. quota."[7] Thus, the foreign sector is in the strategic position of relying upon its own domestic market with highly favorable international sugar prices for the export of a product which was produced in one low-wage economy by a cheap labor force imported from a second, even lower-wage economy: a three-way geographic division between the market, the point of production, and the point of reproduction.

To the extent that migration out of a context of extremely high unemployment serves as a short-term safety valve, both the Haitian and Dominican state benefit from reduced political pressure. The Haitian state, however, is in the position of receiving a direct economic payoff from the Dominican state corporation, a literal kickback from the benefits derived from the availability of perhaps the cheapest labor force in the hemisphere, a benefit not awarded the Dominican state in the case of Dominican emigration.

These distinctions serve to underscore the basic argument that what is a "labor surplus" in a peripheral context is a highly heterogeneous phenomenon. Dependent development can produce *simultaneously* a relative labor surplus and a relative labor shortage, both of which express the contradictory features inherent in this pattern of development. An adequate account of the functions associated with a given international labor transfer must begin with an analysis of the position in the international division of labor of the society which exports part of its native labor force, imports a foreign labor force, or, as in the Dominican case, does both simultaneously.

ACKNOWLEDGMENTS

The author wishes to acknowledge the financial support received as a postdoctoral fellow from the National Institute of Mental Health (S F 32 MH0)7909-02) during the writing of this article and from the National Institute of Child Health and Human Development (1 R01HD 14298-01).

NOTES

1. Bosch (1979:263) has estimated that the Trujillo sugar empire alone was worth more than $120,000,000 in 1961.
2. "Acuerdo sobre la Contratación en Haiti y la República Dominicana de Journaleros Temporeros Haitianos," 1952, 1959, 1966, Mimeos.
3. The figures cited here are based on the contracts signed in 1978 and 1979. Consejo Estatal del Azúcar, "Contrato Suscrito Entre el Gobierno Haitiano y el CEA," mimeo.
4. Veras, Ramón Antonio, 1981, personal correspondence.
5. Parsons, Programa para la rehabilitación, modernización y diversificación de la industria azucarera del Gobierno Dominicano, Vol III, 1–3, cited in Corten et al,, 1976:19.
6. The author presently is engaged in analyzing data from a survey of three migrant communities in the Dominican Republic, which constitutes part of a larger interdisciplinary study conducted with Dr. Patricia Pessar.
7. Bernardo Vega, "Inversión Extranjera Casos y Situación Dominicana," *Ahora!* no. 346, June, 1970, cited in Del Castillo et al. 1974:163 (translation mine).

REFERENCES

Alba, Francisco
    1978 "Mexico's international migration as a manifestation of its development pattern." International Migration Review 12:502–513.
Acosta, Mercedes
    1976 "Azúcar e inmigración Haitiana." Pp. 9–84 in André Corten, Carlos M. Vilas, Mercedes Acosta and Isis Duarate (eds.), Azúcar y Politica. Santo Domingo: Taller.
Bach, Robert L.
    1978 "Mexican immigration and the American state." International Migration Review 12:536–558.
Bonacich, Edna
    1976 "Advanced capitalism and black/white relations: a split labor market interpretation." American Sociological Review 41: 34–51.
Bosch, Juan
    1979 Composición Social Dominicana. Santo Domingo: Alfa y Omega.
Burawoy, Michael
    1976 "The functions and reproduction of migrant labor: comparative material from Southern Africa and the United States." American Journal of Sociology 81:1050–1087.
Cabral, Manuel José
    1975 "Inflación, Distribución del Ingreso y Empleo." Ciencia y Sociedad 1·4–48.
Cardoso, Fernando Henrique, and Enzo Faletto
    1979 Dependency and Development in Latin America. Berkeley: University of California Press.
Castells, Manuel
    1975 "Immigrant workers and class struggle in advanced capitalism: the Western European experience." Politics and Society 5:33–66.

Castles, Stephen, and Godula Kosack
  1973 Immigrant Workers and Class Structure in Western Europe. London: Oxford University Press.
Cornelius, Wayne
  1979 "Mexican and Caribbean migration to the United States: a report to the Ford Foundation." Unpublished discussion draft (April).
Corten, André
  1976 "Haiti: Estructura Agraria y Migración de Trabajadores a las Centrales Azucareros Dominicanos." Pp. 85–114 in André Corten, Carlos M. Vilas, Mercedes Acosta, and Isis Duarte (eds.), Azúcar y Politica. Santo Domingo: Taller.
Corten, André, Mercedes Acosta, and Isis Duarte
  1976 "Las Relaciones de Producción en la Economia Azucarera Dominicana." In André Corten, Carlos M. Vilas, Mercedes Acosta, and Isis Duarte (eds.), Azúcar y Politica. Santo Domingo: Taller.
Del Castillo, José
  1978 La Inmigración de Braceros Azucareros en La República Dominicana 1900–1930. Santo Domingo: Universidad Autonoma de Santo Domingo.
Del Castillo, José, Miguel Cocco, Walter Cordero, Max Puig, Otto Fernandez, and Wilfredo Lozano
  1974 La Gulf y Western en República Dominicana. Santo Domingo: Universidad Autonoma de Santo Domingo.
Demas, Willian G.
  1965 The Economics of Development in Small Countries with Special Reference to the Caribbean. Montreal: McGill University Press.
Dominguez, Virginia
  1978 Statement prepared for hearing on "Illegal Aliens: Implications for U.S. Policy in the Western Hemisphere." Subcommittee on Inter-American Affairs of the House International Relations Committee, Washington, D.C., May 23.
Dore y Cabral, Carlos
  1979 Problemas de la Estructura Agraria Dominicana. Santo Domingo: Taller.
  1980 "Reforma Agraria y Luchas Sociales en la República Dominicana: 1966-1978." Estudios CentroAmericanos 25: 91-123.
Duarte, Isis
  1979 "La Super-Población Urbana en Santo Domingo: Las Chiriperos y Los Trabajadores Independientes." Paper presented at the Latin American Conference on Labor and Living Conditions, San José, Costa Rica, October.
Frank, Andre Gunder
  1967 Capitalism and Underdevelopment in Latin America. New York: Monthly Review Press.
Furtado, Celso
  1964 Development and Underdevelopment. Berkeley: University of California Press.
Gomez, Luis
  1979 Relaciones de Producción Dominantes en la Sociedad Dominicana 1875/1975. Santo Domingo: Alfa y Omega.
Gutierrez, Carlos Maria
  1972 The Dominican Republic: Rebellion and Repression. New York: Monthly Review Press.
Hoetink, Harry
  1965 "Materiales para el estudio de la República Dominicana en la segunda mitad del Siglo XIX." Caribbean Studies 5
  1971 El Pueblo Dominicano: 1850–1900. Santiago: Universidad Católica Madre y Maestra.
Immigration and Naturalization Service
  1976 Annual Report. Washington: I.N.S.
Kayal, Philip M.
  1978 "The Dominicans in New York: Part II." Migration Today 6:10–15.

Knight, Melvin Moses
- 1937 Los Americanos en Santo Domingo. Cuidad Trujillo: Universidad Autonoma Santo Domingo.

Leahy, Peter J., and Sam Castillo
- 1977 "Making it illegally: 'wetbacks' in the social and economic life of a southwestern metropolitan area." Unpublished paper presented at the Annual Meeting of the Society for the Study of Social Problems, September.

Logan, Rayford W.
- 1968 Haiti and The Dominican Republic. New York: Oxford University Press.

Lopez, Jose Ramón
- 1973 "La Cāna de Azúcar en San Pedro de Macoris, desde el bosque virgen hasta el mercado." Ciencia II (3).

Lundahl, Mats
- 1979 Peasants and Poverty: A Study of Haiti. London: Croom Helm.

Maldonado-Dennis, Manuel
- 1980 The Emigration Dialectic. New York: International Publishers.

Marino Hernandez, Frank
- 1973 La Inmigración en la República Dominicana." Eme Eme: Estudios Dominicanos 5 24–56.

Marrero Aristy, Ramon
- 1978 Over. Santo Domingo: Taller.

Mejia-Ricart, Marcio
- 1980 "La Importación de Haitianos," El Sol (15).

Moya Pons, Frank
- 1978 Manual de Historia Dominicana. Santiago: Universidad Católica Madre y Maestra.

O'Connor, James
- 1973 The Fiscal Crisis of the State. New York: St. Martin's Press.

Oficina Nacional de Estadística
- 1971 6to Censo Nacional Agropecuario. Santo Domingo: ONE.

Patterson, Orlando
- 1978 "Migration in Caribbean societies: socio-economic and symbolic resources." In William H. McNeill and Ruth S. Adams (eds.), Human Migration: Patterns and Policies. Bloomington: Indiana University Press.

Portes, Alejandro
- 1978a "Migration and underdevelopment." Politics and Society 8: 1–48.
- 1978b "Modes of structural incorporation and present theories of labor immigration." Revised version of paper delivered at the conference on Internation Migration Studies, the Rockefeller Foundation, June 1978, Belagio, Italy.
- 1978c "Toward a structural analysis of illegal (undocumented) immigration." International Migration Review 12:469–484
- 1979 "Illegal immigration and the international system, lessons from recent legal Mexican immigrants to the United States." Social Problems 26:425–438.

Ramírez, Nelson, Pablo Tactuk, and Minerva Breton
- 1977 La Migración Interna en la República Dominicana. Santo Domingo: Alfa y Omega.

Sassen-Koob, Saskia
- 1978 "The international circulation of resources and development: the case of migrant labour." Development and Change 9:509–546
- 1979 "Formal and Informal associations: Dominicans and Colombians in New York." International Migration Review 13:314–332.

Schoenrich, Otto
- 1977 Santo Domingo, un Pais con Futuro. Santo Domingo: Editora de Santo Domingo.

Sierra, José
- 1981 "Dice que zafra del 1981–82 comienza en forma normal." El Sol:4.

Ugalde, Antonio, Frank Bean, and Gilbert Cárdenas
    1979   "International migration from the Dominican Republic: findings from a national survey." International Migration Review 8:235–254.
Ultima Hora
    1980   "CEA." Ultima Hora:10
Vega, Gustavo and Enmanuel Castillo
    1980   "Economía y Política: La 'Nacionalización' de la Ley 299." Santiago: Universidad Católica Madre y Maestra, mimeo.
Veras, Ramón Antonio
    1980   "Trabajadores Migratorios, su Situacíon de Trabajo y Seguridad Social en Iberoamérica." Paper presented at the Congreso Iberoamericano de Derecho del Trabajo, Santiago, The Dominican Republic, mimeo.
Vilas, Carlos Maria
    1976   "La Política de la Dominación en la República Dominicana." Pp 155–234 in André Corten, Carlos M. Vilas, Mercedes Acosta, and Isis Duarte (eds.), Azucar y Politica. Santo Domingo: Taller.
Weisskoff, Richard
    1978   "Puerto Rico and the Caribbean Economies: models and patterns." Unpublished paper presented at the seminar on Political and Economic Choices in the Contemporary Caribbean, Washington, April.
Weisz, Vilma
    1973   "Causas de las Migraciones Dominicanas al Exterior." Unpublished thesis, Universidad Nacional Pedro Hendrizuez Ureña.
World Bank
    1978   Dominican Republic: Its Main Economic Development Problems. Washington, D.C., World Bank.

MIAMI'S GARMENT INDUSTRY AND ITS WORKERS

Madeline J. Haug

I. INTRODUCTION

A dual-economy perspective which highlights divisions within national industrial structures has become increasingly popular among researchers. The results of efforts adopting such an approach have led to the conclusion that the monetary rewards of labor force participation are unequally distributed across industries. Workers employed in industries within what has been termed the "competitive" or "periphery" economy (O'Connor, 1973; Piore, 1975; Averitt, 1968) receive low immediate returns and few long-term benefits. The periphery economy attracts and recruits the more vulnerable segments of the labor force—legal immigrants, undocumented workers, and members of racial, ethnic, gender, or age minority groups.

Differences exist not only between economies but among industries within a single economy as well. Wage differentials among industries may be due to characteristics of the work force employed in an industry as well as characteristics of the industry itself, as suggested by split labor market interpretations (Bonacich, 1972, 1976). The organization of production and technological development within an industry also can affect the distribution of work within it, allowing some industries to rely more easily on workers who produce goods at home. The garment or apparel industry is a classic case in point. This low-wage industry has survived through the use of at-home workers tied to the formal economy through an interlocking familial and often ethnic-based network of recruitment and distribution of work.

The purposes of this study are: (1) to document the recent development of the apparel industry within the Miami area; (2) to link the industry's growth to regional conditions conducive to low-wage industry—right-to-work legislation and the presence of an easily exploitable supply of labor; and (3) to describe the organization of apparel work within the Miami area. While accounts in the popular press (Alder et al., 1980) emphasize the unprecedented "success" of Cuban emigres in the United States, the experiences of the female component of this immigrant flow within the Miami area suggest that a gender bias in research exists. This description of Miami's apparel industry and its female Cuban workers is an attempt to correct this bias. Data on which this study is based come from a variety of sources, including government documents, existing studies of garment manufacturers and workers, and interviews with sources within the Miami area. This paper is a preliminary report of an ongoing research project being conducted by the author.

II. THE GARMENT INDUSTRY IN THE UNITED STATES

A. Historical Overview

The use of immigrant labor in the apparel industry has been well-documented historically. The garment industry within the United States, while not begun by immigrant labor, grew under the direction of former immigrants and the hands of more recent arrivals. With the invention of the sewing machine in 1846, demands for ready-made clothing from the U.S. War Department and southern slaveholders could be pursued on an economy of scale (Foner, 1979). Independent tailors and seamstresses were soon replaced by sewing-machine operators employed within a factory setting as clothing manufacturers began to construct garments for sale to the growing urban population in northeastern cities.

Technological improvements and innovations, however, were not the main impetus for this industry's growth. The massive and continuous flow of immigrants to the United States in the late 1800s is credited with establishing a source of inexpensive and experienced labor which could help the industry to flourish.

The 1860 census listed 188 women's apparel firms employing 5,739 workers nationally. In less than 20 years the numbers had risen to 562 firms with 25,192 workers. By 1900, more than 83,000 workers in upwards of 32 states were employed in the women's garment industry. The number of workers approached one million by the 1930s, the garment industry becoming the country's largest single industrial employer in terms of number of employees (Hardy, 1935).

New York City, the port of arrival for the vast majority of Europe's immigrants, emerged as the leading center for the construction and distribution of wearing apparel. By the turn of the century the clothing industry was the largest single employer of both males and females within the city. Not surprisingly, the vast majority of its work force was foreign-born. In 1907-1908, a U.S. Department of Labor survey revealed that 85% of New York City's female workers in the men's clothing industry were foreign-born and another 10% were native-born of foreign parents. Similar patterns existed in Chicago and Philadelphia as well, where 94% and 83%, respectively, of female garment workers were either immigrants or children of immigrants from Germany, Russia, or Italy (Dickinson, 1975).

B. Structure of the Industry

The garment industry clearly can be classified as part of the periphery economy. It is a highly competitive industry and it has been forced often to react to environmental forces—changes in immigration laws, tariff regulations, competition from foreign imports and government regulation of labor organization, collective bargaining and wages—that are largely outside of the control of the vast majority of manufacturers. As Averitt (1968:8) noted in his description of a peripheral economy, firms within this competitive sector operate under the principle that "a penny saved is still a penny earned." The garment industry is no exception to this rule. Its strategy to keep costs low has been to employ the cheapest available labor. Females and recent immigrant arrivals, preferably female immigrants, continue to represent often the most desperate, and hence the most easily exploited and least expensive, labor available.

The growth and organization of Miami's garment industry and its labor force is another, and most recent, example of the survival strategy of periphery firms. Employers within the apparel industry have displayed a continuous tendency to migrate away from larger and more highly organized garment-producing areas to smaller ones where a "plentiful, unorganized labor supply can be uninterruptedly exploited with no union to interfere" (Hardy, 1935:157). Although intended as a description of the industry in 1935, this statement accurately portrays the more recent migratory movement of apparel firms. The southward migration of the garment industry has been a reaction of manufacturers to union organization of workers in the urban industrial centers of the Northeast and Midwest and the passage of right-to-work legislation[1] in the South and Southwest (Wrong, 1974;

Colberg, 1978; NACLA, 1977). The manufacturing of wearing apparel in the Miami area was initiated in the late 1940s, shortly after Florida became a right-to-work state. However, metropolitan Miami did not emerge as a significant garment-producing center until the late 1960s, after the flow of over 100,000 Cuban emigres into the Miami area.

III. THE GROWTH OF MIAMI'S APPAREL INDUSTRY

A. Right-to-Work Legislation and Southward Migration

In discussing problems of labor organization within the Miami area, the manager of the local International Ladies Garment Workers Union (ILGWU) emphasized that the state's right-to-work law has been a major impediment (Ruano, 1980). While an obstacle for organized labor, right-to-work laws have functioned as incentives for industry, particularly low-wage industry, to relocate in right-to-work states. Voluntary unionism states' share of the country's manufacturing employment increased from 19% in 1958 to 25% in 1972 (Colberg, 1978). Regional trends in apparel employment mirrored those for total manufacturing employment. While accounting for only 15% of apparel employees in 1950, southern states accounted for 39% by 1970 (Wrong, 1974)—a 160% increase within the 20-year period.

The southward movement of the apparel industry was at the expense of employment in the many highly unionized and higher-wage states in the North. The Middle Atlantic region's share of apparel employment declined from 55% to 38% in the same 20-year period. Declines in employment of up to 50% occurred in the urban centers of New York and Philadelphia in the Northeast and Chicago in the Midwest (Wrong, 1974).

The state of Florida holds the distinction for passing the first right-to-work legislation in the form of a constitutional amendment in 1944. This did not prevent unionization of apparel workers in the area, but it has, along with other factors, curbed unions' growth. The first Miami local of the ILGWU was chartered in 1949, but by 1979 ILGWU members in the area numbered 2,500, or about 10% of apparel employees.

The lack of union problems, the climate, and the relatively developed system of air transportation initially attracted the apparel industry to the Miami area. Northern owners attempting to escape the higher wages and urban problems of New York moved their operations to Miami. Nearly continuous increases in apparel employment in the Miami Standard Metropolitan Statistical Area (SMSA) from the late 1950s to the mid-1970s, as shown in Table 1, were accompanied by continuous decreases in employment within the New York area. With fewer than 4,300 employees in 1958, Miami reached the distinction of being the third-largest garment-producing center (behind only New York and Los Angeles) by

Table 1. Number of New York and Miami Apparel and Textile Products (SIC Code 23) Employees

Year	New York SMSA (in thousands)	Miami SMSA (in thousands)
1958	284.4	4.3
1959	286.2	4.9
1960	274.9	5.0
1961	262.8	5.2
1962	261.7	6.1
1963	254.5	6.5
1964	249.0	7.0
1965	249.3	8.2
1966	246.0	9.5
1967	239.3	11.5
1968	236.8	13.5
1969	230.8	15.7
1970	210.4	16.3
1971	197.2	18.2
1972	191.0	20.5
1973	185.9	22.4
1974	167.8	20.9
1975	146.9	17.9

Source: U.S. Department of Labor, Bureau of Labor Statistics, *Employment and Earnings, States and Areas 1939-1975*. Washington, D.C.: U.S. Government Printing Office, 1977.

1970 with 16,300 employees. At present, the apparel industry in the area employs approximately 23,000 workers, and Florida's Department of Labor and Employment Security (1980) projects 38,000 workers by 1985.

The impact of right-to-work legislation on levels of union membership and industrial wages explains, in part, the success of Miami's garment industry. Wages for production or nonsupervisory apparel workers in the South have consistently lagged behind those of workers in the Northeast. A comparison of weekly wages in New York and Florida from 1950 to 1975 (see Table 2) at times reveals differences exceeding $20 per week. The discrepancy becomes even more glaring when average hours worked per week are taken into account. During this period, Florida apparel workers averaged between 35 to 38 hours per week, while New York workers remained within the range of 34 to 35 hours (U.S. Department of Labor, 1977). Average weekly wages within the Miami area exceeded those for the state as a whole but remained 15% less than the average for workers in New York State and an estimated 20% less than those for workers within the New York metropolitan area. In an industry in which payroll costs equal almost 60% of the value produced (IRDA, 1978), the ability to hire workers at lower wages is an important component of industrial location.

While the legal conditions to attract the apparel industry to the Miami area

Table 2. Average Weekly Earnings of New York and Florida Production or Nonsupervisory Apparel Workers by Year

	Average Weekly Earnings		
Year	New York	Florida	Miami
1950	54.52	36.53	
1951	57.10	36.77	
1952	57.93	40.20	
1953	59.19	40.97	
1954	59.19	40.74	
1955	61.93	43.04	
1956	63.97	47.60	
1957	65.59	47.03	
1958	66.44	48.06	
1959	68.48	50.65	
1960	69.91	51.10	
1961	71.33	53.39	
1962	73.84	56.70	
1963	74.82	57.15	
1964	77.38	60.54	
1965	79.57	59.47	64.36
1966	83.31	65.80	67.50
1967	88.70	66.91	72.58
1968	95.05	73.48	81.53
1969	100.18	76.49	82.08
1970	104.49	80.57	85.65
1971	108.61	84.13	89.54
1972	115.15	87.79	95.38
1973	121.43	91.50	105.66
1974	127.31	94.52	109.37
1975	136.02	102.60	116.49

Source: U.S. Department of Labor, Bureau of Labor Statistics, *Employment and Earnings, States and Areas 1939-1975*. Washington, D.C.: U.S. Government Printing Office, 1977.

were provided by the state's right-to-work legislation and its later declaration of the agency shop[2] as unconstitutional, the industry could not grow without a large pool of labor willing to work for low wages. The massive inflow of exiled Cubans into the Miami area in the early 1960s provided the labor necessary to move Miami to its status as a major garment-producing center.

B. Cuban Immigration to Dade County and Apparel Employment

Surveys of manufacturers, local planning reports, and the popular press (IRDA, 1978; City of Miami Planning Department, 1979; Silva, 1976b; Fabrica, 1973) agree on the source of Miami's rise in the garment trade—the number of willing workers provided by the influx of Cubans into the Miami area. In 1960, there were approximately 4,200 Cuban refugees in Dade County. By 1966, the number had risen to nearly 128,000, with the largest gains registered from 1961 to 1962 (12,900 to 76,500) and 1962 to 1963 (76,500 to 124,000) (Research Institute for Cuba and the Caribbean, 1967). The number of Hispanic residents in Dade County (approximately 85% of whom are Cuban) reached 296,820 by 1970, accounting for 23.4% of the total, and by 1978 these figures had reached 537,700 and 35.2%, respectively (Dade County Planning Department, 1979).

Thus, similar to earlier experiences in New York and Chicago, the growth of Miami's garment industry coincided with an increase in the number of immigrants within the area. However, few Cuban males found their way into employment within the garment trade. Since the early 1960s between 85% and 90% of the apparel workers in the Miami area have been female, and the vast majority (since 1965, 85%-90%) are Cuban (IRDA, 1978).

Prior to the Cuban "freedom flights" of the 1960s, there was a slight increase in the percentage of black females employed in Miami's garment industry. Although usually targeted as low-wage workers, historically black females have not been considered by employers as "ideal" garment workers. Blacks were brought into the industry in 1917 as strikebreakers by Chicago garment manufacturers and again during World War II when female immigrant labor was not available.

Conditions in the South until 1965 were such the black females were deliberately not recruited for apparel employment. State employment agencies adhered to segregationist placement patterns in both the textile and apparel industries. Blacks were not placed in factory employment unless specifically requested by employers (Wrong, 1974). From 1960 to 1970, however, blacks as a percentage of female garment workers increased in most southern cities. The two exceptions were San Antonio and Miami, both cities in which female immigrant labor was easily available.

Surveys of apparel employers in New York City (Wrong, 1974) and Miami (IRDA, 1978) indicate that immigrant females are considered superior employees in comparison to blacks. Employers argue, for example, that Puerto Rican (and, later, Cuban) women in New York and Cuban-born women in Miami often are better educated, more docile, and have been socialized in the needlework tradition; thus, they are said to require less training. An additional, but less frequently mentioned, rationale is that blacks have access to welfare and other government programs which make them less likely to remain as *steady* employees within the low-wage apparel industry.

Not surprisingly then, as the percentage of Cuban-born females in the Miami area rose, there was a concomitant increase in their representation in apparel employment and a decrease in the percentage of Miami's female apparel workers who were black. While about 6% of Miami's female garment workers in 1960, blacks comprised only 4% in 1970. Thus, the hiring preferences of Miami's apparel employers did not deviate from those in other areas of the country—immigrants with some prior sewing experience and little or no access to other sources of employment or permanent income or aid were preferred over black workers. In terms of the characteristics and needs of the Cuban refugees entering the Miami area, they formed an almost ideal population from which to draw apparel workers.

The gender composition of the population of early Cuban refugees to the Miami area nicely fit the needs of the small but growing apparel industry. Over 65% of airlift arrivals in 1966 were students, children, or housewives. The typical registrant at the Cuban refugee center was female, with no prior occupational experience (Prohías and Casal, 1974).

In the summer of 1964 some 3,700 women "without men" had applied for public assistance at Miami's refugee center. A study based upon a sample of these applicants provides a description of perhaps the most vulnerable of Cuba's refugees (Mayer, 1966). Over 30% of the women had no prior occupational experience, although their average educational level of nine years was higher than that for Cuba's population in general. Over one-half (58%) had dependent children living with them and almost three-fourths had little or no ability to speak English. They also expressed what has been termed an "exile mentality" toward their future life in the United States. Most believed Castro and communism would be overthrown in Cuba within two years, and almost all (94%) said that they would return to Cuba at that point. These were women who expected their stay in the U.S. to be temporary.

The attitudes and conditions of these women reflect those of Miami's Cuban immigrant population in general in the 1960s. Most were desperately in need of employment and were willing to accept jobs below their educational and occupational skill levels for a "few years" until they could return to Cuba. Little relationship existed between the human capital which Cubans brought with them and their placement within the U.S. occupational structure (Rogg, 1974; Prohías and Casal, 1974). Cuban-born women without men relied upon public assistance, family aid, or easily obtainable employment. Their prior sewing experience in Cuba as housewives or daughters was welcomed by Miami's garment manufacturers. Married female Cuban emigres, eager to help their families and husbands who suffered what two researchers have argued to be "a catastrophic loss of occupational status" (Prohías and Casal, 1974:65), found employment as sewing machine operators and finishers both within garment factories and at home. The majority of Miami's Cuban apparel workers are married women living with their husbands.

Both the numbers of Cuban refugees and the sex composition of the refugee population in the Miami area benefitted employers. Weighted toward females with little occupational experience or prior experience as clerical workers or teachers with little or no knowledge of English, Cuban women had few alternatives to apparel employment. The gender role ideology of both Cuban male and female emigres reinforced the belief of employers that women are superior garment production workers. For manufacturers, the best labor force is one that is reliable, inexpensive, experienced, and unwilling to organize. Miami's female Cuban population displayed all of these characteristics plus a strong tendency to look upon the employment of females as "temporary," "secondary," and simply a means to help the family out. As studies of Cuban emigres in Miami and other areas of the United States have consistently confirmed (Rogg, 1974; Fox, 1973; Ferree, 1979), the high labor force participation rates of Cuban-born women in the United States have not changed their orientation nor that of their husbands toward female employment. As one reporter explained, most of Miami's Cuban garment workers do not expect a future or career from their jobs—they simply want to help their husbands and families financially (Silva, 1976a). They do so by finding and keeping employment within a traditionally "female occupation."

IV. ORGANIZATION OF WORK WITHIN THE MIAMI APPAREL INDUSTRY

A. Low Wages

The organization of production within Miami's garment industry was described by one frustrated reporter as "like 'the Dark Ages'" (Gjebre, 1970). Although legally workers must receive the minimum hourly wage, enforcement is difficult for workers who produce garments at home. Those employed within a factory setting in general receive the minimum hourly wage plus incentive piece-work increments. Increments in hourly wages have been slow, as evidenced in Table 2. One 48-year-old Cuban sewing machine operator employed for 15 years with the same company reported earnings of $1.00 per hour in 1961 and $2.75 per hour in 1973. After three years with the same company a finisher saw no increase at all in her hourly wages (Silva, 1976b).

Although working conditions and wages in Miami's apparel industry lag behind those in other manufacturing industries, the consensus within the Miami area is that they have improved since the early 1960s. Reports abound of workers who earned less than $30 per week (Fabrica, 1973) and some at-home producers who received less than $5.00 for at least 30 hours of work (Guinness, 1980).

The inflow of Cuban refugees into the Dade County area in the early 1960s is considered one explanation for the low earnings of Miami's apparel workers. As a whole, unemployment rates within Dade County between 1961 and 1963 consistently surpassed national averages. If, however, the Cuban refugee population is excluded, Dade County unemployment rates drop approximately to the national average (Prohías and Casal, 1974). As the refugee population grew, competition for jobs within the garment industry also increased (Research Institute for Cuba and the Caribbean, 1967) and factory workers also found themselves competing with an ever growing number of even lower-wage workers—at-home producers.

While average hourly earnings within the Dade County apparel industry did register a gain of 17% from 1959 to 1966 (from $1.54 to $1.86 per hour), those within manufacturing as a whole rose 21% during this same period (Prohías and Casal, 1974). This suggests that competition within the garment industry was intense and perhaps did act to keep the already low wages from increasing at the same rate as did those in manufacturing as a whole.

B. At-Home Production

1. Explanations for Its Growth

The Cuban migration to the Miami area also is cited by employers, government workers, and union officials (Gjebre, 1970; Fernandez, 1980; Fabrica, 1973; Ruano, 1980; Guinness, 1980) as encouraging the growth of at-home versus factory production of garments. It is unfair, however, to place the blame entirely on the presence of Cuban immigrants The garment industry both nationally and locally had been experiencing high rates of failure and increased competition from both foreign imports and the continued movement of sewing operations "offshore" to low-wage countries in Central America and the Caribbean. The value of apparel imports to the U.S. rose 354% from 1962 to 1972, with a total value of $1.7 billion by 1972 (Wrong, 1974). Increased competition from foreign factories and lower-priced garments produced by American firms using foreign labor—whose cost averages about 20% of that of Florida apparel workers (Fabrica, 1973)—found manufacturers in the Miami area more than willing to leave the problems of labor and its cost to contractors. One manufacturer in the Miami area noted that if he did not subcontract the sewing of garments his number of employees would rise from 150 to 1,000. He explained his preference for a subcontracting system:

> It is a cleaner operation.... [W]e don't speak Spanish so we don't have to worry about the labor force, and we have enough people to worry about... (Fabrica, 1973:26a).

Neither Miami nor its Cuban refugees, however, invented the subcontracting system. The use of subcontracting within the apparel industry has been a tactic of manufacturers to reduce the cost of labor and avoid labor problems since before the turn of the century. It has alternatively been termed the "contract" system, "at-home production," or the "sweatshop" or "sweating system." It plagued union organizers and labor in both New York and Chicago as early as 1880. The operation of the sweatshop system or contract system has been defined as follows:

> the term "sweating," or "sweating system" originally denoted a system of subcontract, wherein the work is let out to contractors to be done in small shops at homes. In practice...sweating consists of the farming out of competing manufacturers to competing contractors of the material for garments, which in turn is distributed among competing men and women (Commons, 1901:12).

It is a system which fosters competition among manufacturers, contractors, and workers. The monetary advantage to manufacturers is high—it can save up to 50% of their payroll costs. Since a system of subcontracting allows little opportunity for quality control in the construction of garments, it has been used primarily in lower-line apparel and the production of women's and children's clothing. Approximately 72% of apparel firms in the Miami area concentrate in these two segments of the industry (U.S. Bureau of Census, 1976), increasing the likelihood that a contract system would be used in the area's industry.

Thus, the existence of the subcontracting of apparel sewing and finishing which in the Miami area primarily consists of production of garments in the homes of Cuban women is the result of a variety of circumstances—increased foreign competition, increased competition from American-owned firms with sewing operations offshore in low-wage countries, the types of garment produced in the area, and the presence of women willing to work at home.

2. The Extent of At-Home Production

Despite agreement that at-home production is an important component of Miami's apparel industry, the extent of it at present and in the past only can be estimated. Undoubtedly, these estimates vary considerably. In 1973, estimates ranged from 1,000 to 5,000 at-home workers, approximately 5%-25% of total employment. Union estimates tend to be higher than those of the government. The ILGWU appears to have consistently adhered to the belief that 25% of Miami's "real" apparel employees are at-home workers, which would indicate that there are at least 5,000 at-home workers in Dade County at present. The chairman of the board of one of the area's largest children's wear firms estimates that they contract out about one-third of their work (Kantor, 1980). The amount of work which is produced in contracting establishments where sewing is done on the premises versus in the home, however, is not known. Figures have not been consistent over the years, with increases in at-home production reported after a recession in 1974 when workers were laid off from their factory jobs (Silva, 1976a). Table 1 shows a drop in apparel employment in Miami from 1973 to 1975.

3. Organization of At-Home Work and Characteristics of Workers

Although not the bulk of production in the area garment industry, the importance of at-home production is reflected in the highly organized nature of the operations at present. While earlier at-home workers reported to contractors or manufacturers to pick up their piece goods for wages of less than $30 per week, at-home workers in 1976 had their piece goods delivered to and picked up from their home for wages of about $60 to $90 per week (Silva, 1976a). Factory workers were earning about $92 per week at that time. Vans could be seen leaving Miami's garment district in the early morning and returning with finished goods later in the day. Homeworkers frequently are paid in cash or checks made out to cash.

Unlike at-home producers in New York (NACLA, 1979), most of Miami's at-home workers are legal U.S. residents. The majority have been married Cuban women with either dependent children or relatives in their homes. At-home work allows these women with strong family attachments to care for their children and relatives, avoid the cost of outside elderly or child day care, while simultaneously increasing their family's income. The large number of elderly Cubans in Dade County and their lack of participation in organized activities during the day (Prohías and Casal, 1974) makes at-home production a preferred alternative to low-wage employment as operatives within a factory setting for many Cuban women.

Most at-home workers at present are believed to be former factory workers who were laid off from their jobs as sewers and stitchers during the 1974 recession within the industry (Guinness, 1980; Silva, 1976a). The movement from factory to at-home work required only a place in which to sew and a moderate monetary investment in a sewing machine. New single-needle machines could be purchased in over a dozen Miami shops for as little as $35.00 down payment with no questions asked. Machines could be rented at the rate of $75.00 for three months and the rental fee could be converted into a down payment if the machine was eventually purchased. Used machines also were available for as low as $40.00, and the resale value on sewing machines is reasonably high (Silva, 1976a). Thus, the initial investment for at-home garment work was not prohibitive, and the returns in terms of income were comparable to those in factory employment in the mid-1970s.

Not all of these workers prefer at-home jobs because of family responsibilities. For some it is a means to supplement income derived from unemployment or public assistance payments (Ruano, 1980; Fabrica, 1973; Silva, 1976a). Contractors will often list their at-home employees as independent contractors, which exempts contractors from paying payroll taxes while making it easier for workers to continue on public assistance. An IRS probe of homeworkers in 1976 found that almost all were incorrectly listed as independent contractors (Rosenblatt, 1976). Earlier estimates of the amount of wages at-home workers were shortchanged under this system were as high as $150,000 per year (Gjebre, 1970).

Although workers in general suffer some loss of wages under a contract system, it may be the only alternative available to supplement their family income. Other workers prefer the freedom of setting their own hours or caring for their family more conveniently. The work schedule, however, can be grueling. An at-home worker may have to spend some 14-16 hours per day at her machine to produce the quantity of goods she contracted for in her production schedule. She must add to these hours all the time required to care for the home, children, and elderly relatives (Silva, 1976b).

The contract system operates through a network of friends and relatives, and most workers have little difficulty finding work. Recruitment of factory workers occurs in a similar manner, with family or friends locating jobs for relatives new to the area (Fernandez, 1980; IRDA, 1978; Kantor, 1980).

Movement from factory or at-home worker to garment contractor also is one route to increased economic returns for some Miami apparel industry workers (Guinness, 1980). In an industry that offers little opportunity for occupational advancement for its female workers, contracting out work to family and friends is a viable option due to the limited amount of investment that is required.

The success of Cuban contractors in the area recently has caused concern among the larger Anglo-owned manufacturing firms (IRDA, 1978). Considered one of the ten fastest-growing occupations in the Miami SMSA, sewer and stitcher also is now ranked second in terms of occupations with the most job openings (Florida Dept. of Labor and Employment Security, 1980). At-home production and the lack of any significant increase in the industry's labor supply have left many factory owners with positions that they cannot fill. As Cubans have increasingly moved into the roles of manufacturer and contractor as opposed to employee within Miami, the problems of the larger Anglo-owned firms in attracting labor have increased. Between 1969 and 1972 the number of Hispanic-owned manufacturing firms in all industries within the Miami area increased from 166 to 267, with a 200% increase in the amount of total gross receipts (Dade County Planning Department, 1975). Of the 203 apparel manufacturing firms (about one-third of the total firms) in the Miami area listed in the 1980 Florida Industries Guide, approximately one-fourth were owned by Cubans. Of those firms designed as contractors or subcontractors, approximately 40% were Cuban-owned.[3] The situation has begun to develop into a system in which earlier immigrants employ later arrivals, a condition which existed among Jewish immigrants in the apparel industry in the early 1900s (Howe, 1976; Commons, 1950; Carsel, 1940).

4. Enforcement of Minimum-Wage and Hours-Worked Legislation

Despite increased competition among Anglo and Cuban manufacturers and contractors for labor, the at-home system of production and low wages continue to exist within the industry. At-home production makes unionization difficult, and union organizers consistently blame at-home workers as well as right-to-work legislation for lower wages and lack of labor organization in the Miami area (Ruano, 1980). The enforcement of laws dealing with at-home work appears to be beyond the scope of Miami's Wage and Hour Division. Government workers within this division emphasize compliance with minimum wage and overtime requirements, but few at-home workers or contractors keep records of hours worked per day. Failure to maintain adequate records is not a legal infraction, and thus it is almost impossible to substantiate illegalities relating to at-home work. With four government workers assigned to handle reports of violations within the Miami area and a backlog of over 500 cases (Guinness, 1980), it is unlikely that government action will prevent the underpayment of at-home workers in the near future. The Wage and Hour Division is dependent upon union officials and workers to bring their attention to violating contractors, but many at-home workers are erroneously led to believe that they are in violation of the law as well. As a result, a few complaints are filed and even fewer women are willing to testify against a contractor.

The contracting system contains within it an internal means of correction. The frequent violators of minimum-wage requirements for at-home work are often small contractors who, due to their lower wages, attract the least-experienced workers. As a consequence, the quality of work is low, production schedules are not met, and contractors in violation frequently are forced out of business by their own mistakes (Guinness, 1980; Gjebre, 1970; Fabrica, 1973). Recovery of at-home workers' back wages through legal prosecution is problematic, as many contractors cannot produce resources to repay employees. Thus, even if prosecution occurs, the contractor may go out of business and back wages are lost. As one source commented, the system of bidding among subcontractors within Miami is highly competitive—many subcontractors "bid themselves into hopelessness" (Guinness, 1980) and business failure.

V. CONCLUDING REMARKS

The Miami apparel industry and its labor force is neither unique nor aberrant within the histories of the garment industry or immigrant labor in the United States. As indicated in Section II, these histories often have overlapped. Miami's apparel workers, however, represent a portion of south Florida's Cuban immigrants and labor force who are employed in a low-wage industry with few opportunities for occupational advancement. They personally have not shared in the success of the industry's growth in the area nor in the economic or occupational advancement of their immigrant group.

Miami's Cuban-born female garment workers provide the labor in a system which benefits both manufacturers and consumers. Area wages continue to lag behind those for the nation as a whole, representing a considerable savings and profit for manufacturers. The importance of "fresh" immigrant female labor to the industry is borne out by the suggestion of some employers in 1978 to reinstitute Cuban freedom flights into the area to solve problems due to the shortage of low-wage labor. Lower wages for apparel workers, in turn, are translated into lower prices for clothing for consumers. If the wages of textile and apparel workers within right-to-work states were raised to levels commensurate with those of workers in more highly unionized regions, price increases of close to 10% in the typical family's clothing budget would result (Colberg, 1978).

While continued growth of the industry within the Miami area is projected for the future (Florida Department of Labor and Employment Security, 1980), the social organization of production will undoubtedly change. Despite the recent arrival of thousands of Cuban and Haitian refugees to the area, overrepresentation of males in these immigrant groups and the lack of sewing experience on the part of the females (Fernandez, 1980) do not make these recent arrivals attractive sources of labor for garment manufacturers. Cuban-born women, in turn, discourage their daughters from seeking employment as sewing-machine operators, clearly recognizing the limitations of their occupations (Silva, 1976b; IRDA, 1978).

Although the local government is taking action in initiating training programs to attract black females to the industry and in revitalizing Miami's garment district (City of Miami Planning Department, 1979), area economic studies project that an increasingly large proportion of garment production in the future will be accomplished offshore (IRDA, 1978). As the focus of the garment industry within the Miami area moves toward the design and distribution of wearing apparel, lower-level operative positions within the industry are transferred to low-wage countries in Latin America or the Caribbean. Thus, the benefits to manufacturers and consumers previously produced by the labor of low-wage, Cuban-born, female at-home and factory workers within the national economy will be produced by the labor of even lower-wage, female workers in underdeveloped countries. Transfers of subsidies to consumers which occurred on an intranational level will occur internationally.

NOTES

1. Section 14(b) of the Taft-Hartley Act amendments to the National Labor Relations Act was passed in 1947 over a presidential veto. The Taft-Hartley Act outlawed the closed shop, but permitted the union shop in collective bargaining agreements. Designation as a union shop permitted the hiring of nonunion persons, but carried the requirement that union membership must be acquired within a specified time period. Section 14(b) of the amendment, however, gave states the right, in effect, to outlaw union shops and establish a system of voluntary unionism. Workers could not be required to join unions in order to keep their jobs. Florida passed its voluntary unionism law before the enactment of the Taft-Hartley amendments. By July 1976, 20 states had passed right-to-work laws (Colberg, 1978).

2. Agency shop clauses in collective bargaining agreements were interpreted in 1962 by the Florida Supreme Court essentially as evasions of right-to-work laws and declared unconstitutional. These clauses required nonunion members to pay fees, in an amount equivalent to union dues, to unions for their collective bargaining efforts with employers (Colberg, 1978).

3. These figures were compiled by the author from entries in the 1980 Florida Industries Guide. Firms were categorized under broad census industry codes, and all firms listed as apparel and textile manufacturers (SIC Code 23) were included in the calculations. Cuban ownership was determined on the basis of Spanish surname, and 85% of the owners with Spanish surnames were estimated to be of Cuban origin.

REFERENCES

Alder, J., M. Lord, E. F. Newholl, S. McGuire, and V. Coppola
    1980 "The new immigrants." Newsweek Magazine XCVI:26-31.

Averitt, Robert T.
  1968 The Dual Economy. New York: W.W. Norton.
Bonacich, E.
  1972 "A theory of ethnic antagonism: the split labor market." American Sociological Review 37:547-559.
  1976 "Advanced capitalism and black/white relations: a split labor market interpretation." American Sociological Review 41:34-51.
Carsel, W.
  1940 A History of the Chicago Ladies' Garment Workers Union. Chicago: Normandie House.
City of Miami Planning Department
  1979 "Garment center/fashion district redevelopment plan." Mimeographed report, July.
Colberg, M.
  1978 The Consumer Impact of the Repeal of 14(b). Washington, D.C.: The Heritage Foundation.
Commons, J.R.
  1901 "Contractor is at the heart of the sweating system." Reprinted in M.D. Danish and L. Stein, (eds.), I.L.G.W.U. News History 1900-1950. Atlantic City, N.J.:I.L.G.W.U.
Dade County Planning Department
  1975 "Minority-owned businesses, Miami, Florida." Mimeographed report, July.
  1979 "Dade county facts." Mimeographed report, August.
Dickinson, J.
  1975 The Role of Immigrant Women in the U.S. Labor Force 1890-1910. Unpublished doctoral dissertation, University of Pennsylvania.
Fabrica, J.
  1973 "Willing workers lure garment makers." Miami Herald, March 5.
Fernandez, F.
  1980 Personal interview, City of Miami Planning Department, Miami, October 23.
Ferree, M.M.
  1979 "Employment without liberation: Cuban women in the United States." Social Science Quarterly 60:35-50.
Florida Department of Labor and Employment Security
  1980 "Employment in manufacturing." Mimeographed report.
Foner, P.
  1979 Women and the American Labor Movement, from Colonial Times to the Eve of World War I. New York: The Free Press
Fox, G.
  1973 "Honor, shame and women's liberation in Cuba: views of working-class emigre men." Pp. 274-290 in A. Pescatello (ed.), Female and Male in Latin America. Pittsburgh: University of Pittsburgh Press.
Gjebre, B.
  1970 "Miami garment industry like 'the dark ages.' " Miami News, December 9.
Guinness, J.
  1980 Personal Interview, Department of Labor, Wage and Hour Division, Miami, November 24.
Hardy, J.
  1935 The Clothing Workers. New York: International Publishers.
Howe, I.
  1976 World of Our Fathers. New York: Harcourt Brace Jovanovich.
Industries Guide, Inc.
  1980 The Florida Industries Guide '80. Orlando, Fla.: Industries Guide, Inc.
International Resource Development Associates, Inc. (IRDA)
  1978 "The textile/apparel industry in Miami: problems and prospects, final report to the City of Miami." Mimeographed report, March 21.

Kantor, S.
    1980   Personal interview, Florida Children's Wear Manufacturers' Guild, Miami, November 25.

Mayer, J.
    1966   Women without men: selected attitudes of some Cuban refugees. Unpublished Master's thesis, University of Florida, June, 1966.

North American Congress on Latin American (NACLA)
    1977   NACLA 11 (March).
    1979   NACLA 12 (November-December).

O'Connor, J.
    1973   The Fiscal Crisis of the State. New York: St. Martin's.

Piore, M.J.
    1975   "Notes for a theory of labor market stratification." Pp. 125-150 in R.C. Edwards, M. Reich, and D.U. Gordon (eds.), Labor Market Segmentation. Lexington: D.C. Heath.

Prohías, R., and L. Casal
    1974   The Cuban Minority in the United States. Boca Raton, Fla.: Cuban National Planning Council.

Research Institute for Cuba and the Caribbean
    1967   The Cuban Immigration 1959-1966 and its Impact on Miami-Dade County, Florida. Coral Gables, Fla.: University of Miami.

Rogg, E.M.
    1974   The Assimilation of Cuban Exiles, the Role of Community and Class. New York: Aberdeen Press.

Rosenblatt, G.
    1976   "IRS probes garment industry taxes." Miami Herald, November 29.

Ruano, M.
    1980   Personal interview, International Ladies' Garment Workers Union Locals 415 and 475, Miami, November 7.

Silva, H.
    1976a   "Garment worker's home now her factory." Miami News, September 14.
    1976b   "Union label rare in garment trade." Miami News, September 15.

U.S. Bureau of the Census
    1976   1972 Census of Manufactures. Volume II, Areas and States. Washington, D.C.: U.S. Government Printing Office.

U.S. Department of Labor, Bureau of Labor Statistics
    1977   Employment and Earnings, States and Areas 1939-1975. Washington, D.C.: U.S. Government Printing Office.

Wrong, E.
    1974   The Negro in the Apparel Industry, Report 31. Philadelphia: Industrial Research Unit, The Wharton School, University of Pennsylvania.

MONASTIC OCCUPATIONS:
A STUDY IN VALUES

George A. Hillery, Jr.

> ...for then they are truly monks when they live by the labor of their hands, as did our Fathers and the Apostles.
>
> St. Benedict, *The Holy Rule*

I. INTRODUCTION

Nowhere is the concept of vocation more perfectly exemplified than in monastic occupations. In the traditional sense of the word, as defined by *The Oxford Universal Dictionary* (Little et al., 1955), a vocation is "The action of God in calling a person to exercise some specific...function...." From this point of view, the entire way of life of a monk thus becomes his vocation, of which his occupation is only a part.

This paper will examine monks' occupations as part of their total lifestyle. The analysis begins with a discussion of the method of data collection, then an overview of the monastic way of life. Next, the analysis focuses on the economic sphere, after which the occupation and the monks' values are explicitly examined. As will be seen, however, such sharp delineation is not always possible.

Throughout the discussion, the purpose is to relate the occupation, or the job narrowly considered, to the rest of the monk's life—and in particular to his value structure.

II. COLLECTION OF DATA

The data for this study have been collected over an 11-year period that commenced in 1969 with participant observation. Structured interviews have also been used, as well as documents and questionnaires administered by both the author and the monks themselves. Participant observation has been applied mainly in one monastery, called here by the pseudonym of Palisades Abbey. The author spent approximately seven months living with the monks, for periods ranging from a few days to several weeks (most of the visits were of ten days' duration). For most of this time (six months) the author worked and ate with the monks but slept in the guest house.

Though the focus of this study is on Palisades Abbey, it is of importance to note that Palisades was not studied in isolation. Eleven of the twelve established abbeys for men (Order of Cistercians of the Strict Observance) in this country were visited, and three of the five Cistercian monasteries for women. Various types of data (participant observations, documents, interviews, and questionnaires) were gathered for most of them. The author lived at the other monasteries for four months. One other abbey is selected for comparative purposes in the section on "The Occupation and the Vocation," called here Jericho Abbey. Approximately two weeks were spent at this monastery. It was chosen because it is of a comparable size and age to Palisades Abbey. (For more detail on methodology, see Hillery, 1981.)

III. THE WAY OF LIFE

The day of a monk in Trappist-Cistercian monastery begins at 3.15 A.M. when he prepares for the "night office," the first of seven "offices" he will recite during the day. These offices consist of the singing of psalms, prayers, and devotional readings and last from 10 to 45 minutes. The number of monks at any given office varies, ranging from 20% to 90% (some monks recite their office privately). There is, in addition, a daily Mass.

Work normally begins at 8:00 A.M., though some monks may start later. In most monasteries, work lasts from four to six hours, six days a week. The bulk of the remaining time (approximately four hours) is spent in prayer and meditative reading (also known as lectio divina). After the final office of Compline, the monks retire at 8:00 P.M. Complete silence is to be kept in the monastery until 8:00 A.M. the next day (except while performing Mass and the different offices).

These three functions, liturgy (especially in the "office"), labor, and lectio divina, constitute the essential vocation of the monk. These functions are the reasons why he is in the monastery: to praise God, to pray, and to work for a living. Though prayer is considered by most to be the most important part of this triad, one also prays in praise and at work. A man joins a monastery not simply to pray or to praise but to live as a monk, which definitely includes labor. Nevertheless, no monk is ever "hired," that is, he never is chosen for his occupational specialty. He may never practice his trade in the monastery, though he will do so if occasion demands. I have known writers, lawyers, cooks, accountants, physicians, printers, farmers, professors, and priests who practiced their occupation both as a "layman" and a monk, but each of these held other jobs as well. In fact, it is characteristic of a monk that at any given time he will hold several jobs, and usually the longer he is in the monastery, the more different kinds of jobs he will be exposed to.

Although the monk forsakes the world and is largely separated from it by means of the cloister (that part of the monastery where only monks are permitted), the outside world impinges at many points, particularly through the occupation. Chief roles through which contact is made are the guestmaster, who receives all guests and is immediately responsible for their needs; the porter, a kind of assistant to the guestmaster who is usually the first to greet visitors; the cellarer, who manages the internal economic affairs; the procurator, the monastic business agent; and the chaplain, who cares for the religious needs of the guests.

A few words should be said about priests, who comprise about half the population of monks (the other monks are called brothers). The main functions of the priests are saying Mass, hearing confessions, and acting as chaplains for guests. In addition, according to the canon law of the Church, only priests can be abbots, though a brother may be (and has been) ordained priest if the community feels that he could be their superior. At one time the separation between priest and brother was sharper, only priests (and those so destined) singing in choir. The brothers wore different habits than the priests and more manual labor was expected of them. Now the dress of the two is indistinguishable, as are, generally speaking, the work expectations. Today, from the monastic point of view, no special status is conferred by the priestly office (which does not mean that some monks do not individually confer additional status on priests). Both priests and brothers take the same monastic vows, and neither is deemed more "holy" than the other (Della Fave and Hillery, 1980). In fact, priests oftern enter the monastery as priests, and they are then treated as any other novice, except that they are expected to say Mass and assume other priestly duties, as required.

At one time, relatively strict silence was observed in Trappist-Cistercian monasteries, and the monks employed a sign language. The sign language is still used, but speaking is now permitted generally during the daytime, except at certain times and in certain places. The monastic economy is also well integrated with the outside society. The monks, however, are not permitted to beg. To be a Cistercian monk, one must work, and preferably he should work with his hands (though not all perform manual labor). Agriculture in some form is also a preferred pursuit, but no monastery is exclusively agricultural. The economic products of Palisades Abbey', alone, include or have included religious arts and crafts, beef cattle, grain and hay, fruit and vegetables, honey, bread, pottery, candles, and polished stones. In addition, other monasteries produce cheese, fruitcakes, jams and jellies, stained-glass windows, religious vestments, flowers, ornamental trees, shrubs, eggs, milk, prunes, and walnuts, and one monastery even depends for its living primarily on making concrete blocks.

Several monasteries operate gift shops, selling their own produce as well as various religious articles, books, and records. Both the monasteries to be considered here have gift shops, but many monasteries have closed them, either because they had a disruptive effect on the monastery (some guests coming only to purchase gifts instead of to worship) or because it was felt that commercialism should not be so important at the monastery. Nevertheless, the economy itself provided frequent and regular contact with people outside the monastery, whether through selling the monastery's produce or buying supplies. Visitors, of course are a regular feature of the guesthouse, and though contact with the monks is not permitted within the cloister, in many ways the guesthouse may be considered a hotel. The most important difference from a hotel is that guests do not have to pay, though contributions are welcomed (and perhaps to some degree expected).

Cistercian monks have five vows: chastity, conversion of manners, stability, obedience, and poverty. Chastity means also celibacy, and this means, as far as occupations are concerned, that no woman is employed in any way. The monks take care of all their personal needs. Celibacy also means there are no children to support, though the aged and the infirm are fully cared for. Conversion of manners requires that the monk always attempts to bring his life into closer harmony with the requirements of his faith. Stability limits the monk to the monastery to which he made his vows, or wherever the abbot wishes to send him. Obedience is to the abbot. Poverty means that the monk receives no pay for his work, and everything the monk owns is provided by the monastery. He literally owns nothing. At one time these monks did not even have rooms but slept in dormitories. Now they have rooms, and it is a basic rule of the monastery that one's room is to be kept strictly and privately his.

Obedience and poverty are probably most pertinent to understanding monastic occupations. No monk "owns" any job, technically speaking. Though some monks may consider a certain occupation "theirs," this practice is not felt to be in the best interest of the monastic vocation, the monk's occupation will usually be changed rather frequently. Poverty also means not living lavishly, and many of the monks constantly examine their material level of living with the purpose of avoiding extravagance. In practice, poverty becomes translated into simplicity. Thus, the monk will have well-made clothes but few of them; he will live in good buildings, soundly constructed, but plain; and the pictures and other ornamentation will be kept simple. Similarly, the food is plain (vegetarian), though prepared tastefully.

Recruitment in Trappist-Cistercian monasteries is essentially passive. The monks seldom make lecture tours or similar efforts to obtain new monks. In fact, tradition has it that the first inquiries of a prospective monk are to be refused. One who wishes to become a monk at Palisades Abbey applies first to be an "observer." He lives for a month with the monks. He then returns home for a period of one month, during which time he decides whether he wishes to return. If he does so decide, he contacts the abbey, and he then learns whether the monks have decided favorably toward him. If the feeling is mutual, he begins as a postulant (for six months), then becomes a novice (for two years), then a "simply professed" (for another three years). At the end of this period (which may take even longer), the community votes whether to accept him, and only after receiving a favorable response can he take his final vows and become one of the "solemnly professed."

During the novitiate, the novice has very little contact with the outside world and thus would not normally have jobs in the guesthouse, nor would he be the cellarer or procurator. He will be instructed in monastic life by a novice-master, although during the earlier years of this study this duty at Palisades Abbey was undertaken by a "formation team." Generally, only men age 20 to 40 years are accepted, but 90% of those who become postulants do not take final vows. In the vast majority of cases, the decision to leave is primarily that of the person involved (postulant, novice, or simply professed). Though it has happened, seldom is the monk voted "out of the monastery" by the community when he asks to be admitted for solemn profession. If he is asked to leave, he will have been asked usually long before he would take his final vows.

Since the renewal of the Roman Catholic Church initiated by the Second Vatican Council (1962-1965), a great many Trappists have left their monasteries. In Palisades Abbey alone, the population has declined from a high of 142 monks in 1960 to its present population of approximately 50, most of them leaving in the earlier years. No detailed study has been made of those who left (though see SanGiovanni, 1978), but impressionistically there were several factors. (1) Some monks have been raised in Catholic institutions all of their lives, and when a decision was required concerning what to do with their lives the wisest choice seemed to be to continue in some kind of Catholic institution. The renewal encouraged them to try other alternatives. (2) It had been a Catholic tradition, at least in some areas, that the "religious" life was the spiritually best life. The Second Vatican Council liberalized this viewpoint, and many monks left simply because they felt that they should (and could) be married. (c) Some monks left because they felt they were not being fulfilled personally, and often this decision was related to their choice of a job.

During the 1960s, there was a flurry of small, experimental monasteries established in various parts of the country. There were founded mostly in response to the third point noted above. Monks were "looking for community," which they felt could be found in a smaller, more intimate group. Only two of these experiments continue today. None of the established houses have been closed or appear in danger of becoming so. There is, in addition, a recent increase in observers, postulants, and novices in many of the monasteries.

IV. THE MONASTIC ECONOMY

Before the monastic occupational situation can be understood, one must first understand something of the monastic economy. This condition is made necessary because the most important thing about being a monk is the entire way of life—the liturgy, the prayer, *and* the labor. In fact, for most monks the *particular* job is of relatively little concern. What is of concern is that one be a monk, which in turn means seeking God. This concern in no measure should be interpreted to mean that the monks do not care about their jobs.

Economic matters have always seemed to be one of the most volatile subject in the monastery. Many of the personal problems of the monks have arisen out of things relating to work and income, and the monastery's administrative problems essentially revolve around the economy. This is especially true, according to one brother, of a monastery that has been struggling for some time. He went on to note that "a lot of times the things we do [here] are not just working for efficiency, and a study of these decisions brings out the value structure. We have a paradox here. Ideally, the most important thing is to be as little concerned about mundane affairs as possible and [to be] living in the eschatological affairs of Christ." And yet, economics occupies many if not most of their problems. It is significant that it was the economy that was responsible for the monks making a self-study, in which this monastery was a pioneer among American Cistercians.

The initial question to be answered in this section is "How do the monks make their living?" The very asking of that question, however, inevitably leads to others, such as the emotional impact of the interplay between economics and prayer, economics and authority, etc. The answer to the initial question will thus have to be interpreted in terms of the attitudes of the monks and the problems they face outside of the economic area.

The base year for the data for this section is 1971. This year is chosen because it is the one closest to the self-study, including the data on attitudes (see Table 2), and it is also represents the year by which the author had participated enough in the monastery to have some understanding of what was happening. It is not a representative year—no year is. The monastery is constantly changing. Since 1971, for example, the formation team has been eliminated in favor of a novice-master, a new abbot has been installed, the dehydration plant has been eliminated, and a new church as been built.

Most of the monastery's production activity revolves around agriculture. The farm department mainly sells corn, the beef department sells purebred Angus. The dehydration department (dehy) produces pellets from alfalfa obtained from the farm department. Mention should also be made of the service department, not shown in Table 1 because strictly speaking it produces no income and its expense is allotted to the other departments. This department is engaged primarily in servicing the various machines operated by the monastery, including tractors and automobiles. In addition to the garage, its various functions are electrical maintenance, carpentry, plumbing, and painting. The expense of this department is allocated among the others: approximately 40% to the farm 30% to the abbey, 25% to the dehy, 4 percent to beef, and the remainder to the miscellaneous departments. The abbey "department" may be regarded as a type of general financial clearinghouse for the monastery.

Table 1. Income and Expenses for Palisades Abbey, 1971*

Income		Expenses	
PRODUCTION DEPARTMENTS		COMMUNITY LIVING EXPENSES	
Farm	$ 83,000	Recurring:	
Dehy	9,000	Food	$ 21,500
Beef	−(73,000)	Medical	15,000
Bakery	8,000	Heat, Power	9,500
Miscellaneous	16,000	Services	9,000
	$ 43,000	Maintenance	7,000
OTHER SOURCES OF INCOME		Travel	4,000
		Clothing	3,000
Interest	43,500	Insurance	3,000
Stipends	24,000	Gasoline, Oil	3,000
Contributions	6,000	Supplies	3,000
Retreats	20,500		
Miscellaneous	13,000	Mail	3,000
	$107,000	Library	2,000
		Payroll taxes	1,000
Receivables	10,000	Miscellaneous	19,500
Liabilities	7,000		−($103,500)
		Extraordinary:	
		Building	40,000
		Machinery and Equipment	2,500
		Feed and Fertilizer	500
		Contributions	16,000
			−($ 59,500)
Total income:	$167,000	Total expense	−($162,500)

Note: *The figures shown are on a cash basis. This excludes depreciation, includes capital expenditures, and excludes inventory adjustments.

In 1971, as in past years, the production departments were not as important as other sources of income, especially income from interest and dividends and from Mass stipends (these stipends are gifts made by various persons to have one or more Masses said for someone or some purpose). Contributions also formed an important source of income, both in the form of outright donations and in the form of contributions made by persons who go on retreat. The income from the retreats department should not rightly be termed "fees" or "payments," since there is no fixed amount that retreatants contribute, and many who visit the monastery pay nothing at all, not even for meals. It is of some interest that the food bill for the guests and retreatants is almost half of that for the monks themselves.

Some regard the retreats department as producing acceptable income (even perhaps in the same class as production departments). Others would rather see no charges made at all, and all retreatants would then be treated in reality as guests (i.e., making no payments). A similar difference appears with Mass stipends: some regard them as legitimate offerings, others do not approve of them in principle. Whether they should be treated as income or contribution depends on one's perspective.

Expenses were widely divergent. They may be roughly divided into recurring and extraordinary. Of the recurring expenses, only food amounted to more than 20%. Outgoing contributions were the third-largest item of all expenses. And although not shown separately in Table 1 (since the expense is divided among the various departments), the monastery pays approximately $13,000 each year in property taxes alone. This is an important point to remember when it is realized that the monks send no children to school, none to old-age homes, receive virtually no social security payments, and contribute no deviants to asylums or jails.

How, then, do the monks make their living? As is apparent, even with this vastly simplified presentation, the question is a difficult one (and it should be noted that, whatever the answer, the result depends to some extent on the type of accounting system used). Nevertheless, in a crude and very brief fashion, three types of activities figure most prominently in the monastery's economic picture: agriculture, interest, and contributions (including retreats as well as other types). The single largest source of income (farm department) as well as the largest "expense" (beef department) were agricultural, and agricultural concerns were prominent in several other areas (dehy, honey, orchard, etc.). In contrast, interest gained through various financial sources resulted in more income that from all of the production departments combined in 1971. Though this was an unusual year in view of the heavy cattle purchases by the beef department, the comparison is helpful in showing the importance of interest in the Monastery's economy. Finally, contributions were also important both as income and expense. Indeed, the significance of contributions is probably greater than shown in the statistic, since much of monastery's hospitality expenses are debited against the retreats department.

Thus, in spite of mechanization, industrialization, and urbanization, the monks are still largely farmers. But they are also living to a large extent on the financial accumulations of past years. Finally, they are heavily concerned with charity, both giving and receiving.

One must keep in mind that the monks are not primarily concerned with profits. Their more important economic objective is to establish sufficient security to enable them not to be overburdened with financial cares. Their income in excess of expenses in 1971 reflects this—approximately $4,500 (for a community of that time of 70 persons). But on a profit-and-loss computation (which is figured differently than on the cash basis used here), the monastery has shown a net loss during four of the past ten years.

Some monks are rightly concerned about their economic security. Some are concerned over the source of their income. They would prefer fewer investments and less reliance upon contributions in any form. And some cannot help but think (even if naively) that, regardless of the economic complexities, somehow money continues to find its way into the abbey's bank account.

Discussion of decision-making in the economic sphere also merges into discussion of monastic government. The structure of the decision-making bodies in the monastery is presented in the accompanying diagram. As can be seen, there are essentially five aspects: the abbot, the treasurer and the accountant, the business council, the department heads, and the community. Major decisions are made both by the abbot and the business council. The council, in turn, consists of three members appointed by the abbot and three elected. The treasurer and the accountant both act as resources for the abbot and the council. That the community is also involved will become apparent, but let it be said most simply that it would be difficult indeed for a communal organization as small and as relatively closely integrated as this one to be run by anything approaching a dictatorship. As is suggested by the *Holy Rule*, "Whenever any important business has to be done in the monastery, let the abbot call together the whole community and state the matter to be acted upon."

From this point, the *Rule* goes on to specify a stronger position than the abbot in fact took in 1976. The abbot is ultimately accountable only to God, "knowing that beyond a doubt he will have to render an account of all his decisions to God, the most just Judge" (*Holy Rule* Chap. 3). In fact, the abbot would not go against the best-intentioned wishes of the monks themselves. But more, the abbot who was in office at the time of the study preferred to rule by indirection and sought out the monks' collective opinion as often as possible. Judging from conversations with some of the monks, the abbot's exercise of his authority generated an interesting mixture of respect and dissatisfaction. On the one hand, some monks believed that the abbot was deficient in economic matters, that the "direction" of his decisions was unclear, and that he was not consistent in following his own policies. On the other hand, with almost no exceptions, the monks showed genuine fondness and respect for him. It would seem that his policy of rule by indirection (particularly in attempting to have the monks assume as much responsibility as possible) had the effect of making at least some of the monks uncomfortable.

In real sense, then, the fact that the abbot serving at that time *shared* his authority with the business council was as much a function of his personality as it was the wishes of the community.

Figure 1. Organization Chart of the Monastery's Economic Structure.

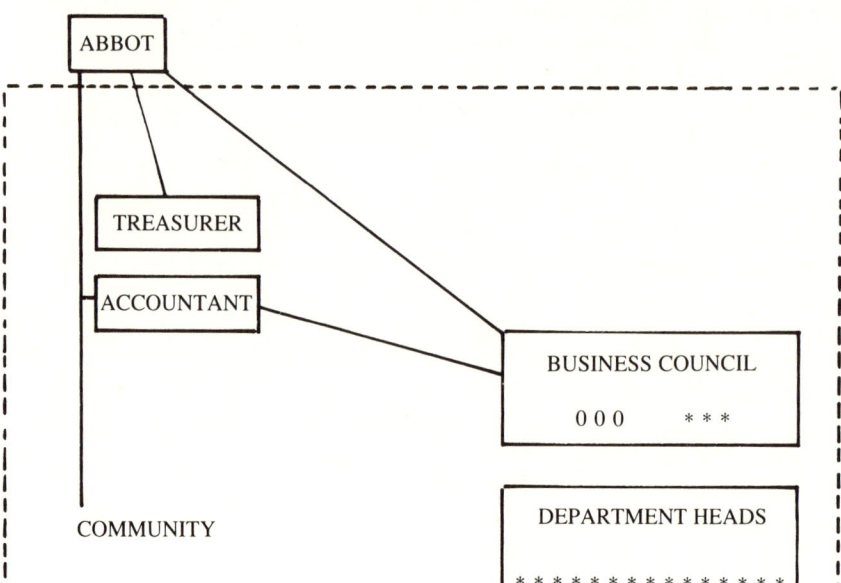

Notes: * = appointed
 0 = elected

The business council was composed of the following monks:

- A brother who was the subprior, a member of the formation team, and who worked with the heating equipment and the septic tank
- A priest who worked at the gatehouse and was the buyer for the monastery
- A brother who was the infirmarian
- A brother who worked in the beef department and was studying for the priesthood
- A priest who was the head of the farm department
- A priest who was the head of the beef department

The abbot is not a member of the business council at all but "shares his authority in matters of temporal administration with the business council." These last words were referred to by one monk as "the magic words." Some matters are initiated by the abbot, and on some he seeks advice. In some matters the business council takes its own initiative. For example, an expensive piece of work equipment was available at a bargain price, and one monk wanted very much to have it purchased. But the council decided against it for a number of reasons, the most important in their eyes being that the piece of equipment would not be in the best spiritual interests of that monk.

The initiative expressed by the business council in this instance, however, was unusual. Some have thought about extending the council's initiatives to other economic matters, but this is not being done.

The positions of treasurer and accountant are fairly autonomous. They are not members of the business council.

One of the chief functions of the business council concerns the assignment of monks who are not part of a more permanent work force. The subprior has the main responsibility here. In earlier times the abbot would assign each man his job at the start of each day. This would take at least five minutes. Some people would be assigned the same job day after day, but still the job would be "called out" by the abbot in the morning.

The monks work approximately 4–5 hours per day, though this varies. In earlier years they worked considerably more, and in fact this monastery had a reputation among the other monasteries for being a work-oriented house. Four outside laborers were employed, specifically in the service, farm, and beef departments, with the service department having the largest payroll, the beef department the smallest. During 1970 more than $26,000 was paid out in wages by these three departments.

Most of the monks (37) have only one job, but 46% (31) have two or more. Some of these other jobs are really responsibilities that are carried as an extra assignment, such as being a student for the priesthood (although some are full-time students), working in the garden, and conducting retreats.

The specific jobs in the monastery are of a wide variety, as the listing in Table 3 below suggests. Additional jobs in Palisades Abbey not listed in Table 3 are accountant, buyer, lawn worker, Mass secretary, chaplain, incense maker, gardener, greenhouse keeper, and various administrative positions, such as laundry manager, cleaning manager, and orchard manager.

The following discussion concerns information on attitudes that was gathered during the monastery's self-study conducted in 1969. Only those questions are used which proved to be of some interest (see Table 2). The first question shows a strong degree of adherence to one of the basic Trappist values, that of self-support. The third question concerns one of the problems in the monastery, the feeling that insufficient communication exists between the community and those concerned with the monastery's economic affairs. It was this dissatisfaction that led to the present business council. The sixth question reflects a continuing type of behavior expressed by the monks; an economic activity is not necessarily followed because it is efficient or profitable. The dehy (in this case) is noisy, demands time of the monks, and produces a distinctly unpleasant odor. For this reason most monks who have an opinion would prefer that it be discontinued, and in fact operations were soon after drastically curtailed and then terminated altogether. However, there is a decided minority (seven persons) who felt strongly

Table 2. Attitudes Concerning the Economy, March 1969

Question	Per Cent				
	Strongly agree	Agree	Neither agree nor disagree	Disagree	Strongly disagree
1. We should strive to be fully self-supporting.	33	46	4	4	5
2. Generally speaking, I feel that the members of our community are given work which suits them.	2	52	19	12	4
3. I can now obtain as much information regarding our economy as I need.	12	40	13	17	12
4. I feel that work time taken for individual projects is hindering community work.	12	40	27	12	2
5. The practice of poverty in our community is generally satisfactory.	4	44	5	31	12
6. I feel that, if possible, the Dehy should be discontinued.	25	15	23	17	13
7. Each monk should be free to work as much as he cares to, over and above what is assigned.	4	35	17	35	10
8. If I had my choice, I'd prefer to do work other than that which I do now.	8	6	35	37	4

Note: 52 replies were obtained, in all. However, some monks did not respond to all of the questions. Percentages were computed with 52 as the base. The remainder is thus composed of those who did not answer.

otherwise, and thus the dehy was a point of contention. The important consideration, however, is that this problem was considered and acted upon, rather than avoided or subjected to unilateral decision.

There are two polarizing questions: the fifth and the seventh. The monks are divided on the question of poverty and the permissibility of excess work. Neither question, however, is seriously polarizing: there are not two camps, each of which is strongly opposed to the other, but the monks simply disagree on these points and are about evenly divided.

The questions concerning work provided an important picture. The last question shows that, as far as the individual monk is concerned, he is not dissatisfied with what he is doing. Many do not care (35% neither agreed nor disagreed with the question, and another 10% did not answer), which is probably in keeping with monastic values. A monk does not take a job. He follows a call to a way of life.

Similarly, the monks feel that their fellow monks are given work which suits them (Question 2). But they do *not* feel that each monk should be allowed to work as much as he wants, and they feel even more strongly that time taken from individual projects is hindering community work. There was a feeling, then, at the time of the survey that, though work was important, and though the individual needs should be given consideration, some monks were carrying their work (or projects) too far.

Several other questions are important for showing the monks' values, especially in relation to poverty. When asked to state the social class to which their present standard of living compared, 50% of the monks checked the "lower-middle class," and 37% checked the "upper-middle class" (10 percent checked "wealthy"). But when asked to state the class to which the monks *should* compare, 27% said the "poor" and 61% said "the lower-middle class." (None said "wealthy.") Thus, there is a decided discrepancy between where the monks think they are vis-a-vis the social strata of the general society and where they think they should be. Regardless of whether they may differ regarding their definitions of "middle class," "poor," etc., poverty is still a value.

Generally speaking, the monks felt at the time of the self-study that their overall financial position was "fairly secure" or better (77%). Although there was some dissatisfaction, in that half of the monks felt that the production departments were not producing all that was needed, most felt that the income from all sources was sufficient or more than sufficient. This does not mean, of course, that all the monks are satisfied about their financial situation. Some were worried and were (and are) quite vocal about it, but the concern does not extend throughout the monastery (which of course serves only to increase the anxiety of those who are worried).

V. THE OCCUPATION AND THE VOCATION

In 1980, the author had open-ended interviews with 22 monks concerning their jobs and their perceived relationship to the monastic vocation. Of these interviews, 17 were conducted at Palisades Abbey and five at Jericho Abbey. Six questions were asked: (1) What are your main jobs here in the monastery? (2) How long have you been doing them? (3) What other jobs have you done in the monastery? (4) What kind of jobs did you have before you came to the monastery? (5) What do you see as the relationship of your jobs to your monastic vocation? Do they help, hinder, or neither? (6) What problems do you see with your jobs now, if any?

An effort was made to focus on a wide variety of jobs, and special attention was given to key jobs, specifically superior and novice-master. For these two jobs, in particular, interviews were conducted at both abbeys. The position of the interviewee, together with related occupational information, are shown in Table 3.

Table 3. Occupation Information on Selected Monks
(From the Open-Ended Interviews Conducted in 1980)

Monastery	Main Positions	Years in Job	Other Monastic Jobs	Jobs Outside the Monastery
Jericho	Superior	1	Wardrobe, submaster, guestmaster, dean of residents, student, assistant cellarer	Factory making various instruments, student
Palisades	Superior	3.5	Librarian, assistant infirmarian, painting, farmer, cattle	Student, janitor
Jericho	Gift shop manager	1.5	Prior, student	—
Palisades	Gift shop manager	44	Utilities, organist, teacher, sacristan, orchard, guestmaster	Farmer
Jericho	Novice master	14	Manual labor, crafts, cleaning	Teacher, chaplain
Palisades	Novice master	2.5	Wardrobe, laundry, janitor, plumbing, painting, orchard farmer, kitchen	Student, grocery clerk
Jericho	Cook (for the monastery)	2	Packing food products	Sheet metal worker
Palisades	Cook (for the guests)	15	Cook (for the monastery)	Cook
Jericho	Tailor, odd jobs	4	Retreat master, vocation director, sub-prior, prior	Teacher, professor
Palisades	Organist, librarian, refectorian (guest house)	16 2 3	Refectorian, cattle, odd jobs	Student, worked in a bicycle shop
Palisades	Assistant guest master	0.5	Farmer	Farmer
Palisades	Plumbing and maintenance	20	Construction	Stock clerk
Palisades	Procurator	0.5	Sacristan, cook, asst. guest master, honey, novice master, prior, odd jobs	Delivered papers, bus boy, kitchen helper, radio repair
Palisades	Farm, fence repair carpentry, mail	13 13 1 6	Quarry worker, laundry, general cleaning	Student, construction worker
Palisades	Guest house	> .5	Baker, cook	Student
Palisades	Guest master gardener, book binding	0.5 2.0 "Many"	Truck driver, stone mason, quarry worker	Bus boy, student, caddy

(Continued)

Monastic Occupations

(*Table 3.* Continued)

Monastery	Main Positions	Years in Job	Other Monastic Jobs	Jobs Outside the Monastery
Palisades	Submaster for novices, secretary	2 0.5	Orchard, maintenance	Student
Palisades	Cantor, farm manager, secretary	12 2.5 13	Common work, farm	Farmer, student, typist
Palisades	Printer	10-15	Farmer	Printer
Palisades	Odd jobs, baker	— —	Odd jobs	—
Palisades	Infirmarian	2	Farm, cleaning, porter, common work	Navy, medic
Palisades	Heavy equipment operator, welding, fire chief	21 12 13	None	Student

A few words about the occupational composition of this sample should be helpful. First, the variety of jobs is wide, ranging from superior to odd jobs (also called common labor). Second, though most of the monks (13) could list one main job, all the others (41%) had more than one job, and virtually all the monks had had different jobs at some other time during their stay in the monastery. Third, only 9% of the monks were doing the same job in the monastery as they had done before they became monks. One additional monk had done the same job inside the monastery as outside, but he was not doing that job at the time of the interview. Further, almost one-third had been or were doing some related job. Thus, nearly half (45.5%) have never performed the same job in the monastery as they had on the outside. (The jobs outside the monastery for the remaining monks were not known.)

Analysis of the replies of the monks reveals that work is considered to be a valuable endeavor in its own right. Most of the monks feel that work, in itself, contributes to the monastic vocation. Only one of the 22 monks interviewed appeared indifferent (but he was not interviewed in depth). Three monks felt that work both helped and hindered the monastic vocation (i.e., in some ways it helped, in some ways it hindered), and two were uncertain. Thus, 19 monks felt that work had a positive value relative to the monastic vocation, at least in some ways, and 16 felt that the contribution of work was unquestionable.

The range of attitudes was accordingly from expressions of uncertainty to positive affirmations. The only negative attitudes expressed were by monks who felt that some jobs were valuable and others not so valuable, but even here those jobs that did not contribute directly to a monastic vocation were still regarded as necessary for the monastery. They had to be done. No more than three monks fell into this category, as mentioned.

The positive replies show a wide variation. The most positive was from Jericho Abbey, specifically from the novice-master and the superior. The novice-master regarded his job as primarily inspirational. "I see the formation of novices," he said, "to be the transmission of my own life to the novices by example, and this gives me the impetus each day to live my life as a monk." Novices have told him that they derive more from his example than from what he says. Perhaps of most importance, this monk sees his job as intimately related to his life of prayer. He feels that after a period of deep prayer he is much more able to share his outlook with the novices. "It overflows."

But it is not just this job that imparts the inspiration—that is, the inspiration does not come to just anyone who works with novices. Compare this man's remarks with those of the novice-master in Palisades Abbey, who is also a deeply religious monk. He felt that his job "expressed" his monastic vocation— he did not know if it helped or hindered it. By this he meant that his job was simply a part of the monastic life. One could not talk of helping or hindering (from his point of view). His job simply *was* that of being a monk. Pressed for an answer, he said, after a moment's reflection, "I have to say, 'help it,' " but this response was most probably prompted by the fact that this was simply his job at that time. It should probably be noted that he did not ask for the position, and he would have preferred another, but he felt that doing this job (which he was doing very well) was fulfilling his monastic vow of obedience.

For two other monks their jobs are also intimately related to monasticism in their eyes. One of them, a printer, saw his job as "one of the essential elements of monasticism." The monk's job, he felt, "began with the pen." It wasn't that printing was holy or had any other special attributes. He felt that, if the monks did not have printing, they would have to find some other way to express themselves. Though this monk was alone in giving such special emphasis to printing, others would agree (though still a minority) about the need for a creative outlet.

For the other monk, his job was essentially what he wanted to do: "work outside and [work] with things." He felt that it would be a "terrific onus" if he had to represent the community before people. It was not that he did not like working with people—working with *outsiders* is what he considered so burdensome.

For other monks, the value of the job was precisely working with people, and not in the job itself. One of the monks was an assistant to the guestmaster, and so the relationship to people is part of the job. The other monk, however, was a cook, and thus the relationship of the job to people was most probably due largely to his own efforts. In other words, again the value of the job was not something intrinsically part of the job itself, but instead something the monk brought to the job.

Four monks saw their jobs as an outlet, a break from the monastic routine, and the job had value in that sense. As several of the monks said, "You can't pray all day." In this connection many saw work per se, *any* kind of work, as having intrinsic value. The classic monastic statement, repeatedly made, was *ora et labora*, prayer and work. One monk specifically mentioned that work was good because ipso facto, it was mentioned in *The Holy Rule* of St. Benedict.

Nevertheless, part of this intrinsic value was the contribution that work made to the total way of life, particularly as a source of variety. "A bow bent too tightly will snap," as one monk said. Work was seen as a "psychological balance for a life of prayer" by another.

Accordingly, work is seen as something good in its own right and in providing a break in routine. But given these values, the attitude a monk brings with him to his work is extremely important. The same job, as with the example of the novice-master, may prove a source of inspiration or may be seen simply as part of the way of life, a way that requires a monk to work. Here it should be noted that manual work is especially valued, and one of the novice-masters is part of the common work pool. For, according to *The Holy Rule*, "for then they are truly monks when they live by the labor of their hands, as did our Fathers and the Apostles" (Chap. 48).

The importance of attitude is probably most clearly seen in the remarks of the superior of each of the abbeys. One of them said simply, "I'm an optimist, so I have to say it helps." The other superior answered in a more involved way. Administrative details, he felt, hindered his life as a monk, as did some of his pastoral duties (which included counseling). Yet both of these aspects of his job (administrative and pastoral) required him to exercise a discipline and an inner detachment that were, in themselves, monastic virtues.

One can consider the monastic vocation as a whole, or one can consider the vocation in its various aspects. Between the main parts of the monastic life (labor, liturgy, and lectio) there are usually rather distinct boundaries. One normally goes from liturgy to lectio, that is, to a different place, and one goes from work to liturgy, etc. This is true for most of the monks. And yet, there are definitely cases where the boundary is blurred. The cantor, for one, has as part of his job that of leading the choir when the psalms are sung. The organist, as another example, plays the organ as one of his jobs. In such jobs, labor and liturgy mingle.

Further, for some there is a mingling between labor and prayer. One monk noted that "repetitious jobs like hoeing or housekeeping lend themselves to conscious prayer. [For example] I can recite and memorize the Psalms." Others have expressed similar points of view. In one monastery (which was neither of those being considered here), a monk told me he enjoyed candling eggs because he found the quiet and the rhythm of the job conducive to prayer.

Another monk, however, probably summed up the experience of most: prayer, he said, "is a conscious activity, where you set aside time to do just that." But, he continued, there is also prayer in another, broader sense, in which it becomes "the continuous condition of any Christian who is trying to praise God. In one sense, I'm leery of people who say, 'my work is my prayer,' but there is a certain something to it. It's like a husband working for his family. He may not be conscious of loving his family when he's at work, but that's what he's doing."

Thus, there are roughly three kinds of relationships between work and prayer. (1) One prays at one time and works at another. This is probably true of most monks most of the time. (2) One prays while he works. (3) One prays in his work. Each of these is a radically different condition. Some jobs simply do not facilitate a mixture of prayer and work (though they may allow prayer *in* work). The task of the superior seems to be one of these. One of the superiors remarked that his time was not his own and that one must have time to cultivate prayer. The other superior remarked, "I don't have as much time for prayer as when I'm doing a regular job. My prayer now, rather than being extensive, is intensive."

There is a distinct sense, however, in which labor, like prayer, can pervade much of a monk's life, even beyond the bounds of work. Many monks who are *concerned* about their work paradoxically at the same time maintain a detachment from it. This attitude of detachment is one of the major values of monasticism. A monk is in the world but not of it. And while all monks do not exhibit this state of mind, many do.

There are several expressions of detachment relative to work. One monk said, "I think I could be doing something else, and it would make very little difference." Or, as he put it later in the interview, commenting jokingly on one of his jobs, " I would not be unhappy if I were not doing it." The idea of detachment arises also in complying with the vow of obedience. A monk will be asked to do a job, even to leave one he likes, and, if he is thoroughly imbued with the monastic ideal, he will comply, even to the extent of throwing himself wholeheartedly into his new job. Not all monks are this detached, of course. Some monks are allowed to have the same job year after year because it is so much a part of them. One monk is jokingly referred to as the "proprietor" of his particular monastic shop, and as another monk remarked, "if the abbot moved him, it would probably kill him." But that monk would nevertheless give up that job, even if it did kill him.

Detachment, however, in no way reduces concern. This is shown by an analysis of the problems the monks perceive to be connected with their jobs. Some of the monks (4 of the 22) saw no problems at all. Two of them were doing what they most wanted to do. Five other monks, however, viewed whatever difficulties they had as part of the life:

> All my spiritual growth in great part has been due to my work. Sticking to it...I've had to trust in God. My work helped me to do that.

> I've found that work is essential to our way of life. Without it, 90% of those who try the life would not survive.

> An old abbot said once, there are two places where a monk reveals himself: in choir and at work. You can hide everywhere else, but you can't hide there.

> Part of the monastic vocation is difficulty. I'm very much aware that this might be the very [kind of job] I need to grow. It's probably the Lord's doing. It makes me aware of the amount I need to grow.

> The problems go in all directions. But they are normal. It's part of the life.

> The chief problems are things that make one impatient or angry. But I guess that's why we're here—to confront them. They are problems but they are part of why we are here—to face up to what we are, even to the point of being overwhelmed.

Thirteen of the monks had more specific problems, problems that were related only to the particular job at which they were working. Only two or perhaps three monks could be judged to have complaints which arose from purely personal or psychological difficulties. All the rest (ten) stemmed from the desire of the monks to do a better job of the kind of work to which they had been assigned. Thus, the superiors wanted to relate better to the men, the novice-masters were concerned with the internalization of monastic values by the novices (with themselves being better examples), one of the cooks felt somewhat frustrated because he was not able to cook with meat, and so on. Such concerns are evident even, and at times especially, among those who also have shown detachment.

VI. CONCLUSIONS

The most important theme of the monastic vocation is that of holism. It is simply not useful to think of the monk's job as occurring in only a segment of his life. He works in order to pray and praise, but his work is also part of his prayer and praise, not only literally in many cases but as part of the monk's way of life. To be a Trappist-Cistercian monk, one must do all three: pray, praise, and work.

But, as important as work is, the monk should not become too attached to any specific form of work. Though such attachment does occur, it is considered not in the best interests of the monk. No outward stigma is attached to any monk because of his attachment to his job, but the attachment is noted nonetheless. The ideal, which occurs frequently, is for a monk to be shifted from job to job, as the needs of the community change, and for the monk to embrace each new job with dedication and enthusiasm.

Accordingly, no job is rated as better than any other, again ideally. This means that there is no stratification system in the monastery, though there are status inequalities (Della Fave and Hillery, 1980). But the status differences among monks, when they exist at all, are due largely to the manner in which one follows the monastic way of life, not the particular occupation.

REFERENCES

Della Fave, L. Richard, and George A. Hillery, Jr.
    1980 "Status inequality in a religious community: the case of a Trappist Monastery." Social Forces 59: 62-84.

Hillery, George A., Jr.
    1981 "Triangulation in religious research: a sociological approach to the study of monasteries." Review of Religious Research 23:22-38.

Little, William, W. Fowler, J. Coulson, and C.T. Onions
    1955 The Oxford Universal Dictionary on Historical Principles. Third edition. London: Oxford University Press.

St. Benedict
    [520] Rule of Monasteries [The Holy Rule]. Trans. by Leonard
    1948   J. Doyle. Collegeville, MN: The Liturgical Press, St. John's Abbey.

SanGiovanni, Lucinda
    1978 Ex-Nuns: A Study of Emergent Role Passage. Norwood, NJ: Ablex.

WOMEN'S PAID LABOR IN THE HOME:
THE BRITISH EXPERIENCE

Jane Hoy and Mary Kennedy

I. INTRODUCTION

It is well known that women have not been paid for their domestic labor in their own homes. However, there is a long tradition of women doing paid work in the home which because of notions of family privacy has largely been hidden and therefore ignored by governments, employers, and trade unionists. We have chosen to look at homeworkers and childminders who, though a minority of the growing number of part-time women workers, nevertheless share similar characteristics of low pay and low-status work with poor conditions of employment. The overwhelming majority of women doing paid work in the home have domestic responsibilities. The "age of children has a marked effect both on the proportion of women who work and the proportion who work full time"—50% of women with dependent children are employed in the labor force, only 16% of whom work full-time; there is evidence to show that the age of the youngest is crucial in determining not only whether they work in paid employment but where they work (HMSO, 1980a).

Given that there is considerable evidence on the connections between the sexual division of labor in the family and women's opportunities in the labor market, a crucial area of our analysis will be how this is reproduced in the workplace. As Maxine Molyneaux has argued (1979:22), there is no invariable or necessary relationship between women, work, and family: "[T]he terms of the debate have to be broadened [and] an attempt made to analyse the complex combination of material relations through which women's subordination is mediated: such an analysis would include in addition to the domestic sphere, consideration of the sexual division of labour, reproduction, the labour market, changes and variations in the value of female labour power and the role of the state in maintaining women in a dependent position within the family..."She adds that it also entails consideration of intersexual and interfamilial relations. We shall focus in this paper on discrimination against women in employment as reflected in traditional attitudes and practices by employers and workers, and briefly mention the inadequacies of the Equal Pay Act, which came into force in 1975. It also appears that family policy and current preschool provisions reinforce the ideology that women are primarily responsible for children and home life.

In Britain both homeworkers and childminders are employed to do paid work in their own homes, although their respective relationships with their employers differ. The official definition of a homeworker is "a person who contracts with a person, for the purposes of that person's business, for the execution of work to be done in a place not under the control or management of the person with whom he contracts" (DOE, 1979). Childminding is a long-established form of private day care for which there is some statutory provision. A parent agrees with a minder to pay a fee in return for having the child looked after the childminder's home for an agreed time during the day. Where children are considered to be "priority" cases the Local Authority Social Services Department is empowered to help parents meet costs by direct payment of the childminder (HMSO, 1973).

Our interest in these two apparently dissimilar forms of work was stimulated by one of us who has a long-standing involvement in research with homeworkers. Also, as workers in a department of adult education, we began to contact local groups of women, amongst whom were childminders. It became increasingly apparent that they were experiencing particular difficulties with their jobs in terms of their conditions of employment and opportunities for the future. The preference of many women for paid work outside the home is reflected in current research (Fonda and Moss, 1976; Hunt, 1968) as well as among the childminders we interviewed.

Much of the current research on childminders has concentrated upon the quality of child care being offered. Information has been gathered through in-depth interviews of individual minders which have often avoided the question of the status of their employment in the context of day-care provision. During the mid-1970s, however, minders were coming together in groups for social and educational purposes and various programs had been piloted which aimed at obtaining resources for community forms of day care. For women tied to their homes and children the collective experience and group identity gained through membership in minders' groups is clearly of importance for the development of occupational identity. Also, as child-care workers at the bottom end of the preschool hierarchy, they have had experiences which throw a different light on the employment problems of women who are or have been mothers. We chose therefore to have a series of exploratory discussions with four selected childminder groups from inner-city and suburban areas of London. The results of these discussions form the basis for this review, locating their work experiences within current social policies and research on women workers and the family.

Homeworkers are difficult to identify, for they continue to be scattered and isolated despite attempts to organize. In the past six years there have been a number of surveys on the pay and conditions of homeworkers which have led to some active public campaigns and the beginnings of greater trade union involvement (Low Pay Unit, 1974-1980; Hope et al., 1976; Hakim, 1980; Hodge, 1980). Much current research avoids any examination of the influence of cultural and familial patterns on the experience of homeworkers. For this study we had in-depth interviews with four specialists working on the problems of homeworkers, for there are few local groups of homeworkers. Attention needs to be drawn to gaps in these studies in order to indicate the persistence of beliefs about women's work and activities in the home.

This review paper also undertakes a brief evaluation of economic explanations of women's disadvantaged position in the labor market which have not yet offered an adequate explanation of the complex relationship between women, work and family policy.

II. SHARED CHARACTERISTICS

Both homeworkers and childminders have long, hidden histories (Thomas Hood's *The Song of the Shirt*, Charles Dickens' *Our Mutual Friend*, and Charles Kingsley's *Alton Locke*, for examples in literature) which have periodically been brought to public attention through research and media exposure of extreme cases of exploitation. But apart from this they have several characteristics in common. They do essential jobs for people who need to supplement their income, particularly those at the bottom of the social, economic, and educational scale. They usually provide a service or services that are local, flexible and informal in organization, and that suit the needs of women with family commitments who feel they must base their work at home.

During the 1970s the general trend in women's employment in Britain and Europe has been towards a decline in full-time women workers and a corresponding increase in the number of part-time women workers: from 30% of women workers in 1960 to 41% in 1976 (Robinson, 1979:63). Although one in every five people now works part-time, only 2.1% are male. The vast majority are married women who, by 1975, accounted for 88.3% of all women part-timers in the United Kingdom (Hanley and Sawbridge, 1980:32). In addition 35% of mothers with children under 16 were doing part-time work by 1978, compared with 30% five years earlier, while the percentage of mothers working full-time has fallen by 1% in the same period (HMSO, 1980b). Part-time women's employment is found chiefly in clerical work and the public and service sectors; it is declining in manufacturing.

The link between our two groups is primarily their acceptance of and responsibility toward their families. In this respect both minders and homeworkers, while proud of the work they do and the modest financial independence they earn, identify themselves as mothers and wives first, and as secondary not primary providers for the family. So the husbands' work comes first and, in general, any work that the wives do must not interfere with their husbands' needs and wishes. Many of our sources said the same thing: "My husband doesn't mind [the minded children] as long as his dinner is on the table when he comes home." Or an Asian homeworker who explained that she did not machine between the end of supper and the time her husband went to bed, however urgent the work, as this would disturb his television watching and he needed " time to rest after his day's work" (BBC, 1981). This image of their own paid work as being secondary to that of the husband, and by implication not being a measurable day's work because it is fitted in around the household needs, is mirrored in the low and peripheral status accorded it in the marketplace. The existence of dependent children and the availability of child care is a critical element in determining whether women work outside the home (Mackie and Pattullo, 1977:52). Our sources would have preferred outside employment if adequate day care had been available.

Since the 1960s there has been an abundance of sociological literature on the extent and persistence of poverty, particularly in families where the main breadwinner is employed full-time. A recent discussion of the family wage indicates that increasing numbers of women work out of economic necessity in order to supplement the family income (Townsend, 1979). Minders and homeworkers have confirmed that their work is crucial in maintaining an adequate standard of living.

Low rates of pay are a common characteristic of both groups (Crine, 1979; NCMA, 1980). In addition, homeworkers and minders carry the cost of overheads, lighting, and heating, which they often fail to take into account when assessing their weekly earnings. Another reason for low pay is the irregularity and insecurity of employment.

Both homeworkers and childminders are dependent upon the employer's supply of work. This is often affected by seasonal demand, the fashion and Christmas trade, for example, or depends upon the supply of children to mind in areas where the mothers and/or parents may have variable employment or the children are ill. The Merton childminders' group said that sometimes the job was seasonal: "If we lose a child in the late autumn then there are usually no more children until Easter."

Both groups have in common the experience that their work is assessed as part-time—even if they do over 40 hours a week in it—because they work at home and at the time they decide upon, compared with those who go out to work for a set space of regulated time. Like all part-timers they suffer from comparison with the norm, which is full-time work differentiated into measurable units.

Definitions of the employment status of both groups remain ambiguous. Childminders are considered to be self-employed, and only in a few cases are they employees of a local authority (National Child Care Campaign, 1980). Yet they are in theory subject to regulation and registration by the local Social Services departments. Homeworkers, on the other hand, consider themselves to be employees in direct contradiction to the employers' view that they are self-employed. Neither group has been able to establish full rights to paid insurance, sickness and unemployment benefits, or paid holidays, although some minders get a proportion of pay if a child is ill and for holidays—a sort of retainer fee—and homeworkers in custom tailoring and some parts of the garment trade get proportional holiday pay based on their annual earnings.[2] Indeed, it seems that where trade union organization is strong conditions are improving. Furthermore, there is a reticence about interfering in areas of women's work in the privacy of the home, which is tied into their traditional family role and domestic housework. Homeworking and childminding are known to exist, but because they are part-time and fitted in around the household tasks, they can be invisible in the official statistics.

Homeworkers are often hard-pressed to attend to their children when they have rush jobs to finish, and sometimes minders have little time to give to their minded children in the midst of the housework. Even full-time married women workers, who were shop stewards in their trade union, "accepted that they had to cook the supper and wash and iron in the evenings, not because they thought such activities right and proper for women, but because they saw no way out of it: their acceptance of the domestic role was pragmatic rather than ideological" (Purcell, 1979:129). Thus the working mother is trapped in the triple role of wife, mother, and worker in a domestic setting where ostensibly she is free to pace her day's work and commitments as she chooses. But it is important to realize that such work at home means almost no leisure time for the woman. It has been estimated that women in part-time jobs spend an average 35 hours a week on household tasks, and those not in paid work 45 hours (Young and Willmott, 1973:113). What is interesting to observe is how the problem is perceived. In general the reaction is one of shock at the continuation of nineteenth-century conditions of work and status in a seemingly affluent society rather than a questioning of why women are trapped into doing this kind of work. The ideology of the autonomy of the family and its right to privately regulate its affairs is rarely examined, except by feminists. Public awareness shies away from an analysis of the role of the family in relation to the custom and practice of wage work inside and outside the home, and how this affects women who are still seen primarily as wives and mothers. Women form nearly 50% of the work force, but there remains a deep-seated reluctance to accept and provide for their integration as full members of it (cf. Sweden) (Adams and Winston, 1980:201).

From our observation it is evident that the sort of woman who does homework or childminding is not highly educated or trained, and does not have much confidence about finding better work opportunities. Whatever training there is occurs on the job or is based on the practical experience of motherhood and womanhood. Therefore she has little choice over the type of work available locally or near her home. This feeling of constraint was corroborated by the minders' groups: "It was there"; "what else could we do with young children?"; "I needed the money and could not leave home." Apart from the lack of employment opportunities it may be asked why these women continue to accept such poor conditions of employment. Most of them are unskilled or untrained, and it is possible that even if employment were available outside the home the prospect of being "your own boss," "controlling your own time," and "looking after your own children" [3] to some extent would offset the disadvantages of their pay and status. A further reason, which is often referred to in research studies and by trade unions, is the problem of isolation within the home so that they are often unknown to their fellow workers and collective action to improve their situation is difficult. Furthermore, they are in a one-to-one relationship with their employers or parents, with the fear that if they demand better pay they will lose the job to others competing for the same work. Only childminders, with their own local associations in some places, are beginning to be able to change this situation by setting an agreed minimum charge in that area.

Equal-pay legislation has failed to fundamentally alter the position of the low-paid, despite a series of government interventions in pay and incomes policies since the 1960s (Playford, 1980). There is no national minimum wage, and under the Equal Pay Act it has not been possible, so far, to raise women's wages, which remain at two-thirds of the average male wage. The problem remains in the segmentation of women in the labor market, for the principle "of equal pay for equal work" cannot be applied where there is no comparability between men's and women's work. Such is the situation for homeworkers and childminders.

The women workers in our study share all the characteristics of the secondary sector of the dual labour market, in which (1) labor is divided into higher-paying and lower-paying segments, (2) mobility across the boundary of these sectors is restricted, (3) higher-paying jobs are tied into promotional or career ladders, lower-paid jobs offer few opportunities for vertical movement, and (4) higher-paying jobs are relatively stable, lower-paid jobs unstable. Conditions of employment such as fringe benefits, sick and holiday pay, and job security are all adversely affected (Barron and Norris, 1976:49). These disadvantages are of course shared by other categories of labor such as the unskilled or ethnic groups. Women, however, suffer from cultural assumptions about the sexual division of labor, the distinctions drawn between jobs suitable for men and those appropriate for women. The majority of women work in the service and public sectors and are clustered into occupations where there are few men doing equivalent jobs, such as clerical work (HMSO, 1980b:10). There is not only a separation between jobs, for dualism also cuts through firms and industries: "it is possible for a single employer or industry to contain both primary and secondary labour markets" (Barron and Norris, 1976:49).

Dualism in the labor market is therefore associated with social characteristics which are often confused with the individual and personal characteristics of the employee. It is commonly assumed that women are dispensable and unreliable workers (for they are working only for "pin" money) and that they lack interest in training and are reluctant to show solidarity with fellow workers in demands for better pay and conditions. Employers, trade unionists, and researchers alike have viewed women employees as a problem, for they do not fit into the category of the "normal" worker, i.e., the adult white male (Brown, 1976; Mathieu, 1977). Contrarily, employers often say they prefer married women employees for they are thought to be more dependable owing to their family responsibilities. But to focus on these attributes directs attention away from the process by which women are allocated to particular jobs in the labor market. The difficulties they face as employees—isolation in small firms, neglect by trade unions, and discrimination by employers—are the products of social relations at the work-place structured by assumptions about the primary responsibilities of women to their families. For childminders and homeworkers the disadvantages of the secondary labor market are compounded by their classification as part-time workers and severe fluctuations in the availability of work.

III. WOMEN AS MARGINAL WORKERS

Workers experiencing the conditions of a secondary labor market are often defined negatively and are thought to be of peripheral importance to the economy. Economic explanations of women's position within the labor force, derived from economic models of a dual labor market, have argued that women's marginality is inevitable and will increase. The divergence of the two sectors will result in a massive pool, a "reserve army of labor" (RAL) consisting mainly of women who will become increasingly unskilled. Although there are differences in approach, both dual labor market and radical analyses attribute this shift to technological developments under capitalism which will result in the displacement of labor due to the need of capital to control the work force by "divide and rule" (Rubery, 1980; Cutler, 1978).

Breugel (1979:13) argues that women employees are also more likely to suffer from "a greater propensity to dismiss females in preference to males in a redundancy situation." Even women in traditionally secure occupations such as clerical work may find themselves threatened by rationalization due to micro-technology (Barker and Downing, 1980). Women, therefore, become a cheap and flexible labor supply, particularly women with families or married women who are dependent on husbands (Beechey, 1979). However, mechanistic theories of segmentation in the dual labor market ignore the relationships between different forms of capital and the way in which small firms and monopolies are tied together within the economy. Many small firms in the retail and service sectors operate on small profit margins and may be in a subcontractual relationship to the large monopoly firms. These small firms are often found in declining industrial areas where large firms have moved out, or in the inner city, and it is here that homeworking exists, often in its worst forms. Although this review focuses on women's paid work in the home and the relationship between child care and employment opportunities, it would seem to be essential for future research to look at the pattern of local employment and community resources in the context of industrial change in a specific urban area (CDP, 1979, 1978). This would permit a clearer understanding of the structuring of women's work inside and outside the home. Radical theories of wage distribution have used the concept of the RAL to explain segmentation of women in the labor market. However, there have been extensive critiques of the RAL which suggest it has a limited use. Firstly, the RAL is intended to refer to movement within a working population and the creation of unemployment. Secondly, the RAL "cannot differentiate groups of human subjects" and is therefore unable to explain why it consists largely of women and/or immigrants, and why women, for instance, are found in specific low-paid occupations (Anthias, 1980; Cutler, 1978).

The women in our research may receive low wages, which are the *effect* of their disadvantaged position, but an *explanation* of these wages also requires an analysis of a variety of discriminatory practices at the level of the workplace which reflect and reinforce the sexual division of labor in the home. If we are not to assume women's marginality we need "to understand the importance of women's employment for advanced capitalism—as cheap labour and as a relatively unorganized and passive element in the work force" (Anthias, 1980). One approach has been to discuss the employment of women doing unpaid work in the reproduction of the labor force. The narrow focus of this debate (known as the "domestic labor debate") on women's economic functions for capital has directed attention away from other forms of production and reproduction. Provision of child care, for instance, affects the availability of women for paid work both inside and outside the home (Kuluzynska, 1980:27).

Working class women have always worked, yet the view that they are not "serious" wage earners is often reflected in the attitudes and practices of employers and trade unionists. Homeworkers and childminders, as paid workers, face the continual problem of low pay and irregular work. But to locate the causes of this within the family not only relegates women to a marginal position in the home but also ignores the way in which their ghettoization within the labor market may be a result of the structure and organization of the industries in which they find themselves. More specifically, it is a result of attempts to control the labor process by organized labor and management through practices which may covertly reinforce women's subordination.

The degree to which labor can defend or transform its position depends on the degree of control over entry (training or apprenticeship schemes) and promotion within occupations. The battle over skill definitions is particularly important in terms of the entry and status of women in employment for a variety of historical reasons, not least of which are the ways in which management and trade unionists may operate with assumptions about the primary responsibilities of women in the home. This is covertly reinforced by education and government-sponsored manpower training and retraining policies.

An example of these practices has been shown in a recent study of the relationship between wages and skill in the paper box industry where "men and women work a similar process [but] men are recognised as semi-skilled rather than unskilled workers." Accordingly, the men were paid a higher wage (Phillips and Taylor, 1980:79).

It has been argued that the traditional demand by trade unions in the United Kingdom for a "family wage" maintains wage differentials between men and women. This leads to the marginalization of demands for equal pay, reinforcing beliefs about the low status of women's work. It is of course assumed that women are dependent upon men, who therefore can legitimately claim they need more money (Barrett and McIntosh, 1980:51).

The "sexualization of skill" (Phillips and Taylor, 1980:85) affecting the relationship between gender and low wages is an example of the way in which the material effects of such ideologies exist in traditional trade union practice and are not necessarily derived from gender relationships alone. The problem for the majority of low-paid workers, of whom many are women, is that they are concentrated in sectors or small firms where there are few men working in comparable jobs. Discrimination over pay is not, therefore, always obvious; its discovery requires intervention from outside, since wage negotiations at the workplace are largely irrelevant in firms where there is a low level of cohesion between workers.

The preferred means of wage determination by trade unions in the United Kingdom is through free collective bargaining, which relies on negotiation between management and labor at the level of the workplace. Obviously this situation does not yet apply to childminders and homeworkers. However, as minders become more organized and integrated into the structure of the local social services, they will be encouraged to join with other local authority workers in a public sector trade union (e.g., National Union of Public Employees, National Association of Local Government Officers).

Another agency is the Wages Councils, set up by government to monitor mainly manufacturing industries and trades where wages are low and the labor force (including homeworkers) is fragmented. Each council has equal numbers of employers and trade unionists with an independent chairman, and their job is to fix the statutory minimum rate (equivalent to a minimum wage). It has been argued that labor's reluctance to demand effective statutory legislation such as minimum-wage rates and incomes policies is attributed to its fear of increasing control by the state and capital. Consequently, there is little interest in making Wages Councils more effective as a means of implementing better conditions and pay for the low-paid (Tomlinson, 1979). Despite various pay policies aimed at the low-paid over the past 15 years, there is evidence that not all low-paid workers have benefited equally. Although the overall relative wages of the low-paid have risen, the degree to which the Wages Council has been effective in implementation of these pay rises has varied (Playford, 1980). On the whole, Wages Councils have not been very active in setting reasonable wage rates, except where backed by trade union support. (See Homeworkers Section). Childminders, for instance, being outside any Wage Council industry, have not been affected by any such wage policies.

Cases of discrimination at work and claims for equal pay are heard at Industrial Relations Tribunals. These are courts for employment, headed by a legally qualified chairperson assisted by two lay people (one trade unionist, one employer). Only 3% of chairpersons are women. Cases do not set precedents, so each one has to be fought anew.

The majority of recent tribunal cases have concentrated on dismissal and redundancy disputes, and the success of claims for equality at work has been minimal. The question of opening up access to occupations for women and immigrants is rarely raised. Indeed, Snell has observed that "the employer's right to choose" is embodied in industrial relations law and reflected in the negative and passive approach of sexual discrimination legislation. The major problem of the Equal Pay Act and the high failure rate of equal-pay claims is that the act operates on the principle of equal pay for equal work, which does not usually help many women for they are not in jobs comparable to men's. In practice, indirect discrimination exists through the segmentation of the labor market, and criteria such as merit, skill, nightwork, etc., have often been used by employers and trade unionists (mainly male) to justify pay differentials in the courts (Snell, 1979:37).

The legacy of assumptions about women's responsibilities in the home dies hard, but it is only by reference to the process and practice of discrimination that we can understand the ideological marginalization of women and their disadvantaged material position in the labor force.

IV. FAMILY AND CHILD CARE POLICY

In the United Kingdom day care for children is provided on an ad hoc basis, for the traditional assumption is that it remains primarily the responsibility of parents. There is, however, a limited amount of day care provided by the state, the majority of which is in the form of nurseries or nursery schools for children over three. There has been little variation in this provision since World War II, despite the widespread belief that during the war years the state encouraged the massive development of nursery facilities for women involved in the war effort. Recent research has shown that in fact wartime provision of day care is reflected in the present pattern. By 1941 there were a few 24-hour nurseries and 1,000 day-care nurseries, most of which were closed after the war. Day care was arranged by the mother, who was encouraged to use the equivalent of a childminder, who in order to avoid the stigma attached to minders was called a "volunteer housewife." In cases of special need a "daily guardian" was paid 6d a day by the Local Authority and 6d by the parent to do the same task (Summersfield, 1981).

Similar ideas about the sexual division of labor are reflected in family and day-care policies today. The persistent rejection of demands for full day care by the state certainly has an effect on the allocation of women to disadvantaged sectors of the labor market. Nevertheless, the state does provide a minimal amount of day care, the allocation of which is based on policies aimed at special categories of families deemed to be "deprived" or "at risk" in some way.

In the United Kingdom there is no integrated set of family policies. Sweden, in comparison, has planned provision for day care which is part of legislation designed to encourage women to work full-time and to increase their commitment to employment (Adams and Winston, 1980:201). There are, however, coherent sets of assumptions about "both the pattern of family responsibilities and dependencies within marriage and the duties of parents for their children and vice versa" which are implicit in British legislation (Land and Parker, 1978:331). The long history of laissez-faire, self-help, and ambivalence about the degree of state control over the family are reasons for the persistence of traditional views about the sexual division of labor in the family (Thane, 1978:11), despite the appearance of increasing numbers of one-parent families and changing family structures: in the 1971 census 30% of families were headed by women, 30% were nuclear families, i.e., parents and children, and 20% were childless couples. Policies are therefore aimed at the individual even though she/he may have a family. Fiscal, social security, child care, housing and employment policies differentiate between family members yet try to preserve a family form (nuclear) which is already beginning to break down (Wilson, 1977). Land and Parker have discussed how the dependence of women upon the male head of household is ensured: married men can offset a larger allowance against their taxable income than single men, yet married women do not have a similar concession; unless the wife has opted for separate assessment, only the husband can sign the joint income tax form; married women are excluded from the noncontributory invalid care allowance if caring for disabled relatives; and if living with a man, the woman is not eligible for supplementary benefit in her own right (Land and Parker, 1978).

Together with the privileging of the male head of household goes a widely held belief in the privacy of the family, as an arena for purely personal activities and a haven from the outside world. Indeed, the popularity of marriage persists in the face of evidence of increasing tension and stress for women who remain isolated at home with young children (Brown and Harris, 1978). This modern grouping concerned with the emotional self-realization of its members is regarded with some political diffidence in Britain. Debate over state intervention ranges from the necessity to preserve the privacy and autonomy of the family to the need for intervention to prevent the social and economic collapse of families, which are thought to be failing to fulfill their responsibilities toward themselves and society. Welfare policies in Britain, then, are not monolithic. They represent a continual struggle over the allocation and degree of state support.

Yet radical analyses of social policy have been split between those who view state legislation as an extension of state control over specific sectors of the population and those who view it as the result of working-class struggle. In the first view women, for instance, are defined and controlled through legislation as dependents of men; the working class is split into "deserving" and "undeserving" poor. Welfare benefits are not a right of individuals but are allocated according to specific criteria which may be seen as palliatives for social unrest, and as an attempt to incorporate groups demanding social reforms. Education, health, and social reforms are seen as the direct result of the needs of capital to maintain a healthy and semi-educated work force. In the second view the process of struggle is recognized as a formative influence on policy through the success of trade union and labor demands for institutions such as the National Health Service and pensions (George and Wilding, 1976).

This tendency to polarize is the result of interpreting the impact of legislation in terms of either capital or labor. This directs attention away from the possible impact of other ideological and political elements such as voluntary groups, pressure groups, and women's organizations. An overly deterministic view of policy formation and implementation also cuts off any possibility of identifying opportunities for change. Similarly explanations of the persistence of the family in terms of its value for capitalism emphasize the coherence of the family unit and its function of biological and social reproduction for capitalism. The family, structured by various state social and economic policies, provides a supply of labor for the labor market (Harris, 1979). Married women, because of their dependence upon the male head of household, are a particularly cheap and flexible supply of labor, for in periods of recession they "disappear" back into the family. Like other explanations of social policy which rely on the economic logic of the needs of capitalism, this one assumes a static and monolithic view of the state and family structure which ignores the way in which many women are independent of men yet experience discrimination. We need to know more about why specific categories of women are drawn into the labor market and their experiences at work, i.e., the way in which women are conceptualized as biological givens through ideological practices embodied in legislation and the labor process (Anthias, 1980).

The historical transformation of the family and the emergence of contemporary childbearing patterns have been discussed elsewhere (Aries, 1972; Shorter, 1977). In this brief review it is not possible to document the traditions of child care outside the family in the United Kingdom, except to note that there is a long-standing tradition for working women to leave their children under the care of others. Yet the belief that young children should remain at home with the biological mother persists, at the level of policy and the level of individual belief and preference.

Land and Parker have shown how women's dependence within the family is assumed in current practices. Donzelot (1979) argues that the family is a point of confluence, a crossroads for different social policies. Although he avoids any discussion of the father, he argues that the mother has been constructed as the carrier of a uniquely privileged role in the modern family unit, with a special responsibility for ensuring the health and adequate social reproduction of family members. This construction is not carried out through the intervention of the economy or through the diffusion of bourgeois ideals about family organization and the role of the mother. It is the result of interventions from various social, philanthropic, and state agencies, which are incorporated into the family and differentiable between family members. The family is not seen as a cohesive unit but as an agency where the mother, together with the state, takes charge of responsibilities for health, education, etc. Bourgeois families, however, are allowed considerably more autonomy regarding family activities than are working-class families. Donzelot argues that the continual failures of the latter to conform to public standards of health and education enables the state to increase its control through compensatory policies. The family, then, is constructed as both a public and private group (Donzelot, 1979).

This brings us a little nearer to ideas underlying day-care provision today and its present split between the state, voluntary sectors, and the family. The extent of day care cannot be understood purely in terms of the shifts in supply and demand for women workers in response to the needs of the economy. During World War II, the state temporarily increased the number of nurseries but the majority of child care provision was provided, as it is today, on the open market. Child care is virtually nonexistent for children under two. At the same time, since the 1960s there have been a number of recommendations for preschool provision in order to compensate for perceived increases in social and economic deprivation, particularly in inner-city areas. Massive postwar slum clearances and ensuing housing and employment policies had a considerable social effect. The rediscovery of the widespread persistence of family poverty casts doubts on the distribution of welfare benefits (Titmuss, 1963; Townsend, 1979). Education reports reflected the growing concern of the 1960s and 1970s with the problems of the inner city and the need for compensatory education (HMSO, 1980b). The Seebohm Report in 1968 recommended a shift toward family and area policies: "social work with individuals alone is bound to be of a limited effect in an area where the community itself is a major impediment to healthy development" (HMSO, 1968).

The 1975 Children's Act assumed that, although 3-to 5-year-olds might benefit from educational programs in preschool centers or nursery classes, the appropriate place for the young is with the mother, confirming the emphasis on the responsibility of the family for preschool care.

The current interest in minders is justified largely in terms of their suitability as "surrogate mothers" and the home environment is assumed to be the best place for children under two. Thus, the state recognizes the social and environmental deprivation of many young children, but is prepared to offer only minimal facilities, mainly educational, for those most socially "at risk". This allows an educational intervention which is not seen as an invasion of family responsibilities, for educational provision has long been seen as a legitimate task of the state. The refusal to "share *care*" is related to the fear that the family might abdicate most of its responsibilities for children in favor of state support. A "precarious balance" (Land and Parker, 1978:358) is maintained at the expense of working women with husbands, who are highly unlikely to obtain any state day care even if they are under considerable stress from isolation in the home. Single mothers are more likely to get a nursery place, for it is assumed, in terms of family pathology, that being fatherless requires compensation. Childminders fill the gap in state provision, meeting what is clearly a social need but being poorly rewarded. Moreover, present trends toward community care are not likely to be supported by adequate funding. A recent study reveals that the care of the elderly, sick, and disabled is likely to be relegated to the home, where indications are that in practice women will be taking the main responsibility for care of family members (Finch and Groves, 1980) as a low-cost solution.

The autonomy and privacy embodied in concepts of family responsibility perpetuate the sexual division of labor within the home and also reinforces women's view of the uniqueness of their own position vis-à-vis children. The current recommendations aimed at integrating minders into the structure of social services fail to challenge received views on the needs of young children and their mothers, merely extending the mothering role to minders. Present fiscal policy also reflects this emphasis on family responsibility through such mechanisms as family allowances, tax concessions, and child benefits.

V. CHILDMINDERS IN TRANSITION.

In the United Kingdom, preschool services are split between the Department of Health and Social Security (DHSS) and the Department of Education and Sciences (DES), a split which creates practical and ideological divisions in childcare provision. There is also a strong voluntary sector in the form of the Preschool Playgroups Association. Childminders operate predominantly in a private, free, and largely unregulated sector, where wages are very low. In the London and South East region the average is £15 per child for a week which is often over 40 hours; the national range is from £12 to £15.

In the United Kingdom there are state nursery schools and classes, reception classes attached to primary schools, playgroups and day nurseries (state and private), childminders and workplace nurseries. Together these provided 914,676 places in 1977—298 places for every 1,000 children under five (mostly 3-to-4 years olds). Some 1.25 million of 3 million under fives are unofficially catered for, most children being in voluntary playgroups organized by the Preschool Playgroup Association. The major problem is that most facilities are available to children over three on a part-time basis; state care is poorest in all day-care places and in the care of the children under two, the group who are to be found with minders or other family members. Some 90,000 children are with registered minders, with an estimated 100,000-300,000 with unregistered minders. The latter remain unknown and unsurveyed, the hidden part of the minder's world, and are the ones who tend to give minding its poor nineteenth-century image of "baby-farming." Regional provision varies from only 2% of 3-to 4-year-olds in mainly rural and affluent counties to 42.5% in Manchester, a large industrial center. Class bias in preschool provision also affects availability of day care. Children of professional or managerial parents are most likely to have a place in a playgroup or private nursery, and in the past decade the state sedór has taken an increasing number of children from families in need (HMSO, 1978). A recent survey in the London borough of Haringey[4] with a high ethnic population (19%) reveals the following distribution of places available for a population of 14,000 children under five.

Full-Day Care Places: 920 (not open to children under three), of which 280 were Local Authority, 560 registered childminders, and 80 nursery centres.

Part-Time Day Care: 1,520 nursery schools (4-year-olds); playgroups; 2,230 4-year-olds in nursery schools.

The survey also confirmed the findings of academic researchers (Fonda and Moss, 1976) that 7 out of 10 mothers with children under five and 9 out of 10 with school-age children would like to work if good day care were available. This view was confirmed by many of our minders, although some firmly believed their place was at home with young children.

Some of the findings of the Haringey study are reflected in an earlier survey in Birmingham, where it was found that the quality of care varied in relation to social and environmental circumstances. In these areas minding is often an inadequate form of day care due to poor housing and linguistic and cultural deprivation:

> The bill for this neglect of facilities in terms of apathetic and understimulated children and disturbed home situations is being paid every day in the inner city (CRC, 1975).

In recent years there has been a substantial amount of public and media interest in childminding, particularly in the more lurid activities of minders living in poor conditions and caring for too many children. It was largely public pressure which led to the 1968 amendments to the Nurseries and Childminders Regulation Act of 1948, although this only resulted in more "policing" of minders (Jackson, 1976) to register and conform to public health and safety requirements in the home. Minders are allowed to register for three children, apart from their own.

Local Authorities vary in their activities with minders, but some have established local links through day-care organizers and community workers, resulting in discussion groups and education classes. The emergence of local voluntary groups resulted in the formation in 1977 of the National Childminders Association (NCMA) organized by and representing the interests of 4,300 childminding members.[5] There are also various national and international organizations concerned with child-care provisions, for example, National Child Care Campaign, One Parent Families, Child Poverty Action Group, and Save the Children Fund. In 1979 The European Economic Community criticized the United Kingdom for the worst provision for children under five in Europe, apart from Eire (EEC, 1979).

Current research on childminding has referred critically to the quality of care offered by minders, evaluated within the framework of debates about maternal deprivation and the psychological needs of young children (cf. Mayall and Petrie, 1977; Bone, 1977; Rutter, 1972). However, our research confirms conclusions suggested by recent surveys that emphasize the sense of responsibility minders have for their charges. As one minder said: "You wouldn't surround yourself with kids all day if you didn't like them." Childminders were conscious of the value of the service they provided while being resentful of their poor public image. On a number of occasions minders have been exposed to racist and sexist remarks in the street, particularly if they have a racially mixed group of children.

Minders felt that the problems they faced derived mainly from the irregularity of their work, which often affects relationships with social services and parents. Without exception they valued opportunities to meet with other minders, and the experience of sharing common problems has led to a number of developments: an agreed-upon local fee; drop-in centers; toy libraries; and projects for linking day care with other community groups.

However, the deficiencies of existing provision are still being documented, particularly in the context of decreasing public expenditure and evidence that recent governments have favored "low-cost forms of provision in the community." Critics have advocated the inclusion of minders in local authority day-care provision, where, it is argued, childminding is ideally suited to meet the needs of a disadvantaged and weak sector of the labor force. However, this is where parents share the poor conditions and status of the minders themselves (Hughes, 1980:246).

Present governmental policies embody a number of beliefs in family and social policy which affect not only working women as parents but also those employed as child-care workers. For example the present junior minister at the Department of Health and Social Security said in an interview in the *Guardian* (October 17, 1978) before taking office: "We are committed to the concept of equal opportunity but once the rights exists in law, the practice must be left to the individual.... The financial responsibility for a child must be theirs.... We favour an easing of taxation so there is a little more in the family coffers to allow people some choice." Such sentiments throw the responsibility for child care back onto the family, which is increasingly likely to have to find its own ad hoc solutions. Recent official recommendations are disturbing in their ambiguity toward childminding. They recognize that "children who are merely minded are more likely than other children to be denied social and intellectual stimulation...," so they advocate closer voluntary cooperation with social services, nursery schools, and play groups (DHSS, 1976). But if minding is inadequate, does this mean it is acceptable for children under three for whom minding is specially recommended, i.e., as an extension of the mothering role? There is very little provision anyway for this age group.

Governmental proposals for the closer integration of childminders with preschool arrangements ignore the lack of funding and the scarcity of local organizers to coordinate child care. It is not clear how minders could fit into the present structure of day care, which is divided between informal voluntary playgroups, nurseries, and the educationally oriented nursery schools. In the mid 1970s research in Scotland on cooperation in preschool provision identified the main problem as "lack of corporate identity," which on the whole would exclude minders (Watt, 1977). The division between health, education and social services has led to a fragmentation of resources which Hilary Land relates to the way in which interventions in family and child care are justified (Land and Parker, 1978).

Local Authorities have a statutory duty to administer the registration of childminders. Depending on staffing levels, they may also supervise minders; they are empowered to enter the home if necessary. Minders have complained of unnecessary intrusion on their privacy from fire and safety staff; Social Services may be bureaucratic and keep out-of-date registration lists, inconveniencing parents and minders alike; registration is often refused on what are perceived by the minders to be arbitrary grounds. In return, Social Services staff complain that minders are unreliable, have a high turnover, find registration irrelevant, and possess an 'us and them' attitude (Mayall and Petrie, 1977). Yet, as minders point out, there is little incentive to register. However, some Social Service departments which have offered better employment opportunities to minders and integrated their work with that of local centers and schools have found that minders tend to stay longer (National Child Care Campaign, 1980).

Although many Social Services departments provide baby buggies, safety equipment, and toy libraries and may also organize drop-in centers for minders and children, few resources are available. Some have appointed specialist daycare organizers, and this works well if they win the confidence of the socially mixed minders. Occasionally however there may be a clash between the professional ethos of the social worker and the desire for independence of minders' groups (Watt, 1977). Where minders have had some autonomy to develop their own ideas, they have succeeded in making applications for urban aid grants for special projects managed by themselves.[6] The opportunity to visit local day centers in particular is important for minders, who are often criticized for not providing enough stimulation for their minded children.

One of the most crucial problem areas is the relationship between minders and parents. Payment of fees has to be taken on trust. Few minders and parents have formal contracts, due largely to the free market of childminding, which may lead to undercutting as parents search for the cheapest minder. The NCMA has now devised a simple contract which is binding in law; this sets out pay, holiday, and sickness arrangements.

An even more difficult area is communication—it might almost be described as a silence in which parents and minders find it difficult to discuss a particular child's development. The minder is conscious of the prerogative of the parent. On the other hand, the parent is reticent about being critical of the mothering qualities of the minder whom she/he is paying to look after a child, particularly as it might be seen as an invasion of the privacy of the minder's home. This may be why the majority of parents would prefer nursery care, where relationships are more neutral. In mixed ethnic areas there are also difficulties compounded by language and cultural differences.

If childminders are to be fully integrated into the preschool sector and are to achieve better conditions of work and therefore a recognized status, then a more systematic educational program is needed. At the moment there are a variety of informal training and discussion groups and classes which give no recognized qualification. Minders are often put on courses which are designed for a variety of special groups—e.g., nursery nurses and playgroups—which they find irrelevant to their needs and interests. The Trade Union Congress (TUC) has called for an end to the present distinction between "care" and "education" in preschool services (TUC, 1976). A recent working party on Integrated Training for Under Five Workers recommended flexibly structured courses which would incorporate the theoretical and practical experience of adults and students, one which ensures a level of movement across to other more specialized fields and "one which caters for a wide variety of entry and concedes the great variety of people who might wish to train in this field" (National Child Care Campaign, 1980:10). Another project has been worked on by the Open University and the NCMA which interestingly will be aimed at both parents and minders, for as minders have often indicated it may also be parents who need to know more about their children's development.

If childminders are in a process of transition toward becoming skilled child-care workers, there may, however, be problems in taking on full professional status, for, as Land and Parker observe, there is a "Rubicon which once crossed places skill and competence with the professionals thereby... devaluing the capabilities of ordinary families, especially women. The relationship of the professions and families seems to reflect and reinforce that of the state and families" (Land and Parker, 1978:332). If integration is not to antagonize both registered and unregistered minders, then positive support services are required, together with the recognition that minders, like other community groups, would prefer to control their own day-care centers.

VI. HOMEWORKERS: ON THE INCREASE?

In the long history of concern over homeworking there have been optimistic pronouncements that it is on the decline and will eventually disappear. As the Chief Inspectorate of Factories and Workshops wrote in his annual report for 1925: "There is a consensus of opinion that homework is on the decline... [There is] not much room for casual work in modern industry; moreover outwork in the past has not usually been well organized as it has been difficult to secure that the work has been properly done and delivered at the right time. Formerly these disadvantages were probably counteracted by the cheapness of their form of labour...." Despite the nineteenth-century belief in progress, the separation of home and work, and the changes in monopoly capitalism, homeworking still remains an unsolved problem. The fact that homeworking has been done and is still being done mainly by women is reflected in the assumption that women's paid work in the home is of peripheral importance to the economy.

But there is evidence that "the numbers of people working at home, and of homeworkers more specifically, appears to be increasing, with a wider variety of white-collar jobs now being done at home. Between 1921 and 1971 the number of people who reported themselves as working at home in the population census increased from 250,000 to 1.5 million, that is, from 1.4 percent to 6 percent of the labour force" (Hakim, 1980:1110). It should be pointed out that probably the majority of those working at home, according to these figures, have skilled or professional occupations and therefore would be in a higher socio-economic group than homeworkers, who are usually classified as unskilled or semi-skilled.

More specifically there is the problem of calculating numbers of homeworkers. Estimates vary, mainly because the majority of homeworkers do not pay tax or national insurance, are not eligible for sickness or unemployment benefits, are rarely registered by their employers with the local councils, and are not organized into local groups or trade unions. A generally accepted estimate is 100,000-150,000 homeworkers in the United Kingdom, but other estimates have been as high as 250,000 (Townsend, 1980:463-465; Hakim, 1980). Even within London it is difficult to find an agreed-upon estimate to work from. For example, local experts in the London boroughs of Hackney, Haringey and Lewisham estimate their number of homeworkers at 4,000, 5,000, and 1,000, respectively, but in 1978 Lewisham Council had only 53 homeworkers officially registered. Even these figures could be confused because employers often draw their homeworkers from a catchment area outside the borough where their businesses are located, if special skills are needed. It is a noticeable trait that homeworkers are reluctant to reveal themselves for the fairly well documented reasons that they may be caught by officialdom, may lose their jobs to competitors, may annoy the employer, or are ashamed to let the neighbors know they take in homework.

Homeworkers are a heterogeneous group working in a variety of jobs which can range from the traditional (such as sewing for the garment industry; knitting and crocheting; making jewelery, curtains, lampshades, toys, and Christmas crackers; assembling items; and packing) to childminding, typing, envelope addressing, punching computer cards, electrical and plastic assembly work, spot welding, printing, or using visual display units (a recent innovation in Britain that is expected to increase). There are a growing number of redundancies in office work due to the introduction of word processors, which could lead to an increase in part-time home-based clerical work (Barker and Downing, 1980).

The experience and skill of workers vary, as do employers' rates of pay even within firms. It is difficult to summarize earnings, for there is a further complication that homeworkers tend to emphasize their weekly pay, being vague about the number of hours worked due to the pressures and interruptions of family life. Being outside the primary sector and isolated in the home, homeworkers usually feel that they should accept whatever pay is offered, which does not take into account such overhead items as heating, lighting, and upkeep costs. This is often overlooked by workers when calculating their wage. Although they may be aware of publicity over low pay, they have no bargaining power vis-à-vis the employer. Pay can vary from 20p. to £1.50 per hour for sewing or related work, with the hours worked ranging from 20 to 80 per week, and 25p to £1.50 per hour for manufacturing work (Hakim, 1980:1107). A Lewisham study (1980, unpublished) estimates a rate of 30p to something over £1 per hour for homeworkers in that locality. The 1978 ACAS report on the Toy Manufacturing Wage Council discovered that 82% of the 159 homeworkers interviewed earned less than the statutory piecework basic time rate of 86p and over 50% less than 50p per hour (ACAS, 1978).

The great majority of homeworkers are women, predominantly married and/or mothers with dependent children and sometimes adults. Most single women who do homework—they are in a minority—are pensioners, disabled, or responsible for children or elderly or dependent relatives.

Within the general category of homeworkers are groups of women from the ethnic minorities whose language and cultural differences make it difficult to find employment outside the home. Even less is known about such women than the native homeworkers, as often they get their homework jobs through their husbands' networks, within the local ethnic community and sometimes do not even know the names of their employers. Such arrangements would appear to be a repetition of the economic world outside the home: while the women machine and sew, the men manage and develop the business side. Within the southern European and Bengali communities, wives are expected to contribute to the household income through their sewing and machining work. Such patterns of work in the garment industry are typical for immigrant groups in Britain (Hetherington and Siddiqui, 1977:3-5; Hope et al., 1976:88-108; Shah, 1975).

There are cultural differences in attitudes toward homework, as expressed by women from the ethnic groups and British women. Both groups put their family responsibilities first but needed to do homework for economic reasons. However, those from the minority groups were unlikely to envisage doing paid work outside the home until their children had finished school (Hope et al., 1976).

British women were more likely to see lack of child care as the main reason for doing homework as well as the need to supplement the family income. In a 1978 report on the toy industry, 159 homeworkers were interviewed; 58% gave lack of child care as the main reason for doing homework, and 61% did it out of financial necessity (ACAS, 1978). This figure reflects the dependency of many families on a second income, for, if married women did not work, "the proportion of families of women in full-time work who are in poverty or near poverty would increase by over 50 percent." (Townsend, 1980:631). As one homeworker, interviewed in a recent survey of 50 homeworkers, said: "Well, it helps out—especially when it comes to the kids' shoes; they always need shoes all together. You can work it out; you knit one garment for one pair of shoes, sort of. That's how it helps me." Another homeworker from the same survey discussed her husband's attitude (and her own view of the work): "He's in favour. Doesn't feel as though I'm really working 'cos I'm in the house. Not like going out to work; he accepts it" (Hakim, 1980:1106-1107).

One of the main problems affecting homeworkers is the lack of coordinated supervision of their conditions of work. There is a confusion of regulations and authorities, often unchanged since they were first devised in the early years of the twentieth century as a response to public fears about the spread of disease from goods made in the home. For example, under the 1961 Factory Act, and even harking back to the 1911 Health Act, employers are supposed to register the names of their homeworkers with the environmental health officer of the local borough council. But this is irregularly done, for councils usually do not check and employers are only liable for a £20 fine. Homeworkers, like other workers, should be protected under the Health and Safety At Work Act (1974) from dangerous and toxic substances. However, various proposals are being discussed which may lead to the exclusion of clerical homeworkers, for example, from the operations of this act, thus weakening the extent of the existing modest supervision. One vital reform needed is a clarification of the legal employment status of homeworkers. Are they self-employed, as employers hold, since this means the employers are not responsible for paying their share of national insurance, nor for paying sickness, holiday, or redundancy pay, nor the homeworker's overhead costs? Or are they employees, as homeworkers believe? Under the main acts covering employment—the Redundancy Payments Act (1965), the Employment Protection Act (1975), and the Employment Consolidation Act (1978)—the homeworker can only be considered to have employee status if this is conferred by the employer or by decision of individual industrial tribunals. Recent rulings by two industrial tribunals appear to confirm that homeworkers are employees,[7] but these rulings do not constitute case law applicable to all homeworkers. Not every homeworker can take her case to legal arbitration, lacking the money, the time, and the knowledge. The Taxation Laws and Social Security Act (1975) also assumes that homeworkers are self-employed. However, it is possible in Britain for an individual to be both self-employed under tax law and employed by a contractor under labor law.

The executive arm charged with monitoring the conditions and pay of homeworkers is the Wages Councils. There are 19 of these at present, but due to government cuts and the decline of some industries several are being abolished in the next few years. They are meant to set a statutory minimum rate (SMR) for workers in their industries—estimated to cover 25,000 to 30,000 homeworkers, only a small proportion of the total number of homemakers; but they often are slow to raise the SMR, which is well below the national wage average, and they do not always make sure that both employers and workers know the rates of pay, for the orders are particularly complex (Jordan, 1977; Winyard, 1976). All too often homeworkers do not even know they have a Wages Council. The Government Wages Inspectorate should, in theory, check up on homeworkers and their conditions of pay and employment. In practice, they fail to do so partly due to understaffing and also because of their responsibilities for the other low-paid factory workers covered by the appropriate Wages Council. This may improve now that there is a special Homeworkers Unit with 16 inspectors attached to it, set up in July 1978. However, it does not appear that this implies any real change in the approach traditionally followed by the Wages Inspectorate. For example, wages inspectors have responsibility for registration of the firms employing Wages Council workers, not the employers. Their role is conceived of as educative, aiming at cooperating with employers in order not to antagonize them, and prosecutions are rare (Jordan, 1977; Winyard, 1976; CDP, 1977). One example of how this operates is shown in the published result of a special investigation of 486 garment trade homeworkers' pay in south London and the town of Walsall (in the English Midlands) carried out by the Wages Inspectorate in 1979. They found that no homeworkers were underpaid, according to the statutory minimum rate set by the appropriate Wages Councils, except for a mere 8% (34 homeworkers) who were "deemed to have an output less than normal." Queries have been raised about the criteria used for assessing the output of those 34 homeworkers in relationship to the other homeworkers in the same investigation (DOE, 1979).

It is clear that government supervision, local and national, covers only a minority of homeworkers, and even that not effectively. To join a trade union would be the best course for homeworkers' interests, but the majority of homeworkers are unaware of their existence or suspicious of their usefulness. Since 1978 the trade unions, led by the TUC, have moved from their historic anti-homework position and advocacy of its abolition in favor of the family wage into a recognition that homework will not disappear. "The decision of the Trade Unions to improve the position of homeworkers rather than simply to abolish the practice, is strongly influenced by the knowledge that the social circumstances which cause homeworking cannot be redressed overnight" (TUC, 1978). But it still remains a difficult problem to contact individual homeworkers who live and work so privately, especially when trade union staff are already overworked and used to organizing collective groups in factories, offices, and workplaces. Indeed one of the problems about joining a trade union for a homeworker will be the way in which trade unions are structured for protecting the interests of full-time workers. Moreover, trade union representatives are predominantly men who do not carry the main responsibility for running a home. Union meetings scheduled after the normal working day, the weekly union subscription on a small, irregular pay packet, and lack of practice in the politics of work and union organization can be intimidating for the home-based woman. These organizational problems are also compounded by the perceived way in which wages are allocated. Homeworkers suffer from the way jobs are defined and classified in the workplace by employers and trade unions in the process of negotiation. Although this varies from industry to industry, there is evidence, for example, that in the garment trade and paper box industries similar functions are graded higher for men than for women (Hope et al., 1976:107; Phillips and Taylor, 1980:84). So far only a beginning has been made in successfully using trade union skills and muscle to improve conditions for homeworkers. One example was the unionization of the homeworking glovemakers in the small Devon town of Torrington in 1976-1977, where the General and Municipal Workers Union negotiated a 35% increase in the piecework rate, bringing the homeworkers to within 20% of the rate paid in the factories. This is believed to have been the first trade union branch for homewokers in the country, and the conditions were not typical: small town, localized industry, and homeworkers knowing one another. The effect of this rural condition is reflected in a report of attempts to organize low-paid workers and homeworkers in Canning Town in inner London, where problems of isolation existed. Effective organization relied not only on trade unions themselves but also a network of contacts with other cultural and community groups who encouraged collective action over low pay and trade union membership (CDP, 1977). In the Longsight Moss Side (Manchester) Community Action Project in the mid 1970's a group of Pakistani homeworkers was encouraged to join together to make and sell dolls, cushions, and clothing as a short-term experiment. This venture was psychologically successful though not economically viable

(Hetherington and Siddiqui, 1977). These projects, small-scale and tentative though they were, show the possibilities of new ways of reaching homeworkers, but they also highlight the problems of changing markets and jobs. There seems to be a need for publicized, local drop-in centers where homeworkers could find out details of jobs available, the pay and their employment rights. These could be run by trade unions or community groups or as a joint activity.

Since the 1970s there have been a variety of pressure groups such as trade unions and community organizations that have combined to lobby for better protection for homeworkers, to inform homeworkers of their rights at the local level, and to keep the issue before the public (notably, the Low Pay Unit in 1974, the National Homeworker Action Groups in 1976, the London Homeworking Campaign in 1976, the Homeworkers Association set up by the Low Pay unit, and the appointment of the first homeworking officer by a local council, that of Hackney, in 1979). A homeworkers' charter on rights has been produced and a private bill, the Homeworkers Protection Bill, although unsuccessful, was put before Parliament in 1979. In fact, the various governmental bodies concerned with employment have been busier than in the past 80 years in investigating homeworking conditions, and a Homeworking Advisory Committee of Members of Parliament and representatives of the various voluntary campaigns has been appointed. In spite of these many attempts to demarginalize homeworkers and improve their status and pay, coordinated legislation and action are still needed to establish their status as full members of the work force.

VII. END TO MARGINALITY?

The work of childminders and homeworkers is a necessity for them and is an important part of the local economy. This creates the triple disadvantage of being wife, mother, and paid worker in the home. Although the majority of women would prefer to go out to work, the lack of adequate child care leaves them little choice but to stay in the home; they therefore become available for various forms of low-paid work.

In this review we have been looking at some of the issues around women, the family, and the labor market. Large numbers of women have always worked. But there is an ambivalence in family policies and preschool child-care provision which contains an implicit recognition that some women go out to work but that the majority are caught in the part-time trap with few rights and little protection. The perpetuation of ideas about family autonomy and privacy is reflected in a variety of social policies which confirm the belief that the primary responsibility for children lies with the family. In practice intervention is limited to families "in need," however defined: in general, the mother or surrogate mother is defined as the most suitable person for the care of the very young child.

The fluctuating pattern of women's participation in the labor market, and of homeworkers and childminders in particular, is due mainly to the family life cycle, and secondly to the irregularity and seasonal nature of work generated by small firms in the local economy. Homeworkers are an ineffectively regulated sector of the private labor market, and remain isolated within their homes. Childminders, on the other hand, are in the process of moving out of the free child-care market into a closer relationship with local public sector day care.

The present disadvantages experienced by these kinds of workers reflect conventional views about the organization of the working day and the split between home and work. Both employment and trade union discriminatory practices construct women as marginal workers, and perpetuate the view that their place is in the home. Perhaps changes in employment patterns, due to the continuing threat of structural unemployment in Britain and new technologies, may encourage more positive attitudes toward flexible working time. These would be more attuned to the experience of women workers, and they might begin to break down the sexual division of labor at home and work. However, this should be within the framework of effective legislation recognizing the need for full employment status and an adequate wage for all workers.

Given the present problems of organization, due to the lack of workplaces and the current financial stringency, there is a need to know more about the links between local communities, labor organizations, and industries. Homeworkers and childminders operate within local family and cultural networks, and these have been, and could be, mobilized to work for more community resources. Community day centers for childminders, and neighborhood work centers or cooperatives for homeworkers, would bring them out of the isolation of their homes and involve them in a flexible and collective work experience.

ACKNOWLEDGMENTS

We would like to thank the following for all the generous help they gave us in preparing this paper: the childminder groups of Balham, Finsbury, Haringey, and Merton; the Lewisham Women's Employment Project; the staff of the Community Development Project in Haringey, and of Corporate Planning in Lewisham; Helen Eadie of the London Homeworking Campaign; Brian Hodge, homeworking officer in Hackney; Daisy Hurran, homeworker and trade unionist; Jane Maughan of the National Childminders Association; and Joyce Mosley, Social Services Department, Islington.

NOTES

1. Interviews with childminders in Finsbury and Haringey, autumn 1980.
2. Retail Bespoke Tailoring Wages Council, notice of increased statutory minimum earnings, 8 June 1979.
3. Childminders in Balham, Finsbury, and Merton, autumn 1980.
4. London Borough of Haringey: Area Management Team Report. 1980.
5. Full membership figures are 4,600. Annual Report, National Childminders Association, 1980.
6. Haringey, Lambeth and Merton childminders groups. 1978-80.

7. Industrial Tribunal decisions: (a) Case 32512/77 (5 December 1977) and Appeal EAT/75/78 (28 June 1978). The case of Mrs. Delia Cape and Airfix Footwear Ltd., where Mrs. Cape won her claim that she was an employee. (b) Case 11168/79 (18 May 1979). The case of Mrs. Doreen Spinks and D. Maclares Ltd., where Mrs. Spinks was deemed to be entitled to redundancy pay.

REFERENCES

Adams, C. Teich, and K. Teich Winston
   1980   Mothers at Work. New York: Longman.

Advisory, Conciliation and Arbitration Service (ACAS)
   1978   Report on the Toy Manufacturing Wages Council, Report No. 13. London.

Anthias, F.
   1980   "Women and the reserve army of labour: a critique." Capital and Class 10:50-63.

Aries, Philippe
   1973   Centuries of Childhood. London: Penguin.

Barker, Jane, and Hazel Downing
   1980   "Word processing and the transformation of patriarchal relations of control in the office." Capital and Class 10:;64-99.

Barrett, Michele, and Mary McIntosh
   1980   "The family wage." Capital and Class 11:51-72.

Barron, R.D., and G.M. Norris
   1976   "Sexual divisions and the dual labour market." Pp. 47-69 in Diana Leonard Barker and Sheila Allen (eds.), Dependence and Exploitation in Work and Marriage. London: Longman.

Beechey, Veronica
   1977   "Some notes on female wage labour." Capital and Class 3:45-66.

Bone, M.
   1977   Pre-school children and their need for day-care. London: Her Majesty's Stationery Office (HMSO).

Breugel, Irene
   1979   "Women as a reserve army of labour: a note on recent British experience." Feminist Review 3:12-23.

British Broadcasting Corporation (BBC)
   1981   "Hemmed In." Television film transmitted on 11 January. Director: Jenny Morgan.

Brown, George William, and Tirril Harris
   1978   Social Origins of Depression: A Study of Psychiatric Disorder in Women. London: Tavistock.

Brown, Richard Kemp
   1976   "Women as employees: some comments on research in industrial sociology." Pp. 21-46 in Diana Leonard Barker and Sheila Allen (eds.), Dependence and Exploitation in Work and Marriage. London: Longman.

Community Development Projects (CDP)
   1977   Limits of the Law. London: CDP.
   1978   North Shields: Women's Work—North Tyneside CDP. Final Report, vol. 5. London: CDP.
   1979   The State and the Local Economy. London: CDP.

Community Relations Commission (CRC)
   1975   Who Minds? A Study of Working Mothers and Childminding in Ethnic Minority Communities. London: CRC Publications.

Crine, Simon
   1979   The Hidden Army. London: Low Pay Unit.

Cutler, A.
   1978   "The romance of labour." Economy and Society 7, No. 1.

Department of Employment (DOE)

1979 Wages Council Act, Section 28. London: DOE.
1979 Press releases on homeworkers survey, 21 August. London: DOE.
Department of Health and Social Security (DHSS) and Department of Education and Science (SES).
1965-78 Joint Circulars, Nos. 13/65, 37/68, and 1978 (no number).
Donzelot, Jacques
1979 The Policing of Families. New York: Pantheon.
European Economic Community (EEC)
1979 Sevres conference report.
Finch, J., and D. Groves
1980 "Community care and the family." Journal of Social Policy 9 (October).
Fonda, Nickie, and Peter Moss
1976 Mothers in Employment. London: Brunel University.
George, Victor, and Paul Wilding
1976 Ideology and Social Welfare. London: Routledge.
Hakim, Catherine
1980 "Homeworking: some new evidence." Employment Gazette: 1105-1110. London: Department of Employment.
Harris, C. (ed.)
1979 New Directions in the Sociology of the Family. Sociological Review Monograph. London.
Her Majesty's Stationery Office (HMSO)
  1968 Seebohm Report on Allied and Personal Social Services. London: HMSO.
  1970 Children and Their Primary Schools. London: HMSO.
  1973 Children and Young Persons Act, Section I. London: HMSO.
  1978 Central Policy Review Staff. Services for Young Children with Working Mothers. London: HMSO.
  1980a Office of Population and Census Surveys (OPCS). London: HMSO.
  1980b General Household Surveys, 1973 and 1978 in Social Trends. London: HMSO.
Hetherington, R., and N. Siddiqui
1977 Longsight Moss Side Community Project Report (March). Unpublished paper, Manchester.
Hodge, Brian
1980 Bibliography on Homeworking. London: Borough of Hackney.
Hope, Emily, Mary Kennedy, and Ann de Winter
1976 "Homeworkers in North London." Pp. 88-108 in Diana Leonard Barker and Sheila Allen (eds.), Dependence and Exploitation in Work and Marriage. London: Longman.
Hughes, Martin, Berry Mayall, Peter Moss, Jane Perry, Pat Petre, and Gill Pinkerton
1980 Nurseries Now. London: Penguin.
Hunt, Audrey
1968 A Survey of Women's Employment. London: Her Majesty's Stationery Office.
Jackson, Brian
1976 "Childminding: the breakthrough point in the cycle of deprivation." In Department of Health and Social Security (DHSS), Low Cost Day Care Provision for the Under-Fives. London: DHSS.
Jordan, D.
1977 The Wages of Uncertainty. Report No. 6. London: Low Pay Unit.
Kuluzynska, Eva
1980 "Wiping the floor with theory: a survey of writings on housework." Feminist Review 6:27-40.
Lambeth
1978 The Groveway Minders Scheme. London: Lambeth Social Services Department.
Land, Hilary, and R. Parker
1978 "Family policy in the U.K." Pp. 331-61 in A.J. Kahn, and S.B. Kammerman (eds.), Government and Families in Fourteen Countries. New York.

Mackie, L., and P. Pattullo
 1977 Women at Work. London: Tavistock.
Manley, P., and F. Sawbridge
 1980 "Women at work." Lloyds Bank Review (Jan.): 29-40.
Mathieu, N.C.
 1977 Ignored by Some, Denied by Others: The Social Sex Category in Sociology. London: Women's Research and Resources Centre Publications.
Mayall, B., and R. Petrie
 1977 Minders, Mother and Child. Studies in Education, 5. Institute of Education, University of London.
Molyneaux, Maxine
 1979 "Beyond the domestic labour debate." New Left Review 116:3-27.
National Child Care Campaign (NCCC).
 1980 "Integated Training for the Under-Fives Workers." Working Party Report (unpublished) London: NCCC.
National Childminders Association (NCMA).
 1978 Pay and Conditions of Childminders. Working Party Report (September) (unpublished). London: NCMA.
 1980 Annual Report. London: NCMA.
Phillips, Angela
 1978 Interview with Mrs. Lynda Chalker, M.P. The Guardian (17 October).
Phillips, Anne, and Barbara Taylor
 1980 "Sex and skill: notes towards a feminist economics." Feminist Review 6:79-88.
Playford, C.
 1980 Low Pay Policies. Report No. 2 (October). London: Low Pay Unit.
Purcell, Kate
 1979 "Militancy and acquiescence amongst women workers." Pp. 112-133 in Sandra Burman (ed.), Fit Work for Women. London: Croom Helm.
Rutter, Michael
 1972 Maternal Deprivation Reassessed. London: Penguin.
Robinson, Olive
 1979 "Part-time employment in the EEC—a marginal labour force?" Three Banks Review 122: 61-76.
Rubery, Jill
 1980 "Structured labour markets, worker organisation and low pay." Pp. 242-70 in Alice H. Amsden (ed.), The Economics of Women and Work. London: Penguin.
Shah, Samir
 1975 Immigrants and Employment in the Clothing Industry: The Rag Trade in London's East End. London: Runnymede Trust.
Shorter, Edward
 1976 The Making of the Modern Family. London: Collins.
Snell, Mandy
 1979 "The equal pay and sex discrimination acts." Feminist Review 1.
Summersfield, Penny
 1981 "Child-care during the 1939-45 War." Paper (unpublished) given at the Social History Society conference at Winchester, U.K., January.
Thane, P. (ed.)
 1978 The Origins of British Social Policy. London: Croom Helm.
Titmuss, Richard
 1963 Essays on the Welfare State. London: Allen and Unwin.
Tomlinson, J.
 1979 State Agencies and the Labour Market. Mimeograph. London: Brunel University.

Townsend, Peter
   1979   Poverty in the U.K. London: Penguin.
Trade Union Congress (TUC).
   1976   The Under Fives. Report of a TUC Working Party. London: TUC.
   1978   Statement on Homeworking. (January) London: TUC.
Watt, Joyce S.
   1977   Co-operation in Pre-School Education. Monograph. London: Social Science Research Council.
Wilson, Elizabeth
   1978   Women and the Welfare State. London: Tavistock.
Winyard, Steven
   1976   The Weak Area of the Law. Report No. 13. London: Low Pay Unit.
Young, Michael, and Peter Willmott
   1973   The Symmetrical Family. London: Routledge.

THE TOURING TENNIS PROFESSIONAL:
A MIGRATORY WORKER

Nancy G. Kutner

The touring tennis professional, whether ranked 5th or 200th, must be committed to tennis as a full-time occupation. However, career length tends to be relatively short, and in this sense tennis is a peripheral occupation for most touring tennis pros. This is especially true for the majority of players who make up the lower stratum of professional tennis, i.e., those who play in the "satellite" or "feeder" circuits. Only the most talented and persistent players are able to move from satellite circuits into the upper stratum, qualifying for major tournaments which comprise the Grand Prix circuit for men or the Colgate and Avon circuits for women. Players who are successful at the upper level may earn enough money to guarantee their future financial security or may move into lucrative careers which are built on their contacts and experience as a tennis pro. Players whose experience is limited to the satellite circuits frequently become coaching professionals, for which the increased popular interest in tennis as a participant sport has created a large demand.

Four categories of tennis players have been recognized since 1968 by the International Lawn Tennis Federation (ILTF): (1) amateurs, who do not receive, directly or indirectly, financial advantage by playing, teaching, or demonstrating tennis; (2) coaching professionals, who receive fees for giving instruction in the game; (3) registered players, who may play for prize money but acknowledge the authority of their national tennis association; and (4) contract professionals, players who contract to a particular promoter. These definitions are subject to further interpretation by member countries of the federation.

This chapter focuses on tennis pros known as "playing professionals" (registered players and contract professionals), who are migratory workers. Although some coaching professionals vary their work location on a seasonal basis, the majority are permanently located at private clubs or public tennis facilities. Amateurs are migratory, but they are unpaid workers. Differences, as well as linkages, between the four types of playing status can be clarified by reviewing the history of professional tennis in the United States.

I. THE DEVELOPMENT OF PROFESSIONAL TENNIS IN THE UNITED STATES

Professional tennis in the United States officially began in 1926, when an industrialist, C.C. ("Cash and Carry") Pyle, asserted that professional tennis could and should be considered theater and envisioned a nationwide professional tennis tour. Pyle signed contracts with six top men and women players from the United States and Europe. His first tour earned $83,000, but gate receipts declined during successive tours, indicating that the public would not support matches involving the same set of players.

In the early 1930s, promotion of professional tennis was taken over by Bill Tilden, one of the most impressive players in the history of American tennis. In addition to displaying brilliant tennis, Tilden has been described as having "a touch of the theatrical in his makeup" (Perry, 1974:60). Tilden and two tennis colleagues organized a very successful tour in 1934, adding new names from time to time. Tilden thereby established the pattern of a tour during which contract pros played a series of matches throughout the country that determined a professional champion, with a continuing effort to recruit the top amateur players to join the tour. A contract was signed between the promoter and the player which guaranteed the contract pro a set figure or a share of the gate receipts for a tour of the United States and/or other countries.

The early pro movement encountered many obstacles, however. Tours took place during the winter months, and it was difficult to arrange the necessary indoor facilities. Large facilities were dominated by more-popular spectator sports, basketball and ice hockey, which were able to draw large crowds. University and high school facilities furnished much less desirable playing conditions. Touring was physically exhausting for players because of the need to travel by train or car—air travel was not an alternative available in the 1930s. But the most frustrating obstacle was the clash between the new professionals and the established amateur power structure represented by the United States Lawn Tennis Association (USLTA).

> Professional tournaments were scarce. Few clubs would risk the wrath of the USLTA by permitting the professionals to use their courts during the tennis season with the amateur circuit in full swing. Detractors were quick to knock this lack of *bona fide* tournaments, classing the tours as exhibitions and demonstrations. Amateurs—champions in their own right—who had joined the professionals were no longer welcome at amateur events or at tennis clubs affiliated to national LTAs. The confrontation was absolute. Amateurs were not permitted to play against professionals except in official matches. Needless to say, permission was seldom given...(Perry, 1974:61).

Despite the addition to the professional tour of tennis greats Fred Perry and Donald Budge in the late 1930s, gate receipts for professional tour events did not meet expectations. By 1940, the advent of World War II effectively halted the pro movement for several reasons: (1) expansion of tours to other countries, one means of generating increased public interest and revenue, was impossible; (2) newspaper publicity, a vital requirement for all sporting tours, was scarce; and (3) the public mood did not include patronizing tennis matches.

Immediately following the war, however, public interest in the professional tennis tour revived. The acknowledged pro champion, Donald Budge, was challenged in a 1946-1947 series of matches by Bobby Riggs, the 1939 (amateur) Wimbledon champion. Riggs emerged the new pro champion, and Jack Kramer, the top amateur, was signed to challenge Riggs in 1947-1948. Kramer dominated that series and continued his reign as pro champion by defeating new challengers, Pancho Gonzalez and Pancho Segura, in 1949-1950, 1950-1951 series. These particular players have had a continuing influence on the development of pro tennis in the United States, over and above their popularity as tour participants. Bobby Riggs was in 1973 to play a widely televised match against women's champion Billie Jean King, which was won by King and boosted public interest in the women's pro tour. Pancho Gonzalez helped to popularize the power tennis game and bullet-like serve which now characterizes many top men players. Pancho Segura's "cute" shots and rapport with the crowd foreshadowed the use of the theatrical element by players such as Jimmy Connors and Ilie Nastase. Jack Kramer became the organizing force behind postwar professional tennis tours from 1953 to 1962, during which time "almost every kid who won either Wimbledon or Forest Hills turned pro..." (Kramer and Deford, 1978:26). Jack Kramer was also to become the first executive director of the Association of Tennis Professionals (ATP), a players' union organized in 1972.

In 1962, survival of the pro movement again seemed to be in doubt. Kramer withdrew from being a full-time promoter. The style of the then-current pro champion, Ken Rosewall, did not attract crowds. Top amateurs did not want to commit themselves to an uncertain pro career, especially when lucrative under-the-table rewards were abundant. Rosewall and Lew Hoad were considering retiring, but they decided to make a personal guarantee of $125,000 for a one-year tour to fellow Australian Rod Laver, who had just won the French, British, Australian, and U.S. championships. Impressed by their sincere belief that "if we could just keep it going some day pro tennis would thrive as a significant sport" (Collins, 1974:65), Laver accepted their offer, and his share of the gate receipts in 1963 exceeded the guarantee.

A significant impetus for the development of modern pro tennis occurred in 1964 when a Boston bank assumed sponsorship of the U.S. Pro Championships at prestigious Longwood Cricket Club in Boston. This endorsement enabled the pros to secure several other sponsors for a short summer tournament circuit offering about $80,000 in prize money. Professional tennis could then shift its emphasis from "roving one-night stands" to conventional tournaments, thereby reducing the difference between the structure of amateur and professional tennis. The concept of "open competition," i.e., matches open to both amateur and professional players, was a logical extension of this structural change.

In 1967, promoters established World Championship Tennis (WCT) and the National Tennis League (NTL), which quickly signed fourteen of the world's top professional and amateur players. The International Lawn Tennis Federation responded to this pressure by finally accepting open competition in 1968. However, subsequent relationships between ILTF and the promoters' leagues were strained, largely because the promoters required payment of a management fee for the service of delivering players for each tournament. Disagreements between the ILTF and WCT, which had taken over NTL, led to the temporary cessation of open tennis during early 1972. By the late summer of 1972, however, the organizations reconciled their differences, permitting WCT pros to participate in the U.S. Open at Forest Hills.

At the same time, a yearly World Championship of Tennis was being organized, with twenty $50,000 events from which the top eight finishers would emerge for a $100,000 tournament leading to a $50,000 first prize. Professional tennis could now promise significant financial rewards to its "workers."

Television coverage of WCT matches in the winter of 1972, the first time that tennis had been televised on a regular series basis by an American commercial network, "seemed to establish the pro game once and for all with the American public who had been unaware of pro tennis only a few years before" (Collins, 1974:67). Pro tennis stars now had access to the recognition and prestige which were denied to the marginal men who comprised Jack Kramer's touring group. Finally, job security within pro tennis was strengthened by the emergence in 1972 of the Association of Tennis Professionals, a player's union organized to oversee playing conditions, prize money, tournament qualifications, retirement schemes, and other issues affecting professional players' careers.

A. Development of Women's Professional Tennis

Except for the inclusion of two women players, Suzanne Lenglen and Mary K. Brown, in Pyle's pioneering 1926 tour, participation by women in professional tennis prior to 1971 was limited to sporadic exhibitions at clubs or sparsely filled arenas. Pauline Betz and Sarah Palfrey Cooke had a financially unsuccessful tour in 1947. Gussie Moran and Pauline Betz played a series of pro exhibitions with Kramer and Segura in 1950-1951, but the women generated little public interest. Althea Gibson and Karol Fageros signed with the Harlem Globetrotters' games during the winter of 1958-1959, but Gibson consistently overpowered Fageros, and the women's financial rewards were less than expected. Similarly, the four women who were among the players signed by the NTL in 1967 (Billie Jean King, Rosemary Casals, Françoise Durr, and Ann Jones) proved to be poor gate attractions.

At the conclusion of their contract with NTL in 1970, King, Casals, Durr, and Jones continued to play as independent pros in American and European tournaments, but prize money never exceeded $4,000, which was far below the amount available to men players. Women players became incensed when Jack Kramer offered $50,000 in prize money for the men's event and only $7,500 for the women's event at the Pacific Southwest Championships in August, 1970. With the growth of feminist awareness in the United States, the climate was right for the emergence of a women's pro tour.

Led by outspoken Billie Jean King, 19 of the top women players signed with Gladys Heldman, editor of the magazine *World Tennis*, for a series of contract pro tournaments during the 1971-1972 winter and spring season. This was the beginning of the World Tennis Women's Pro Tour and the Virginia Slims Prize Money Circuit (the Philip Morris Company had decided that backing women's tennis would be a good way to advertise their new slim cigarette). Although the USLTA soon voted to allow the women to qualify again for all official teams and rankings, disagreements about playing conditions continued between the WT Women's Pro Tour and the USLTA.

At the U.S. Open late in the summer of 1971 the women's cause received important institutionalized backing when the chairman of the board of Philip Morris threatened to withdraw TV sponsorhip of the U.S. Open if the USLTA continued to discriminate against WT women pros. Further support came in early 1972 when two of the most influential men in U.S. tennis, Jack Kramer and Donald Dell (the Davis Cup captain), negotiated a contract giving autonomy to the Women's Pro Tour under the USLTA. There was growing awareness that women's pro tennis had a potentially lucrative future ahead; it is interesting that Donald Dell was later to manage the career of Tracy Austin, who had earned $1 million before her eighteenth birthday. By September of 1972, the USLTA decided to get on the bandwagon and organize its own Women's Pro Tour. The

WT Women's Tour responded by creating its own professional organization, the Women's International Tennis Federation. Finally, in 1973, the two organizations agreed to allow all women players to compete against each other. Virginia Slims retained sponsorship of individual tournaments, but the "Virginia Slims Circuit" was replaced by the "USLTA Circuit." Perhaps the clearest indicator of the strength of the women's movement within tennis was equalization in 1973 of prize money for women and men competing in the U.S. Open. However, a marked differential continues to exist in the total earnings of men and women pros.

II. THE EVOLUTION OF TENNIS PRO CAREERS

Changes in the structure of professional tennis since its inception in 1926 have in turn affected the nature of tennis pro career patterns. The adoption of open tennis in 1968 was an important turning point, finally eliminating the pro's marginal status as a tennis player.

A. Careers of the Pre-1968 Contract Pros

The early tennis pros toured the country as contract pros only after they had become recognized champions by winning major amateur events, especially Wimbledon and the U.S. Championship. The number of contract pros was relatively small, therefore. Players such as Jack Kramer considered themselves the best in the world and felt it was "ludicrous" that contract pros were barred from competing in championship events. Although Kramer reported that seven of his touring pros were making more than $50,000 in 1959-1960 (more than most baseball and football players at the time), lack of acceptance of the pros by the amateur official power structure was a deep source of frustration.

A number of the early pros later turned to nonplaying tennis careers, becoming coaching professionals (e.g., Pancho Segura and Pauline Betz), TV tennis commentators (e.g., Tony Trabert), or tennis organization executives (e.g., Jack Kramer and Butch Buchholz, executive directors of the Association of Tennis Professionals). Pancho Gonzalez, Ken Rosewall, Frank Sedgman, and Rod Laver continued their playing careers into the late 1970s, competing on the men's pro circuit, the "Grand Masters" circuit for older players, and World Team Tennis. Ken Rosewall retired from tournament competition in 1979 at age 45; he then began to set up tennis centers at two resorts in Australia and planned to begin a junior tennis development program there.

B. Careers of the Pre-1968 "Amateur/Pros"

From the early 1960s to 1968, many players held an ill-defined status somewhere between amateur and professional. Only "amateurs" could participate in the prestigious Australian, French, British, and U.S. championships, but these players received unofficial payments. This practice, which came to be called "shamateurism," characterized smaller tournaments as well.

> If your ranking was high enough that they knew who you were, you were in like Flynn. You just wrote and said, "I'd like to come to your tournament. How much can you pay me?" They'd write back with an offer: "We'll give you $300." You either agreed or tried to make a better deal someplace else (Barry Phillips-Moore, quoted in Lorge, 1978d:61).

> [T]hose of us who were attempting to make a living out of the game were... obliged to wheel and deal our way around the globe, airing our talents in the sunshine and accepting our rewards in some dark, secret place (Marty Riessen, quoted in Lorge, 1978d:58)

Top players did well financially, receiving cash payments as well as free rackets, strings, and other equipment from manufacturers. Although clothing companies founded by former players Fred Perry and Rene Lacoste furnished tennis attire to most players on the circuit, players who were not among the top 35 in the world frequently had a difficult time covering the travel expenses associated with tournaments.

In the pre-open era, upset of a top-ranked player in a tournament was likely to evoke negative sanction; for example, Barry Phillips-Moore, an unheralded Australian, found that "in the tournaments that I had my best results, I wasn't asked back" (Lorge, 1978d:61). Although players who experienced the pre-open era have termed it "absurd" and "chaotic," some have expressed nostalgia for the camaraderie and the relatively relaxed atmosphere of the competition in smaller tournaments. Because of the scarcity of big prize money, players either combined their tennis with another job, tennis-related (e.g., importing gut for rackets) or non-tennis-related (e.g. carpentry), or became true "tennis bums" enjoying the local sights and hospitality of Paris, Monte Carlo, and other alluring tournament locations.

Some of the best-known players of the 1960s were Barry MacKay, John Newcombe, Roy Emerson, Fred Stolle, Manuel Santano, Bill Alvarez, Arthur Ashe, Stan Smith, Dennis Ralston, Chuck McKinley, Cliff Richey, and Donald Dell. They were among the "special designated players" from their respective countries who were guaranteed a certain amount of money at events such as Wimbledon. However, their national tennis associations exercised strict control over them, allowing players to stay only a specified length of time before or after tournaments in other countries and penalizing them for violating these association rules. Players have reported feeling that they were unwelcome aliens when competing in another country: "... the Americans felt that way when they played on the clay in Europe, and I'm sure the Europeans felt the same way when they came to America" (Cliff Richey, quoted in Lorge, 1978d:63). Players were imported, so to speak, to broaden the field and increase the appeal of major tournaments. After the tournament they were quickly returned to their home country, just as migrant laborers are returned to their home when they have completed the work they were brought in to do.

A few players from the amateur/pro group, such as Stan Smith at age 34 and Marty Riessen at age 38, continue to be successful competitors. Several of the pre-1968 amateur/pros are active in tennis-related careers. Dennis Ralston coached several top pros before becoming head tennis coach at SMU. Barry MacKay promotes a yearly tournament in the San Francisco Cow Palace and conducts courtside interviews for telecasts of Grand Prix tournaments around the country. John Newcombe left the singles circuit at age 31 to set up his own tennis resort. While playing the circuit, he was a volunteer instructor at tennis camps for several weeks during the summer and was able to use his contacts and evaluation of existing programs in starting his own business. Newcombe also serves as a TV tennis commentator and has a syndicated column.

Arthur Ashe and Donald Dell are two amateur/pros who have been very influential in shaping the structure of modern professional tennis. They are also colorful personalities whose careers have received considerable media attention (Bookman, 1980; Lorge, 1978b, 1978c). Arthur Ashe is a past president of the Association of Tennis Professionals and continues to serve as a board member; he is one of three player representatives on the Men's International Pro Council. After a heart bypass operation in late 1979, Ashe officially retired at age 37 from competitive pro tennis and began to write an autobiography and an instruction book. He plans to accept engagements as a TV sports commentator. His business commitments include advertising for a racket company and for a clothing and shoes company, minority recruiting for Aetna Insurance, public relations appearances for Philip Morris, and a magazine column for Miller Beer. Although Ashe remained very busy after retiring from competition, he acknowledged that his tennis career had left him with no "special skills":

> I know how to talk. I know how to think. I know right from wrong. But I can't run a business. I couldn't even run my own tennis shop in Washington, D.C. I am no retailer. I wouldn't know how to represent a player. Even though I'm a business graduate, that was fifteen years ago (Arthur Ashe, quoted in Bookman, 1980:30).

Ashe still enjoys the nomadic lifestyle he knew as a player, "getting on 747s and blasting off to new places to meet new people and do new things" (Bookman, 1980:26). Although no longer playing tennis, Ashe expects to continue traveling to participate in pro tennis policy-making.

Donald Dell has been described as "undoubtedly the No.1 power broker in tennis" (Bud Collins, quoted in Lorge, 1978b:18). Dell played the international circuit in the early 1960s while working on a law degree but gave up tennis to join a law firm in 1965. In 1968 he resigned from the law firm to captain the Davis Cup team. Donald Dell served as an informal business adviser to his players and informed the USLTA in 1969 that his team would not play the U.S.

The Touring Tennis Professional 249

summer circuit for covert appearance fees instead of prize money. He then founded a $25,000 prize money tournament which became the first event of the summer circuit and helped to induce the other tournaments on the circuit to offer prize money instead of appearance guarantees. After resigning his position as Davis Cup captain in 1970, Dell began to represent four of his Davis Cup players as legal counsel; by 1980, Dell and his partners represented more than 50 tennis pros and were promoting and managing tennis tournaments around the world. Perhaps this statement best sums up Dell's career goals: "...My objective, and I am fanatical about it, is to make tennis the biggest professional individual sport in America...I want to see it swallow golf, and I believe that in the next five or ten years it will" (Donald Dell, quoted in Lorge, 1978c:61).

C. Post-1968: Modern Tennis Pro Careers

1. The Financial Incentive

After open tennis was adopted in 1968, professional tennis became not only a legitimized but also a potentially lucrative career option for a much larger number of players. To date, 19 men and 6 women pros have earned $1 million or more in tournament prize money. The top men players receive more money than any other athletes, and women pros as a group are the highest-paid women athletes. In addition to prize money, potential off-court earnings for tennis pros were boosted by the tremendous growth in popularity which tennis enjoyed in the 1970s, both as a participant sport and as a spectator sport.

> The $10 million Grand Prix series, satellite circuits, big-money TV specials and exhibitions, the endorsement bonanza, and the whole idea of tennis as a lucrative career for more than a handful of players are all part of a Brave New World that has been discovered and cultivated within the last decade...(Lorge, 1978d:58).

The Association of Tennis Professionals and the Women's Tennis Association maintain a computerized ranking of playing pros which reflects their performance in competition. The higher a player is ranked relative to other players, the more he/she is likely to earn from nontournament activities such as exhibitions and endorsements. It has been estimated that by becoming one of the top ten ranked players, tennis pros increase their earnings by 50%. Players with established top ten rankings are likely to derive the majority of their income from nontournament activities, as illustrated by Bjorn Borg's estimated 1979 income distribution:

$1 million	tournament prize money
$1 million	use of Donnay racquet
$1 million	fee for being "resident pro" for a few weeks at a tennis club in Spain

$500,000	exhibition fees
$400,000	wearing Fila tennis clothes
$300,000	wearing Diadora tennis shoes
$200,000	fee for being touring pro for Caesars Palace
$125,000	exclusive photo rights to his wedding
$1 million	miscellaneous endorsements of products and services.

For a fee, agents negotiate endorsements, which enable players to tap a "ready-made market"; unlike baseball or football stars, the products that tennis pros use when they play are the products that consumers use also. A player who has won a major title such as Wimbledon can continue to benefit from endorsements even after retiring from competition. The most impressive example is Arthur Ashe, who earned $3-$4 million while retired in 1980.

Although women tennis pros are the highest-paid women athletes, only 35 women earn $100,000 or more a year in prize money while approximately 75 men pros earn that amount each year. Because the public recognizes more men pros' names than women pros' names, endorsement opportunities exist for a significantly larger number of men than women.

It appears that the financial incentive which professional tennis now represents will lead talented amateurs, especially girls, to "turn pro" at increasingly younger ages. Tracy Austin became the first athlete to earn $1 million before reaching age 18. Andrea Jaeger at age 14 became the youngest tennis pro and the youngest athlete ever to endorse a product.

2. *Entry Into a Professional Tennis Career*

Most of the top playing pros began to play tennis before they were teenagers, some as early as age 5 or 6. Parental encouragement was generally strong for these players; a parent or sibling often served as first coach and/or practice partner. Many top players possess all-around athletic ability and seriously considered careers in other sports, e.g., swimming, ice skating, gymnastics. In the United States, players tend to come from white, upper-middle-class families who can afford the expense of lessons and tournament travel. An additional factor which may become increasingly characteristic of top players in the future is having attended a "tennis academy." Summer tennis camps have been available since the 1950s, but the tennis academy is a new idea, operating for nine months of the year and attempting to create a total tennis environment for talented junior players aged 10 to 17. Students from a Florida academy have been very successful in winning junior championships, and 90% of the academy's graduates earn college tennis scholarships.

Because of a difference in the ages at which girls and boys reach their physical (and perhaps emotional) maturity, talented junior girls are likely to be ready to turn pro at an earlier age than junior boys. Two additional explanations which have been offered for girls' early success in tennis as compared to boys' are a sex-role difference—i.e., girls have fewer approved outlets for competition than do boys—and "the young girl's classic desire to please her father" (Bodo, 1979b:41). Paternal approval was a strong motivating force for Suzanne Lenglen, as it is for Chris Evert, Andrea Jaeger, and several of the most successful junior girl competitors.

A successful record as a college player is frequently the catalyst for a young player's decision to turn pro. Those who have not completed their degree when they turn pro may have to sacrifice their original career plans, e.g., switching from pre-med to a less demanding major, as Victor Amaya did. Despite the potential financial reward, some talented players are not in a hurry to "turn pro." Players may want to concentrate on both a college education and tennis, realizing that they won't be playing tennis their whole lives. Players may also value the peer support and recognition available to them in college. The highest-ranked amateur man in 1980 and the star of the Stanford tennis team decided to complete college before turning pro, explaining that "I could refine my game under that pressure, get my degree in psychology and hang out with friends my own age..." (Peter Rennert, quoted in LaMarche, 1980b:103).

Although the majority of prospective playing professionals are amateurs, some coaching professionals also decide to try their luck on the minor tournament circuits. Their incentive is the thrill of successful competition and enjoyment of travel rather than financial reward per se:

> I could teach in Chicago, Las Vegas, and make $600, $700 a week starting tomorrow. I gotta give it this shot though. What regrets can I have? I've met successful, important people. I've lived in places people dream of visiting. I've been to Europe twice, and will probably go to Asia and Australia this next year. Tennis is my life and already it's given me things I couldn't imagine getting anywhere else....I like teaching but if you can support yourself playing that's got to be the greatest thing (Ray Murphy, quoted in Metcalfe, 1979:28).

The United States Tennis Association (USTA) has prepared an information sheet for prospective pros, which states at the outset that "there is no simple route to becoming a playing pro." Only the finest players are able to make the circuits. The major criterion is one of developing your game to the level necessary to play top tennis and getting the visibility and recognition needed to get into the minor, then major, professional circuits.

What are some of the initial steps you should take to further your aspirations? Assuming that you are already a player of some proficiency:

1. Join the USTA. The USTA provides and manages a framework of tournament competition for both the amateur and professional player at every age level. Membership in the USTA gives you the right to play in sanctioned USTA tournaments and be ranked by the USTA. Such tournaments are sponsored by the USTA on a national, sectional and district level. The USTA is divided into 17 sections and further subdivided into 50 districts.

2. Begin your competitive career by playing in local tournaments sponsored by your USTA district or sectional association.... Try to play in as many tournaments as possible for competitive experience.

3. Be sure that you check your section's guide or yearbook for information on how to work toward a ranking in your section or district. Yearly rankings of players are computed by the USTA on the district, sectional and national levels, based on the players' tournament records.

4. Once you have established yourself as a top junior player in district and sectional competition, you will become eligible to be endorsed by your section to play in national competition. By competing in USTA national championships, you increase your chances of being nationally ranked, and also have the opportunity to play the best junior talent in the country for experience and improvement in your game. It is important that you work toward the highest national ranking possible if you are aspiring to become a pro player. A high national ranking will facilitate your entry into the minor professional circuits, where you then may earn enough "points" to qualify for major pro tournament participation (USTA Education and Research Center, 1980).

The effort involved in becoming a high-ranking tennis pro is hidden from the general public:

> Sometimes you come across people who think they know something about tennis and always they will ask you, 'So how is it just playing tennis and going around the world?' And they say, "I would like my son to do it, but there is so much traveling."... Ninety-nine percent of the people, they think it is not a matter of breaking through but only a matter of *deciding*. They think you *decide* you are going to be a tennis player so you do it. You enter a tournament. They don't know about the hundreds or thousands behind, because the press never tells you about them. They don't realize that there is qualifying and pre-qualifying to get into the qualifying, and it is unbelievably tough (Wojtek Fibak, quoted in Lorge, 1979:62).

3. *Job Opportunities*

a. Major and minor circuits. The major circuit for men pros is the Grand Prix, organized in 1971, which includes more than 90 tournaments around the world. The series has had as its sponsors the Pepsi, Colgate-Palmolive, and Volvo companies. In addition, tennis clubs and businesses in the local area sponsor individual tournament events. Major circuits for women are the Colgate series, organized in 1977 and including over 40 major tournaments, and the Avon 12 week winter circuit, which in 1979 replaced the Virginia Slims circuit.

Both men's and women's tournaments are classified into categories based on the total prize money offered. The higher the prize money category, the more points players can earn as winner, runner-up, losing semifinalist, losing quarter-finalist, and loser in the round of 16, 32, or 64. All men who compete on the Grand Prix circuit must play at least six events, excluding the "Grand Slam" events (the French, British, U.S., and Australian championships), three of which have minimum prize money of $175,000 and three of which offer prize money between $50,000 and $125,000. Players and their agents determine which tournaments players will compete in, basing their decisions on player preferences for tournament spacing and on performance in past events.

Players frequently move back and forth between the major circuit and a minor, or "satellite," circuit, depending on their tournament records. Players' acceptance into major tournament events around the world is based on their ranking by the Association of Tennis Professionals or the Women's Tennis Association. The number of players ranked by the ATP grew from 200 in 1975 to almost 1,000 in 1980. Only players ranked in the top 110 by the ATP play the Grand Prix circuit, and players ranked in the top 45 play the two women's circuits. The bulk of competition for "computer points" takes place on 27 satellite circuits around the world. In the United States, aspiring men pros compete on the Penn circuit, which was organized in 1979 and has been compared to the old minor league of professional baseball. Aspiring women pros compete on the Avon Futures circuit, organized in 1977, or a feeder circuit organized by the USTA in 1980.

The men's Penn circuit has six segments, each with four tournaments followed by a "Masters" event. Penn Athletic Products, the circuit sponsor, contributes $1,500 to each tournament, and the local club hosting the tournament is responsible for raising the remainder of the $7,000 prize money. Sixty-four men compete in each tournament except for the Masters event, which has a 32-man draw. Players must compete in all the events of a segment to be eligible for computer points. Playing one match in the Masters tournament earns a player one ATP computer point, which in turn gives a ranking of approximately 680th in the world—a position shared by some fifty players.

The Avon Futures circuit has three levels of competition. Prequalifying events, open to anyone, are held six times during the season. The top eight competitors from the prequalifying become eligible for a week on the next level, which is a qualifying round of 64. A player reaching the round of eight in any one week on the qualifying level is then eligible for one of the eleven main tournaments, which have a draw of 32 and $20,000 prize money. As is true for the men's satellite circuit, the promoter of women's satellite events contributes a portion of the prize money in return for advertising exposure; and a local club, resort, or individual furnishes the remaining amount.

Although most satellite circuit players stay in private housing arranged by the tournament committee, it is also common for players on the men's Penn circuit to squeeze into a crowded motel room or sleep in a van or car (Danzell, 1980). Players have been known to sleep on the lounge chairs around the pool adjoining the club's tennis courts. Car pooling from tournament to tournament is common.

Some players travel long distances to be "on-site alternates," hoping that they can take the place of registered players who fail to show up for the tournament. These are likely to be individuals who must economize on travel expenses, and they have been described as a "nomad population" which transforms the host tennis club's parking lot into a campground filled with tents, mobile homes, trailers, and vans (Danzell, 1980).

Most of the satellite competitors are young players, eager for competitive experience. There are few spectators at the satellite tournaments, and the players have no ball boys or linesmen to make their work easier. Satellite tournaments are usually not held in exotic locations. Blanton and Ross (1980:4) note that there are a "surprisingly large number of players who travel with spouses or girlfriends," but this probably represents a means of trying to combat the tension and loneliness which players frequently experience. One satellite player has reported seeing the same movie "about 26 times last summer just to get out of the hotel room" (Ray Murphy, quoted in Metcalfe, 1979:28). Another frequent pastime on the satellite circuit has been called "malling": "hitting the local shopping mall as soon as you have a free moment; browsing in bookstores, girl watching, trying to get your mind off the fact you might be bounced from the draw at the last minute if a bigger name shows up..." (Metcalfe, 1979:28).

b. Exhibitions and endorsements. Regardless of the promise they show, young pros must prove their ability by winning on the major circuits before they can successfully command exhibition fees and endorsement contracts. Having done this, however, they can earn large sums of money much more quickly through exhibitions than through tournament competition. For example, Connors and Borg receive $25,000 or more for a single exhibition. The Men's International Pro Council attempts to schedule major tournaments to allow top players free time to take advantage of this source of income. Some observers argue that tennis pros may be tempted to devote too much time to exhibitions, showing a lack of responsibility to the sport (Lorge, 1978c; Bodo, 1980c). On the other hand, an exhibition may provide the only opportunity for fans in smaller cities to see one of the top players in person.

Although the practice is contrary to Pro Council rulings, some players accept "appearance money" which "guarantees" that they will participate in a certain tournament. Guarantees may be disguised as exhibition arrangements coinciding with the event or as endorsement deals accompanying entry to a tournament. Appearance money deals are viewed by many as dysfunctional because players may be less motivated to work hard in a tournament which they have been paid to enter.

Endorsements are an important means to additional income. Although only the top players are likely to have multiple endorsement contracts, the opportunity for some kind of endorsement (rackets, apparel, or shoes) exists for the top forty women pros and the top 120-130 men pros. Endorsement of non-tennis-related products (e.g., cars, watches) is only feasible for the "superstars," i.e., names readily recognized by the commercial public.

Management firms such as the one run by Donald Dell and his associates perform a crucial role in negotiating endorsement contracts and in arranging exhibitions or appearances for their player-clients. Because athletes generally have a relatively short earning career, the management firm seeks to help players earn as much as possible and conserve as much as possible in order to establish their financial security (Gamarekian, 1980).

4. *The Decision to Retire*

Tennis pros in good physical condition can continue to compete successfully against significantly younger opponents. Two good examples are Marty Riessen and Billie Jean King. As of 1980, Riessen, age 38, was ranked 37th in men's singles and 3rd in men's doubles; King, age 36, was ranked 5th in women's singles and 24th in women's doubles. Both acknowledge that avoiding serious injury and staying in shape have been significant factors in their long playing careers. While Riessen has stressed enjoyment of the financial rewards as a primary reason for not retiring from pro tennis, King has stressed enjoyment of the game as her primary reason. It has been speculated that Riessen, rather than turning to an alternative profession, will eventually move into tours for older players such as the "Grand Masters" and "Legends" and that King will become the coach of a promising young pro, Andrea Jaeger.

Tennis pros who have reached an age at which it is difficult to compete successfully in singles matches against younger players may concentrate on becoming doubles specialists. Because the game of doubles requires less running, older players (e.g., Marty Riessen, Stan Smith) may be able to maintain high doubles rankings. However, a high ranking as a singles player is more prestigious than a high ranking as a doubles player, which encourages pros to compete on the singles circuit as long as possible.

Top tennis pros who compete in exhibitions and special events and who are featured in TV coverage of tournaments acquire a celebrity/entertainer role as well as an athletic competitor role. Dislike of the former role may lead a player to quit the pro tour; according to one former pro:

> You have to be a certain type of person to fit into all of this. You are put on a stand and people look at you. That's what I have trouble with (Terry Rocavert, quoted in *Tennis*, 1980:14).

Other players relish the celebrity/entertainer role. Ilie Nastase is a particularly good example; at age 34 he no longer seems able to win a major tournament, but he is clearly reluctant to retire:

> I like people recognizing me in a restaurant and getting a table when it's crowded. It will bother me... when that stops. (Ilie Nastase, quoted in *Tennis*, 1980:14).

For women tennis pros, marriage and/or family considerations may be the reasons for retirement or temporary retirement, which explains why very few of the top women pros are married and few of those who are married have children. After Chris Evert at age 24 married British tennis pro John Lloyd, speculation immediately began about how much longer her career would continue. Evert has acknowledged her desire to have a family as well as to spend more time traveling with her husband on the men's tour, but she demonstrated at age 25 that she was not ready to retire by fighting her way to the championship of the U.S. Open. Evert notes that it is very difficult to give up something that has dominated her life since she was six years old.

Evonne Goolagong Cawley, mother of a 3-year-old daughter, won the Wimbledon championship at age 28:

> Before I had Kelly, I thought a family life might end tennis for me. If it had to come down to a choice between the two, I would drop tennis right away. But now that Kelly's become...a person, I realize I want to play the game again (Evonne Goolagong, quoted in Bodo, 1979a:50).

However, Goolagong does not want to play the tour on a regular basis; she hopes to perform well enough in selected tournaments to sustain a high ranking.

Karen Hantze Susman returned to competitive tennis at age 34 when her daughter had become a teenager. Susman won Wimbledon titles in 1961 and 1962 and the U.S. doubles title in 1964, but then left the circuit to devote full time to marriage. She competes on the Avon Futures circuit, playing tournaments located close to her home, and is ranked among the top 80 women:

> It's the challenge I like. I don't have a goal to be in the top 50 or 20, although I would like to be around 70 so it would be easier to get into the satellite draws... (Karen Susman, quoted in Doherty, 1980:24).

III. CONCLUSION: ASSESSING THE REWARDS OF A PRO TENNIS CAREER

Inherent in the changes which have taken place in professional tennis since 1926 is a changing reward structure.

Despite their high earnings, the pre-1968 (men) contract pos were migratory, seasonal workers who experienced physical hardships. According to Rod Laver, the last champion of the pro tour, "traveling around from state to state, getting caught in snowstorms and changing clothes in the car—that was the game as it was" (Trees, 1978:45). An even greater hardship was the pros' status as marginal men: players who were the best at their trade but who were barred from traditional tournament competition and were generally unnoticed except by tennis fans in the cities they happened to visit. The operation of Jack Kramer's tour has been described as analogous to the operation of professional wrestling, except that matches were not "fixed" (Lorge, 1978a).

The Touring Tennis Professional

Before large "secret" payments became customary for top amateurs in the 1960s, a top player could only choose between obscurity as a touring contract pro and financial hardship as an amateur. Vic Seixas was one of the few major championship winners who opted not to join Kramer's tour:

> People always asked me what my full-time job was. We were always scrounging, getting expenses, but we couldn't make any money.... It forced a lot of players out of tennis.... I left at age 34 to go into the brokerage business.... (Vic Seixas, quoted in Moore, 1980:22).

During the 1960s, about 35 of the top men received financial rewards for their tennis, but within a noninstitutionalized structure. There were few opportunities for upward mobility or financial rewards for players who were not among the top 35. Most players who participated in the "amateur/pro" years are critical of the dishonesty and lack of organization which characterized tennis. However, there were some enjoyable fringe benefits which accompanied their tournament work:

> Three or four nights there were functions to go to. People had house parties that all the players went along to.... We used to socialize with [the tournament organizers], with the local people, have a nice meal and some wine, maybe practice leisurely for an hour in the morning and play a match at two in the afternoon.... (Bob Carmichael, quoted in Lorge, 1978d:62).

After 1968, the tennis pro's work became significantly less peripheral to the main economy, influencing purchases of tennis-related and non-tennis-related products and visible to a wide public through TV coverage. Financial rewards and prestige became available to a much larger number of tennis pros—women as well as men. Individuals such as Jack Kramer and Donald Dell were able to accumulate power as well as financial rewards and prestige through professional tennis. However, elements of the earlier days of professional tennis are still visible. Appearance money is available outside the institutionalized prize money system. Most important, the number of marginal pros, especially among the men, is larger than ever. These are the satellite circuit competitors, who have been described as going up and down a one-way street (McDermott, 1980) but who continue to hope for a lucky break. Many of these players experience physical hardships in their efforts to minimize tournament expenses.

It is interesting to assess the rewards of professional tennis relative to the rewards of the other major individual sport in the United States, professional golf. The structure of the two sports is similar; players compete on "mini-tours" and must earn their "tour card," the equivalent of a computer ranking in tennis, in order to qualify for the Professional Golfers Association tour, which is the major circuit of golf. As in professional tennis, players are not supposed to accept appearance money. Financial rewards from prize money and endorsements have increased dramatically in recent years:

> Instead of traveling two to a Ford coupe from one tournament to the next, and sharing cramped quarters at a roadside motel..., today's golfers go by jet, live in luxurious quarters...and

get to see themselves in magazines and newspapers, and on television selling soap suds, clothing and golfing equipment (Bisher, 1980:23).

Colgate has sponsored women's golf as well as women's tennis, and a star such as Nancy Lopez can earn impressive amounts of money, but the rewards of professional golf for a woman are lessened by its tradition as a male sport. For both women and men, professional golf does not offer the same challenge of competing head-to-head as does professional tennis.

Although top tennis pros have year-long employment opportunities in exhibitions, special events, and endorsements, the opportunity for paid work, i.e., winning prize money in tournaments, is intermittent for the majority of players. However, nonpaid work, practicing, is constant for all tennis pros. Tennis is a full-time job for touring pros, both at the major circuit and the satellite circuit levels. With the exception of coaching professionals, most touring pros do not earn money from other jobs. Players may receive financial assistance from their families; players who have achieved a good record as juniors may receive financial backing from their local tennis association.

The touring pro must be "unbelievably single-minded" (Benton, 1980). He or she must adjust to "the constant travel, the dragging of equipment from city to city, the hotel rooms...." (*Tennis*, 1979:13). Life is not necessarily glamorous, even for tennis's most highly paid professional, Bjorn Borg. For the nine months of the year during which they live in hotels, Borg's wife has provided this description of their typical daily routine:

> We get up and order breakfast from room service. Then we practice, come back to the hotel and order room service. Then Bjorn practices again, if he's not playing a match, and then we come back and order room service. Very glamorous, isn't it? (Mariana Borg, quoted in Phillips, 1980:59).

Although the financial incentive cannot be discounted, the primary rewards of a pro tennis career, for players at the top or near the bottom of the pro-ranks, stem from a love for the game:

> I really don't enjoy the travel. I miss my home and friends. But I enjoy the sport very much.... (Ivanna Madruga, 16th-ranked woman, quoted in LaMarche, 1980a:102).

> It's a lot of hard work, a lot of ups and downs. But the highs are so high that they make the lows a lot easier to handle. (Mary Carillo, 40th-ranked woman, quoted in *Tennis*, 1979:12).

> If given the choice between a million dollars or playing the circuit, there is no question as to what I'd do—I would play. (Mark Hardy, satellite circuit player, quoted in Danzell, 1980:43).

The thrill of successful competition, whether yielding a number-one ranking or one computer point on the satellite circuit, is the strongest attraction of the peripheral world of work which is professional tennis.

ACKNOWLEDGMENTS

Information for this chapter was gathered through interviews with the USTA Women's Coordinator and with the Vice President of Marketing and the Director of Public Relations of ProServ, Inc. The author has informally followed tennis pro careers since receiving coaching from Pauline Betz and competing at the state and national levels in junior tennis.

REFERENCES

Adams, Susan B.
    1980 "Chris Evert Lloyd takes stock at 25." World Tennis 27: 24-26, 53.
Benton, Ray
    1980 Personal communication (December 6).
Bisher, Furman
    1980 "Women at play-for-pay." Sky Magazine 9: 20:22, 24.
Blanton, Dewey and Tom Ross
    1980 "To Wimbledon via Rockwall." International Tennis Weekly 5: 4-5.
Bodo, Peter
    1979a "Evonne Goolagong: the rebirth of a champion." Tennis 15: 50-51, 54, 56, 58, 60, 63-64.
    1979b "Why women's tennis is producing those whiz kids." Tennis 15: 39-41.
    1980a "The eternal youth of Marty Riessen." Tennis 15: 88-89.
    1980b "Where is pro tennis headed?" Tennis 16: 24TV-30TV.
Bookman, Ron
    1980 "Arthur Ashe: still classy after all these years." World Tennis 28: 26-30.
"Chris Evert Lloyd: Her Last Hurrah?"
    1980 Tennis 15: 10.
"Chris' Future"
    1979 Tennis 15: 8, 10.
Collins, Bud
    1974 "The postwar pro game." Pp. 63-67 in The Encyclopedia of Tennis. New York: The Viking Press.
Cubbedge, Robert
    1980 "Net profits: you'll be astounded at how much the pros make." Tennis 16: 34, 36-37.
Danzell, Bill
    1980 "The sun never sets on the satellite player." World Tennis 28: 39-43.
"Disappearing act"
    1980 Tennis 16: 10
Doherty, Donna
    1980 "Karen Susman: glad to be back." Tennis 16: 24.
"Do marriage and professional tennis mix?"
    1980 Tennis 15: 8.
Gamarekian, Barbara
    1980 "Dell, Craighill: lawyer racqueteers." New York Times 130: III-8.
Heldman, Gladys M.
    1974 "The women's pro game." Pp. 68-71 in The Encyclopedia of Tennis. New York: The Viking Press.
Kramer, Jack and Frank Deford
    1978 "A little hanky-panky, but no fixes." Sports Illustrated 48: 26-30, 71.
LaMarche, Robert J.
    1980a "Player to watch: Ivanna Madruga." Tennis 16: 101-102.

1980b "The campus champs: Peter Rennert and Wendy White named 1980 college players-of-the-year." Tennis 16: 103.

Lorge, Barry
 1978a "The way we were, the way we are." World Tennis 26: 19-22.
 1978b "Meet the most powerful man in tennis." World Tennis 26: 18-22, 25.
 1978c "'Donald Dell is like E. F. Hutton: when he talks, you listen.'" World Tennis 26: 61-64, 66, 68, 70-72.
 1978d "Whatever happened to the tennis bums?" World Tennis 26: 58-63.
 1979 "How a pro finds happiness on $384,663 a year." World Tennis 27: 61-63.

McDermott, Barry
 1980 "Starting out or ending up." Sports Illustrated 52: 86-90, 92, 94, 96, 98, 100.

Metcalfe, Steve
 1979 "The donkey circuit: it's a long way to the top of the tennis world." Racquet 69: 24-28.

Moore, Judy
 1980 "Goodness Seixas." World Tennis 28: 22.

Morgan, Park
 1980 "King: someone willing to take risk." The Atlanta Journal/Constitution: 19D.

"Passing Shots"
 1979 Tennis 15: 14.

Perry, Fred
 1974 "The start of the pro game." Pp. 60-62 in the Encyclopedia of Tennis. New York: The Viking Press.

Phillips, B. J.
 1980 "The tennis machine." Time 115: 54-59.

"Quotes-of-the-month"
 1979 Tennis 15: 12.
 1980 Tennis 16: 14.

Trees, Susie
 1978 "Here's to the winners." World Tennis 25: 43-47.

USTA Education and Research Center
 1980 "Are you interested in becoming a playing professional?"

Wilson, Sally
 1980 "Lloyd's at the top of her game." The Atlanta Constitution (September 24): ID, 4D.

Wiltse, David
 1980 "Inside tennis' toughest school." Tennis 16: 43-45.

SELF-EMPLOYMENT AS A CYCLICAL ESCAPE FROM UNEMPLOYMENT: A CASE STUDY OF THE CONSTRUCTION INDUSTRY IN THE UNITED STATES DURING THE POSTWAR PERIOD

Marc Linder

The lateral and vertical advance of industrial capitalism during the past two centuries has ousted economically "independent" producers from their key positions within the economic system, transforming them into occupants of a distinctly peripheral role.[1] That significant numbers of unemployed workers periodically seek refuge in various kinds of self-employed activities to tide themselves over until new employment opportunities arise, underscores the subordinate macrosocial status to which self-employment has been reduced.

Some controversy has surrounded the empirical issue of cyclical changes in self-employment in the United States during the post-World War II period.[2] Although it has been suggested that aggregate self-employment does behave countercyclically (Bregger, 1963)—that is, rising during periods of growing unemployment—other research has urged caution in drawing such a conclusion (Ray, 1975).

A major obstacle to meaningful empirical studies of the behavior of aggregate self-employment derives from the extraordinary heterogeneity of the self-employed as a socioeconomic stratum. Encompassing such disparate occupational agents as surgeons, corporate lawyers, athletes, and entertainers receiving the highest "earned" incomes offered by society, wealthy farmers and poverty-stricken sharecroppers, merchants, independent artisans, craftsmen and mechanics, taxicab drivers and peddlers, this grouping represents an ensemble of "life chances" as diversified as that of society as a whole. A category of socioeconomic agents defined by their ownership and operation of a business irrespective of whether they employ workers or whether their income exceeds that of an unskilled employee[3] is ill designed as the object of an empirical study that presupposes the existence of a uniform and unitary response to socioeconomic stimuli.

In order to avoid some of these pitfalls, the present study focuses on a delimited and hence more homogeneous sphere of self-employment—the construction industry. The trades constituting this industry, which have accounted for one-ninth to one-sixth of all nonfarm self-employment during the postwar period (Table 1; Ray, 1975:Table 1 at 51; Employment and Earnings 22, no. 7, January 1976:148; Employment and Earnings 24, no. 1, January 1977:153; Employment and Earnings 25, no. 1, January 1978:155; Employment and Earnings 26, no. 1, January 1979:174; Employment and Earnings 27, no. 1, January 1980:176) represent the largest contingent of the manual self-employed (Bregger, 1963:Tables 4 and 5 at 40; Ray, 1975:50). In addition to eliminating discrepancies arising from the characteristic differences in employment security between blue-collar and white-collar workers, an examination of the construction industry with its traditionally sexually homogeneous labor force (Anderson and Davidson, 1940:178; U.S. Bureau of Labor Statistics, 1975:Table 39 at 105 and Table 44 at 115) helps to disentangle the issue of female "attachment" to the labor force in general from that of cyclical changes in self-employment.[4]

Self-employment has long played a prominent part in the building trades (Bridenbaugh, 1950:75-76; Weyforth, 1917:181-192; Montgomery, 1927:155; Derber, 1953:I, 673, 707; Bertram, 1966:2; Beeks, 1887:123; Myers, 1945:81; The Carpenter 6, no. 6, 1886:3; The Carpenter 13, no. 8, 1893:3; The Carpenter 25, no. 6, 1905:12-13; The American Architect and Building News 82, no. 1505, 1904:33). Even today, relatively minimal capital requirements in carpentry, painting, plumbing, electrical work,[5] and particularly in repair and maintenance work (U.S. Bureau of Labor Statistics, 1949:4) place single proprietorships[6] within the potential reach of large numbers of skilled craftsmen (Immer, 1962:15). In view of the comparatively high levels of cyclical as well as seasonal and frictional employment experienced by contract[7] construction workers (Mills, 1967; U.S. Bureau of Labor Statistics, 1970), temporary shifts to self-employment may offer a means of escaping unemployment for some building tradesmen (Landay, 1957:6; Strasser, 1970:9; Enquete über die Bauwirtschaft, 1973:II, 159-161).

In order to determine how realistic this possibility is, year-to-year changes in construction self-employment may be compared with those in unemployment. Such an approach is, to be sure, problematic inasmuch as construction workers do not represent the only source of the self-employed in construction trades whereas some formerly self-employed construction workers may seek wage-employment in other branches or leave the labor force entirely.[8] Nevertheless, given the skills required to perform construction work on one's own account, employees of the construction industry represent the source and destination of most self-employed construction workers in transition (cf. Foster, 1970; Sommers and Eck, 1977). In the following discussion the self-employed will be examined in connection with the narrow category of "construction workers" (including working supervisors), i.e., production workers.[9]

Between 1948 and 1979, the self-employed in construction as a share of the total of the self-employed and construction workers declined from 26.5% to 23.4% (the lowest value—18.7%—was reached in 1969). This decline resulted from an increase of 92.7% in the number of construction workers, as compared with a rise of 62.7% in the number of self-employed (see Table 1). In contrast, aggregate nonagricultural self-employment accounted for a much smaller share of nonagricultural employment at the outset of the period (12.0%) and declined more precipitously (to 7.7% in 1979). Although the absolute number of nonfarm self-employed rose by 8.9%, this increase occurred exclusively between 1976 and 1979; as late as 1976 there were 420,000 fewer self-employed than in 1948.[10]

Between 1948 and 1975[11] the share of self-employment in the construction industry rose in ten of the years; eight of these increases corresponded to a rise in the rate of unemployment among wage and salary workers in private construction.[12] Similarly, eight of the eleven annual increases in the rate of unemployment were accompanied by a rise in the share of self-employment.[13] Of these eight years, six were characterized by absolute increases in the number of self-employed;[14] and of these six, in turn, five were additionally characterized by absolute decreases in the number of construction workers.[15]

The foregoing data suggest a pronounced countercyclical development of self-employment in the construction trades. Correlation analysis of unemployment and self-employment supports this conclusion. For the years 1948 to 1975 the rate of unemployment and the share of self-employment are positively correlated; the coefficient of determination (r^2) is 0.26. For the shorter period between 1956 and 1969 the coefficient of determination is 0.91.[16] For the entire nonagricultural sector, on the other hand, a negative correlation obtains for the years 1948 to 1975, resulting in an insignificant coefficient of determination of 0.01.[17] A comparison of the absolute number of unemployed and self-employed in the

Table 1. The Self-Employed, Unemployed, and Construction Workers in the Construction Industry in the United States, 1948-1979

Year	Self-Employed (1) (000s)	Construction workers (2) (000s)	(1) as a percent of (1)+(2) (3)	Unemployed (4) (000s)	Rate of unemployment (5) (percent)
1948	695	1,924	26.5	207	8.7
1949	687	1,919	26.4	352	13.9
1950	696	2,069	25.2	329	12.2
1951	691	2,308	23.0	196	7.2
1952	687	2,324	22.8	194	6.7
1953	655	2,305	22.1	206	7.2
1954	699	2,281	23.5	367	12.9
1955	727	2,440	23.0	333	10.9
1956	708	2,613	21.3	301	10.0
1957	736	2,537	22.5	367	10.9
1958	745	2,384	23.8	543	15.3
1959	769	2,538	23.3	481	13.4
1960	758	2,459	23.6	483	13.5
1961	727	2,390	23.3	564	15.7
1962	724	2,462	22.7	483	13.5
1963	748	2,523	22.9	476	13.3
1964	768	2,597	22.8	407	11.2
1965	730	2,710	21.2	378	10.1
1966	696	2,784	20.0	298	8.0
1967	648	2,708	19.3	275	7.4
1968	664	2,786	19.2	259	6.9
1969	685	2,973	18.7	234	6.0
1970	686	2,951	18.9	394	9.7
1971	710	3,023	19.0	447	10.4
1972	741	3,166	19.0	466	10.3
1973	803	3,325	19.5	417	8.8
1974	864	3,234	21.1	499	10.6
1975	827	2,761	23.0	831	18.1
1976	863	2,814	23.5	718	15.6
1977	933	3,021	23.6	607	12.7
1978	1,072	3,388	24.0	541	10.6
1979	1,131	3,708	23.4	548	10.2

Sources: Column (1). Self-employed in construction. 1948-60: Lebergott, 1964:Table A-7 at 516; 1961: Bregger, 1963:Table 4 at 40; 1962-75: information provided by the U.S. Bureau of Labor Statistics to the author, dated January 1976; 1976: Employment and Earnings 24, no. 1, 1977:154; 1977: Employment and Earnings 25, no. 1, 1978:156; 1978: Employment and Earnings 26, no. 1, 1979:175; 1979: Employment and Earnings 27, no. 1, 1980:177.

Column (2). Construction workers in contract construction. 1948-73: U.S. Bureau of Labor Statistics, 1975: Table 41 at 108; 1974-75: Employment and Earnings 22, no. 7, 1976:164; 1976-79: Employment and Earnings 27, no. 1, 1980:205.

(*Table 1.* Continued)

Column (4). Experienced unemployed private wage and salary workers in construction. 1948-52: U.S. Bureau of Labor Statistics, 1970:Table 53 at 52. Unemployed wage and salary workers in construction. 1953-59: ILO, 1960:203; 1960-61: ILO, 1964:256; 1962-75: information provided by the U.S. Bureau of Labor Statistics to the author, dated January 1976; 1976: Employment and Earnings 24, no. 1, 1977:150; 1977: Employment and Earnings 25, no. 1, 1978:150; 1978: Employment and Earnings 26, no. 1, 1979:169; 1979: Employment and Earnings 27, no. 1, 1980:171.

Column (5). Rate of unemployment among private wage and salary workers in construction. 1948-74: U.S. Bureau of Labor Statistics, 1975:Table 73 at 172; 1975-77: U.S. Bureau of Labor Statistics, 1979:213; 1978-79: Employment and Earnings 27, no. 1, 1980:167.

construction industry yields a considerably higher positive correlation: for the years 1948 to 1975 the coefficient of determination is 0.54.[18] The aggregate nonfarm sector once again exhibits a negative correlation without statistical significance ($r^2 = 0.002$).

For the years 1975 through 1979, the highly positive corelation between self-employment and unemployment in the construction industry ceases to apply:[19] an unprecedented increase in self-employment of 304,000 stands against a decrease of 283,000 in the number of unemployed. Two factors may have contributed to this new pattern. First, whereas the very high level of aggregate unemployment during these years may have encouraged the unemployed from other branches to seek employment and self-employment in construction, it discouraged those who might have left the construction industry from seeking employment elsewhere. Second, the number of new nonfarm, one-family private housing starts also grew at an unprecedented rate.[20] Since this subbranch of the construction industry has traditionally provided the greatest competitive opportunities for small firms (U.S. Bureau of Labor Statistics, 1970:134-135; Sumicharast and Frankel, 1970; Lasch, 1946:10, 83; Laitila, 1969-1970; National Association of Home Builders, 1959; U.S.Bureau of Labor Statistics, 1954; Colean, 1944; Foster, 1974), the self-employed presumably benefitted disproportionally.[21]

Figures 1 and 2 present a schematic overview of the model of cyclical labor flows which was sketched above. During a recession/depression additional self-employed construction tradesmen are recruited from the ranks of construction workers and the unemployed in construction as well as from outside the industry (i.e., from among other workers and unemployed workers and those outside the labor force such as the retired). Those construction workers who cannot or do not wish to remain in the industry as self-employed become unemployed, enter other industries, or leave the labor force. Competitive conditions will also enforce a certain amount of turnover among those who were already self-employed in construction prior to this time, compelling them to make decisions similar to those of construction workers.[22]

During a cyclical upswing, on the other hand, rising demand for, and wage rates of, skilled construction workers cause their ranks to be swelled by the

Figure 1. Schematic Model of the Cyclical Recruitment and Discharge of the Labor Force in the Construction Industry: Recession/Depression Phase

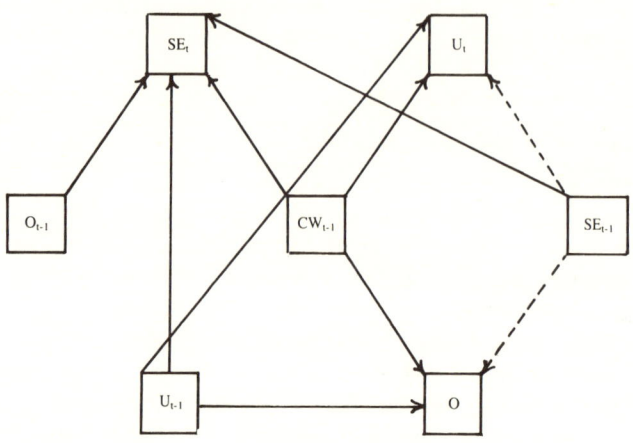

Notes: CW: construction workers O: others
SE: self-employed in construction U: unemployed in construction
t: this period t-1: previous period
main flow ⟶ subsidiary flow ---⟶

marginally self-employed in construction as well as by the unemployed and workers from other industries. Some unemployed construction workers and self-employed, still unable to find employment in construction, will leave the industry. A small segment of construction workers from the previous period will retire or lose their jobs (either to more-efficient workers or as a result of shifts in demand for certain types of skills).

The relative insensitivity of aggregate self-employment to changes in unemployment must be viewed in the context of the aforementioned heterogeneous composition of this stratum. Among the highly trained and well-compensated professional occupations (such as medicine and law) macro-economically determined, cyclical, intragenerational shifting between self-employment and salaried employment has traditionally been uncommon.[23] For different reasons two-way shifting within the wholesale and retail trade sector is also unlikely to be widespread: it is implausible that significant numbers of small owners close their businesses during upswings in order to take advantage of salaried employment as managers, clerks, or salespersons in larger corporate entities, planning to reopen their stores during the next period of unemployment.[24] Such behavior would be more common in service establishments requiring minimal capital investment; in particular less-skilled members of the labor force may be expected to display persistent shifting patterns.[25]

Construction workers, on the other hand, have proven to be one of very few

Figure 2. Schematic Model of the Cyclical Recruitment and Discharge of the Labor Force in the Construction Industry: Prosperity Phase

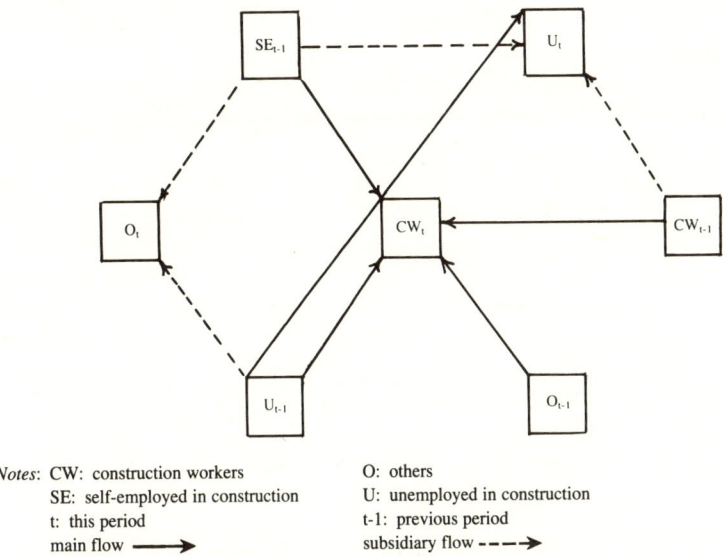

Notes: CW: construction workers   O: others
SE: self-employed in construction   U: unemployed in construction
t: this period   t-1: previous period
main flow ⟶   subsidiary flow ---⟶

occupational groups engaged in recurrent intraindustry two-way shifting between self-employment and wage-work. Three peculiarities of the construction industry have contributed to this blurring of socioeconomic class lines (cf. Strauss, 1958:69; Seidman et al., 1958:54). First, the retardation of capital-intensive methods of industrial production (Fitch, 1948; Gangl, 1970; v. Gottl-Ottilienfeld, 1923:58: Stone, 1966; Schon, 1967:156-158; Batelle, 1967; Report of the President's Committee on Urban Housing, 1968) has preserved a quasi-artisanal skill structure among building tradesmen (Perry, 1965; U.S. Bureau of Labor Statistics, 1959: 5, 28; U.S. Bureau of Apprenticeship, 1954). Second, the concomitant absence of phenomena of concentration and centralization of capital and labor [26] has provided these skilled workers with a relatively high degree of access to self-employment in general. Third, the seasonal and casual nature of employment in contract construction (Scheuch, 1951:41-42, 172; Gordon et al., 1973; U.S. Congress, 1968; Wittrock, 1967; Myers and Swerdloff, 1967; Rothschild, 1965) has induced workers to avail themselves of the opportunity to employ themselves in order to avoid unemployment without being forced to relinquish exercise of their skills.

Although the self-employed tend on the average to receive lower annual incomes than skilled building tradesmen (U.S. Dept. of Health, Education and Welfare, 1965:36, 44; Bregger, 1963:42; Ray, 1975:49), the fact that they may receive more than unemployment benefits (U.S. Dept. of Health, Education and Welfare, 1965:44; U.S. Bureau of the Census, 1975a:Series H 309-310 at 354;

U.S. Bureau of Labor Statistics, 1970:56) doubtless encourages some construction workers to form their own businesses. But in spite of the tenacity with which the self-employed attempt to maintain their status (Steindl, 1945:61; Mayer and Goldstein, 1964:550), prolonged depressions such as that of the 1930s hasten the exodus from and inhibit the flow into small proprietorships.

Dual-class careers in the construction trades have exerted an enduring influence on the attitudes of construction workers and the character of industrial relations. Experience as owners of the means of production with the ultimate authority and responsibility for the fulfillment of contractual obligations and—in some cases—as employers of other workers may engender a degree of understanding for the viewpoint of employers among construction workers who have been self-employed.[27] Given the disruptive effect of cyclical self-employment on the "permanent and stable organization" (Dunlop, 1948:184) of the labor market by trade unions as well as the divisiveness involve in enforcing union standards in the case of subcontracting members (Haber, 1930:215-217), some building trades unions have prohibited members from joining the ranks of contractors (The Carpenter 10, no. 11, 1890:4; The Carpenter 11, no. 2, 1891:1; The Carpenter 12, no. 9, 1892:3; cf., however, U.S. Senate, 1885:I, 410-411).

ACKNOWLEDGEMENTS

John Bregger and Alan Paisner of the U.S. Bureau of Labor Statistics helped the author in collecting data; Leonel Corona of the Graduate Dept. of Economics, National Autonomous University of Mexico (Mexico City), provided computer services for the correlation analysis.

NOTES

1. For Marx the peripheral or quasi-extraterritorial status of independent commodity production within the capitalist mode of production was not only empirical but also categorical (1861-1863:382-384; cf. Harris, 1939:328-356). On the notion of independent commodity production as an autonomous mode of production, see Linder, 1975:151-175; cf. Blaug, 1968:238.

2. On the period prior to World War II, see Woytinsky, 1953:330-331.

3. On the so-called proletaroid self-employed, see Sombart, 1954:455-458; Geiger, 1972:30-47.

4. In 1979, for example, women accounted for 29.1% of all nonfarm self-employed but only 2.2% of the self-employed in the construction industry. Self-employed males in the construction industry accounted for 23.4% of all nonfarm self-employed males (Employment and Earnings 27, no. 1, January 1980:176-177).

5. In 1972 the average gross book value of depreciable assets for individual proprietorship establishments of single-unit companies with payroll for the four trades mentioned in the text amounted to $4,771, $4,985, $14,985. and $11,940, respectively (U.S. Bureau of the Census, 1975b:Table 2 at 12-13, 15). The establishments without payroll, for which no data on assets were collected, are only one-fifth to one-seventh the size of the establishments with payroll in terms of receipts (U.S. Bureau of the Census, 1975b:Table 1 at 4-5). In the same year the average special trade constractor with 10-19 employees possessed depreciable assets of less than $50,000 (U.S. Bureau of the Census, 1975c:Table B4 at 1-13).

6. Neither the monthly data on the self-employed collected by the Bureau of the Census for the Bureau of Labor Statistics nor the annual Business Tax Returns published by the Internal Revenue Service distinguish between employers and those who work "on own account" without employees. The postwar Census of Construction Industries has, however, collected data on establishments with and without payroll. Thus, in 1972 70.5% of all individual proprietors owned construction establishments without payroll (U.S. Bureau of the Census, 1975B:Table 1 at 4). Beginning in 1967 the Bureau of the Census reclassified proprietors who had incorporated their businesses as employees of their new corporations (Ray, 1975:50).

7. "Contract" construction workers exclude those who work for nonconstruction businesses as well as for the various levels of government.

8. The Social Security Administration can tabulate such data (Svolos, 1966:38; cf. U.S. Bureau of Labor Statistics, 1970:42).

9. Nonprivate wage workers have been disregarded because they experience considerably less unemployment (U.S. Bureau of Labor Statistics, 1970:38, n. 31). Elimination of unskilled workers would sharpen the focus of the study.

10. On the long-term trend of aggregate self-employment, see Denison, 1974:Table C-6 at 173; Lebergott, 1964:514, 516; Phillips, 1962.

11. The years 1975 to 1979 are discussed later.

12. The two exceptions were 1963, when a minor decline in the rate of unemployment occurred, and 1973, when the decline was steeper.

13. The three exceptions were 1949, 1953 and 1961. The mass influx of World War II veterans into construction self-employment may, by having exhausted the source of new entrants temporarily, have been responsible for the development in 1949 (Mangum, 1964:233). The Korean War curtailed opportunities for self-employment in general.

14. The exceptions were 1960 and 1975.

15. The exception was 1971.

16. Both are significant at the .01 level. The data on proprietors collected annually by the Internal Revenue service and published in its "Statistics of Income—Business Income Tax Returns" do not exhibit the same pronounced cyclicity as do the data collected by the Bureau of the Census. The definitional basis differs between the two agencies.

17. For the years 1956-1969, the correlation is positive and the coefficient of determination is 0.56.

18. Multiple correlation analysis, including lagged unemployment as a variable, revealed a still higher positive correlation.

19. For the whole period between 1948 and 1979 the correlation between the absolute number of self-employed and unemployed is positive; the coefficient of determination is 0.38.

20. Between 1975 and 1977 they rose from 892,000 to 1,451,000, or by 62.7%, to the highest level ever recorded (U.S. Bureau of the Census, 1975a:Series N 159 at 639: U.S. Bureau of the Census, 1980:3). The somewhat lower level—1,194,000 units—recorded in 1979 had, prior to 1977, been exceeded only once.

21. Data from the Census of Construction Industries on single-family housing contractors are not available; among firms with payroll in 1972, such contractors employed on the average five employees compared to 9.5 for the whole industry (U.S. Bureau of the Census, 1975c: Table A1 at 1-2 and Table B1 at 1-8; cf. Kaplan, 1958).

22. In point of fact, comparatively few self-employed are registered as unemployed (Bregger, 1963:42).

23. For personal professional reasons lawyers and physicians may, of course, practice individually or for institutions, corporations, or governments successively—or even concurrrently. Some professions are also subject to a long-term, permanent absorption into the salariat. Lawyers in individual private practice, for example, declined from 58.3% of all practicing lawyers in 1948 to 36.9% in 1970 (U.S. Bureau of the Census, 1975a:Series H 1046-1061 at 416).

24. It is more plausible, however, that in businesses operated by (unpaid) family members some of the latter leave periodically while the enterprise itself remains intact.

25. More highly skilled employees who earn a secondary income in a self-employed capacity may also have recourse to the latter for full-time work when they lose their primary employment (Ray, 1975:51). This mechanism has been repeatedly documented for part-time farmers in the Federal Republic of Germany (Preuschen, 1969).

26. In 1970, manufacturing corporations with assets in excess of $50 million accounted for 79% of all corporate assets in manufacturing; the corresponding figure for construction was approximately 14% (U.S. Internal Revenue Service, 1970:35-36). In 1972, companies in manufacturing industries employing more than 10,000 employees accounted for 45.2% of all employees in manufacturing; the corresponding figure for constructing companies was 2.9% (U.S. Bureau of Census, 1977:142, 144, 148). Similarly, 55.6% of construction companies in 1972 employed no one, in contrast with 7.8% of manufacturing companies (U.S. Bureau of the Census, 1977:142, 144, 148).

27. A study of West German industrial workers who also worked part-time in a self-employed capacity pointed out that industrial enterprises desired employees who appreciated the social significance of privately owned productive property (Wagener et al., 1959:98; Linder, 1974).

REFERENCES

American Architect and Building News
   1904   86,no. 1505:33
Anderson, H. Dewey, and Percy E. Davidson
   1940   Occupational Trends in the United States. Stanford, Cal.: Stanford University Press.
Batelle Memorial Institute
   1967   The State of the Art of Prefabrication in the Construction Industry. Columbus: Batelle.
Beeks, James.C.
   1887   30,000 Locked Out. Chicago: Grindele.
Bertram, Gordon W.
   1966   Consolidated Bargaining in California Construction. Los Angeles: University of California.
Blaug, Mark
   [1962] Economic Theory in Retrospect. Homewood, IL.: Irwin.
   1968
Bregger, John
   1963   "Self-employment in the United States." Monthly Labor Review 86 (1):37-43
Bridenbaugh, Carl
   1950   The Colonial Craftsman. New York: New York University Press.
Carpenter, The
   1886-
   1905
Colean, Miles
   1944   American Housing. New York: Twentieth Century Fund.
Denison, Edward
   1974   Accounting for United States Economic Growth, 1929-1969. Washington, D.C.: Brookings.
Derber, Milton
   1953   "Building construction." Pp. 659-785 in W. Ellison Chalmers et al. Labor Management Relations in Illini City, Vol. I. Champaign: University of Illinois.
Dunlop, John T.
   1948   "The development of labor organization: a theoretical perspective." Pp. 163-93 in Richard A. Lester, and Joseph Shister (eds.), Insights into Labor Issues. New York: Macmillan.

Employment and Earnings
    1977-
    1980
Enquete über die Bauwirtschaft
    1973   Commissioned by the Federal Minister of Economics. Vol. II. [West] Berlin.
Fitch, James M.
    1948   American Building. Boston: Houghton Mifflin.
Foster, Howard G.
    1970   "Labor force adjustments to seasonal fluctuations in construction." Industrial and Labor Relations Review 23:528-40.
Foster, Howard G.
    1974   Manpower in Homebuilding. Philadelphia: University of Pennsylvania.
Gangl, Norbert
    1970   "Die Engpässe für eine konsequent industrialisierte Wohnbauwirtschaft—Ansätze zu einem Modell der industrialisierten Wohnbauwirtschaft." Diss. Hochschule St. Gallen.
Geiger, Theodor
    [1932] Die soziale Schichtung des deutschen Volkes.
    1972   Darmstadt: Wissenschaftliche Buchgesellschaft.
Gordon, Jerome, et al.
    1973   Year-Round Employment in the Construction Industry. New York: Praeger.
v. Gottl-Ottlilienfeld, Friedrich
    1923   Wirtschaft und Technik. Tübingen: Mohr.
Haber, William
    1930   Industrial Relations in the Building Industry. Cambridge, Mass.: Harvard University Press.
Harris, Abram L.
    1939   "Pure capitalism and the disappearance of the middle class." Journal of Political Economy 47:328-356.
Immer, John R.
    1962   Starting and Managing a Small Building Business. Washington, D.C.: Small Business Administration.
International Labour Office
    1960   Year Book of Labour Statistics, 1960, Twentieth Issue. Geneva.
    1964   Year Book of Labour Statistics, 1964, Twenty-Fourth Issue. Geneva.
Kaplan, Lawrence J.
    1958   "Factors affecting productivity in the homebuilding industry." Dissertation, Columbia University.
Laitila, Edward E.
    1969-   "The small home builder in today's economy."
    1970   Small Business Administration Economic Review 3 (1):9-16.
Landay, Donald M.
    1957   "Characteristics of unemployment in contract construction, 1956-1957." Construction Review 3 (12):4-8.
Lasch, R.
    1946   Breaking the Building Blockade. Chicago: University of Chicago Press.
Lebergott, Stanley
    1964   Manpower in Economic Growth. New York: McGraw Hill.
Linder, Marc
    1974   "Bauern als 'selbständige' bzw. 'kleine' Warenproduzenten." Hohenheim University (Unpublished).
    1975   Reification and the Consciousness of the Critics of Political Economy. Copenhagen: Rhodos.

Mangum, Garth L.
  1964   The Operating Engineers. Cambridge, Mass.: Harvard University Press.
Marx, Karl
  1861-
  1863   Theorien über den Mehrwert. Vol. 26, Part 1 in Karl Marx and Friedrich Engels, Werke. 40 vols. Berlin [DDR]: Dietz, 1958-1968.
Mayer, Kurt B., and Sidney Goldstein
  1964   "Manual workers as small businessmen." Pp. 537-50 in A.B. Shostak, and W. Gomberg (eds.), Blue-Collar World. Englewood Cliffs, N.J.: Prentice-Hall.
Mills, Daniel Q.
  1967   "Factors determining patterns of employment and unemployment in the construction industry of the United States." Dissertation, Harvard University.
Montgomery, Royal
  1927   Industrial Relations in the Chicago Building Trades. Chicago: University of Chicago Press.
Myers, Richard R.
  1945   "The building workers. The study of an industrial sub-culture." Dissertation, University of Michigan.
Myers, Robert J., and Sol Swerdloff
  1967   "Seasonality in construction." Monthly Labor Review 90 (9):1-8.
National Association of Home Builders
  1959   The NAHB Membership Survey: A Study of Builders and the Homes They Build. Vol. I. Washington, D.C.: NAHB.
Perry, Herbert Anthony
  1965   "A study of the procedures for training manual skills at a time of technical change in the contemporary construction of the United States with some comparisons relating to that of Great Britain." Dissertation, University of London.
Phillips, Joseph D.
  1962   The Self-Employed in the United States. Urbana: University of Illinois.
Preuschen, Gerhardt
  1969   Landwirtschaft im Nebenerwerb. Hamburg and [West] Berlin: Parey.
Ray, Robert N.
  1975   "A report on self-employed Americans in 1973." Monthly Labor Review 98 (1):49-54.
Report of the President's Committee on Urban Housing.
  1968   Technical Studies. Vol. II. Washington, D.C.: U.S. Government Printing Office.
Rothschild, K.W.
  [1954] The Theory of Wages. Oxford: Blackwell
  1965
Scheuch, Richard
  1951   "The labor factor in residential construction." Dissertation, Princeton University.
Schon, Donald A.
  1967   Technology and Change. New York: Delta.
Seidman, J., J. London, B. Karsh and D.L. Tagiacozzo
  1958   The Worker Views His Union. Chicago: University of Chicago Press.
Sombart, Werner
  [1903] Die deutsche Volkswirtschaft im neunzehnten Jahr-
  1954   hundert. Darmstadt: Wissenschaftliche Buchgesellschaft.
Sommers, Dixie, and Alan Eck
  1977   "Occupational mobility in the American labor force." Monthly Labor Review 100:3-19.
Steindl, J.
  1945   Small and Big Business. Oxford: Blackwell.

Stone, P.A.
   1966   Building Economy. Oxford: Pergamon.

Strasser, Arnold
   1970   "Annual earnings in construction." Construction Review 16 (3):4-10.

Strauss, George
   1958   Unions in the Building Trades. Buffalo: University of Buffalo.

Sumichrast, Michael, and Sara Frankel
   1970   Profile of the Builder and His Industry. Washington, D.C.: NAHB.

Svolos, Sebastia
   1966   "Measures of labor mobility and OASDHI data." Social Security Bulletin 29(4):38-45.

U.S. Bureau of Apprenticeship
   1954   A Study of Census Data of the Craftsmen Population of the United States 1870-1950. The Skilled Labor Force. Technical Bulletin T-140.

U.S. Bureau of Labor Statistics
   1949   Bulletin 967: Employment Outlook in the Building Trades. Washington, D.C.: U.S. Government Printing Office.
   1954   Bulletin 1170: Structure of the Residential Building Industry in 1949. Washington, D.C.: U.S. Government Printing Office.
   1959   The Construction Worker in the United States. Washington, D.C.
   1970   Bulletin 1642: Seasonality and Manpower in Construction. Washington, D.C.: U.S. Government Printing Office.
   1975   Bulletin 1865: Handbook of Labor Statistics 1975. Washington, D.C.: U.S. Government Printing Office.
   1979   Bulletin 2000: Handbook of Labor Statistics 1978. Washington, D.C.: U.S. Government Printing Office.

U.S. Bureau of the Census
   1975a   Historical Statistics of the United States, Colonial Times to 1970, Bicentennial Edition. Washington, D.C.: U.S. Government Printing Office.
   1975b   Census of Construction Industries, 1972, Special Report Series, Type of Operation and Legal Form of Organization, CC72-S-1. Washington, D.C.: U.S. Government Printing Office.
   1975c   Census of Construction Industries, 1972, Industry Series, United States Summary, CC7 2-I-1. Washington, D.C.: U.S. Government Printing Office.
   1977   1972 Enterprise Statistics, Part 1: General Report on Industrial Organization. Washington, D.C.: U.S. Government Printing Office.
   1980   Construction Reports, Series C20. February.

U.S. Congress, House of Representatives, Committee on Education and Labor, Select Subcommittee on Labor
   1968   Seasonal Unemployment in the Construction Industry: Hearings on H.R. 15990. 90th Congress, 2nd Session.

U.S. Department of Health, Education and Welfare, Social Security Administration
   1965   Handbook of Old Age, Survivors, and Disability Insurance Statistics: Employment, Earnings, and Insurance Status of Workers in Covered Employment, 1957. Baltimore: HEW.

U.S. Internal Revenue Service
   1973   Statistics of Income—1970, Corporate Income Tax Returns. Washington, D.C.: U.S. Government Printing Office.

U.S. Senate
   1885   Report of the Committee of the Senate upon the Relations between Labor and Capital. Vol. I. Washington: U.S. Government Printing Office.

Wagener, H., H.J. Diehl, and W. Thamm
   1959   Verbreitung, Situation und Bedeutung der landbesitzenden Industriearbeiter im Einflussbereich verschiedenartiger Industrien. Bonn: Forschungsgesellschaft für Agrarpolitik und Agrarsoziologie.

Weyforth, William O.
　1917　The Organizability of Labor. Baltimore: Johns Hopkins University.
Wittrock, Jan
　1967　Reducing Seasonal Unemployment in the Construction Industry. Paris: OECD.
Woytinsky, W.S.
　1953　Employment and Wages in the United States. New York: Twentieth Century Fund.

DRUGS AS WORK

Peter K. Manning and Lawrence J. Redlinger

I. INTRODUCTION

Modern work is primarily viewed as occupationally based work that is named and classified, full-time, nonseasonal, urban, and of a legitimate sort. This perspective diverts attention from seasonal work, from rural work in general, from work that is not labeled, from part-time work, from illegitimate work and work in the "grey market"—or, as it is called in Scandinavian societies, the "black purse"—that is based on barter, exchange, and quid pro quo. Further excluded are "odd jobs" (Miller 1978), household labor (by both spouses and children), and coerced work like that found within prisons. These types of work are sometimes described as being in the secondary or tertiary sectors of the labor market, a classification which separates them from the rest of work activities and blurs their essential relationship to the overall fabric and social organization of work.

Historically, the patterning of work has created a quasi-legal grey market in goods, services, and considerations and a more clearly defined illicit market which parallels legitimate wages and considerations. Ditton (1977), for example, analyzed the types of "invisible wages" associated with work and noted that many salaried workers are permitted to take additional emoluments by "wage theft," or pilfering from the workplace, from the cash flow, or by the conversion of time to personal use. Other workers in what have traditionally been seen as blue-collar service occupations are given a set of "wage opportunities" or granted wage pilferage. As the risks of being caught are small, these quasi-legitimated payments on the side are thought of as an integral aspect of the work role. Where there is an institutionalization of perks, or satisfactions thought to inhere in the role, one finds "wage-perks" that are rigorously and extensively codified.[1] Whereas lower-level service workers must call in sick, lie about their well-being and whereabouts, or steal for invisible wages, middle-level persons are able to take "personal leave days"—legitimate time from work with pay—and some workers are able to come and go with impunity, having been guaranteed the freedom from obtrusive control over their work.[2]

Drug work provides an excellent example of work carried out in both primary and secondary (or tertiary), licit, and illicit, sectors of the labor market. Because of legal definitions, some drugs are legally marketed while others are produced, distributed, bought, sold, and consumed illegally. Yet, activities required to import, distribute, promote, and sell in both licit and illicit market contexts are work and have similarities to each other. Participants in licit markets such as physicians, nurses, drug manufacturers, sales people, chemists, pharmacologists, and those who regulate such activity [e.g., the U.S. Food and Drug Administration (FDA)] are all engaged in licit drug work. Their livelihoods derive directly from drugs, their creation, production, distribution, and wholesale and retail sale. Likewise, in illicit drug markets, there are workers who derive their income from producing, distributing, wholesaling, and retailing drugs. (It should be noted that participants in licit markets may assume any of these roles more easily than those in illicit work; for example, a pharmacist can dispense drugs both legally and illegally.) There are persons engaged in full-time or nearly full-time criminal activities: illegal drug producers and chemical laboratory workers; importers; wholesalers and retailers; those who buy and consume illicit drugs. Moreover, those who seek to eradicate these markets [e.g., the U.S. Drug Enforcement Agency (DEA), Customs and Immigration, Treasury, and state and local drug police] penetrate and participate in them.

Our focus in this chapter is on the political economy of regulation/eradication as it shapes the market structure and the kinds of differentiated work roles people perform in controlling and participating in the illicit markets. For while dealing illicit drugs is a "crime," it is also an occupation. Implicit in this perspective, which has been outlined elsewhere (Manning and Redlinger, 1977; 1978; Manning, 1980), is that the market shapes and patterns law enforcement, and enforcement shapes and patterns the market. That is, as in legal markets, there is an interdigitation between regulators and the regulated. Traditionally it has been assumed that enforcement primarily shapes, patterns, and occasionally even eradicates some markets for drugs, while the market has little effect on enforcement. However, evidence of the complexity of market/enforcement interrelationships is still appearing (see Wilson, 1975; Redlinger, 1977; Manning, 1980), and suggests that it is difficult, if not impossible, to sort out the direction of causality. Rather, drug dealers and police are part of an organizational network concerned with drugs and mutually affect each other. One of the principal reasons why traditional assumptions about enforcement effects have not been carefully examined is that the press and the public have credited police statements about their effectiveness and efficiency in illicit drug market regulation uncritically and without question (see Manning, 1980).[3] Furthermore, the distinction between drug workers and narcotics agents is blurred insofar as the police hire and support drug market participants. They hire people to inform for them, to make drug buys under their supervision, and to recruit other informants. These persons may be paid ad hoc rewards for especially good information, paid flat fees for particular tasks, put on a salary plus expenses (which does not eliminate the possibility of receiving other payments as well), given reduced charges, have arrests dropped, be protected against arrest on other charges while working for the police, and given other payments in kind such as drugs, food, or liquor. These routine practices shape the pattern of employment of marginal workers in drug markets.[4]

In this analysis we touch only briefly upon the social organization of consumption because technically consumption is not "work" (although there are some persons hired by dealers in heroin who work as "tasters" and are paid in kind for their services). Our principal concerns are the social organizations of illegal markets and the means by which market adjustments are made, rather than the psychosocial aspects of identity that arise within the occupational and/or organizational context.

II. LICIT AND ILLICIT DRUG MARKETS

Analytically it is clear that the concept *occupation* does not denote just legal or licit work. Form defines "occupations" as "relatively continuous patterns of activities that provide workers with a livelihood and define their general social status. Occupations emerge whenever a division of labor is associated with a monetary economy and labor and commodity markets" (1968:245). Whenever a society is organized around occupations, it is an "occupational society" (Form, 1968). The markets in which goods and services are exchanged are controlled in a variety of ways in occupational societies. Among the most important distinctions is that between *regulation*, wherein an attempt is made to modify the price and output curves or the point at which they meet while sustaining a viable market structure and conventional means of market adjustment, and *eradication*, wherein the aim is to destroy the market and eliminate the participants therein, or reduce the capacity of the organizations to sustain the market on an ongoing basis.[5] In effect, however, either by attempting to create a legal, regulated drug market or by eradicating an illicit market, one creates its opposite number.

Consider that the existence of a legal market in morphine and other opiates protects that market from penetration by nonlicensed participants and by those who do not subject themselves to similar regulatory costs. As Schelling (1967) notes, on the other hand, "the black market gets protection against all competitors unwilling to pursue a criminal career." Ironically, the "protection" is usually in the form of higher risk costs to participants in the illegal market. It should be appreciated that the intersection of the two markets produces a marginal grey market in which products are bartered whose existence is morally ambiguous (drug paraphernalia), where a law is occasionally applied by stretching a point (pornography), or where informal practices are subject to a variety of social definitions ("scalping" tickets). Occupations and occupational practitioners can participate in all three markets from time to time.

Within markets, the degree of *competition* varies from oligopolistic and monopolistic to highly fragmented, competitive market situations. Most commonly in the trade in opiates there are tendencies toward oligopolistic and/or oligopsonic markets, although this may be less true for other drugs.[6] There are legal and illegal means to produce order in both legal and illegal markets. For example, Schelling (1967) defines criminal activity primarily in terms of the use of illegal means to organize a legal market. The defining characteristic of *racketeering* is that it involves criminal means to control an otherwise legitimate market. Violence, denial of the law, and "criminal practices" in general characterize illegal markets. He notes that there are monopolies which are achieved by legal means, others which are legal but which are regulated by antitrust and other laws intended to control competition, and some that are criminal. Racketeering is designed to produce a monopoly by destroying the competition through criminal means. However, another sort of monopoly is that produced by *extortion*, wherein the operation or business "lives off" another business by the threat of violence or of criminal competition (Schelling, 1967, 1971). Clearly, within the drug world, protection is provided by criminal practitioners for their own operatives, and violence is used against competition and in general can be used to produce a degree of order in the illegal market. These illegal means can be used to organize a market into a cartel-like conspiracy in restraint of trade. Thus, it is clear that the illegal means of extortion and criminal monopoly can exist within *either* legal or illegal market systems. It is only when they are singularly characteristic of an organization that it can be considered "criminal" in Schelling's perspective.

The degree of *routinization* of action that characterizes the market is important, because in both illegal and legal markets there is need for institutions, conventions, and well-understood practices that are built up to reduce uncertainty.[7] It is, for example, argued by Schelling that large criminal enterprises can maintain peace in the underworld, enforce discipline, arbitrate disputes, supply governance, and be seen as corporate states. Finally, the *number of firms* in competition and their *size* is important in understanding the context within which a given firm operates. In general, market adjustments and occupational practices

Drugs as Work 279

are created by participants in an illegal market where illegal means are commonly used to organize markets.

In this analysis the *law* is critical because it mediates both within and between markets. That is to say, the law as action is the coercive force that shapes both markets, adding costs in both and an additional criminal tariff in the illicit.[8] The penetration of legal norms and processes into the illegal market is primarily in the form of enforcement rather than in the form of taxation, firing, compliance, or even inspectorial strategies. Viewed analytically, there is a surprising sense in which the police are mobilized structurally to act within illegal drug markets in an organizational form that reflects the organization of the market in drugs. The police, once stripped of the canopy of the law, can be seen to be using legal means to achieve criminal purposes. For example, when they "hassle" small-time numbers or policy operators, they protect the sport bettors who work in taverns amongst the white lower and lower-middle class. Schelling (1967) provides the example of the Miami police involvement in protecting gambling and notes that the police can indeed be said to be be in control of a criminal monopoly if they are organized to use the criminal monopoly to achieve their own benefits. This is perhaps better seen as a moot point than dismissed as improbable. It is not at all clear that the police are not acting in this way in their sanctioned control of the lowest levels of the drug trade.[9]

There are some additional *contextualizing* aspects of the drug trade which will continue to come into play in this analysis. They can be listed for later attention:

- The possession, distribution, and sale of heroin are habitual economic crimes which reflect a style of life, a social class and ethnic or racial position, and an ecologically patterned socioeconomic activity (see, for example, Redlinger and Michel, 1970).
- The social structure of dealing is a pyramid of power, prestige, authority, and information. One's position on the pyramid is correlated with one's access to quality opiates (McAuliffe and Gordon, 1974).
- Use is rooted in social relations. In the first instance, initiation of use is by friends for most users. There is a frequently noted connection between kinship and dealing organizations. Neighborhood and school are other bases for association, dealing, and use as well as the repressively produced group coherence of stigmatized, morally marginal, "hard-drug" users.
- Users are frequently arrested (Johnson et al., 1977).[10] They are frequently also participants in other criminal behavioral systems (fencing, pimping, prostitution), and under the umbrella of the law users qua informants are permitted to commit otherwise illegal acts such as buy drugs, arrange drug transactions, and transport and hold drugs. Participants are thus bound together by shared class, ecology, monetary relations, ethnic values, expressive symbols of their lifestyles and their shared vulnerability to police intervention and sanctioning, surveillance, and intelligence operations.

- If economic, social, and moral relationships between members of the system are sound, then there is little possibility that a reported crime will occur. Reported crime results when someone *outside* or *inside* the dealing/using system informs. Inside informing accounts for most of the "important" criminal drug investigations.

III. ON THE STRUCTURE OF ILLEGAL MARKETS

Several observations derived from economic analysis inform this discussion. First, there is little evidence that, aside form the impact of being made illegal through prohibition-based laws and associated enforcement patterns, the economics of illegal markets differ greatly from those of legal markets. Secondly, *regulatory* effects differ from market to market, and overall effects of regulation are likely to be more easily discerned in the nonprice aspects of the market than in pricing per se; in other words, variations in price have not been shown to be the direct result of variations in regulatory strategies and tactics. The incentives toward criminal organization, according to Schelling (1967), are best explained by a theory of the firm which relates costs of business to certain variables such as overhead costs, externalities of competition, price competition, and monopoly control of the market. Heroin markets are not clearly shaped by these principles because the threat of arrest and being put out of business are conducive to small, tightly integrated, face-to-face organizations of people. Monopoly control is unlikely in the heroin market because small firms maximize the capacity to reduce the risk of arrest. The larger the organization, the more vulnerable it is to surveillance and police control, according to conventional theory (see Reiss, 1974; and Reiss and Bordua, 1967). Thus, overhead costs (including security costs) are not necessarily reduced by large operation. The externalities of competition tend to be largely borne by those outside the market. For example, if in a highly competitive heroin market dealers exhaust supplies, addicts must find other sources. They can do so by enrolling in methadone programs (presumably a positive externality) or they can burglarize drug stores (a negative externality). In either case, it is the larger society that bears the costs of competition. Ironically, similar effects can result from successful police intervention causing short-term disruptions of the market which result in external diseconomies (e.g., an increase in robberies of pharmacies). Legal means of controlling competition and supplies through lobbying and trade associations and the like are unavailable, as are other influence channels such as membership in regulatory bodies (Manning and Redlinger, 1977).

The oft-described model of police/heroin market interaction, which has been argued by Moore and Redlinger, among others, to be incorrect, is shown in Figure 1. The assumptions are, in various modified forms, that "expanded enforcement effort" in the form of arrests and seizures increases the risks to dealers;

Figure 1. Casual (or Path) Model of the Impact of Police Action on the Dealing-Using System

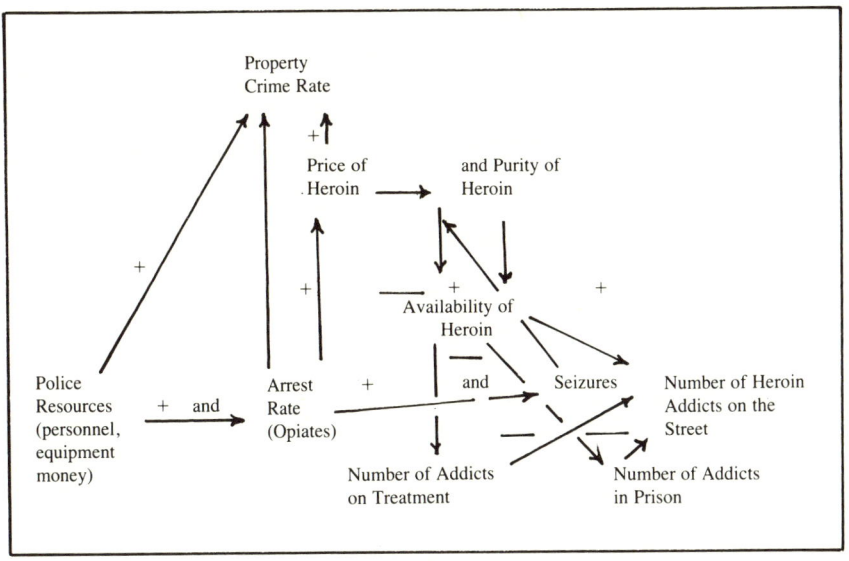

Source: Modified from Levin et al., 1975:58, and reprinted from Manning, 1980:63.

they, in turn, raise their prices (partially to cover increased costs of protection and risks costs); heroin consumption, being inelastic, remains at the same level. The next stage in the flow of consequences is seen in different ways by different analysts. Some argue that the increase in price and profits leads to more crime because users must maintain their habits, and may turn to property crime (see, for example, Greene, 1975). Others argue that the increase in profits leads to more aggressive behavior on the part of dealers to "drum up new business" (see Moore's exposition of a model he rejects, 1977a:6). Moore (1977a) and Wilson (1975) have argued that increased arrests and higher prices make it more difficult for people to obtain the drug and thus use falls off, or that the level of use is elastic and that people reduce their habits and/or substitute other drugs. Moore (1977a) also argues that the increased risks will tend to impact more on lower-level dealers and that these are the people most likely to serve newer clientele. As the new users have more difficulty in finding the drug, they are less likely to continue its use. In any case, as Moore argues, the conventional analysis of Schelling relative to criminal industry is not sensitive to the *technology* of producing heroin outside the United States and the addictive nature of the product. In addition, the actions of enforcement agents have an important effect on the market, namely, in the high markup between first wholesale exchange and the final retail exchange, in the network of highly personalized dealerships that work on a local, face-to-face basis, and in a concentration of dealers at the lowest end of the market process (Moore, 1977a:3).

It has been noted that interdependencies in the shared environment of the drug law enforcers and those who illegally trade in drugs produce isomorphism in the structures of dealing and control.[11] Enforcement units to some degree have grown in response to the market and the character of the social events that drug units must monitor: secret, private, sporadic, and uncertain in their appearance. Enforcement and dealing have also been shaped by the conscious decisions and perceptions of those in control concerning the nature of the environment. There is a sense of the nature of drug work that is shared by officers and by dealers, and there is an imagery of that work as well. Sense, imagery, and the objective features of the environment combine to create and maintain the enacted environment of drug enforcement (see Weick, 1977).

The enforcement world mirrors the illicit world in the following ways. Narcotic dealers must deal; there are pressures to make sales, to be secretive and maintain security against intrusion. Hence they use a personalized mode of dealing. Agents must also produce, maintain secrecy and security, and use a personalized mode of evaluation of their successes and personalized modes of dealing with their informants. Dealers use an entrepreneurial model of success, organize their businesses among trusted underlings with whom they have kinship, partnership, local, or racial ties, and base their actions roughly on a pyramidal structure of authority. Agents also work like entrepreneurs, and some agents even envy the dealer for his success, freedom, and cleverness. They rely heavily on their partners but tend to distrust others in the authority pyramid within which they work. Partnerships are usually based on similarities of ethnicity, age, sex, and background. Dealers distrust others as a mode of doing business, and use lying, deceit, duplicity, betrayal, threat, and violence as dominant interpersonal modes. These are also the dominant modes of operation among drug police. The amounts paid to employees or informants for drugs and the prices charged for drugs are based on trust and interpersonal relations as well as monetary considerations. The prices are typically negotiated and are not necessarily based on fixed or predetermined schedules. The agent, when working with informants, follows the same pricing pattern, the same style of interpersonal negotiation and bargaining over prices paid for services, and rests decisions on an assessment of the person, as well as what informant work the person has done in the past. Because the level of trust is low and dealers lack legal protection in their relationships with other dealers and users, violence and "rip-offs" of each other's dope often occur. Thus, feelings of revenge, envy, and retaliation are not uncommon among dealers. These same feelings suffuse the narcotics agent's world. The agent both envies the dealer and feels a moral distaste for his doings, especially when they involve what he considers to be children, and for the fact that the dealer seems to be above the law, avoids its pressures, and does not have to respect it as the officer feels he must. The agent wants revenge for past situations where the dealer has avoided arrest, been released on bail, beaten a charge, pleaded-out to lesser charges, dealt while still awaiting trial, and the like.

Dealing work, although based on rational systems of accounting, is sporadic, having high peaks and troughs, and is full of uneven demands on one's time. Opiates especially must be used by at least some consumers daily, seven days a week, 52 weeks a year, year in and year out. Often, the work spreads out unexpectedly and involves the person in both day and night work. Agents operate on analogous schedules. They work sporadically and spend enormous amounts of time waiting for phone calls, for deals to go down, for their people to show up at a meeting place, for equipment, for money to appear. The work then may involve bursts of energy extending for days at a time, around the clock. Although the work schedules of enforcement units do not appear to result from information on the pattern of dealing, it would appear that the flexibility in hours and periods of work is a reasonable approximation of the phenomenon they are mandated to control (on this point see Williams et al., 1979). The clientele of the drug dealer can be "turned;" that is, the user can be made an informant for the control agency or can become a double agent. Likewise, the informant utilized by an agent can be also in the employ of a dealer or can be turned by the dealer using the same means (extortion, threats, money, promises of immunity or exemption in the future).

The users of drugs are something like civilians in a war: they suffer the indignities of the two warring parties with few of the benefits associated with "victory." Routinization would appear to be more common the higher one mounts the dealing structures. That is, it is assumed that the larger the dealer, the more rational his methods of accounting, business practices, modes of deception, and prevention of arrest (Moore, 1977a). It would appear that the more enforcement activities become systematic and planned, the more they target large dealers; and the more enforcement is aimed at small dealers, the more proximal, spontaneous, and unplanned are the actions of the agents. The symbolic rewards of the dealing world, according to McAuliffe and Gordon (1974), include not only the respect of other dealers and users but also access to better-quality heroin. Their view is that there is a prestige hierarchy within the dealing world, based on several dimensions. The prestige of the dealing world is mirrored in the prestige structure within the world of control: great prestige accrues to the investigator who makes a "big bust" or arrests a "big dealer," no matter what the circumstances.

IV. THE SOCIAL ORGANIZATION OF DEALING

Economic analyses of the shape of the market and the logical sources of impact on price have been complemented by ethnographic studies of the LSD, marijuana, and heroin markets (see Carey, 1968; Redlinger, 1969, 1975a, 1975b).[12] In order to know something of the nature of drug work, one must look to these ethnographies. For example, the stereotypical "junkie" as portrayed in movies and on television is only one of many types of users that have been identified [see Moore's summary of these types (1977a:67-115)]. Partially because the image and behavior of the user have been stereotyped, the view of the market as being static, except for movement from the bottom due to arrest, imprisonment, and burnout, and the view that demand is inelastic have been perpetuated (see Moore, 1977:6-10). However, demand is less inelastic than previously thought and is similar to that for physician's services. Moore estimates that a 10% increase in cost will produce a 2% decrease in use. An increase in price reduces use but boosts profits within the industry (Moore, 1977a:9). Nevertheless, "disproportionate numbers of heroin users are drug dependent; because of their compulsive use, the demand for heroin is much more inelastic than the overall illicit demand for drugs" (Heller, 1973:389). The most detailed analyses of the heroin market and the work of drug workers can be found in Preble and Casey (1969), Redlinger (1969, 1975a, 1975b), and Williams et al. (1979). These works supply most of the materials we will use to characterize the work at retail and wholesale levels. In general, we can ask "What are the conditions under which a person participates in the heroin business at either the wholesale or retail level?" This includes those who both use and sporadically sell small quantities to partially defray the costs of their own heroin use (in some markets known as "street jugglers"). Typically, street jugglers "cut" the heroin they buy with some neutral substance after taking some heroin out for their own use. They then sell the now lower-quality heroin at the same price. When capsules are used, it is even possible to simply take a small portion out of each capsule and blow into the capsule, creating enough moisture to make the powder that is left appear to be more than what is actually in the capsule. These practices can occur because the standard units in the retail market (e.g., "caps," "papers," "bags," "balloons," "grams," "quarter-pieces," etc.) are symbolically based on heroin of a customary quantity and quality. While the container (e.g., a small balloon or a gelatin capsule) remains the same, the quality and within limits the quantity can vary.

The relationship between quality (percentage of heroin per standard unit) and price is complex. The purity varies, in general, by levels within the system. For example, in five cities studied by Manning and Redlinger (1975) purity at the lowest level ranged from 3%-5% to 9% while at the "piece" or ounce level it ranged from 5% to as high as 40%. Redlinger, on the basis of data from the Phoenix crime laboratory, established that the quantity of heroin had been dropping in samples from 20%-60% purity in 1967 to 3%-15% in 1975. The price in Phoenix as in other cities studied had been generally rising during the same period. That is, while the quality had been steadily decreasing the price had been increasing; in addition, the quantity had also decreased! For Phoenix, Redlinger found, "Five years ago a $10 paper contained 160 milligrams. Today [1975] it contains 60 milligrams. Similarly, five years ago a $25 quarter contained close to 500 milligrams. Today it contains about 150-200 milligrams" (1975b:18). The causes of this change are, perhaps, generally inflationary trends in all consumer goods, the effect of an increasingly nationalized market, increased demand, law enforcement efforts, and dealers' desires to maintain profit levels over time (see Redlinger, 1975b).[13]

A. Retailing

Recruitment to the drug world is similar to that of any other market: one must have the opportunity to see and be familiar with the product, possibly be a user of it, in order to have initial interest in selling it. Some drug markets provide both licit and illicit opportunities for sellers, while others like the heroin market are largely confined to illicit markets. In effect, participants in illicit markets are in the secondary sector of a dual labor market system since entrance to the legal markets for dealing is closed to them. Within illicit markets, there are ethnic and class effects, as well as a stratification system that has consequences for the pattern of recruitment into the work.[14]

There is a precondition for dealing, regardless of the way in which one first has contact with the product: it is familiarity with the drug and/or with business associates who are familiar with the drug. Once familiar, there are generally four other preconditions for retail work in the heroin market. First, retailers must use the drug. This does not mean that they must become addicts, nor that their use be anything more than sporadic. Moreover, in a few instances involvement in retail work precedes use, and a few retailers "back into" selling heroin through trade in other drugs. That is, a dealer's clientele can request heroin from the dealer, and the dealer's business connections allow him access to heroin. In this instance, the dealer usually has a different drug of choice for his own use. Overall, however, most retailers are users. Often the experience of working with another retailer as a mule ("runner") or a sales person also precedes entry. Most dealers are profit-oriented, although some sell only to defray the costs of their own use. Studies show that many participants in the drug market also work at other jobs, legal and illegal (Hughes et al., 1971; Moore, 1977a:Table 2-9). This means, it should be emphasized, that what is viewed as the "second job" may affect the time and energy available for participation in the illicit market.

Second, one must know other retailers and be able to obtain the product. These are two separate matters, for knowledge may not produce trustworthiness, and therefore the product may not be entrusted to the protean dealer even if he has the money and the associates that might lead to an initial contact or interview with a source. One must be credible, and credibility is derived from status criteria: age, sex, ethnicity, and style of life. This can be inferred from statistics on drug users and drug-related arrests, which show a remarkable clustering among blacks and young lower-class men of Mexican or Hispanic descent (Helmer, 1975:121). Trust is critical because the perceived threat of enforcement is great, and the penetration of the market by controllers, especially by means of informants, is seen to be great. In order to protect oneself from informants and the police in general, dealers disassociate themselves from the dope if possible, and thus those to whom the goods are "fronted" or given on commission must be trustworthy. This concern also accounts for the tendency to hire relatives and longtime friends as business associates.

Third, one must be able to finance the operation. This can be managed either from illicit activities or from licit ones such as legitimate jobs with a free cash-flow situation (such as small businesses or self-employment generally).

Fourth, one must locate a place from which to deal and become known as a dealer to potential buyers. The more visible, available, and easily located by buyers, the higher the threat of arrest but the lower cost of the location. For example, one can deal cheaply and easily from a car in a parking lot, but the threat of surveillance or being reported is also high. Retailers, in general, balance location, client, and sale decisions in a satisficing manner since they have imperfect information about their environments (Simon, 1976). However, some firms are able virtually to optimize locational decisions. For example, one of a firm's retail outlets was located within the depths of a public housing project that maximized its insulation from police interference. In addition, they sold only to users from their own ethnic group, and the mode of selling made it impossible to buy from an identifiable individual since between the purchaser and the seller were auditory and visual screening devices.

Once in business, one must learn the practices of the occupation. In order to stay in business, Carey (1968) notes on the basis of his study of LSD and marijuana markets in the Bay area in the 1960s, one must: engender and maintain the trust of a clientele; regularize one's transactions for stability of business and to maintain a loyal clientele; practice deception in relationships with present and potential customers, the police, and potential police agents; and exercise caution in respect to fronting merchandise and money, and in one's lifestyle generally.

Drug dealing is fraught with uncertainties with respect to the quality of the product, the salience of violence and the absence of legal protections, the distribution and flow of heroin within the local market, the variation in numbers of participants, and the moral/political climate of dealing (police occasionally go on "heroin hunts" or "dope drives"). In particular the uncertainties contribute to fluctuation in availability. There are periods when shortages on the retail level induce retailers to raise their prices in the short term or maintain the same price but reduce the purity of the drug, thereby stretching supplies and maximizing profits. In periods of retail glut, street dealers may be forced to compete for customers. Even when the market is stable, dealers often negotiate the price with the user because some users simply do not have enough cash to pay the standard or customary price; in this case, dealers "sell short." Those who work for someone else generally take the cut out of their commissions on sales. In general, the retail heroin market is fraught with uncertainties that affect every relationship.

B. Wholesaling

Wholesale work presumes the existence of retailers to buy the product; wholesalers serve as middlemen between producers, importers, and retailers. Wholesalers need not presently use heroin in order to enter the wholesale ranks (i.e., use is variable). Preconditions for entry and participation are previous experience as a retailer or previous work for a wholesaler. Some of the wholesalers worked previously supplying other drugs. The experiential nexus of trust is important here, for association with fellows in gang relationships, in neighborhoods, or as friends plays a role in recruitment. From these epicenters wholesalers may be recruited.

Establishing a business, as contrasted with initial entry, requires at least four conditions. First, one must know of a potential pool of buyers or customers. This is in large part the result of prior participation in the business oneself, although ethnic, neighborhood, church, school, kin, and friendship ties are also important. Secondly,

> Essential to establishing a wholesale business is getting the "connection" or establishing trade relations with sellers on the Mexican side. In most cases the "introduction" to the connection costs the fledgling wholesaler money. The average cost for an introduction runs around $200-400. Of course, the cost of an introduction can vary depending on the quantity desired. Once the wholesaler knows the name of the connection, the wholesaler is privy to special information, but not special arrangements. To qualify for special arrangements the ability to move the product and keep a "secret" must be demonstrated by the wholesaler (Redlinger, 1975a:343)

Third, the potential wholesaler must be able to finance his first buy. He must have cash in hand or be sufficiently trustworthy to be "fronted" enough dope to open the business. Fourth, he must locate and establish relationships with retailers. Previous involvement in the business at the retail level improves his chances of so doing, and of associating himself with trustworthy underlings. The same characteristics that allow one to enter the retail market and to trade in the wholesale market tend to be sought in one's employees.[15] Doing business requires other characteristics and practices. While the degree of vertical and horizontal differentiation is variable within the market, total vertical integration is unlikely because major wholesalers and those even higher in the market structure wish to reduce informational and other links that can be directly made to themselves. Dealership location is a choice in which the risk of having drugs available for easy access and sales must be balanced against the risk of being caught in possession of the drugs by agents. One mode of protection is to keep one's inventory of available drugs in a "safe house" or a location away from one's self that is largely unknown to others and thus is safe both from police and from other dealers and/or users. Similarly, protective strategies and tactics for selling vary, as Moore (1977a) has analyzed.

As in retailing, wholesale activity is subject to internal and external "pressures," and business or market adjustments can be noted. For example, wholesalers can front or be fronted all or part of a consignment with the verbal understanding that when the goods are sold payment will be made. In addition, wholesalers engage in variable pricing strategies, selling goods for more or less depending upon how well they know and trust their clients. To some degree, then, the price of a standard unit varies independently of the quality of the product. As Redlinger points out, the illegal nature of the product does much to increase the price and also to create pressure upon the dealers both to protect themselves and to maximize per-unit profits (1975a:349-350). It appears that profits in the illegal wholesale market are slightly higher than those in the comparable legal market, in part because the risk cost elevates the cost of goods. Only a portion of the increased cost is actually assigned to security, while the remainder is assigned to profit. The general rise in price and operations costs in the illicit market (a presumed effect of enforcement in particular and the condition of illegality in general) are passed directly to the consumer and result in higher revenues.

V. THE INTERPLAY OF REGULATION AND CAREERS IN DRUGS

Because heroin dealing is seen as a significant political, social, and moral problem, and because we are concerned with the structure of work in the heroin market, we want to assess how the regulatory-eradicative actions of police affect the careers of those involved in the market.

First, the pattern of enforcement influences the risk of working in the illicit market. The condition of illegality increases the risk of doing business because dealers are denied legal protections. In addition, the police can increase risk through enforcement by reacting to (1) drugs found under other circumstances (e.g., traffic stops), (2) citizens' calls, (3) media attention (whether to a real or an imagined problem), and (4) big issues such as a perceived heroin epidemic; or they can actively create cases by (5) using hired informants (some of whom are working off charges or trying to have charges reduced or dropped), (6) making buys themselves, (7) trying to build larger cases by means of antitrust or tax laws or civil harassment, or (8) constructing criminal conspiracy cases (see Manning, 1980).

Second, these risks bear differentially on participants in the distribution system, which is a pyramid of power, profit, and prestige. Higher-level dealers involved in importation and large-scale distribution are least vulnerable to arrest, and even less vulnerable to conviction since they rarely handle the drugs themselves. Those at the highest level in an organized market are also in a position to control prices, to extract higher profits at greater margins, and to restrict their clientele and thus protect themselves from arrest and prosecution to a greater degree than those in the lower levels of the distribution structure. The lower-level dealers, "street pushers," are characterized by opposite features. Most importantly, they are visible and can be observed; they operate at a lower margin of profit; they must deal with strangers or casual acquaintances (some of whom are possible police informants); and often they deal to use. They are often known to the police because of previous arrests or convictions, and they are frequently rearrested (Johnson and Bogomony, 1973; Webster, 1975). Since these dealer-users are disproportionately young black and Hispanic males or lower-class whites with similar neighborhood origins and educational levels and limited opportunities to work in licit markets, the class-power nexus that local drug arrests represent also symbolizes the criminalization of lower-class occupations and lifestyles. If Mack's (1964) data on professional criminals are roughly applicable to drug dealers, they suggest that there are two categories of drug business persons: "top dogs" who are well insulated, legally protected, and rarely arrested; and vulnerable lower-level persons who are arrested repeatedly (see Webster, 1975). The inequities in arrest patterns are reproduced in inequities in charging, in prosecution, in bringing cases to trial, and in sentencing. One effect, then, of the police actions is to perpetuate the power and authority structure of the drug world.

Third, enforcement efforts have economic consequences for the illegal practitioner and for the consumer. The business person must pay the normal costs of business (cost of goods, operating expenses, and transaction costs) plus the risk costs associated with security and precautions to prevent arrest, defense and legal fees, bribery of agents, and loss of goods and work time due to arrest, trial, and imprisonment. Business relationships with clients are characterized by uncertainty in source, quality, quantity, and reliability, and by generally flawed ethical practices (such as "burns," cutting drugs with dangerous substances, "shorting" bags, and betrayal). Business people in the illicit market are denied civil protection or entitlements available to licit business, such as bankruptcy protection, guaranteed loans from the Small Business Administration, and "disaster relief." The protections of legal institutions such as contract, suit, and adjudicatory processes are also unavailable to them. Their involvement in illegal trade denies them the usual protections of the criminal law concerning robbery, assault, or burglary. In addition, as a general practice, police discredit or deny requests made for legal protection by participants in illicit markets. For example, they show neither compassion nor "professional interest" in the light of a drug dealer whose television is stolen. The consumer also suffers from participation. Costs of goods are high, inflated in part by the risk costs passed on to the consumer, there is enormous variation in price, quality, and quantity. The consumer suffers the multiple risks of being arrested, being forced to inform (thus producing risks of being denied drugs, subjected to violence in revenge, suffering loss of status and income), being roughed up by the police, and kept under surveillance. Sources vary, and new relationships ("connections") must be established. Each new venture carries with it additional risk.

Fourth, since drug drives and enforcement are characterized by a high degree of uncertainty, irrationality, and often violence, constant upheavals are the norm amongst small drug businesses, and these reverberate through the network of social relations that is the market. This situation contrasts with ordinary licit business, which is a source of stability, predictability, and daily activity.

However, the actual effects of enforcement practices on the market cannot be accurately evaluated because they are compounded with other forces affecting the supply of and demand for heroin. Besides enforcement effects (discussed below) at least three other sources of change can be identified: exogenous variations in supply; changing taste preferences; and the availability of substitutes. *Exogenous effects* alter the availability of heroin through variations in the amounts produced abroad and the quantities diverted into illicit channels; changes in shipping and distribution channels; political disruptions caused by revolutions, wars, and port or dock strikes; and indirect effects due to general economic (inflationary or recessionary) patterns, etc. *Changing taste preferences* occur, for example, when the demand for cocaine rises or amphetamines become the drug of preference. It has been noted in the liquor industry that taste preferences change rather quickly between a variety of highly priced liquors and unusual "exotic" brands or types of drinks (Denzin, 1977). This type of taste variability as well as the expansion and contraction of consumption levels create fluctuations in demand even in the heroin market. Opinions differ about the degree of inelasticity in the heroin market. Conventional views regard the market as highly inelastic due largely to the addictive character of the drug (see, for example, Reynolds, 1981). However, such arguments generally ignore variations in product purity and consumer use patterns, arguing that users once addicted will pay any amount for any quality product. Since virtually all users of heroin also use other drugs such as alcohol, amphetamines, barbiturates, tranquilizers, cocaine, and marijuana (see O'Donnell et al., 1976), wide variations in the supply of heroin are likely to produce reduced consumption by users and a shift to other drugs (Gooberman, 1974). In addition, when the purity of retail heroin drops below 2%, while the price rises to, say, $40 a paper, it becomes extremely difficult for the consumer to maintain an addiction. Indeed, when the retail purity of heroin drops below 2%, it becomes difficult to argue that consumers using reasonable standard doses (e.g., two papers a day) are addicted at all. Furthermore, *substitutes* such as methadone, LAMM, and others from licit treatment centers and black-market sources ease demand during periods of reduced heroin availability (Green et al., 1975). These data on market fluctuations and consumption patterns indicate considerably less inelasticity than is conventionally assumed. Those who ignore the other forces that impact on supply and demand exaggerate the possibility of control of the market by enforcement efforts, especially in light of constraints placed upon the police.

In actuality, enforcement efforts appear to be limited and inadequate to the task. The procedural limits on police action are so severe that the costs extracted marketwide are largely those of inconvenience and harassment, and those are borne disproportionately by those at the bottom of the market. This is so because police have limited time, money, skills, information, organizational strategies, citizen cooperation, and legal resources. Even though agents operate with the ideal of making the big case against the big dealer, most agents, given the constraints, make cases at the bottom where they are most easily made. That is, given limited resources and pressures to produce, activity is directed at the lowest levels where felony cases can be made with the minimum expenditure of resources. While "dope drives" can be shown to result sometimes in short-term disruptions (a day to perhaps three or four days) of the lower levels of the market, such actions are rarely sustained (on this point see Redlinger, 1975a; Williams et al., 1979). Dope drives exhaust police informational sources, but those at higher levels of the market are most often insulated against penetration. Police, thus, must wait for the market to stabilize so that they can set up informational links to activity. In this and in other senses police activity is reactive to and shaped by events in the market. As a result, it is sometimes argued that police enforcement activities, given the constraints under which they are carried out, are ceremonial activities important to demonstrate to the larger public that something is being done even though what is actually occurring is ineffective. Dealers, for their part, need not comply with any regulations, but rather react to renewed enforcement efforts with greater secrecy, more intricate intelligence systems of their own, bribery, and other forms of agent corruption. Moreover, the heroin market system is international in origin and thus little amenable to national prohibitions. The police can only in a modest, discretionary, circumscribed fashion shape the illicit drug business. Classical notions of legal deterrence are not really relevant to the control of such a lifestyle occupational crime (Hellman, 1975; Chambliss, 1967; for a general review, see Gibbs, 1975).

Many insightful writers have summarized the impediments to the eradication of the market in illicit drugs, using opium as their model (Clague, 1973; Fernandez, 1969, 1973; Heller, 1973; Holahan, 1972; Moore, 1976, 1977a, 1977b; Redlinger, 1977; Rottenberg, 1968). Others approach the problem in more general terms, noting the resistance of certain types of illicit markets to control and the ease with which they are organized by criminal means (Schelling, 1967, 1971). Authors have argued that the world supply of opium is virtually unlimited and that less than 12% of the world's opium production could supply the estimated half-million users in the United States in 1971. They have shown that in areas where opium is cultivated it is a central labor-intensive crop and the source of extraordinary profits (partially as a result of its being illegal) from the initial source to the final retail sales. Within the illicit market system, there appear to be ready replacements for arrested users at the base of the market pyramid and functionaries hired by wholesalers and retailers. There is virtually an endless source of money for infusion into larger firms that dominate local and regional markets. The licit market in prescription drugs contributes to the availability of drugs and volume of use because ethical pharmaceutical houses are difficult to control and refuse to supply data on their production. They continue to produce drugs in this country and in other countries (e.g., Mexico) which are imported and smuggled back into the United States. For example, the "overproduction" of amphetamines has been well known for over a decade, but the government has been ineffectual in attempts to monitor or reduce it (Pekkanen, 1973; Silverman, 1974). Finally, the advertising of pharmaceutical houses, the wish of physicians to "do something" for or to patients, and the patients' belief in the ideology of cure for "emotional problems"—all these produce an enormous flow of licit drugs, some of which are diverted into illicit markets (see Radelet, 1977).

VI. CONCLUDING COMMENT

Although there is a long history of concern with work of various sorts in American sociology, most attention has been given to the study of full-time, labeled, urban, legitimate, salaried work. Professional work has attracted a disproportionate amount of time and attention. Conversely, the odd-job, part-time, or even two-job person, the rural worker, the entrepreneur, and those engaged in illegitimate work have been slighted. A countertheme can be found in the ethnographic studies of criminals done by Sutherland (1937), Maurer (1940), and in more recent times Chambliss (1972), Letkeman (1973), Jackson (1969), and Klockars (1974). These powerful and illuminating studies help to remind us of the need to analyze occupations comparatively, as Hughes (1958) has noted.[16]

Drug work is done in both illicit and licit markets, and in both the controllers and the controlled interface. Some similarities are noted here following the observation that many of the economic principles that operate licit markets are also found within illicit ones. Modes of control and governance, either criminal or noncriminal, are found in both, with violence, interpersonal trust, and personalized dealings replacing the formal role of law within the illicit market. However, the law shapes both types of markets, albeit the illicit with different intent. The importance of "risk costs" is elevated in the illicit market because the contribution of enforcement is said to be generally reflected in the higher costs of operation, especially at the lower and more vulnerable end of the market.

The complex interrelation between the regulators and the regulated has been a topic of scholarly interest in recent times (Stigler, 1975) within both the legal and the illegal markets (see Manning and Redlinger, 1977: Williams et al., 1979; and Manning, 1980). We have some evidence concerning the ways in which enforcers shape the illicit market and the ways in which the market shapes the controllers. The social organization of dealing and the social organization of enforcement are interdependent, and aspects of each are structured by the other so that a degree of isomorphism exists. Yet there are unique variations from city to city as local markets and enforcement patterns adapt to each other and to the larger environment (see Williams et al., 1979; Adler et al., 1976).

Economic models of heroin markets and the behavior of heroin dealers contribute knowledge of the form of drug dealing, while the ethnographic studies of Redlinger, Carey, and others do much to fill in content. However, the economic analysis of illicit behavior, in spite of its strengths, is limited on several grounds. First, it assumes a degree of public consensus concerning the severity of certain crimes, the associated penalties that ought to be attached, and the mandate the public has granted police agencies. Stigler (1970), for example, bemoans the "ambivalence of the public" and the possible lack of consensus, while Gusfield (1980) and Edelman (1971) argue that public wishes and even enforcement are symbolic and ceremonial in nature. This suggests that there is considerable slack between the law, legislative intent, enforcement practices, and the impact of enforcement. Irrespective of this slack, drug crime and illicit drug regulation disproportionately focus on the inept, the powerless, and the poor, using resources approaching a billion dollars a year.

Second, the cost of criminal behavior, even in the drug world, are difficult to establish because costs are based on the value of something foregone, or "opportunity costs." It is difficult to imagine establishing the value of crime that is foregone. The units within which this is measured are so vague that comparisons are somewhat nonsensical. The fact is that many of these entrepreneurs are eliminated from competition in licit markets, and are systematically excluded (some are denied entry because the entry costs are too high).

Third, economists overlook basic moral and political question concerning why certain laws are passed and with what intent. Instead, as Erikson (1969:486) ironically notes, they raise "the question of the propriety of dealing with the topic of optimum coercion as a problem of resource allocation." When questions focus on the optimum level of enforcement rather than on whether enforcement should take place at all, or inquire into the alacrity and severity of sanction rather than what sort of sanctions, if any, ought to be attached to such behavior, expediency rules and can subvert political and social order.

The fact that economic metaphors permit certain observations to be ordered does not mean that the ordering is moral nor that by neglecting sociomoral questions one makes the analysis objective. The licit-illicit dimension is a socially constructed one, fueled and sustained by multiple sets of values and interests that place disproportionate costs on particular members of society. Questions about the values behind enforcement and about whose interests are actually served by the current arrangements still remain.

NOTES

1. Ditton's work (1977a and 1977b) on invisible wages and wage-pilferage is a tour-de-force, but overall the literature is scanty.
2. For a discussion of obtrusive and unobtrusive control in the workplace; see Perrow, 1979.
3. In large part the sort of work discussed here takes place in *crime-dependent environments* in which large numbers of people are involved in one way or another with illegal work, the conse-

quences of illegal work (e.g., fencing property, bail bond work, supplying protective services), or the income generated by illicit enterprise. Thus, indirectly or directly, persons living in low-income areas in large cities are face to face with crime daily. Whether the participants think of themselves as criminal, practice crime full-time, or are dependent on the income for support is somewhat difficult to establish here. However, it appears that addicts are treated with a variety of strategies (education, medicine, rehabilitation, punishment), and they may more likely think of themselves as criminal than do drug retailers or wholesalers (on these points see Geis, 1974; Mack, 1964, 1972; and Williams, 1979).

4. By "marginal," we mean those who are not involved full-time, whose involvement may be avocational, and who move in and out of employment in the drug market, whether the source of their income is the police or criminal practitioners. That is, while a few workers are "professional informers," the majority are not. The problem of marginal workers makes it difficult to determine the actual strength of enforcement forces in the vice-narcotics area because the number of informants fluctuates, they are not carefully supervised nor recorded in files, and their existence is frequently concealed to protect them (see McDonald, 1973).

5. As Mark Moore has noted (1977a:xx-xxi), however, the *intention* of the government in the illicit market in opiates is to *regulate the distribution* of heroin under a policy that *prohibits* all uses of heroin. Perhaps it would be more direct to state that, *regardless* of the symbolic intent and legislative mandate for the control of heroin and other "dangerous drugs," what is possible and in fact attempted is regulation of the distribution of these substances. Whether this differs in economic terms from regulation where the regulatory effect only is intended, or and what precisely regulatory "effects" are (see Stigler, 1975), is subject to considerable debate among economists. The political implications and ramifications are better known (see Edelman, 1971; and Gusfield, 1980).

6. A useful outline of structural differences between the illicit markets in amphetamines, barbiturates, marijuana, and heroin is found in Soref, forthcoming. LSD and marijuana are compared in Carey (1968) while Redlinger (1969) compares heroin, LSD, and marijuana, with a special focus on heroin. Works on the market for heroin are cited above. Goode (1970) has written the most complete study of marijuana dealing (although also see Carey, 1968; Kamistra, 1975; Goldman, 1975; and Adler and Adler, 1976). The most useful study of the market in amphetamines is Grinspoon and Hedblom (1975). Cocaine markets have been analyzed by Woodley, (1971), Sabbag, (1976), and Phillips and Wynne (1980).

7. These include what Durkheim termed "non-contractual aspects of contracts."

8. The concept of crime tariff is explored by Packer (1968).

9. See Webster's argument on this point (1975) and Manning (1980).

10. See DeFleur (1975) for an interesting discussion of drug arrest statistics.

11. Portions of this argument are summarized from Manning (1980:63-73).

12. Studies show that there are several types of market structures for heroin dealing, although the "New York" model of Preble and Casey (1969) is cited as "the market structure in heroin." Until recently, the shape of the market has been assumed, especially by law enforcement agencies, rather than studied.

13. DEA buys that are attempts to monitor the quality and price of heroin tend to be misleading because they are not standardized by level in the buying chain at which the drug is purchased. Prices may be misleading because strangers buy at higher prices than "regulars" (i.e., *who* buys the dope is a variable that affects both quality and price). Judgements concerning the type and source of the heroin (brown, or "Mexican," or white, "Asian") are unreliable because they are made by "eyeballing" the sample and because the color of the heroin is a function of the refinement process and not the area of origin. Finally, as Brown and Silverman note, the price per gram of heroin is inversely related to the size of the purchase made; the larger the volume of the sale, the lower the unit price. However, they disagree with the claim made above concerning the relationship between size of the purchase and quality of the heroin. They suggest that highly potent quantities are transacted in both large and small amounts, and that "large but diluted transactions are more common than might have been expected"

(Brown and Silverman, 1974:602). Since estimates of the price of heroin are made from samples bought almost entirely by agents at the lowest levels in local police units, they tend to overestimate the cost of the product generally. Quality varies in short and long terms because of the exogenous and endogenous effects noted above, as does price. In other words, both price and purity can rise, remain roughly the same, or decrease. The relationship has to be seen for any given time within a ninefold matrix (see Manning and Redlinger, forthcoming). In general, over the last 10 years or so, during which somewhat reliable measurements have been made, the quality of heroin has been dropping while the price has been rising.

14. Access to dealing and to users, like access to medical clientele, is socially patterned [see, for example, Oswald Hall's work on the medical career (1946 and 1948)]. It is known, for example, that *use* is primarily touched off under four different conditions, which produce different types of users and ultimately different role-occupants in the retail dealing structure. First is the condition of *epidemic spread*. Use of and access to a particular drug spreads rapidly through a population involving large numbers of people not usually involved. In contrast are: the *associate model* where users learn the habit from friends and family and where patterns of use are more stable and their diffusion is more predictable (Hughes, 1977; de Alarcon, 1969; DuPont, 1971; and Greene, 1973); the occupationally related model of use based on *access at work* [these include nurses, doctors, medical technicians, pharmacists, and other hospital staff (Hessler, 1974)]; and the *medical-sickness model*, in which use is begun as a result of hospitalization for injury or an operation (Ball, 1965).

15. Kanter (1977) has shown that, under conditions of market uncertainty, people tend to choose others they perceive to be like themselves.. This helps to explain the perpetuation of males at the higher echelons of business, both licit and illicit.

16. One of the most important new developments in the study of crime and criminal work in general has been the recent attention paid by economists. Perhaps the way was charted by von Neumann and Morgenstern (1944) in their outline of the theory of games as a decision-making tool relevant to complex social contests and further elaborated by Schelling (1967). This work has been supported by the analysis of crime and of regulation in general carried out by Stigler (1970), Becker (1968), Ehrlich (1973), Moore (1977a), Reynolds (1981), and others in the new institutional economics tradition [see, for example, the creative work of Leff (1976) and Zald (1970)].

REFERENCES

Adler, P., P. Adler, and J. Douglas
    1976   "Organized crime: drug dealing for pleasure and profits." Unpublished mimeo. University of California, Santa Barbara

Ball, J.C.
    1965   "Two patterns of narcotic drug addiction in the United States." Journal of Criminology and Police Science 56:203-221.

Becker, G.S.
    1968   "Crime and punishment: an economic approach." Journal of Political Economy 76:169-217.

Brown, G.F., and L. Silverman
    1974   "The retail price of heroin: estimation and applications." Journal of the American Statistical Association 69:585-606.

Carey, J.
    1968   The Drug Scene. Englewood Cliffs, N.J.: Prentice-Hall.

Chambliss, W.
    1967   "Types of deviance and the effectiveness of legal sanctions." Pp. 389-407 in W. Chambliss (ed.), Criminal Law in Action. Santa Barbara, Ca.: Hamilton Publishing Co.
    1972   Boxman. New York: Harper Torchbooks.

Clague, C.
    1973   "Legal strategies for dealing with heroin addiction." American Economic Review 63:262-269.

de Alarcon, R.
  1969 "The spread of heroin use in a community." U.N. Bulletin on Narcotics 21:17-22.
DeFleur, L.
  1975 "Biasing influences on drug arrest records: implications for deviance research." American Sociological Review 40:88-103.
Denzin, N. K.
  1977 "Notes on the criminogenic hypothesis: a case study of the American liquor industry." American Sociological Review 42:905-920.
Ditton, J.
  1977a "Perks, pilferage and the fiddle: the historical structure of invisible wages." Theory and Society 4:39-71.
  1977b Part-time Crime. London: Macmillan.
DuPont, R.
  1971 "Profile of a heroin-addiction epidemic." New England Journal of Medicine 285:320-324.
DuPont, R., and M.Greene
  1973 "The dynamics of the heroin addiction epidemic." Science 181:716-722.
Edelman, M.
  1971 Politics as Symbolic Action. Chicago: Markham.
Erickson, E.
  1969 "The social costs of the discovery and suppression of the clandestine distribution of heroin." Journal of Political Economy 77:484-486.
Ehrlich, I.
  1973 "Participation in illegitimate activities: a theoretical and empirical investigation." Journal of Political Economy 81:521-564
Fernandez, R.
  1969 "The clandestine distribution of heroin, its discovery and suppression: a comment." Journal of Political Economy 77:487.
  1973 "The problem of heroin addiction and radical political economy." American Economic Review 63:257-262.
Form, W.
  1968 "Occupations and careers." Pp. 245-257 in International Encyclopedia of the Social Sciences. Volume Eleven. New York: Macmillan.
Geis, G.
  1974 "Avocational crime." Pp. 273 in D. Glaser (ed.), Handbook of Criminology. Chicago: Rand McNally.
Gibbs, J.
  1975 Crime, Punishment and Deterrence. New York: Elsevier.
Goldman, A.
  1975 "What will happen when middle-class America gets the straight dope." New York Magazine 8:28-36; 39-41.
Gooberman, L.A.
  1974 Operation Intercept: The Multiple Consequences of Public Policy. New York: Pergamon Press.
Goode, E.
  1970 The Marijuana Smokers. New York: Basic Books.
Greene, M.
  1975 "The resurgence of heroin abuse in the District of Columbia." Pp. 242-254 in Hearings of Permanent Subcommittee on Investigations of the Committee on Government Operations, U.S. Senate, 94th Congress, 1st Session, June 9-11, Part I.
Greene, M., B.S. Brown, and R.L. DuPont
  1975 "Controlling the abuse of illicit methadone in Washington, D.C." Archives of General Psychiatry 32:221-226.

Grinspoon, L., and P. Hedblom
   1975   The Speed Culture: Amphetamine Use and Abuse in America. Cambridge, Mass: Harvard University Press.

Gusfield, J.
   1980   The Culture of Social Problems. Chicago: University of Chicago Press.

Hall, O.
   1946   "The informal organization of the medical profession." Canadian Journal of Economics and Political Science 12:30-44.
   1948   "The stages of a medical career." American Journal of Sociology 53:327-336.

Heller, J.D.
   1973   "The attempt to control illicit drug supply." Pp. 383-407 in Drug Use in America: Problem in Perspective. Volume III, Technical Papers of the Second Report of the National Commission on Marijuana and Drug Abuse. Washington: U.S. Government Printing Office.

Hellman, A.
   1975   Laws Against Marijuana. Urbana: University of Illinois Press.

Holahan, J.
   1972   "The economics of heroin," Pp. 255-299 in P. Wald, et al. (eds.), Dealing with Drug Abuse. New York: Praeger.

Helmer, J.
   1975   Drugs and Minority Repression. New York: Seabury Press.

Hessler, R.
   1974   "Junkies in white: drug addiction among physicians." Pp. 146-153 in C.D. Bryant (ed.), Deviant Behavior: Occupational and Organization Bases. Chicago: Rand McNally.

Hughes, E.C.
   1958   Men and Their Work. New York: Free Press.

Hughes, P.H.
   1977   Behind Walls of Respect. Chicago: University of Chicago Press.

Hughes, P.
   1971   "The social structure of a heroin copping community."American Journal of Psychiatry 128:551-557.

Jackson, B.
   1969   A Thief's Primer. New York: Macmillan [paper ed., Outside the Law, published in 1972 by Transaction Books].

Johnson, W., and R. Bogomony
   1973   "Selective justice: drug law enforcement in six American cities." Pp. 498-650 in Drug Use in America: Problem in Perspective. Volume III. Technical papers of the Second Report of the National Commission on Marijuana and Drug Abuse. Washington; U.S. Government Printing Office.

Johnson. W., R. Peterson, and L.E. Wells.
   1977   "Arrest probabilities for marijuana users as indicators of selective law enforcement." American Journal of Sociology 83:681-699.

Kamistra, J.
   1975   Weed. New York: Bantam Books.

Kanter, R.M.
   1977   Men and Women of the Corporation. New York: Basic Books.

Klockars, C.
   1974   The Professional Fence. New York: The Free Press.

Leff, A.
   1976   Swindling and Selling. New York: The Free Press.

Letkemann, P.
   1973   Crime as Work. Englewood Cliffs, N.J.: Prentice-Hall.

Levin, G., E. Roberts, and G. Hirsch
 1975 The Persistent Poppy: A Computer-Aided Search for Heroin Policy. Cambridge, Mass.: Ballinger.
McAuliffe, W., and R.A. Gordon
 1974 "A test of Lindesmith's theory of addiction: the frequency of euphoria among long-term addicts." American Journal of Sociology 79:795-840.
McDonald, W.G.
 1973 "Enforcement of narcotics laws in the District of Columbia." Pp. 651-685 in Drug Use in America: Problem in Perspective. Volume III. Technical Papers of the Second Report of the National Commission on Marijuana and Drug Abuse. Washington: U.S. Government Printing Office.
Mack, J.
 1964 "Full-time miscreants, delinquent neighborhoods and criminal networks."British Journal of Sociology 15:38-53.
 1972 "The able criminal." British Journal of Criminology 12:44-54.
Manning, P.K.
 1980 The Narcs' Game: Organizational and Informational Limits on Drug Law Enforcement. Cambridge, Mass.: M.I.T. Press.
Manning, P.K. and L.J. Redlinger
 1977 "Invitational edges of corruption: some consequences of narcotic law enforcement." Pp. 279-310 in P.E. Rock (ed.) Drugs and Politics. New Brunswick, Transaction Books.
 1978 "Working bases for corruption: some consequences of narcotic law enforcement." Pp. 60-89 in A. Trebach (ed.), Drugs, Crime and Public Policy. New York: Praeger.
 1979 "The political economy of fieldwork ethics." Pp. 125-148 in C. Klockars and R. O'Conner (eds.), Deviance and Its Relation to the Ethics of Social Research. Beverly Hills: Sage.
 forth-coming"Observations on the impact of police strategies upon the trade in opiates." Iros: The International Review of Opium Studies. Philadelphia: Institute for the Study of Human Issues.
Miller, G.
 1940 The Big Con. Indianapolis: Bobbs-Merrill.
 1978 Odd Jobs. Englewood Cliffs, N.J.: Prentice-Hall.
Moore, M.
 1976 "Limiting supplies of drugs to illicit markets." Unpublished paper, Kennedy School, Harvard University, November.
 1977a Buy and Bust. Lexington, Mass.: Lexington Books.
 1977b "Reorganization plan #2 reviewed." Unpublished paper, Kennedy School, Harvard University, January.
O'Donnell, J.
 1976 Young Men and Drugs—A Nation Wide Survey. Research Monograph Number 5, National Institute of Drug Abuse. Rockville, Md.: NIDA.
Packer, H.L.
 1968 The Limits of the Criminal Sanction. Palo Alto: Stanford University Press.
Pekkanen, J.
 1973 The American Drug Connection: Profiteering and Politicing in the "Ethical" Drug Industry. Chicago: Follett Publishing Co.
Perrow, C.
 1972 Complex Organizations—A Critical Essay (2nd ed.). Glenview, Ill.: Scott, Foresman and Co.
Phillips, J., and R. Wynne
 1980 Cocaine: The Mystique and the Reality, New York: Avon Books.

Drugs as Work

Preble, E., and J. Casey
   1969 "Taking care of business-the heroin user's life on the streets." International Journal of the Addictions 4:1-24.

Radelet, M.
   1977 "Social factors influencing medicalization of anxiety: a study of tranquilizer use." Ph.D. dissertation, Department of Sociology, Purdue University.

Redlinger, L.J.
   1969 "Dealing in dope: market mechanisms and distribution patterns of illicit narcotics." Ph.D. dissertation, Department of Sociology, Northwestern University.
   1975a "Marketing and distributing heroin: some sociological observations." Journal of Psychedelic Drugs 7:331-35.
   1975b "Hot stuff in the ashes: notes on heroin, crime and law enforcement in Phoenix." Report to Drug Abuse Council. Washington, D.C.
   1977 "Suppression and regulation: notes on the probable futility of the drug laws." Unpublished paper delivered to American Society of Criminology, Atlanta, Ga.

Redlinger, L.J. and J. Michel
   1970 "Ecological variations in heroin abuse." Sociological Quarterly 11:219-229.

Reiss, A.J., Jr.
   1974 "Discretionary justice." Pp. 679-687 in D. Glaser (ed.), Handbook of Criminology. Chicago: Rand McNally.

Reiss, A.J., Jr., and D. Bordua
   1967 "Environment and organization: a perspective on the police." Pp. 25-55 in D. Bordua (ed.), The Police: Six Sociological Essays. New York: Wiley.

Reynolds, H.
   1981 Cops and Dollars: The Economics of Criminal Law and Justice. Springfield, Illinois: Charles C. Thomas.

Rottenberg, S.
   1968 "The clandestine distribution of heroin, its discovery and suppression" Journal of Political Economy 76:78-90.

Sabag, R.
   1976 Snow-Blind. Indianapolis, Indiana: Bobbs-Merrill.

Schelling, T.
   1967 "Economics and criminal enterprise." The Public Interest 7:61-78.
   1971 "What is the business of organized crime?" Journal of Public Law 20:71-84.

Silverman, M.
   1974 Pills, Profits and Politics. Berkeley: University of California Press.

Simon, H.
   1976 Administrative Behavior. 3rd Edition. New York: Free Press.

Soref, M.
   forthcoming"The structure of illegal drug markets: an organizational approach." Urban Life.

Stigler, G.
   1970 "The optimum enforcement of laws." Journal of Political Economy 78:526-536.
   1975 The Citizen and the State: Essays on Regulation. Chicago: University of Chicago Press.

Sutherland, E. [annotated and interpreted]
   1937 The Professional Thief [by a Professional Thief]. Chicago: University of Chicago Press.

von Neumann, J., and O. Morgenstern
   1944 The Theory of Games and Economic Behavior. Princeton: Princeton University Press.

Webster, J
   1975 "Drug enforcement: have the police gone into business for themselves?" Pp. 189-209 in E. Viano and J. Reiman (eds.), The Police in Society. Lexington, Mass.: D.C. Heath.

Weick, K.
   1977   The Social Psychology of Organizing. (2nd ed.) Reading, Mass.: Addison-Wesley.
Williams, J.R.
   1977   Effects of Labelling the 'Drug-Abuser': An Inquiry. National Institute of Drug Abuse Research Monograph #6. Washington: U.S. Government Printing Office.
Williams, J.R., L.J. Redlinger, and P.K. Manning
   1979   Police Narcotics Control: Patterns and Strategies. Washington: U.S. Government Printing Office.
Wilson, J.Q.
   1975   Thinking About Crime. New York: Basic Books.
Woodely, R.
   1971   Dealer. New York: Holt, Rinehart and Winston.
Zald, M.
   1970   Organizational Change. Chicago: University of Chicago Press.

SUCCESS, FAILURE, AND ANOMIE IN ARTS AND CRAFTS WORK: BREAKING IN TO COMMERCIAL COUNTRY MUSIC SONGWRITING

Richard A. Peterson and John Ryan

Aspiring contemporary American commercial musicians, actors, painters, writers, and the like have to learn how to "break in to" their chosen line of work. "Breaking in," "getting a break," and similar oft-repeated phrases suggest a pattern of career entry which mixes aggressive self-assertion, luck, and probably failure. The terms also suggest that the rewards are rich and career success assured once one has broken through the initial barrier.

Breaking in is not the usual means of occupational entry. The first rung on many occupational ladders may be difficult to achieve, but aspirants don't normally talk about breaking in to medicine, engineering, or government work. The training and experience required for entry-level positions are clear and relatively objective. What is more, trainees take numerous tests along the way so they can accurately gauge their progress and prospects. These processes, which make for orderly careers, have been studied in a wide range of occupations, and they have been summarized in the various textbooks on occupations (Hall, 1975; Montagna, 1977; Ritzer, 1977). In contrast, relatively little is known about our subject—the recurrent strategies of breaking in.

To understand better the nature and requisites of breaking in, this research has three goals. The *first* is to describe the three major systems of commercial song production and to show the importance of each in contemporary country music. The *second* goal is to describe what it takes to break in and the four types of adaptation which songwriters employ to cope with the very high probability of failure. Robert Merton's paradigm of modes of adaptation to anomie is employed for this purpose. The *third* goal is to show three distinct ways that orderly careers have been instituted in other areas of arts and crafts production. This review further highlights the socio-structural reasons that songwriters have not been able to enjoy orderly careers.

Illustrations are drawn primarily from the field of country music songwriting. This occupational specialty is appropriate because the field of country music songwriting is continually open to the unschooled novice eager to break in. The field is open for four linked reasons.

First, relatively few country music artists sing songs that they themselves have composed, so there is a continual market for new songs composed by persons who specialize in songwriting.

Second, it is believed that no preparation, training, or special apprenticeship is needed to write good songs. Many of the established writers have no training in music theory, have no great proficiency in playing an instrument, and cannot read music. What is more, country music lyrics appear to be extremely simple so that innumerable people without prior training or experience write songs. Since a few of these *are* recorded, and over the years several have become major hits, other novices are continually encouraged to write and submit their songs to recording artists.

Third, there is no union shop or licensing of proficient writers. There is no clear way of sorting the most prospectful songwriters from the rest. The *next* song of a novice who has shown no great talent may be excellent. Hank Williams, for example, wrote simple derivative songs for several years and then, overnight, began to produce widely acclaimed unique songs such as "Cold, Cold Heart," "Half as Much," and "I'm So Lonesome I Could Cry" in quick succession (Malone, 1968:234-236; Rumble, 1980).

Finally, even the experts are unable to predict in advance which of the hundreds of new songs written each week, whether written by established writers or unknowns, will be successful in the marketplace. The most successful record producers record songs which fail to become popular, and producers can also point to hit songs which they had earlier rejected as having no commercial potential (McNeel and Luther, 1978). For example, novice writer Don Schlitz's "The Gambler," which had been rejected by many major record producers over a three-year period, became an instant hit and "Country Music Song of the Year" for Kenny Rodgers in 1979. That same year, John Conlee had a number-one hit on "Back Side of Thirty," which had failed on its original release in 1976 (Kirby, 1979).

In combination, these four conditions mean that the occupation of country music writing is continually open to the unschooled novice eager to break in.

I. DATA SOURCES

This study is part of an ongoing investigation of facets of the commercial music industry in which both authors are engaged. In addition to this project, they are jointly examining the constraints on creativity experienced by commercial songwriters (Ryan and Peterson, 1982).

Ryan, a songwriter himself, is completing a dissertation on the role of song publishing and music rights organizations in shaping the development of popular music. In addition, he roomed with an aspiring singer/songwriter for six months after moving to Nashville in 1977 and participated in a professional songwriters' workshop in 1980.

Peterson has made systematic observations of the music recording process since 1962, has taken or lectured in four technical music industry courses, has worked as a consultant for a music publishing firm, and has interviewed songwriters and publishers off and on since 1972 as part of his study of the development of the music industry in Nashville. He has also supervised a number of undergraduate students who have provided taped interviews with songwriters in conjunction with their course work.

It is impossible, therefore, to state accurately how many interviews provide the relevant documentary material for this research. It is also nearly meaningless to make such an enumeration because some of the contacts have been casual and fleeting, while others have lasted nearly a decade. Since some of the contacts were made without explicitly telling the informant that their comments might be quoted in print, names are not routinely given, but our primary debts in this regard are listed in the "Acknowledgments."

Finally the authors made a survey of the *Billboard* "Hot Country Singles," a weekly listing of the 100 top-selling records in the country music field. The survey was made in order to see just how open the country market is to novice writers.

The charts for the first week in May and November for 1979 and 1980 were used. These dates were selected to avoid any of the unusual seasons such as Christmas or the doldrums of late summer. Dates six months apart were chosen to make it unlikely that any song would be represented on more than one chart.

The four charts provide 100 chart positions each, but the total sample includes 411 songs because in 11 cases *Billboard* judged that both sides of the record were contributing to sales. All of the songs were classified separately by the two authors with the help of people knowledgeable about the music industry, and the two lists were compared to eliminate discrepancies. The only discrepancies were in the judgments about the degree of prior success which distinguishes what we call the "professional" from the "novice." These distinctions are discussed below.

Fifty-one of the songs, or about 12 on each chart, had enjoyed prior commercial success.[1] The remaining 360 songs, 77% of all those charted, were new in the sense that they had not been hits before. Most had been penned in the 18 months prior to the charted record's release. These 360 songs are the product of the writers being studied here—persons writing for the country music market at the time of the survey.

II. THREE MODES OF SONG PRODUCTION

In order to understand the process of "breaking in," it is necessary to describe the industry being broached. There are three distinct ways in which newly written songs are obtained, whether for the soul, popular, disco, or country music markets. Which method predominates greatly affects the novice writer's chances of breaking in.

First, there is the method of vertical integration that is referred to in the industry as *in-house* production. Here the record company or its executives own one or more publishing firms, each of which has a stable of regular staff writers who provide most or all of the new songs for the singers that the company has under contract. The major record companies in the popular music market successfully operated in this way through the 1940s and the early 1950s (Gillett, 1972; Peterson and Berger, 1972), but the clearest example of successful vertical integration is Motown Record Company in its heyday in the soul and popular music markets of the 1960s (Morse, 1962). Within this system the staff writers have a virtual monopoly of access to company artists, and novices have no regular channel for breaking in.

Second, there is the *singer/songwriter* mode of song production. Here the performing artist or group composes all or nearly all the songs they perform. This style of music writing came to the fore in the pop music market with the Beach Boys, Bob Dylan, and the Beatles in the mid-1960s. To the extent that singer/songwriters write their own songs, the professional songwriter is frozen out of the market.

Third, there is the *job-shop* method of song production. Here the creative elements which go into making each record are assembled from different sources on a record-by-record basis. In such cases a number of independent songwriters, or the publishers who represent them, compete with each other to get their songs recorded by the prominent recording artists.

These competitive job-shop conditions give the greatest opportunity for aspiring songwriters to break in.

III. COUNTRY SONG PRODUCTION

Such job-shop competition can be found in some parts of each sub-field of commercial music production, but it is currently most conspicuous in the field of country music. From the 1940s through the mid-1970s, the writing of country music was dominated by the job-shop rather than the in-house or singer/songwriter modes of song production (Malone, 1968:214; Peterson, 1975; Rumble, 1980).

The relative importance of the three writing systems and the chances of a novice writer's breaking in in 1979-1980 are indicated in the charts sampled for this study.

The singer/songwriter system is most easily identified. Of the 360 new songs, 53 were composed solely by the performer or members of the performance groups featured on the record, and another 21 songs were credited to the performer working with another writer. Thus, 20.6% of the new songs in the country market were written in whole or in part by persons singing on the record.

It is not so easy to assess the importance of the in-house form of song production. No major record company in the country market now keeps a stable of writers to compose the songs to be recorded by its artists, but there are two in-house-type arrangements which restrict the competitiveness of the open job-shop system.

In many cases it is possible to trace links between writers, publishers, producers, artists, or managers that—it is widely held in the industry—restrict the equal access of "unconnected" songwriters. This sort of in-house production includes all arrangements in which the singer, producer, or any other person who could influence the choice among songs to be recorded has a traceable financial interest in the song chosen. Such links can be identified for 9.8% of the sample; this represents a conservative estimate because we and our expert judges could not know the details of all of the financial arrangements.

Numerous small companies make country music records and in most cases employ an in-house system of production in the sense that the songwriter, publisher, and artist are all affiliated with the firm. While exhibiting vertical integration in production, these companies do not have the funds, staff, and facilities to manufacture, promote, and distribute records, so these services are contracted for with one or another of the distributing firms. The performers who record on these small independent labels include artists who once enjoyed success on a major label but fell from popularity after country music marketing was transformed in the mid-1970s (Peterson, 1978) and persons who enjoy a purely local reputation.

Occasionally records made in this way reach a wide-enough audience to be charted by *Billboard*. In our sample, 9.7% of the songs were produced by such companies, but none were in the top one-third of the chart and most were in the bottom quarter, suggesting that they do not pose any competitive threat to the few major firms that dominate the rest of the chart positions. Since these companies are so marginal to the country music market, they do not provide novices a channel for breaking in.

Having reviewed the alternative means of providing new songs, we are now in a position to assess the importance of the independent job-shop system of production. If artists or writers working without co-writers accounted for 14.7% of the new songs on the country charts, and small firms for 9.7%, independent songwriters wrote 75.6% of the popular songs sampled. More accurately, they had a part in writing this proportion of the songs because in 3.3% of all cases the performers are listed as co-writers and in 2.8% of the cases the producer or some other collaborator gets co-writer credit. These figures show that the job-shop system of production utilizing professional songwriters is the most important source of new country music songs.

Clearly, professional songwriters are able to compete successfully in the country music market, but what are the chances of breaking in to this fraternity? To get an answer, professional writers were divided into two groups: established writers (those who have had several songs on the charts in recent years) and novices.

For some, the song in our sample is the first of their songs to have been recorded and to have become popular enough to be charted. Other novices have had up to six songs charted, but they have not had enough commercial success to be rated as established professionals by our music industry judges. Novices are listed on 9.2% of the songs. Of the latter, almost three-fourths credit not only the novice but also an established writer or artist (only 16 songs were written by novices working alone). Even for the novice, then, it is important to have connections. In summary, there is some chance of breaking in to country music songwriting, but the chance is slight.

IV. THE MERTONIAN PARADIGM

A song that reaches the top 10 of the weekly country music charts will earn its writer $5,000-$10,000 in a matter of months—and that is just for one song. A top writer may have three or more songs on the charts at one time. The Tree Publishing Firm estimates that every country music radio station in the United States played a song written by Sonny Throckmorton once every three hours, on average, during the entire year of 1980. According to the music licensing firm Broadcast Music Incorporated, Boudleaux and Felice Bryant had over 1,000 songs recorded with over 200,000,000 records sold between 1949 and 1974, and they are still writing hit songs. The financial lure of song writing is obvious.

There is no way of accurately measuring how many hundreds, or even thousands, of songs are submitted to be considered for recording each month—the experts differ widely in their estimates. Dennis Lecorriere claims to have listened to over 2,000 songs to find the 10 that fit the image and mood appropriate for a

Dr. Hook album. While the songs of many writers were screened, the work of the established writers received more respectful and thorough consideration.

The active competition among many people to achieve high goals with rich rewards, in which some are more likely to fail than others, is a recurrent condition in American society, as Robert Merton (1968:175-214) has noted. He characterizes the resultant condition as a state of anomie.

Merton describes five sorts of adaptations to such stressful conditions. Although he was explaining the origins of deviant behavior in American society at large, and his ideas have been widely critiqued and modified,[2] the original paradigm is useful for understanding the accommodations that are made by persons trying to break in to commercial songwriting because it most nearly seems to fit the conditions found in the commercial music industry. Each of the commercial adaptations represents a different way of accommodating oneself to the success goals and the means that are defined as legitimate for achieving the goals. Thus, to use his paradigm, it is necessary at the outset to define the goals and legitimate means for becoming a commercial songwriter, and to show how access to these legitimate goals and means is blocked for a goodly number of would-be songwriters.

A. Goals

The goal of the commercial songwriter is to have numerous songs recorded, and to have some of these recorded by several different artists. From these songs the writer obtains a hopefully continuous flow of income and creates a measure of renown within the world of commercial music. The commercial writer would like to pen a song which becomes a "standard" sung widely and remembered for generations, but the focus is on the routine production of numerous good songs.

As Harlan Howard, veteran country music songwriter, puts it in characterizing what he calls the professional and what we term the commercial writer: "I don't consider the guy who's just getting records a professional writer. He is getting close, and I certainly don't think you could call him an amateur. He's just a beginner, but he's got a lot of things to learn, plus he's got to prove that he's not just a one-song Johnny, both to himself and everyone else, because we've had a lot of those.... I think the professional is one who makes his living at it, with no other source of income. A guy is an amateur even if he's got a song recorded. He's still an amateur in my opinion until he turns that corner and actually gets into it with both feet, sustains himself and starts working full-time at writing. Then he is a pro" (Gant, 1973:116).

The commercial writer receives acclaim from peers for having a craft-like ability (Peterson and White, 1979; Becker, 1981:Chapter 9); that is, the goal is to write diverse sorts of songs on demand, not needing to await inspiration to create new works. The commercial songwriter does not aspire to become a star whose name and face are recognized by fans. To the degree that stardom is the goal, the individual is something other than, or in addition to, a commercial songwriter as the term is defined in the world of country music. As Harlan Howard noted, "the ones I consider to be really professional are those who do not make appearances [as performers] or do anything else except write. It is like being an author; that's all he does" (Gant, 1973:116).

Even the most successful commercial writers, such as Harlan Howard, Boudleaux Bryant, Ben Peters, Sonny Throckmorton, and Bob McDill, are virtually unknown outside the music industry. Like other essentially anonymous creative people, their songwriting "credits" are mentioned as part of any formal introduction in order to certify their importance to the unknowing. Within the world of country music, the writer must become a performer as well to attain *public* acclaim (Hall, 1979).

This statement of the goals emerges from the interviews, the studies of songwriting and publishing (Gant, 1973; Siman, 1976; Rumble, 1980), and the various books on "how to write a commercial country music song" which have appeared over the past decade (Bart, 1970; Burt and Ferguson, 1970; Kosser, 1976; Baskerville, 1979; Kuroff, 1980).

B. Means

"Talent, perseverance, and a lot of luck, just get the strong song to the right artist at the right time"—that is what it takes to get songs recorded, according to Mickey Newberry, veteran songwriter. The means of increasing the probability of these things happening are described in a number of interviews and how-to books.

The legitimate means of achieving success as a commercial songwriter can be stated as a set of imperatives:

1. Affiliate with an established publishing firm which can facilitate getting songs recorded.
2. Seek out and take criticism and suggestions; this may be facilitated by writing with another, more experienced person.
3. Write in straightforward terms about conventional situations rather than about personal or unique happenings.
4. Write for a specific artist or type of artist.
5. Write to communicate to a particular large category of the audience (usually 30-year-old women).
6. Write regularly rather than waiting for inspiration.
7. Work on several songs simultaneously so that a block on one song does not halt all productivity.
8. Act outgoing and optimistic, meeting as many people as possible without being overbearing, because one never knows what contact will lead to having a song recorded.
9. Learn the fine etiquette of how to "pitch" songs to artists and producers.

10. While doing all the foregoing correctly, expect many rejections rather than quick success and be prepared to be financially supported in other ways for at least two years after moving to Nashville.

Together, these are a prescription for becoming a craftsman writer, what Becker (1976:43-46) calls the "integrated professional."

C. Limited Access

In the job-shop system of song production, hundreds of writers compete with each other to get their own songs recorded by the few major recording artists. The objective chances for success are not great, and they tend to be overestimated not only by the aspiring novice but by other people in the music industry as well (Hodnette, 1974; Siman, 1976; Baskerville, 1979:34).

For example, Tom T. Hall, appearing on the "Mike Douglas Show" in early 1981, was asked by Douglas whether it was possible to make money writing country music songs. Smiling, Hall said, "Oh, yes," explaining that his song "Harper Valley P.T.A." was written in 20 minutes. Recorded by Jeanne C. Riley, the song earned him $40,000 from record sales alone. In addition, he earned 2½ cents each time the song was played on the radio. Recently the lyric has been used in a movie and a television series, so he has earned additional royalties. Facing the camera, Hall concluded, "that's not bad for 20 minutes work!" Numerous stories of this sort circulate, implying that the dream of "rags to riches" is within easy reach of anyone.

In theory the best song will be chosen irrespective of who has written it. But, as noted earlier, it is virtually impossible to distinguish between the potential hit and the large number of good songs. In practice, songs by established writers and songs which the artist or producer has a financial interest in stand a much better chance of being recorded than do the songs of the aspiring novice. Thus, many aspirants who write good songs and who anticipate succeeding face continual failure.

Such sorts of favoritism are common in most social situations. When there is a choice, people tend to choose the familiar, and people go to great lengths to maintain contacts. For example, Peterson and White (1979) describe the tactics that the clique of established musicians, a group they call the simplex, use jointly to exclude novices from competing on an equal footing for the few best jobs. Something very much like the simplex seems to operate to protect the established writers against newcomers. With access blocked using the legitimate means of striving for success, the aspiring writer may turn to any one of the four "deviant" accommodations identified by Merton (1968).

V. THE PARADIGM APPLIED

Many novices actively seek to achieve the goals of songwriting success by employing the legitimate means. Merton (1968) refers to such people as conformists, and Michael Kosser (1976) provides an extended description of the conformist means of breaking in to commercial songwriting. Rather than discuss conformity separately, it will be introduced as appropriate in describing Merton's four "deviant" accommodations: innovation, ritualism, retreatism, and rebellion. Each involves giving up either the legitimate means or the success goals, or abandoning them both.

A. Innovation

Since the success goals are strongly desired, and the chances of success by accepted means are so slight, writers may adapt illegitimate means to achieve the success goals. Merton (1969:195) calls this strategy innovation. Merton recognized that innovation might take novel forms, but that recurrent patterns of innovation usually emerge.[3]

The most prevalent form of innovation among some writers is for novice writers to give up part of the ownership rights to their work in order to get songs recorded. The writer loses royalty payments for each right signed away. Usually this involves assigning the publishing rights to a company owned by the recording artist or the record producer. In more extreme cases, the artist or producer may demand co-writer credit. For example, in 1975 Gene Tubb and D. Lindsey wrote a song "Two Story House." Tammy Wynette, an established country music star, agreed to record the song with her ex-husband, George Jones, on condition that she receive both co-publishing and co-writer credit on the song. Her involvement guaranteed that the song would be well presented and that a major record company would invest enough money in it to produce, distribute, and promote the song properly. In May 1980 the record hit the top of the country music charts. Such singers, producers, and co-writers may, of course, participate in writing the song, but a number of well-known people are notorious for insisting on gaining a financial stake in a song before they will consider recording it (Wood, 1980).[4]

Innovation is so widely practiced that it is sometimes talked of as being necessary to breaking in. "Hey, assigning is just one of those things a beginner has to do to get attention," a successful songwriter told us. "It is all a part of paying the dues. Once you are established, once you have paid those dues, once you are known as a hot writer, *then* you can dictate your own terms; have your own publishing company and all."

Even if it is widely practiced, assigning rights to get a song cut is illegitimate because alternative songs should be judged solely on their merits, according to the ethos of the commercial songwriter (Wood, 1980:68). As Gant (1974:62) notes, "it is the 'deals' and the 'in-house' situation that the writers who were interviewed disliked most about the difficulties of getting one's songs to market."

Those occupations in which breaking in is the standard means of career entry provide various opportunities for innovation. These range from working for less than "scale" wages to the exchange of sexual favors to get a break (Peterson and White, 1979). Such innovation strategies are different from the accommodations to be discussed below in that they are, in effect, self-eliminating. The successful innovator does break in and thus has a chance to succeed using legitimate means.

B. Ritualism

Ritualism, according to Merton (1968), involves conforming to the means of achieving success but, in effect, abandoning the goal of commercial songwriting success. Ritualists go through the motions, doing some of the right things but doing them at the wrong time, or persisting in a particular strategy when it no longer has a realistic chance of success. The epithet "squirrel" has been applied to such people in Nashville.

Examples abound. A writer told us that in 1978 a song of his was quarterfinalist in an International Songwriters' Contest. Rather than moving aggressively to have the song recorded, he wrote another verse and submitted it to the 1979 contest. Several Nashville clubs have regular "writers' nights" at which people can showcase their new songs in the hope of being heard by people influential in the music industry. Some writers are discovered this way, but others perform much the same set of songs for months on end without any commercial success. In time such ritualists become stigmatized as "writers' night habituals" (Lucas, 1979).

Ritualists congregate at writers' nights, songwriting workshops, and certain night spots. They exchange much information, give advice, and provide encouragement for each other. And yet, since they work in pluralistic ignorance, much of the information is false and the encouragement self-defeating.

Ritualists tend to forget that they are trying to write songs which will ultimately catch the attention of a broad audience. Instead, they start to write and perform almost exclusively for each other. To maintain their morale in the face of failure to break in, ritualists tell each other that their songs are as good as those that are being recorded. As Billy Sherrill, noted producer and songwriter, comments, "One trap writers fall into is that they knock each other out with their songs. A lot of writers get together in little groups, and they come up with a line that they all totally freak out over; the man on the street doesn't even know what the hell they're talking about" (MacNeel and Luther, 1978:140).

Ritualists have not given up the attempt to break in using the legitimate means. Buoyed by stories of struggling writers who eventually become famous—for example, that Kris Kristofferson emptied ashtrays for two years at the RCA studio—they look for their lucky break. Ritualists often assert optimistically that it is only a matter of time.

One recurrent assertion is that there is a waiting line in front of the door of success. One Los Angeles writer, in 1977, explained how Jackson Browne had just broken in, and that there were only two persons in front of him in the queue awaiting discovery. This queue theory of success was put in quite mechanistic terms using the symbolism of clockworks by a Nashville writer: "Everything is like wheels in a clock. You're just sitting on your cog, waiting until your turn comes around. Sometimes people fall off before that time comes, and that's it. But if your time is right, there's no way to stop you" (Gant, 1974:19).

Rationalizations for ritualistic activity have been reported widely in similar is employment situations. The idea that one must "pay dues" or spend "time" is perhaps most widely noted. That there is literally a queue of hopefuls awaiting discovery has not been reported elsewhere, but McHugh (1966) notes precisely the opposite theory among hopeful actors in New York City. His respondents asserted that so many actors of more or less equal ability report for open casting calls that, from the aspirant's perspective, the chance of being chosen is purely random. Whether conceptualizing a queue or a random walk, these formulations rationalize ritualistic conformity to the legitimate means in the fact of persistent failure.

C. Retreatism

Retreatism involves giving up both the success goals and the legitimate means of attaining success. There are the hundreds—probably thousands—of people who write lyrics or compose tunes for their own enjoyment. While numerous, they are not part of the commercial music world. There are, however, three sorts of retreatists who work on the edge of that world.

The first includes those who write songs and usually perform them as well without expecting to succeed in the national market. Typically, these people have "regular day jobs," compose music on the side, and play on weekends for audiences near their homes. Curly Dan and Wilma Ann Holcomb provide a case in point. Southern-born, they work in Detroit and play country music in the style of the 1950s in local clubs on weekends. Their own compositions combine a nostalgia for the South and rural ways with tortured references to the "better life" in Detroit. (Curly Dan and Wilma Ann are available on Old Homestead Records, a local label.)

Hundreds of groups of this kind make an annual pilgrimage to Nashville in their vans and band buses for Fan Fair week. They plaster telephone poles with playbills, give away promotional buttons or bumper stickers, and sell a few "custom-pressed" records to people who come from the towns where they play. Typically, these local acts create country music as a hobby and derive great satisfaction from their association with the music.

The second type of retreatist is quite different. These are the individuals who have written a "message song," and try by any and all means to get it to a "big artist" so that their piece of the revealed truth will be heard. Every political or economic disaster brings dozens of these "bugs" to Nashville. Industry officials dislike them because the songs are usually dreadful, and because the writers do not adhere to the rules of pitching songs within the commercial music market. Their zealous mission to get their message across is interpreted as psychotic by people in the money-making world of the music industry. A few of these zealots, like Bill Rogers, author of songs praising Lieutenant William Calley, Audie Murphy, and Richard Nixon while condemning the likes of Jane Fonda, attain the status of notable crank (Bailey, 1974).

The third kind of retreatist is less easily identified than the two considered so far. While the former endeavor to be visible, this third type hides, shunning evaluation. Although these latter retreatist may write many songs and they may come to the major recording centers, they do not aggressively work to get their songs recorded. They may have numerous reasons for this: they need to rework their songs, they need to see someone who is out of town, it is the wrong time of the year, their prime contact has not returned their telephone call, they don't feel well, they are repulsed by what they call the "crass commercial attitudes" of the people in the industry, etc., etc.

When they do find the courage to show their work to others, it may be rejected initially, or reworking of major sections may be requested. All novices face these frustrations, but this type reacts in a distinctive fashion. They retreat further. Convinced of the worth of their songs as they are, these writers refuse to make changes deemed needed to fit the current commercial mold. They may rationalize this by saying that their work is "ahead of its time," implying that the industry may catch up and their talent will be discovered in the future.

Such writers often fix on the fact that there are "cliques" and "deals" and "politics" which link the established writers with publishers, writers, and producers. These arrangements do abound (Peterson and White, 1979; Wood, 1979; Ryan and Peterson, 1982), but focusing on such barriers as the reason for their lack of success encourages these retreatists to ignore the suggestions and advice which might make their songs more appropriate for the commercial market.

Some of these retreatists give up songwriting, but other continue implicitly believing that they, like the avant-garde painters of the early twentieth century, will be discovered and vindicated when the established cliques have had their day. When such individual retreatists seek each other out, and begin to fashion a distinctive aesthetic, they are on their way to becoming what Merton (1968) calls rebels.

D. Rebellion

Merton (1968:209) uses the term "rebellion" to identify the final form of accommodation to the difficulties of achieving success through legitimate means. The defining characteristic of rebellion for Merton is that a group of people collectively substitute new goals and new means for those they have discarded.

The term rebellion may sound inappropriate when applied to songwriting because there are no guns or barricades, but there is much talk of country music "outlaws" and a "writers' underground." While these terms are often used to gain notoriety and increase record sales (Peterson, 1979), they bespeak a singer/songwriter means of music production that, if successful, *would* revolutionize the process of songwriting and destroy the market for conforming commercial songwriters working in the job-shop system. In this sense, the term rebellion seems appropriate.

There is no single revolutionary group of writers. Rather there are a number of loose-knit networks of writers who espouse one or another view of what country music should become or should return to being. These groups of performing writers evolve rapidly as their individual and collective careers develop or disintegrate. Bob Dylan, Kris Kristofferson, Willie Nelson, Tracy Nelson, and Guy Clark all at one time were pivotal members of rebellious circles. Rebels often forsake the label "country music," just as jazz innovators from time to time have denigrated the term "jazz" and revolutionary painters sometimes define their work as "anti-art."

While the kinds of music they espouse may vary widely, rebel songwriters do share the same general goal, namely, to become financially secure and enjoy widespread public acclaim by writing personal songs exploring their own authentic feelings which strike a chord of common humanity. The perceived way of reaching this goal is to become a singer/songwriter and to sing one's own songs in public and on records, creating music in their own authentic style taking aesthetic advice only from other creators. In a word, they seek to be artists in the sociological sense of the term rather than to be craftsmen like the commercial songwriters who work in the job-shop system (Becker, 1981:Chap. 9).

Writers usually do not initially intend to be rebels. Rather, they try to succeed in the usual ways. Failing to break in, rebels do not blame themselves or the cliquish successful writers whom they emulate. Instead, they come to blame the whole mechanical job-shop system of song crafting with its rigid division of labor. Together with others who find the spark of genius in their work, they seek more holistic ways of making a life in music by performing the personal songs they write.

R-D Mowery comments on the changes involved in his transformation from aspiring conformist to rebel. "I came to Nashville. I decided I was going to be a writer for awhile, but I didn't like hustling tunes, and I didn't like writing specifically for other people. I've ended up performing my songs again which I really like to do...[Writing is] just part of what I do. I also sculpt. I also perform....I write songs about people other people don't see, the ones that are overlooked a lot of times. I'm drawn to overlooked situations and people which are stories. My songs don't have any set pattern. They have a tendency to jump right into the subject. There is no big prelude in any of them. They are written just for me to sing" (Goldberg, 1980:14-15).

E. Do Rebels Break In?

The four sorts of accommodations to the difficulties of breaking in—innovation, ritualism, retreatism, and rebellion—have been described for the most part as if they were mutually exclusive alternatives. In practice, novice writers often move from one of these to another. We have noted that frustrated conformists may become rebels. Many other patterns can be traced, but one of the most interesting and important to our concern with breaking in follows the sometimes ironic careers of singer/songwriter rebels.

Only a few writers who also sing have been successful in country music, and *all* of them are either accomplished writers like Tom T. Hall or Kris Kristofferson (who also happens to sing) or are established conventional performers like Merle Haggard, Dolly Parton, and Loretta Lynn (who also happen to write commercial songs). Apparently, to find commercial success singing only one's own songs, as Larry Gatlin does, one must write in the commercial mold, producing songs that other performers might sing just as well. There are no equivalents in country music of the numerous artists like Bob Dylan, John Lennon, Carly Simon, and Jackson Browne who have become stars by writing and singing songs portraying their own unique life experiences and points of view.

One of three things tends to happen to singer/songwriters when they are signed to major record labels. First, the singer/songwriter is allowed to make the record he or she desires, as in the case of James Talley, but then the record company, which is geared to merchandising commercial products, does not actively promote the resulting personal statement. Second, the company may decide to modify the unique sounds of the artist to make them more conventional, as in the case of Marshall Chapman, turning the final product into something which has neither artistic integrity nor commerciality. Third, the singer/songwriter may be completely unprepared to deal with having a performance contract. Here is Lee Clayton's case as he tells it. Two songs, "Ladies Love Outlaws" and "Red Dancing Dress," written by Clayton were big successes, and he was signed by MCA Records in 1973. "They gave me twenty grand to sign and about thirty-five thousand to record and another twenty for a band. I went from being broke to having big bread! I rented a limousine and kept the son-of-a-bitch night and day, chasing women and all that. I was a 'recording star' doing 'the trip.' The money just went.... To make a long story short, within that year I got the money, cut the record which got great reviews, was on the road with the band costing me $40,000 a week, and back off the tour. In January 1974 I was broke and off the label and out on the street again."

What, then, becomes of the singer/songwriter? No study of career paths has been made, but the most frequently traveled routes can be identified. Some few persist. They continue to write and tour small clubs with a band or alone. While most of these troupers give up before they are 40, some continue much longer. In his book *Lost Highways*, Peter Guralnick portrays a number of such honky-tonk troubadours.

Many rebels drop out of the music world. Some are bitter from the rejection and talk of famous people who stole their best song ideas. Many others echo the sentiments of Lee Clayton that they received an invaluable education in "life" and had a lot of fun along the way.

Many would-be singer/songwriter rebels find a place in the commercial music industry. Some become session musicians, others become publishers' representatives, and still others find another type of position working for record companies. From the perspective of this article, however, the most interesting kind of co-optation that occurs consists in singer/songwriters eventually giving up singing and attaining success as conforming commercial songwriters. Their numbers are not inconsiderable. Sixteen individuals who have written songs that are among the 360 on the charts we coded are known to have been (and several still aspire to be) singer/songwriters. It may be that the experience of writing and performing personal songs brings a desirable freshness to the commercial songs written by these would-be singer/songwriters.

Thus, in summary, rebellion proves to be the most ironic of all the five accommodations to the difficulties of breaking in to commercial songwriting. While rebellion does not succeed for country music songwriters, the attempt does provide a training ground for commercial songwriting, as well as visibility and contacts in the industry which facilitate breaking in by *conventional* means.

VI. CREATING ORDERLY CAREERS

At the outset, we accepted the novice writer's premise that there is a wall which must be breached to enter the world of commercial songwriting. Novices *do* see such a wall, but established writers do not perceive a wall at all. They see no single barrier for the commercial songwriter beyond which continuing success is more or less assured.

A. Breaking In: An Illusion?

Asked when he had made it, one established writer answered, "The question is, have I?" Another exclaimed, "I only have had two hits!" Writers repeat the cliche "you are only as good as your last song" and add that the reputation as a "hot" writer fades in a few months without another top-20-charted record.

Kosser (1976) provides a semi-fictionalized account of the difficulties of breaking in as a commercial songwriter. His protagonist has a number of successes, but each one is short-lived or turns sour in a few months. While the writer learns from each of these experiences, he has been able to support himself through the first six years of full-time songwriting only because his wife has a full-time job. At the end of this protracted period the writer is barely on the threshold of possibly attaining sustained success as a commercial songwriter.[5]

Thus, there is no *single* barrier which must be surmounted, but rather innumerable ones. What is more, there is no status such as academic tenure or job seniority to protect the writer who experiences a "dry spell" or "burnout" of his creative ability (Gant, 1974; Kosser, 1976:78-79; Ryan and Peterson, 1982). In this sense, there is no end to the process of breaking in for commercial songwriters working in the job-shop system of song production.

B. Three Ways of Ordering Careers

Not all creative crafts and arts occupations have such unpredictable career paths (Spilerman, 1977; Becker, 1981) as just described. The literature on the sociology of occupations and labor markets suggests that there are three kinds of structures which create orderly careers: the organization, the occupation, and the market (Granovetter, 1974; Hall, 1975; Spilerman, 1977). Each of these will be examined briefly in order to further specify the structural conditions that make for the break-in pattern of career entry.

Careers are sometimes ordered by the operation of the *market* itself. This occurs where the market is tiered with several levels of minor leagues which can lead to the major leagues. A classic case of a tiered market for creative talent is professional baseball.

The occupation of radio announcer (disc jockey) provides another clear example. With little or no training or practice, the novice disc jockey can begin broadcasting at off-prime hours over a station in a small market. Gaining experience and a reputation, the announcer can move to ever more powerful stations in ever larger markets and gain an ever larger income and reputation.

Sidemen in popular music bands move from less well known to better-known and better-paying bands as their reputations develop (Page, 1980). But there is no comparable tiered market in which songwriters can develop and display their talents before competing in the big time. There is only the national market.

Careers are often ordered by *organizations*. The military and the federal government provide obvious cases in point. Recruits progress through the ranks with more or less predictable speed as a function of how well their performance is rated (Hall, 1975; Montagna, 1977). Ballet dancers (Mazo, 1974) and orchestra musicians (Arian, 1971; Couch, 1976) enjoy orderly careers of this sort, as do commercial artists who work for advertising agencies and newspaper photographers (Rosenblum, 1978).

While different in other ways, all these arts and crafts situations require a regular production of more or less standard services. As noted above, songs have been written on an assembly-line basis in popular music since the 1890s in Tin

Pan Alley (Greensberg, 1930; Ewen, 1964), but the vertical integration together with a stable market has never been consolidated sufficiently to guarantee orderly careers in songwriting for any period of time.

Careers are often ordered by the *occupational group* itself (Hall, 1975; Bensman and Lilienfeld, 1973). Guilds and labor unions exemplify craft-based ways of sequencing particular jobs to ensure stable careers. Government-sanctioned academies exemplify art-based ways of ensuring stable careers. Craft unions, guilds, and art academies differ in many ways, but in common they operate to restrict the number of recruits, establish tests of achievement, set wages, define styles of work, and discipline those members who do not comply (Pevsner, 1940; Peterson and White, 1979).

Such occupational peer-based organizations were very influential in medieval and early modern Europe, but they have not had much power to stabilize creative careers for the past century because of the ascendancy of the competitive marketplace for creative products and services (White and White, 1975). Under such competitive conditions, informal circles develop in the arts, and simplexes develop in the crafts to bring some order to careers, but they are effective only for the most successful artists and crafts persons (Peterson and White, 1979).

There are several simplexes in Nashville which bring together many of the most successful active writers. These informal groups operate to discourage and keep out rival songwriters, but, like the musician simplexes analyzed earlier (Peterson and White, 1979), they also help to initiate a few select rookie writers. Typically this involves the senior writers of a publishing firm critiquing and sometimes co-writing songs with novice writers. This may facilitate breaking in (Kosser 1976:61), but it does not guarantee an orderly career development.

C. Conclusion

We have found that the conventional means of breaking in to commercial songwriting require the work routines and rhetoric of craftsmanship. We have also found, using Merton's paradigm, that the unconventional adaptations to the difficulty of breaking in may bring forth the routines and rhetoric of artistic creativity exemplified by the singer/songwriters.

The singer/songwriter system of song production operates to order careers in the rock and popular music fields (Scaduto, 1971; Gillett, 1972; Lipschitz, 1980; Markovitz and Freund, 1981) but does not do so in country music. The vertically integrated in-house system of song production like that found at Motown Records in the 1960s (Morse, 1972) also could order career lines for writers, but the in-house system does not compete successfully in the volatile country music market (Peterson and Berger, 1971; Peterson, 1978; Ryan and Peterson, 1982).

The break-in style of career entry is found in other aspects of art and craft work in which there is an oligopsonistic market, one in which many sellers compete with each other to provide services to a few purchasers of their services (McHugh,

1966; Mukerji, 1976; Powell, 1978; Friedman, 1978, 1981; Peterson and White, 1979; Simpson, 1981; Rosenblum, 1978). In the case at hand, this is exemplified by the job-shop system in which there are many songwriters competing to have their songs selected by the few leading recording artists.

This review suggests that the competitive job-shop system of production itself ensures the continuation of the patterns we have traced: the peculiar phenomenon of "breaking in," the deviant responses we have described here, and in general, unpredictable career paths for commercial songwriters.

ACKNOWLEDGMENTS

The authors gratefully acknowledge the help of the following persons who have provided valuable information, ideas, or critiques of an earlier draft: George Becker, John Brannen, Steve Buchanan, Maggie Cavender, Marshall Chapman, Guy Clark, Jack Clement, Daniel Cornfield, Paul DiMaggio, Terry Fain, Danny Finley, Jack Gibbs, Donna Hilley, Tracy Nelson, Claire L. Peterson, Beth Rabeck, John Rumble, Rick Shields, Deborah Sim, Lisa Silver, Earl Spielman, H. W. Strider, James Talley, Bruce Weigand, and Townes Van Zandt. The authors also appreciate the support of the Kennan Venture Fund during the early stages of the project.

NOTES

1. These recycled songs are of several varieties. Some, such as "Coal Miner's Daughter," are new cuts on country standards; some, such as "September Song," are new cuts on popular standards; some, such as "Chain Gang," as written by Sam Cooke, are older soul songs; some are cover versions of songs currently popular in other fields, such as Billie Jo Spears's remake of the disco hit "I Will Survive"; and finally, several are reissues of records by artists (including Jim Reeves, Patsy Cline, and Elvis Presley) who have been dead for years.

2. Numerous scholars have critiqued and tried to improve upon Merton's paradigm since it was first promulgated in the 1930s. See especially Bierstedt (1938), Dubin (1959), Cole and Zuckerman (1964), and Simon and Gagnon (1976). While these modifications may prove useful in other situations, Merton's formulation presented in *Social Theory and Social Structure* (1968) best fits the situation investigated here.

3. A dictionary definition of the term "innovation" implies uniqueness. Songwriters have indeed invented numerous novel ways of bringing their own songs to the attention of music industry gatekeepers. In the summer of 1980, for example, a personable young writer pushed a sandwich cart along Music Row in Nashville making personal deliveries whenever possible in order to become known. In January 1981 a paraplegic writer placed ads in the local Nashville newspapers informing Waylon Jennings that he had an excellent set of songs composed especially for the country music performer. A vast variety of such tactics could be described, but Merton (1968) defined innovation in a rather special way by focusing on those innovations which are repeated often enough to become predictable as a pattern. We use Merton's term innovation as he intended it, just as with the other types of accommodation to anomie that he described.

4. This form of innovation is hardly unique to the Nashville-based music industry of the 1980s. Similar arrangements were widely practiced in popular music in the 1940s (MacDonald, 1941), in the the 1920s (Goldberg, 1930; Hammond, 1970), and even in the New York Tin Pan Alley and London commercial publishing industry of 1890 (Whitmark and Goldberg, 1975; Pearsall, 1975).

5. The situation for songwriters sounds very much like that described for high school students by

James Rosenbaum (1976). Reviewing the contrast between "contest" and "sponsored" mobility, he finds that neither model fits. Rather, every time a student passes some hurdle, there is another one immediately ahead. Rosenbaum describes the process as a never-ending "tournament."

REFERENCES

Arian, Edward
    1971 Bach, Beethoven, and Bureaucracy: The Case of the Philadelphia Orchestra. Tuscaloosa: University of Alabama Press.

Bailey, Jerry
    1974 " 'Ballad of Richard Nixon' hard to sell on music row." Nashville Tennessean (June 3):1,8.

Bart, Teddy
    1970 Inside Music City USA. Nashville: Aurora.

Baskerville, David
    1979 Music Business Handbook. Los Angeles: Sherwood.

Becker, Howard S.
    1976 "Art worlds and social types." Pp. 41-57 in Richard A. Peterson (ed.),The Production of Culture. Beverly Hills; Sage.
    1981 Art Worlds. Berkeley: University of California Press.

Bensman, Joseph, and Robert Lilienfeld
    1973 Craft and Consciousness. New York: Wiley.

Bierstedt, Robert
    1938 "The means-ends schema in sociological theory." American Sociological Review 3:665-671.

Billboard
    1973 "Songs promote jingles and visa versa." Billboard (July 28):10.

Burt, Jesse, and Bob Ferguson
    1970 So You Want to be in Music. Nashville: Abingdon.

Cole, Steven, and Harriet Zuckerman
    1964 "Inventory of empirical and theorerical studies of anomie." Pp. 243-311 in Marshall Clinard (ed.), Anomie and Deviant Behavior. New York: Free Press.

Couch, Stephen R.
    1976 "The symphony orchestra in London and New York: some political considerations." A paper presented at The Third Annual Conference on Social Theory and the Arts, SUNY-Albany, April 2-4.

Csida, Joseph
    1973 The Music Career Handbook. New York: First Place Music Publications.

Dubin, Robert
    1959 "Deviant behavior and social structure: continuities in social theory." American Sociological Review 24:147-164.

Ewen, David
    1964 The Rise and Fall of Tin Pan Alley. New York: Funk and Wagnalls.

Friedman, Norman
    1978 "The Hollywood actor's search for work." Paper presented at the 73rd Annual American Sociological Association meetings.
    1981 "Auditioning for Hollywood T.V. commercials: an inside view." Presented at The 12th Annual Meetings of the Popular Culture Association.

Gant, Allice M.
    1974 Creating the Nashville Sound. Senior Scholar Thesis, Vanderbilt University, Nashville, Tennessee.

Gillett, Charlie
    1972   The Sound of the City. New York: Outerbridge and Dienstrfrey.
Goldberg, Danny
    1980   "The music gets it every time." Versus 11: 12-18.
Goldberg, Isaac
    1930   Tin Pan Alley: The American Popular Music Racket. New York: John Day.
Granovetter, Mark S.
    1974   Getting a Job: A Study in Contacts and Careers. Cambridge, Mass.: Harvard University Press.
Guralnick, Peter
    1979   Lost Highways: Journeys and Arrivals of American Musicians. Boston: Godone.
Hall, Richard H.
    1975   Occupations and the Social Structure. Englewood Cliffs, N.J.: Prentice-Hall.
Hammond, John
    1970   "An experience in jazz history." Pp. 42-61 in René de Lerma (ed.), Black Music in Our Culture. Kent, Ohio: Kent State University Press.
Hodnette, Pierce
    1974   "Aspiring songwriters: an account of a group of Illinois musicians in Nashville." Unpublished manuscript. Nashville, Tennessee.
Kirby, Kip
    1979   "Stiff now tops chart." Billboard May 5:64.
Korb, Arthur
    1949   How to Write Songs That Sell. New York: Greenberg.
Kosser, Michael
    1976   Bringing it to Nashville. Brentwood, Tenn.: Cumberland Valley Books.
Kuroff, Barbara N.
    1980   Song Writer's Market. Cincinnati: Writers Digest Books.
Lipschitz, Eve
    1980   "The love songs of Carly Simon and Neil Diamond: a content analysis." Unpublished manuscript, Nashville, Tennessee.
Lucas, Scott G.
    1979   "Writer's night: an investigation." Unpublished manuscript. Nashville, Tennessee.
McDonald, Duncan Jr.
    1941   "The popular music industry." Pp. 65-109 in Paul F. Lazarsfeld and Frank N. Stanton (eds.), Radio Research 1941. New York: Duell, Sloan and Pearce.
McHugh, Peter
    1966   "Structured uncertainty and its resolution: the case of the professional actor." Presented at the Annual Meetings of the American Sociological Association.
McNeel, Kent, and Mark Luther
    1978   How to be a Successful Songwriter. New York: St. Martin's Press.
Malone, Bill C.
    1968   Country Music U.S.A. Austin: University of Texas Press.
Markovitz, Andrei S., and Michael Freund
    1981   "So Amerikanish wie Drogen and Apfelkuchen: Andenkungen zum Jubiläum einer Rockband." Dollars und Traüme, in press.
Mazo, Joseph H.
    1974   Dance is a Contact Sport. New York: DaCapo.
Merton, Robert K.
    1968   Social Theory and Social Structure. New York: Free Press.
Montagna, Paul D.
    1977   Occupations and Society. New York: Wiley.

Morse, David
   1972   Motown. New York: Collier Books.
Mukerji, Chandra
   1976   "Having the authority to know." Sociology of Work and Occupations 3:28-32.
Page, Drew
   1980   Drew's Blues. Baton Rouge: Louisiana State University Press.
Pearsall, Ronald
   1975   Edwardian Popular Music. Rutherford, N.J.: Fairleigh Dickinson University.
Peterson, Richard A.
   1975   "Single industry firm to conglomerate synergistics: alternative strategies for selling insurance and country music." Pp. 341-357 in James Blumstein and Benjamin Walter (eds.), Growing Metropolis: Aspects of Development in Nashville. Nashville: Vanderbilt University Press.
   1978   "The production of cultural change: the case of contemporary country music." Social Research 45:292-314.
   1979   "Has country lost its homespun charm?" Chronicle of Higher Education Review (May 29):22-24.
Peterson, Richard A., and David Berger
   1971   "Entrepreneurship in organizations: evidence from the popular music industry." Administrative Science Quarterly 16:97-107.
Peterson, Richard A., and Howard G. White
   1979   "The simplex located in art worlds." Urban Life 7:411-439.
   1981   "Elements of simplex structure." Urban Research, in press.
Prevsner, Nikalous
   1940   Academies of Art of Past and Present. Cambridge, Mass. Cambridge University Press.
Powell, Walter W.
   1978   "Publishers' decision-making: what criteria do they use in deciding which books to publish?" Social Research 45:227-252.
Ritzer, George
   1977   Working: Conflict and Change. Englewood Cliffs, N.J.: Prentice-Hall.
Rosenbaum, James
   1976   Making Inequality: The Hidden Consequences of High School Tracking. New York: Wiley.
Rosenblum, Barbara
   1978   Photographers at Work. New York: Holmes and Meier.
Rumble, John
   1980   "Fred Rose and the development of publishing in Nashville." Unpublished Ph.D. dissertation. Nashville: Vanderbilt University.
Ryan, John, and Richard A. Peterson
   1982   "The product image: the fate of creativity in country music songwriting." Pp. 11-32 in James S. Ettema and D. Charles Whitney (eds.), Individuals in Mass Media Organizations: Creativity and Constraint. Sage Annual Reviews of Communication Research, Vol. 10. Beverly Hills: Sage.
Scaduto, Anthony
   1971   Bob Dylan. New York: Grosset and Dunlap.
Schmidt, Eric van, and Jim Rooney
   1979   Baby, Let me Follow You Down. New York: Doubleday.
Siman, Scott F.
   1976   Modeling the Success of Country Music Records. Senior Scholar Thesis, Vanderbilt University, Nashville, Tennessee.
Simon, William and John Gagnon
   1976   "The anomie of affluence: a post-Mertonian conception." American Sociological Review 82:356-376.

Simpson, Charles R.
   1981   Soho: A Residential Occupational Community. Chicago: University of Chicago Press.
Spilerman, Seymour
   1977   "Careers, labor market structure, and socioeconomic achievement." American Journal of Sociology 83:551-593.
White, Harrison C., and Cynthia White
   1975   Canvasses and Careers: Institutional Change in the French Painting World. New York: Wiley.
Witmark, Isidore and Isaac Goldberg
   [1939]
   1975   The Story of the House of Witmark. New York: DaCapo.
Wood, Jerry
   1980   "Nashville publishers buck producers' song control." Billboard, October 4:1,68,94.

THE EMERGENCE OF PART-TIME FARMING AS A SOCIAL FORM OF AGRICULTURE

Ronald C. Wimberley

I. INTRODUCTION

Farms—there were over 2.7 million of them in the United States as of 1978.[1] If the nostalgic American gothic image is that these are family farms which are worked from dawn to twilight by the operator, spouse, and offspring, this picture is inaccurate for many reasons. One is that many farms are not full-time businesses.

In 1978, 1.3 million or 49% percent of all farms were operated by persons whose principal occupation was, in fact, not farming but something else. Furthermore, 57% of all farm operators worked off their farms to some extent during the year; 46% worked elsewhere at least 100 days.

In other words, practically one-half of the nation's farmers are actually doing something else much or even most of the time. And regardless of whether they call themselves farmers, over one-half work at jobs besides farming. In short, it is part-time rather than full-time farming which is becoming the prevalent form of farm operation in this country.

This study will offer some descriptive information on part-time farming along with information on who these farmers are, where they are, what they do, some contemporary trends in part-time farming, and some issues involved. In addition, part-time farming will be viewed from the wider context of structural changes in American agriculture. Information and analyses on these topics are limited. Therefore, many of the data reported here are drawn from the censuses of agriculture. The focus of this review is to summarize recent findings which call attention to part-time farming and some of its implications for further phases of research and theoretical explanation.

Outside of the limited amount of agricultural research on part-time farming, there has been relatively little empirical or theoretical work on the sociology of agricultural occupations or agriculture in general. For the few dozen sociologists of agriculture, the subdiscipline is typically a part-time career in itself. Such sociological neglect of agriculture seems ironic since the existence of social order, major cultural components, and so much social interaction and organization pertain to the production, distribution, and consumption of food and fiber.

II. OVERLAPPING TYPES OF FARMS: FAMILY, SMALL, AND PART-TIME

Part-time farming is one of many types that are not mutually exclusive. It must be considered in conjunction with several other kinds of farming.

A. Family Farms

Among these is the so-called family farm. Although difficult to define, the notion of family farming is deeply ingrained in American history and has political appeal. This is seen in recent congressional statements including *Status of the Family Farm* (U.S. Senate, 1979), *Status of the Family Farm: Second Annual Report to the Congress* (Economics, Statistics, and Cooperatives Service, 1979), and *Status of the Family Farm: Third Annual Report to the Congress* (Economics, Statistics, and Cooperatives Service, forthcoming). Nevertheless, the ambiguity of what is or is not a family farm hinders use of the concept in research.

In one study, Nikolitch (1972:1-2) examined the family farm, like any other family business, as "a primarily agricultural business in which the operator is a risk-taking manager, who with his family does most of the managerial activities." This definition was operationalized to be those farms using "less than 1.5 years of hired labor because it is assumed that the American family farm supplies 1.5 man-years of labor." While 1.5 work-year equivalents is somewhat arbitrary, such a measure is workable for analytic purposes.

Some family farms are part-time, others are full-time. During the 1960s, part-time family farms were thought to be on the increase. Nikolitch (1972:26-27) took small farms having annual sales of less than $5,000 to be "mainly family operations" and measured part-time status in terms of off-farm income. He found that off-farm incomes rose from 69% of the total in 1960 to 84% in 1969 according to adjusted census data. Therefore, part-time farming would seem to account for a large share of the small-family farm activity.

This type of analysis illustrates the problem of overlap in organizational forms of farming. While family farms, small farms, and part-time farms may be distinguished conceptually, they are empirically interrelated.

B. Small Farms

Arbitrariness in measurement also characterizes research on small farms. Usually a gross annual sales level is the size criterion. For example, small farms commonly are judged to be those with annual sales less than $20,000-$40,000. Agricultural census reports distinguish whether farms sell more or less than $2,500 worth of goods annually. In the preceding example, Nikolitch used a $5,000 limit.

Acreage provides another means of slicing small from larger farm groupings. Fifty acres or less is often one limit, but there is nothing inherently meaningful about any particular acreage designation. A 50-acre wheat farm may be relatively small whereas the same size for a poultry farm would be quite large.

Gross sales are similarly deceptive. A farm earning as much as 10 percent profit on sales of $20,000 clears only $2,000. Such is the nature of most small-farm classifications.

A more recent approach to defining small farms was offered by the U.S. Department of Agriculture (USDA): "All farm families (a) whose family income from all sources (farm and nonfarm) is below the median nonmetropolitan income of the state, (b) who depend on farming for a significant though not necessarily a majority of their income, and (c) whose family members provide most of the labor and management" (USDA, 1979:39; Carlin and Crecink, 1979:933).

It is apparent that this definition would not include all small farms, for it selects those families having incomes in the lower half of the nonmetro families in a state. It includes neither all part-time farms nor all family farms. Like many other definitions, however, it does incorporate small farms with family and part-time farms.

C. Part-Time and Multiple-Career Farms

Perhaps one reason that part-time farming is so vaguely conceptualized is that it is so seldom studied apart from agricultural census data. Therefore, census definitions tend to be the most typically used. In the 1974 Census of Agriculture and again in 1978, three types of census items were directed toward part-time farming.

The primary indicator in the short and long census forms was "At what occupation did the operator spend the majority (50 percent or more) of his work time in [year]?" Responses were "farming" and "other." Operationalized in this manner, " part-time" farms are those operated by persons having a principal occupation other than farming. Those farms operated by persons principally, although not necessarily exclusively, employed as farmers are declared to be "primary farms" (U.S. Department of Commerce, 1977a:A-10). Second, and in the short census form, it was asked what "number of days operator worked off this place in 1974." Responses were "none, 1-49 days, 50-99 days, 100-149 days, 150-199 days, and 200 days or more." The long form inquired, "How many days did each member of the family work OFF the place in 1974?" and used the above response list for the operator or senior partner, spouse, and two other persons (U.S. Department of Commerce, 1977a:C-20). In the 1978 census the question was specified to ask, "How many days did the operator (senior partner or person in charge) work at least 4 hours per day OFF this place in 1978?" The final item was whether off-farm income for the operator and family was greater than that from the year's farm sales.

The census does not distinguish between *seasonal* part-time farming, as might be performed by those growing crops, and that which takes a daily share of one's work activities, as for farmers who tend livestock. This distinction may be crucial for the type of nonfarm employment a part-timer can take.

The issue of family, or at least household, farming enters the definition of part-time farming in another important way. This is in the case where one spouse, or adult household member, operates the farm on a full-time basis and the other may work as much as full-time off the farm. From the perspective of the household, this too is part-time farming; from the perspective of the individual, full-time farm operator, it is not. For such a mix of on- and off-farm labor in the household, this type of part-time farming might be regarded as dual- or multiple-career farming (Coughenour and Wimberley, 1982). Few data exist on multiple-career farming.

Some of the definitional issues on the interrelationships of family, small, and part-time farms will be reflected in the following review of descriptive statistics on part-time farming.

III. A STATISTICAL DESCRIPTION OF PART-TIME FARMING IN THE UNITED STATES

As noted earlier, farmers are now about evenly divided into groups of those who are principally farmers and those who spend at least half their work time as something else. This national pattern of principal occupations among farm operators holds fairly well across all regions of the United States except in the South (see Table 1) where over half are engaged primarily in off-farm occupations and where these "farmers" are most likely to have any or as many as 100 days of

Table 1. Principal Occupations and Days Worked Off Farms for U.S. Farm Operators in 1978 by Regions[a]

	United States (adjusted for undercounts)[b]	United States (unadjusted)	North Central (unadjusted)	Southern (unadjusted)	Western (unadjusted)	Northeastern (unadjusted)
Total N of farms (row percentages)	2,700,554	2,479,866 (100.0)	1,027,319 (41.4)	1,016,070 (41.0)	287,092 (11.6)	149,385 (6.0)
Principal occupation of operator as percent of United States or regional N						
Farming	51	54	63	44	52	53
Other occupations	49	47	37	56	48	47
Days of off-farm work by operator during year						
Any days	57	55	50	60	57	55
≥ 100 days	46	44	38	50	47	45

Notes: [a]North Central = Ill., Ind., Iowa, Kan., Mich., Minn., Mo., Neb., N.D., Ohio, S.D., Wisc.
South = Ala., Ark., Del., D.C., Fla., Ga., Ky., La., Md., Miss., N.C., Okla., S.C., Tenn., Tex., Va., W.Va.
West = Ak., Ariz., Calif., Col., Hi., Idaho, Mont., Nev., N. Mex., Ore., Utah, Wash., Wy.
Northeast = Conn., Me., Mass., N.H., N.J., N.Y., Penn., R.I., Vt.
[b]This column of the U.S. totals is adjusted for undercounts reported in the 1978 preliminary census data as reported in other regional and national totals and as shown in the remaining columns of this table. The adjusted U.S. total includes the unadjusted U.S. total collected by mail plus supplementary data from personal canvasing of an area segments sample.

Source: U.S. Dept. of Commerce, 1978 Census of Agriculture: Preliminary Report

off-farm work. By contrast, nearly two-thirds of the farm operators in the North Central region are principally farmers and barely one-half worked away from their farms at all during 1978.

One reason for these interregional variations is that small farms are proportionately most likely to be found in the South and least in the Midwest. And it is the small farms that are most often part-time. For the nation in 1978, for example, 78% of the operators having farm sales of less than $2,500 were principally in other occupations as compared to only 37% of those with farm sales of higher amounts (U.S. Department of Commerce, 1980a, calculations from adjusted totals).

A. Trends

1. *Principal Occupations*

Farm operators devoting at least half-time to other jobs have increased from approximately 37% in 1974 to the 1978 adjusted and unadjusted agricultural census estimates which run 10%-12% higher. Even with an undercount bias against smaller farms in 1974, this measure reveals a substantial increase in part-time farming in this recent and relatively short period.

2. *Off-Farm Workdays*

For agricultural census questions on days of off-farm work by the operator, increases in part-time farming can be traced further back. Table 2 shows trends from 1929, when the question was first asked, through 1978. The percentage working any days off the farm was fairly stable until 1949 when, perhaps, many operators returning from World War II discovered that supplementary off-farm jobs were needed. Since 1949, the rise in the percentage of farm operators doing off-farm work has continued. It passed the 50% mark in 1969 and reached 57% in 1978.

The percentage working away from away from their farms as much as 200 days per year—the full-time equivalent of as much as 40 or more 40-hour weeks—has risen throughout the period to around one-third of all operators. One hundred or more off-farm workdays has shown a similar increase, to nearly 50% of farmers by 1978.

In general, there has been a long-term and fairly steady trend for the nation's farmers to become part-time in character. This is an historic change in the social organization of farming. Along with the short-term trend toward principal occupations other than farming, these findings suggest that part-time farming is not only well established but is a continually emerging form of farm operation.

Table 2. Off-farm Work by U.S. Farm Operators, 1929-1978

Days of off-farm work	1978[a]	1974[b]	1969	1964	1959	1954	1949	1944	1939	1934	1929
None or not reporting	43	56	46	54	55	55	61	73	71	70	70
≥ 1 day	57	44	54	46	45	45	39	27	29	31	30
≥ 100 days	46	35	40	32	30	28	24	18	16	11	12
≥ 200 days	NA[c]	29	32	26	24	22	18	14	9	6	6

NOTES: [a]Calculation on adjusted base of 2,700,554 farms.
[b]In 1974 there was an undercount of small farms which would tend to be part-time and therefore cause the percentages working off-farm to be lower than the true values. The unadjusted base is 2,279,270.
[c]Not available.

Source: U. S. Dept. of Commerce, *1964 Census of Agriculture*, Vol. II, Chap. 5:518; *1974 Census of Agriculture*, Vol. II, Pt. 3:43; *1978 Census of Agriculture: Preliminary Report*, U. S..

B. Comparisons of Part-Time and Other Farms

As the preceding tables indicate, most descriptive material on part-time farming in the United States comes from the census of agriculture which was taken at five-year intervals until those of 1974 and 1978. Currently, only the preliminary summary data are available for the 1978 census. The only 1978 cross-classifications which involve principal occupations and days of off-farm work are for farms selling less or more than $2,500 per year. However, the final reports of the 1974 census do provide more detailed information.

Agricultural census data, and especially those of 1974, are not without drawbacks. In the first place, the definition of a farm that was initiated in 1974 excludes any having less than $1,000 in annual sales. The definition used from 1959 to 1969 includes places of 10 acres or more which sold at least $50 a year of produce or farms selling at least $250 worth regardless of size. The result of the definition change is that the 1974 and 1978 censuses omit places that might be considered farms but which sell less than the $1,000 threshold used by the Department of Commerce, which conducts the census. Granted, the total amount of farm product sales from such small farms is trivial. Yet, there may be some commercially undeveloped food and fiber potential for these very small farms, and, perhaps more importantly, they produce quantities of food and fiber that are consumed rather than sold. These operations are farming activities, part of the nation's agriculture, and of possible significance for domestic needs. Farm production indexes show that home consumption of crops as well as animal products has reversed a decline measured since 1940 and has been increasing since the early 1970s (Economics, Statistics, and Cooperatives Service, 1979:50).

Omissions of farms due to the change in farm definition are evident in census tables showing that over 152,000 farms in 1974 and at least 470,000 farms in 1978 would have been added had the previous definition been used (U.S. Department of Commerce, November 1980:4,8).

A second drawback is that in 1974 census there was an unusual extent of undercounting. This was associated with the first use of mail questionnaires. Recent estimates (U.S. Department of Commerce, 1980c) put the undercount at 10.7% overall, 4.7% for farms selling at least $2,500, and 25.9% for the smaller farms of $1,000-$2,500 in sales.

Third, the census does not obtain as many social data on farm operators or their households from farms expected to sell less than $2,500 as from farms with higher expected sales. Omitted from the short form on smaller farms, for example, is the information on off-farm income by other family members.

For the purposes at hand, the omission of so many small farms works against an accurate portrayal of part-time farms as well. This bias makes 1974 census reports a conservative estimate of part-time farming and underrepresents part-time farming in comparison to principal farming operations.

There is a fourth limitation to the use of agricultural census comparison of

Part-Time Farming

part-time versus other farms. However, this disadvantage serves to counter the $1,000 sales requirement of the farm definition and is not so affected by the undercount in 1974. Still it is a disadvantage for an accurate and total description. It is this: published cross-classifications obscure part-time farming comparisons across all farms and are directly reported only for those farms of $2,500 or more in sales. As noted here, these data offer a conservative picture of the extent of part-time farming since so many small part-time farms do not have this level of sales. On the other hand, the data on farms of $2,500 or more in sales offer the best cross-classifications readily available.

Table 3 contrasts farm operators who are principally employed as farmers (primary farmers) with those who spend over half of their annual work time in other occupations (part-time farmers). Although the primary farm operators may be considered as full-time, it should be recalled that many of them have off-farm workdays as well.

1. Age and Race

It is observed that part-time farmers are somewhat younger than primary farmers. There are essentially no racial differences between part-time and primary farmers; both are overwhelmingly white.

2. Off-farm Income

Fifty-eight percent of the part-time operators have nonfarm incomes surpassing their farm earnings. Part-time farm families have relatively higher mean nonfarm incomes by a difference of over $8,000 although the mean number of off-farm workers per farm is the same on primary and part-time farms. However, members of part-time farm operator families are more likely to have worked off the farm at all and for as many as 100 or more days.

3. Scale of Farming

The average size of part-time farms is 297 acres, but this is still 150 acres lower than that of primary farms. Concomitantly, small farms of less than 50 acres are proportionately over twice as numerous among part-time farmers. Whereas the average real estate value of part-time farms is nearly one-half that of primary farms, part-time farm sales average only one-third as much as primary farm sales.

4. Commodities Produced

Part-time farmers are relatively more involved with beef cattle and horses. Primary farms tend to be more concerned with dairy cattle, swine, and egg production. The only crops with which part-time farms have proportionately greater involvement are orchards and tobacco. Primary farms tend to dominate production of corn, soybeans, wheat, cotton, hay, and vegetables.

Table 3. A Comparison of Full- and Part-Time Farms with Sales of $2,500 or More in 1974

	Principal Occupation of Operator		
	Farming (Primary farms)	Other (Part-time farms)	Total
Total farms with ≥ $2,500 sales			
N	1,235,852	426,690	1,662,542
(row percentage)	(74)	(26)	(100)
Mean age	52.4	48.3	51.4
Percent white	98	98	98
Mean family off-farm income	$5,876	$14,229	$9,136
Family members other than operator working off-farm			
Off-farm workers per farm	1.2	1.2	1.2
Percent farms with off-farm workdays	14	24	16
Percent farms with ≥ 100 off-farm workdays	11	23	14
Mean farm acreage	547	297	483
Percent of farms of < 50 acres	10	24	13
Value of sales per farm	$47,786	$15,684	$39,547
Commodities produced:			
Percent farms with livestock			
Cattle and calves	65	61	64
Beef cows	42	47	43
Milk cows	23	10	20
Hogs and pigs	24	18	23
Sheep and lambs	5	5	5
Horses and ponies	12	19	14
Laying hens	12	10	12
Broilers	2	2	2
Percent farms with crops			
Field corn	56	37	51
Soybeans	33	24	31
Wheat	33	21	30
Cotton	5	3	5
Tobacco	9	10	9
Irish potatoes	2	2	2
Hay	56	46	54
Vegetables	4	3	3
Orchards	3	6	4
Percent farms with contract labor	43	34	40
Percent farms with hired labor	6	6	6

Source: U. S. Dept of Commerce, *1974 Census of Agriculture*, Vol. I, Part 51, Table 29. Some means and percentages reported here were derived from the base data in the census.

5. Contract and Hired Labor

While over one-third of the part-time farms use contract labor, they are somewhat less likely to do so than are primary farms. Contract labor is needed for such jobs as pesticide and fertilizer applications. The use of hired labor is essentially the same for both types of farms.

IV. FURTHER CHARACTERISTICS AND SOCIAL CONDITIONS PERTAINING TO PART-TIME FARMERS

While such data as the above are available from the agricultural census on part-time farm operations, further information on part-time farming as an occupation is found in several research reports and through Department of Agriculture statistics. Prior to the 1970s there were some analyses by sociologists and economists. The primary focus was upon part-time farming as an exit from or entry into full-time farming. These studies and typologies are treated in a useful review by Bertrand (1967). In the last few years, however, there seems to be a resurgence of research and interest in part-time and multiple-career farmers and their households. Current topics include off-farm occupations and social status, amounts and sources of off-farm income, rural industrialization and reverse migration, quality-of-life and community relationships, household features, and the previous concern for part-time farming as an entry, exit, or stable career pattern for farm operators.

A. Off-Farm Occupations and Status

What is the nature of the other careers of part-time farmers and multiple-career farm households? Needs for this information have been stressed in recent statements on part-time farming (Carlin and Ghelfi, 1979:273; Coughenour and Wimberley, 1981).

In a 1979 survey of registered voters in Kentucky, Coughenour, et al. (1980) selected about 1,100 farmers from a larger sample of respondents and looked at their off-farm employment. These farmers were classified into part-time (44%), dual-career (14%), and full-time (42%) types. Since the researchers used the $1,000 sales threshold, the farmer subsample could be compared to the 1978 Census of Agriculture findings. On similar indicators, a good fit was found between the state sample and the 1978 census results. As was the case nationally, part-time farmers dominated the state's agriculture.

Off-farm occupations for part-time farmers and for the spouses of operators on multiple-career farms were found to range widely and were similar to the distribution of nonfarm occupations in Kentucky's total labor force. In general, the nonfarm jobs of part-time male farmers were 38% white-collar and 62% blue-collar. The respective percentages for the state as a whole were 43% and 57%. For female spouses of multiple-career farm families, 63% were white-collar versus 36% blue-collar, in line with the 68%-32% breakdown for the entire state (Table 4). Therefore, male part-time farmers and spouses on multiple-career farms are slightly less likely to be in white-collar occupations and correspondingly more likely to have blue-collar positions than the general population of this state.

Elsewhere, Coughenour (1980a) reports that part-time farmers in this Kentucky sample were also more likely than other workers to be in the transportation and communications industries (15% versus 9%) and finance/insurance/real estate businesses (5% versus 3%), but less likely to engage in mining (4% versus 6%) and the manufacture of durables (14% versus 11%). Furthermore, part-time farmers in blue-collar nonfarm careers tended to farm less than 100 acres in contrast to white-collar operators who were inclined to operate larger acreages. Off-farm jobs in durable goods manufacturing were associated with part-time farms of less than 50 acres. Part-time farms of 180 acres and larger were most strongly associated with business and professional services and with wholesale and retail trade.

Certainly the sample of Kentucky farmers or those of any other single state cannot be considered to fairly represent the nation. On the other hand, these

Table 4. Off-Farm Occupations of Part-Time and Multiple-Career Farm Families in Kentucky, 1979

Off-farm occupations	*Percent male part-time farmers*	*Percent working wives in multiple-career families*	*Percent multiple-career husbands on farm*
Professionals	10	19	
Managers and proprietors	19	7	
	38 Percent	63 Percent	
Clerical	4	31	
Sales	5	6	
Craftspersons	13	1	
Operatives	23	8	
	62 Percent	36 Percent	
Service workers	6	11	
Laborers	20	16	
Farm	(all)	(None)	93
	100 percent	100 percent	

Source: Coughenour, Stockham, and Christenson, 1980:3.

Part-Time Farming

results cannot be considered entirely atypical. They at least suggest, first, that there is a wide range of complementary off-farm career types for farm commodities produced in the state and, second, that the distribution of these occupational categories is quite similar for multiple-career or part-time farm families and the general population. In addition, the Kentucky research found that off-farm work does enhance family economic well-being.

B. Off-Farm Income

For a farmer or spouse to be employed off the farm is one thing. The amount—large or small—of off-farm income is another matter. Furthermore, farming might be part-time in the sense that it is not the sole source of income whether or not it is the sole source of employment.

1. Amounts

The median 1979 family incomes for the Kentucky farmers were highest for part-time operators ($19,162), although these farms were smallest in terms of sales. Second-ranked were multiple-career family incomes ($15,771), although they had the highest farm sales. The lowest family incomes were for full-time farmers ($10,338) (Coughenour et al., 1980).

In the aggregate, off-farm income in the United States is observed to play a major, if not principal, role in the total family incomes of farm operators (Table 5). While gross family incomes have quite steadily increased from $39 billion to $126 billion in 1978, net farm income has also increased from $12 billion in 1969 to $34 billion in 1978 but at an erratic rate (Economics, Statistics, and Cooperatives Service, 1979:31). This means that the total income of farm operations has also gone up and down, but mostly up from $20 billion in 1960 to $62 billion in 1978. However, variations in these trends are not due to advances and declines in the off-farm incomes. Indeed, off-farm income rose steadily throughout this period, from $8 billion in 1960 to $34 billion in 1978. Whereas the ratio of 1978 to 1960 was 3.2:1 for gross farm income, 2.4:1 for net income, and 3.1:1 for total farm income, these differences were exceeded by a 4:1 ratio of increase in off-farm income.

Since 1964, at least 50% of total farm family income has been from off-farm sources. The only exception was in 1973 when net farm income was at a record high. The all-time high for off-farm income was 62% in 1976 and 1977.

As an alternative to the national aggregate amounts, Figure 1 charts the average farm and nonfarm income for farms of all reported levels of sales in 1978 (USDA, 1981:45). Despite the unequal intervals of the sales classes, it is apparent that, as total farm family income goes up, farm income increases but nonfarm income decreases. This inverse relationship also raises several questions concerning the role of off-farm income. Is it earned to supplement the farm income? Or, is the farm income sought in order to supplement the off-farm resources? In

Table 5. Aggregate U.S. Farm and Off-Farm Income for Farm Operator Families (Rounded to Billions of Dollars)

Year	Gross farm income	Net farm income	Off-farm family income	Total of net and off-farm family income	Off-farm as as percent of total
1960	$ 39 billion	$12 billion	$ 8 billion	$20 billion	42 percent
1961	41	12	9	21	43
1962	42	12	10	22	45
1963	43	12	11	23	48
1964	42	10	12	22	53
1965	47	13	13	26	50
1966	50	14	14	28	50
1967	51	12	15	27	54
1968	52	12	15	28	56
1969	56	14	17	31	54
1970	59	14	17	32	55
1971	62	15	19	33	56
1972	71	19	21	39	53
1973	99	33	24	57	42
1974	98	26	27	53	50
1975	100	24	27	52	53
1976	102	19	30	49	62
1977	109	20	32	52	62
1978	126	28	34	62	55

Source: Economics, Statistics and Cooperatives Service, U. S. Dept. of Agriculture. *Farm Income Statistics*. Stat. Bulletin No. 627 (October 1979): 31.

other words, which is the stronger career commitment of these part-time and multiple-career farm households? Which would they give up if they could?

Perhaps some of the answers are linked with the type of commodity the farm produces. Research by Coughenour (1980b) indicates that those who raise beef cattle seem more strongly committed to farming than those who raise hogs, grains, or tobacco. This does not mean, however, that producers of any particular commodity would necessarily terminate their farm operations in favor of nonfarm careers.

Another response to such questions may lie in the level of total farm family incomes. For example, households at the lower income levels would appear to be in greater need of off-farm resources; those with higher family incomes could get along without the small portion of off-farm income they obtain. But again, would the higher-income households prefer to earn more from the farm if they could? The reasons for farming could be more diverse than reasons for working away from the farm. If so, there is probably no single answer to questions of the relative strength of farm career commitments for part-time farmers and multiple-career farm households.

If the lags in total family income for farms in the $5,000-$19,999 sales

Figure 1. On- and Off-Farm Income per Farm Operator Family by Farm Sales categories, 1978.

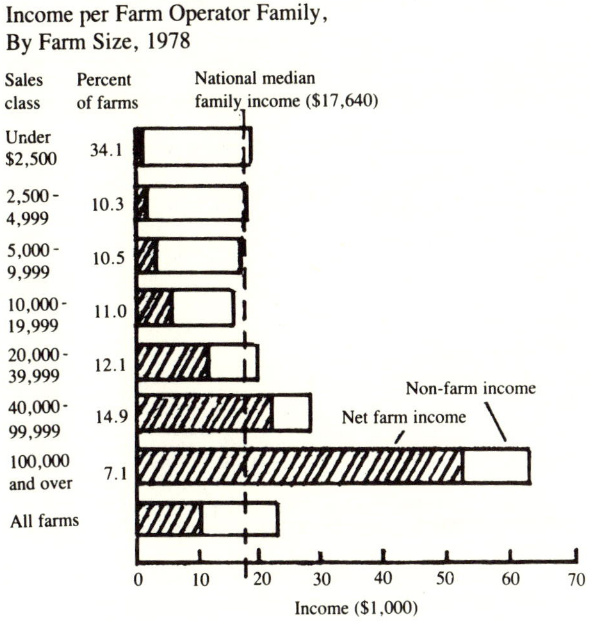

Income per Farm Operator Family, By Farm Size, 1978

Sales class	Percent of farms
Under $2,500	34.1
2,500 - 4,999	10.3
5,000 - 9,999	10.5
10,000 - 19,999	11.0
20,000 - 39,999	12.1
40,000 - 99,999	14.9
100,000 and over	7.1
All farms	

National median family income ($17,640). Net farm income / Non-farm income. Income ($1,000).

Source: Economics and Statistics Service, USDA and as presented by USDA (1981):45

categories (Figure 1) are an indication, there must be some dilemmas in combining farm and nonfarm careers. For these sales categories in particular and for whatever reasons, the interaction effect of farm and nonfarm careers seems negative on total income per family.

In essence, data on aggregate and average farm/nonfarm incomes show that off-farm sources have come to dominate the incomes of farm families. From the standpoint of farm families, part-time and multiple-career farming seem to be interlocked with other sources of income.

2. Sources

The five categories of off-farm income used by the agricultural census are shown in Table 6 with the 1974 per-farm mean averages for operations selling at least $2,500 of products. Highest is income from nonfarm businesses. This average is followed by salaried employment and at a distance by pensions, rentals, and returns from investments. By far the most important source of income for the most farms is the 60% reported from off-farm employment other than businesses. Nonfarm businesses are somewhat more lucrative on the average but account for just 20% of the off-farm receipts. The remaining sources from such things as interest, social security, and rents amount to another 20%. These data indicate that, in terms of income, part-time or multiple-career farming may occur to an appreciable extent in the absence of employment at nonfarm business or salaried jobs.

Table 6. Sources of Off-Farm Income for U.S. Farms Selling $2,500 or More, 1974

Sources	Mean per farm	Percent of total per source
Nonfarm businesses	$10,455	20
Wages, salaries, commissions, tips	8,836	60
Interest, dividends, royalties	2,507	12
Social Security, pensions, retirement, etc.	2,852	6
Rental of nonfarm property	2,651	2
Total per farm =	$ 9,136 (972,121 farms)	100 percent ($8,882 million)

Source: U.S. Dept. of Commerce, *1974 Census of Agriculture*, Vol. I, Part 51. Table 16, p. I-14. Percentages calculated from reported data.

C. Part-Time Farming, Rural Industrialization, and the Reverse Migration

The relationship of farm to nonfarm employment by part-time farmers or multiple-career households is also an issue in rural industrialization. Rural industrialization has an intuitive policy appeal for improving employment, income, and living conditions in rural areas and has been advocated for these purposes. Not only should there be direct benefits from new jobs, but there should be multiplier effects on other types of jobs and on the local economy at large.

It has been thought that low-income farmers could gain industrial employment that would enable them to cease farming or, if they wished, could continue to work their farms on a part-time or multiple-career basis. Rural industrialization has probably served this purpose for some and helped to prevent a degree of rural-to-urban migration from both farm and nonfarm rural residents. Moreover, in what appears to be a major reversal in this migration pattern, the United States nonmetropolitan population began to increase at a higher rate than that in metropolitan areas during the 1970s (Brown and Wardwell, 1980; *Social Science Quarterly*, 1980). Some of this is attributed to the decentralization of industries into rural areas, In addition, moves by retirees, the expansion of colleges and universities in rural areas, and rural recreational developments have contributed to the reverse migration (Beale, 1975).

Firms moving into rural and farming regions often bring many employees from the outside rather than drawing extensively upon the indigenous population (Summers, 1982). On the other hand, it is not characteristic of industries to relocate in rural areas in order to pay higher wages to local people or higher taxes to local communities. Therefore, the existing commitments of farmers to that career may be to the advantage of off-farm employers in several ways. First, farmers can afford to work for low wages since they already have another source of income. Second, many of the farmers are committed to their farms and may not want to move away from their property for jobs. Third, they may also be required to share the burden of increased taxes needed to serve the larger industrial work force.

Besides off-farm employment possibilities which might serve to enhance the transition toward part-time and multiple-career farming, part-time farming may increase in relation to the influx of migrants. First, those retirees who stay or relocate in sparsely populated areas may choose to do some farming as a pastime or as an additional source of income. Second, some people who move into rural areas for jobs in industries, to schools, to other service jobs, or to recreational communities may likewise enter part-time farming for pleasure if not business.

D. Part-Time Farming and the Community

On the one hand, nonfarm jobs may help to retain farm residents in a locality and, on the other, they may become alternative careers for those who move into farming regions. In either event, the number of part-time farms households may grow. Their continued and increased existence in and around small communities and outside major metropolitan areas may have effects beyond the farm households themselves.

In a comparison of part-time and full-time farmers in south-central Missouri, Heffernan and Green (1980) found similarities on most measures of community integration, community goals, and reasons for living in rural communities. The mild-to-moderate differences that were observed occurred primarily among those farmers who had lived in the communities less than seven years. Such variations as were found may have been largely attributable to the facts that the part-time farmers were younger, better educated, and of higher incomes. The study did not compare full-time, part-time, and nonfarm residents to see which kind of farmers most resembled the nonfarm population or to determine whether the presence of either mode of farming mattered in the social conditions of the area.

Findings by Coughenour and Christenson (1980) on the sample of Kentucky residents found that full-time, part-time, and multiple-career farmers were also quite alike in personal and community satisfaction. In combination, however, all three types of farmers were more satisfied than nonfarm residents of the state.

Therefore, what is known about the impact of part-time farming in communities is sketchy. But if anything, it is speculated that recent migrants who are part-time farmers do differ from full-time farmers and that farmers in general may differ somewhat from nonfarmers. More information is needed before the community role of part-time and multiple-career farming can be adequately understood.

E. Part-time Farming and Household Characteristics

The literature reviewed here has not been found to contain reports of household or family characteristics for part-time and multiple-career farm units other than the occupational and income variables that have been discussed. It is unknown whether or how these families may differ from those of the full-time and nonfarm populations in size, marital status, extended family residence, fertility, or age-gender composition. Neither is it clear whether part-time or multiple-career farm households experience more or fewer interpersonal problems.

In addition, what should be the implications for changes in the number of these families for society? Are there advantages to raising children under these kinds of work arrangements? A 1981 tax break for children on farms may be an advantage that will encourage part-time and multiple-career farming (Economics and Statistics Service, 1981) as well as similar mixes of nonfarm employment and businesses.

F. Part-Time Farming as the Beginning, End, or Continuation of a Farm Career Commitment

Given a long-term decline in numbers of farms (Table 7), the shift toward part-time farming as measured by days worked off the farm (Table 2), and the recently documented trend toward principal occupations other than farming (Table 2), it would seem that part-time farming might represent a transition out of farming altogether. This was an implicit assumption in many earlier studies of part-time farming (e.g., Fuguitt, 1959; Bennett, 1967). Indeed, the trend which can be documented since the 1930s for many farm operators to work away from their farms (Table 7) corresponds to the national decline in the number of farms since their peak around 1920.

The exit function of part-time farming is perhaps best seen in a Canadian agricultural census panel analysis by Steeves (1979). He found that between 1966 and 1971 the percentage of operators who left farming increased steadily with the number of days worked off the farms in 1966. While 22% of those with just one to six off-farm workdays in 1966 had left farming by 1971, 46% of those who worked away for 229 or more days left during this period of only five years. This compares to 36% of all operators and 34% of the full-time farmers who quit. Part-time farmers exceeded this rate if they had worked at least 127 days off-farm during the base year. Therefore, it would seem that part-time farming does serve as a transitional phase out of farming for those who spend substantial proportions of their time doing other jobs.

On the other hand, part-time farming may be viewed as an entry to full-time farm careers. Steeves provides information on this aspect as well. As the number of off-farm workdays increased among those who did any farming during 1971, so did the percentage who started farming since 1966. While 19% of those working away only one to six days had begun farming during this span, 43% who worked away at least 229 days in 1971 were not farming at all in 1966. Overall, 24% of all farmers had taken full- or part-time farms since 1966 and 20% of the full-time farmers in 1971 were newcomers to the job.

Steeves concluded that off-farm labor provides an important two-way stepping-stone for entering or leaving farming and that both farm and nonfarm labor markets are interdependent. While numerically there are fewer part-time farmers, calculations from the Canadian data suggest proportionately more stepping in than out. Whereas 27% of the 166,000 part-time farmers in 1966 had left this career by 1971, 46% of the 88,000 who entered farming by 1971 were doing so on a part-time basis.

Unfortunately, the U.S. Census of Agriculture does not lend itself to this type of panel analysis that is required to assess the extent to which part-time farming is the initial or terminal phase of farm careers. No doubt part-time farming in the United States serves both roles; and, no doubt, farming in certain regions of the United States may resemble that of Canada or of other industrialized societies. However, such data do not appear publicly available for a panel analysis of U.S. agriculture at this time.

For Kentucky, at least, Coughenour and Gabbard (1977) do find that in the early 1970s part-time farming seemed to have become more a path into farming than a way out and into other occupations. The evidence that part-time farmers are somewhat younger than full-timers (Table 3) further suggests this phenomenon.

Just as part-time farming would appear to serve as a point of both entry to and exit from farming, it must offer a third option: that of a relatively permanent career pattern combining farming with other forms of work and income. Again, national data are lacking to provide a picture of the relative stability of part-time farm careers. Rather, some information is available from state studies. For example, Coughenour and Gabbard (1977) discovered that part-time farmers in Kentucky had been so for over eight years. In Illinois, a study by Hanson and Spitze (as reported by Carlin and Ghelfi, 1979) found that only 6% of the part-time farmers anticipated a complete shift to off-farm jobs within five years. This leaves a sizable majority who plan to continue. A recent USDA review of several such studies surmises that many part-time farms are not transitional forms of farm operations nor are they economically stressed. It (USDA, 1981:38) concludes that "Part-time farming has apparently developed as a permanent institution, with a different character than the one attributed to it in years past." Thus, part-time farming is no longer to be considered merely as a halfway house for those operators leaving or entering farm careers.

V. STRUCTURAL CHANGES IN AGRICULTURE

A Social Structure: The Population, Farms and Farm Workers

The relationship between population size and the labor required to produce food and fiber has experienced a social transformation in this century. Several indicators of these changes are shown in Table 7. While the U.S. population has continued to increase, the number of farms and employment in farming have decreased.

1. Population

In 1920, when the United States population was about 106 million, the population living on farms was about 32 million, or 30% of the total. By 1979, the national population had more than doubled to 220 million. Conversely, the farm population had declined by 80% to around 6 million, or only 2.8% of the total population. This 2.8 percent represented one farm resident for every 35 citizens in the country.

2. Farms

As the population balance shifted from being predominantly rural in 1910 (54% rural) to more than one-half urban in 1920 (49% rural), the number of farms was at an all-time high at 6.5 million. But in 1978 there were only 2.7 million farms. During these 58 years, the average number of persons per farm had surged from 16 to 81—an increase of 506 percent!

3. Farm Employment

Simultaneously, farm employment dropped. It stood at about 12.5 million in 1930 but, according to various data sources, was only around 3.3-3.5 million by the end of the 1970s. Rather than one farm employee for every 10 people in 1930, there was one for about every 60 or more people in 1979.

Recorded data on those working for farm wages or salaries (Table 7) show their number to have been highest in 1950 and 1960 at 1.6 and 1.8 million, respectively, then declining in 1970 to 1.2 million and gradually rising to approximately 1.4 million by 1979.

If the information from the *1980 Handbook of Agricultural Charts* is used for a guide, only 2.5 million were family workers on farms in 1979. Another 1.3 million hired workers brings the farm labor force to 3.8 million. From 1970 to 1979, there was a decline of .8 million family workers and a gain of .1 million hired employees for a net loss of .7 million. Sixty-three percent of the farm workers were self-employed, as compared with 11% in other industries.

It is evident that drops in the farm labor force cannot continue to be anything near .7 million per decade for very much longer. The ratios of farm units per

Part-Time Farming 345

population may widen, but the trends in farm and farm population numbers may now continue to level off if not fluctuate.

4. Part-Time Farm Work

Still, this has been a dramatic shift in the social resources needed to meet the basic human requirements that farms and their workers produce. The output per worker is even more impressive when one considers that so many of the farm operators and employees work only part-time and/or on a seasonal basis. As noted earlier, 49% of the farm operators in 1978 had a principal occupation other than farming. A General Accounting Office report (1978:55) indicates that 2.8 million farm laborers in 1966 amounted to just 1.1 million full-time equivalent (FTE) positions. Therefore, the effective number of FTEs is only about 39% of the total positions. These workers plus the farm operators—of whom 49% are principally working as something other than farmers—are the core of the farming activity.

This puts the effective ratio of FTE farm workers to the dependent population at a much wider ratio of one position per 58 or so citizens estimated for 1979 in Table 7. An arbitrary and probably optimistically high estimate that 75 percent or 2.85 million of the 3.8 million farm positions are FTEs would make the ratio of farm workers to population about 1:77 or less.

Indexes of total farm output and of farm production per work hour may reflect the effort of the largely part-time and seasonal farm work force with greater sensitivity (Table 7). Both indexes are adjusted to 100 in 1967. The total output index gained 40 points from 1910 to 1954 and as much again by 1978. Hourly production rose about 90 points from 1910 to 1967 and has nearly doubled since that time. These indicators reflect the mechanization and associated technologies of the twentieth-century revolution in food and fiber production which has released people from the farm work required to meet the growing demand.

Regardless of the trends toward a smaller farm population and labor force, agriculture took a stronger role in the U.S. economy during the 1970s when farm exports not only exceeded imports but rose sharply from about $10 billion in 1970 to $35 billion in 1979. This has served to offset deficits in nonagricultural sectors and has helped to stabilized the national balance of trade (USDA, 1980:63). Of course, this does not directly indicate the success of part-time farmers since most of the exporting is probably from the larger, full-time, commercial farms.

B. Farm Structure: Size, Concentrations, and Organizational Complexity

Declines in the number of farms, farm population, and farm labor force along with the rise of agricultural productivity and a growing population of consumers are only several of the structural changes in American agriculture. Additional transformations include trends toward larger average acreages for the fewer

Table 7. Trends of Structural Change in U.S. Agriculture

	1	2	3	4	5	6	7	8	9	10
Year	U.S. population (1000s)	Farm population (1000s)	Farm population percent of U.S. total	Number of farms (1000s)	U.S. persons per farm	Total farm employment (1000s)	Farm wage & salary workers (1000s)	U.S. persons per total farm employment	Index of farm output 1967=100	Index of farm production per work hour 1967=100
1850	23,192			1,449	16					
1880	50,189			4,009	13					
1900	76,212			5,737	13					
1910	92,228	32,077	34.8	6,362	14					
1920	105,711	31,974	30.2	6,448	16					
1930	122,755	30,529	24.9	6,289	20	12,497		9.8	43	13
1940	132,166	30,547	23.1	6,102	22	10,979		12.0	51	14
1950	151,326	23,048	15.2	5,388	28	9,926	1,630	15.2	52	16
1954				3,711	34	8,651			60	20
1960	179,323	15,635	8.7		48	7,057	1,762	25.4	74	34
1964				3,158	61	6,110			80	42
1969				2,730	74	4,596			91	65
									95	81
									102	110

346

Year							
1970	203,810	9,712	4.8		4,523	1,152	45.1	101	115
1971	206,219	9,425	4.6		4,436	1,161	46.5	110	128
1972	208,219	9,610	4.6		4,373	1,216	47.6	110	136
1973	209,859	9,472	4.5		4,337	1,254	48.4	112	130
1974	211,389	9,264	4.4	2,622[b]	4,389	1,349	48.2	106	136
1975	213,051	8,864	4.2		4,342	1,280	49.1	114	152
1976	214,680	8,253	3.8		4,374	1,318	49.1	117	162
1977	216,400	7,806	3.6		4,155	1,330	52.1	121	173
1978	218,228	6,501[a]	3.0	2,701[b]	3,973	1,418	55.4	121	183
1979	220,099	6,241[a]	2.8	81	3,297	1,413	66.8		
1979[c]					3,467	1,506	63.5		
1979[d]					3.8 million	1.3 million	57.9		

Sources for columns of data: 1. USDA, *A Time to Choose* (1981):35.
2. 1959 *Census of Agriculture*, for 1910 population; USDA, *A Time to Choose* (1981):35, for 1920-1979.
3. Calculated from cols. 1 and 2.
4. *Statistical Abstract of the United States*; 1926, for 1850-1900; various years for *Census of Agriculture*.
5. *1974 Census of Agriculture*, Vol. II, Pt. I:15; *1978 Census of Agriculture: Preliminary Report*.
6. *Statistical Abstract of the United States*, 1979:681.
7. USDA, *A Time to Choose* (1981):35.
8. Calculated from cols. 1 and 6. See also source for cols. 9 and 10, page 57, for domestic and foreign persons supported.
9. Economics, Statistics and Cooperatives Service, *Changes in Farm Production and Efficiency, 1978*, Bulletin No. 628, 1980: 6-7.
10. Same as col. 9 source, p. 46.

Notes: [a]1974 agricultural census definition of farm.
[b]Respectively adjusted for 1974 census undercount and for supplementary area sample count in 1978.
[c]U. S. Dept. of Commerce and USDA, *Current Population Reports. Farm Population of the United States: 1979*, Series P-27, No. 53 (1980):5.
[d]USDA, *1980 Handbook of Agricultural Charts*, Handbook No. 574 (1980):25.

remaining farms; the disappearance of middle-sized farms; specialization in technology; specialized labor; changing patterns of farm ownership; increased hired labor requirements; new forms of tenancy; increased energy and petroleum needs for fuels, fertilizers, and pesticides; new land-use patterns; the increased criticality of water; new contractual arrangements and vertical integration; plus other changes (Economics, Statistics, Cooperatives Service, 1979a, 1979b; General Accounting Office, 1978; U.S. Senate, 1979; Shertz et al., 1979; Lin, Coffman, and Penn, 1980; McDonald and Coffman, 1980). Several of these farm-level changes will be considered here with implications for part-time farming.

1. Changes in Size

Consider, for example, the opposite trends of decreases in numbers of farms and increases in their mean acreages. From a high of 6.5 million farms in 1920, the number has dropped to an unadjusted total of 2.5 million (an adjusted total of 2.7 million) in 1978 (Table 7 and U.S. Department of Commerce, 1977a; 1980a). Simultaneously, mean farm size rose from 175 acres in 1940 to 303 in 1959 and to an unadjusted high of 440 acres in 1974 (416 in 1978). In less than 40 years there has been a loss of 3.6 million farms, or a 59% decrease in numbers, with a corresponding increase of 138% or 241 acres in size.

The current sizes of these farms seem to be larger than household labor forces could typically operate. The larger ones appear to be corporate farms. Still, corporate farms may be held by families. In 1978, there were roughly eight family corporate farms for each one owned by unrelated persons (U.S. Department of Commerce, 1980).

2. The Disappearance of Middle-Sized Farms

To the extent that part-time farming is more characteristic of smaller farms, these structural trends suggest that the share of commercial output from part-time farms may likewise decline. However, the picture is not entirely a gloomy one for small farms. Their staying power—and that of the many part-time farms they coincidentally represent—seems more secure than that of moderate-sized operations although not necessarily as good as that for the larger-than-family-sized commercial operations.

This trend toward the disappearing middle of the farm size distribution is another vital structural change for small, family, and part-time farming. Harper et al. (1980) found that there had been an increase in farms of less than 50 acres between the 1969 and 1974 agricultural censuses for all regions except the South. In the North Central region, this was a reversal of a trend toward fewer such small farms from 1959 to 1964. All four regions showed appreciable declines in middle-sized farms of 50-999 acres from 1969 to 1974, while larger farms became more numerous everywhere except in the West.

Comparing preliminary 1978 agricultural census figures with those of 1974 indicates a similar national trend toward the disappearance of 50-499 acre farms

Part-Time Farming 349

whereas there are increases in farms either larger or smaller than this middle category. The pattern is especially prominent in the Midwest and is now becoming apparent in the South. It is not so clear in the Northeast and West. Yet, in all regions farms or less than 50 acres seem to be holding their own or better in numerical strength.

In gross sales, 1974 and 1978 census comparisons show national declines among farms selling $10,000-$39,999 worth of produce and increases among farms selling $2,500-$9,999 and $40,000 or more. The next couple of decades look much the same for the size distribution of farms according to their gross sales. Lin et al. (1980:10) state: "[T]he projections further reveal that future farm numbers are likely to follow a bimodal distribution—a large population of small farms, an ever increasing proportion of large farms, and a declining segment of medium size farms." As noted here for the 1974-1978 period, the middle group of farms with $10,000-$39,999 in sales is predicted to experience shrinkage.

3. Concentration of Production

Another example of structural change shows the concentration of production in fewer large, commercial farms. Similar statistics are offered by a variety of recent sources (General Accounting Office, 1978:57; Schertz, 1979:27, 41-42; Economics, Statistics, and Cooperatives Service, 1979a:52-54; Schertz et al., 1980:14-20; McDonald and Coffman, 1980:8-9; and Experiment Station Committee on Policy, 1981:3-6). In 1960, the 50,000 largest farms accounted for 23% of the sales; in 1967, they received 30%; by 1977, they claimed 36% of the sales (U.S. Senate, 1979:11). To put it another way, by the mid-1970s the largest 5% of the farms had 50% of the sales whereas the smallest 50% of the farms had only 5% of the sales (General Accounting Office, 1978:55-58)

No matter how it is said, the structural difference is that the bulk of the farms command only a small amount of commercial agriculture. The concentration of production is increasing among the few largest farms.

The projections are that this concentration will continue. While the largest 20% of the farms contributed 80% of the production in 1974, for example, by the year 2000 it is estimated that the largest 12% of the farms will produce 80% of sales. Or, the largest 1% of the farms in the year 2000 will furnish 50% of the agricultural goods whereas the smallest 50% will provide only 1% of the farm product (Lin et al., 1980:12; McDonald and Coffman, 1980:8-9).

4. Land Concentration

Although it is difficult to establish trends in farm and other types of land ownership (Lewis, 1980), some information over time is available on amounts of farmland operated by given numbers of farms (Lin et al., 1980:14). For example, 54% of the farmland was controlled by farms of more than 1,000 acres in 1969. This figure grew to 58% in 1974. By the year 2000, the nation's 1,000-acre farms are projected to control 71% of the land. As a second example of trends in farmland concentration, the largest 50,000 farms operated 30% of the land in 1969, 35% in 1974, and are projected to be operating 50% by the year 2000 although such farms should comprise just 3% of all farms at that time. In brief, trends are toward control of more farmland by fewer farms.

5. The Role of Part-Time Farming in Structural Changes

Although commercial production and land are becoming more concentrated in the very largest farms, small and primarily part-time farms seem to have a promising future. Indeed, it may be part-time farming that gives small farms their tenacity in the face of the large-farm concentrations. And since part-time farms are by no means all small, part-time farming might also significantly contribute to and grow in importance for the survival of the beleaguered farms in the middle categories of acreage and sales.

If part-time farming has now become the typical form of small, family farming, it should therefore become an even more common occupational mode in small-and medium-sized farming. Of course, the collective commercial impact of such farms is still likely to be insignificant in comparison to big agriculture. But while part-time farmers may find some economic rewards in terms of supplementary household incomes or for household consumption needs, the more important rewards may be social and psychological.

In any event, increases or decreases in part-time farming as an occupation could have marked effects on other kinds of structural conditions of agriculture including the farm population, the farm labor force, the total concentration of agricultural production in the hands of the few, the number of farms, and farm sizes, to say nothing of the impacts on underemployment, unemployment, the domestic and local food supplies, family food expenditures, and rural and community development.

6. Organizational Complexity

Using principal occupation other than farming and having more off- than on-farm income, an analysis of North Carolina census data on farm structure finds that part-time farming factors into a dimension with individual or family ownership of farms, operation by the full owner, off-farm residence, and farm indebtedness (Wimberley and Belyea, 1979). By its nature, a part-time farm has an added element of structure complexity. It has a division of labor, decision-making, and time use which any full-time organization does not have. This complexity exists at the level of a part-time operation and at the level of a multiple-career household. Likewise, an increased role complexity is the nature of a part-time farming career. For either the farm organization or the part-time career role, however, the complexity should not be considered necessarily as a disadvantage; the joining of farm and nonfarm components also serves to increase the external linkages and options for each. In the case of part-time farm operations and part-time farming careers, some of these options include a means of transforming one type of career into another. Furthermore, these advantages brought about by complementary part-time activities may provide a permanent arrangement for increasing income, a buffer against hard or uncertain times, the keeping of a preferred residential location, or the continuity of a lifestyle.

On the other hand, two or more occupational commitments may become interdependent social investments which restrict career or residential mobility whenever one of the career lines offers greater potential as a full-time career commitment.

VI. CONCLUSIONS

This paper has attempted merely to explore and to describe certain aspects of part-time farming as it is currently found in our society. The purpose has not been to analyze the data in the service of any preconceived theory. Rather, the intent has been to introduce a topic which deserves further empirical and theoretical attention. The hard analytic and explanatory insights are yet to be formulated.

Some of the findings summarized here are, first, that part-time farming has become a dominant force in this nation's agriculture during this century. This appears to be an historic transformation in how farm units are socially organized for the production of essential food and fiber needs.

Second, part-time farmers differ from other farmers in being somewhat younger, having farms of smaller acreage and real estate value, being less likely to use hired labor, and producing different types of commodities. However, full- and part-time farmers are similar in racial composition and in the use of contract labor. Data from one state suggest that part-time male farmers tend to be slightly more blue-collar in their off-farm jobs than are citizens in general. So are the female spouses on multiple-career farms. This plus other community characteristics suggest that part-time farmers and their households are integrated into their social surroundings.

Third, off-farm incomes have become increasingly significant for farm families. The dominant sources of off-farm income are employment and businesses, with interest income, pensions, and rents being lesser contributors.

Fourth, both private sector relocations of firms and the new patterns of nonmetropolitan migration are potential contributors to part-time farming activities. On the one hand, the labor resources of farmers might be an attraction for firms to relocate in farming areas and, in effect, tend to transform some into part-timers. On the other hand, the reverse migration may also serve to bring nonfarm people into part-time farming.

Fifth, part-time farming serves as a way into, as a way out of, and as a fairly stable career pattern of farm operation. Whereas in earlier decades from the 1930s into the 1960s part-time farming may have been predominantly an exit from farming altogether, it may now be proportionately more of a portal into farming on a full- or at least a stable part-time basis. However, conclusive panel data on the United States are lacking on these speculations.

Sixth, part-time farming may also play a role in structural changes in American agriculture by offsetting tendencies toward the concentration of farm sales, production, land, and other resources under the control of relatively few large farms, in certain forms of commodity production at least.

Furthermore, household consumption of farm products from part-time farming may be beginning quietly to offset some purchases of food among part-time and dual-career farm households.

Several areas of research on small and part-time farming have been summarized by Coughenour and Wimberley (1982) and are offered here with regard to part-time operations.

1. *Data needs.* Descriptive data are needed on part-time farmers whose operations are smaller than the census definition includes. A public-use sample of census data is needed to further analyze part-time farm units in addition to the county-level data usually available. Furthermore, national and regional panel data could help determine the entry, stability, and exit rates of part-time farmers.

2. *Opportunities and barriers.* In what ways does part-time farming create opportunities as well as barriers to the expansion of farming operations and to full-time nonfarm employment?

3. *Association for political and economic interests.* To what extent are part-time farmers willing to participate with others to further their political and economic interests?

4. *Social interactions with others.* How are part-time farm career patterns associated with the nature of off-farm career opportunities, personal and family rewards or costs, and the social structure of communities in which these households are found?

5. *Part-time farming in society.* What is the effect of part-time farming on the nature of the larger society? For example, how does this form of agriculture influence social and cultural change, population movement, industrialization and development, farm and nonfarm labor markets, energy use and supplies, conservation and the environment, the food supply, consumership, and lifestyles?

In addition to these areas are the impacts of part-time or multiple-career farming on structural changes in agriculture and vice versa. Among these is the role of part-time and multiple-career farming in the concentration of ownership, production, and control of land or other farming resources.

In general the sociology of food and agriculture may be a "black hole" of the sociological discipline. Just as the alleged gravity of black holes in space lets them emit no light which would call attention to them, the sociology of food and agriculture is also conspicuous for its absence. Unnoticed as it may be to sociologists, the need for food must be among the strongest of social gravities that enable society and culture to operate. It seems eerie that so little sociological research and theory is directed toward its understanding.

Among the prime prerequisites for the continued existence of social life are air, water, and food. The environmental movement has recently caught the attention of some social scientists and turned them to the study of natural resources. While some may assume that rural sociologists have been studying agriculture, this is rarely the case. Only in the past few years have even a minority of rural sociologists renewed interests in the sociology of agriculture. Yet the sociology of food and agriculture goes beyond the customary boundaries of rural sociology or any other of its subdisciplines.

Many sociologists have researched many types of organizations and many types of career patterns—often exotic organizations and deviant careers. Yet very seldom have farms been studied as complex organizations and rarely is farming studied as an occupation or career. And if the study of farms as organizations and the study of farming as an occupational career are in a relative void, so is the study of part-time farming. Such is the nature of black holes.

Large-scale agriculture is dependent upon fuels, fertilizers, chemicals, and the transportation of both farm supplies and products. With the coming of potential energy crises and increased demands for food, the emergence of part-time farming might lend some protection against vulnerabilities in the food chain for households and certain localities. However, to the extent that part-time farms are specialized in one or a few commodities, the potential security of part-time farming is limited. Also, acute energy and food crises—or genetic weaknesses of plant varieties and animal species, worsening environmental conditions, hired farm labor problems, increased costs of transport of commodities, and the like—may not allow time to develop part-time farm operations further in time to meet even minimal short-term food needs.

ACKNOWLEDGEMENTS

While I am responsible for any faults of this review, many of the ideas have benefited from my regional research colleagues in the South and Midwest and especially from Milton Coughenour. Therefore, this paper may be considered in part a contribution toward USDA Science and Education/Cooperative Research Project S-148, "The Changing Structure of Agriculture: Causes, Consequences, and Policy Implications," through North Carolina Agricultural Research Service Project NC11148.

NOTES

1. These figures are from the *1978 Census of Agriculture Preliminary Report* (U.S. Dept. of Commerce, 1980) and are adjusted for undercounts in the county totals. See Tables 1 and 2 for a summary of the statistics used in these introductory paragraphs.

REFERENCES

Beale, Calvin L.
  1975 The Revival of Population Growth in Nonmetropolitan America. ERS-605. Washington, D.C.: Economic Research Service, USDA.
Bennett, Claude F.
  1967 "Mobility from Full-Time to Part-Time Farming." Rural Sociology 32:154-164.
Bertrand, Alvin L.
  1967 "Research on Part-Time Farming in the United States." Sociologia Ruralis 7:295-304.
Brown, David L., and John M. Wardwell
  1980 New Directions in Urban/Rural Migration. New York: Academic Press.
Carlin, Thomas A., and John Crecink
  1979 "Small Farm Definition and Public Policy." American Journal of Agricultural Economics 61:933-939.
Carlin, Thomas A., and Linda M. Ghelfi
  1979 "Off-Farm Employment and the Farm Sector." Pp. 270-273 in Structure Issues of American Agriculture. Washington, D.C.: U.S. Department of Agriculture.
Coughenour, C. Milton
  1980a "The Impact of Nonfarm Occupation and Industry on the Size and Scale of Part-time Farms." In W. Frese (ed.) Rural Sociology in the South: 1980. Mississippi State: Mississippi State University.
  1980b "Farmers, Location, and the Differentiation of Crops from Livestock in Farming." Rural Sociology 45: 569-590.
Coughenour, C. Milton, and James A. Christenson
  1980 "Is Life on the Small Farm Beautiful? Agricultural Structure and Quality of Life in the United States." Paper presented at World Congress of Rural Sociology, Mexico City. Lexington: Department of Sociology, University of Kentucky.
Coughenour, C. Milton, and Ann V. Gabbard
  1977 "Part-Time Farmers in Kentucky in the Early 1970s: The Development of Dual Careers." RS-14. Lexington: Department of Sociology, University of Kentucky.
Coughenour, C. Milton, Ann Stockham, and James A. Christenson
  1980 "Kentucky Farm Families." Community Development Issues 2: No. 5.
Coughenour, C. Milton, and Ronald C. Wimberley
  1982 "Small and Part-Time Farmers." Chapter 27 in D.A. Dillman and D.J. Hobbs (eds.), Rural Society: Issues for the 1980s. Boulder, Colorado: Westview Press.
Economics and Statistics Service
  1981 Farmers' Newsletter: General. Washington, D.C.: Economics and Statistics Service, USDA, March.
Economics, Statistics, and Cooperatives Service
  1979a Farm Income Statistics. Statistics Bulletin No. 627. Washington, D.C.: U.S. Dept. of Agriculture, October.
  1979b Status of the Family Farm: Second Annual Report to the Congress. Ag. Econ. Report No. 434. Washington, D.C.: U.S. Dept. of Agriculture, September.
  1979c Small-Farm Issues: Proceedings of the ESCS Small-Farm Workshop. ESCS-60. Washington, D.C.: U.S. Dept. of Agriculture, July.
  1980 Changes in Farm Production and Efficiency, 1978. Statistics Bulletin No. 628. Washington, D.C.: U.S. Dept. of Agriculture, January.
  Forth-Coming Status of the Family Farm: Third Annual Report to the Congress. Washington, D.C.: U.S. Dept. of Agriculture.
Experiment Station Committee on Organization and Policy
  1981 Research and the Family Farm. Ithaca, N.Y.: Cornell University.

Fuguitt, Glenn V.
  1959 "Part-Time Farming and the Push-Pull Hypothesis." American Journal of Sociology 54: 375-379.
General Accounting Office
  1978 Changing Character and Structure of American Agriculture: An Overview. Washington D.C.: U.S. General Accounting Office.
Harper, Emily B., Frederick C. Fliegel, and J.C. van Es
  1980 "Growing Numbers of Small Farms in the North Central States." Rural Sociology 45; 608-620.
Heffernan, William D., and Gary Green
  1980 "Part-Time Farming and the Rural Community." Paper presented at Rural Sociological Society meetings, Ithaca, New York. Columbia: Department of Rural Sociology, University of Missouri.
Lewis, James A.
  1980 Landownership in the United States, 1978. Washington, D.C: Economics, Statistics, and Cooperatives Service, USDA.
Lin, William, George Coffman, and J.B. Penn
  1980 U.S. Farm Numbers, Sizes, and Related Structural Dimensions: Projections to Year 2000. Bulletin No. 1625. Washington, D.C.: Economics, Statistics, and Cooperatives Service, USDA.
McDonald, Thomas, and George Coffman
  1980 Fewer, Larger U.S. Farms by Year 2000—and Some Consequences. Agriculture Information Bulletin No. 439. Washington D.C.: Economics, Statistics, and Cooperatives Service, USDA.
Nikolitch, Radoje
  1972 Family-Size Farms in U.S. Agriculture. ERS 499. Washington, D.C.: Economic Research Service, USDA.
Schertz, Lyle P., et al.
  1979 Another Revolution in U.S. Farming? Washington, D.C.: U.S. Department of Agriculture.
Social Science Quarterly
  1980 Social Science Quarterly 61 (3&4).
Steeves, Allan D.
  1979 "Mobility Into and Out of Canadian Agriculture." Rural Sociology 44: 566-583.
Summers, Gene F.
  1982 "Industrialization." Chapter 20 in D.A. Dillman and D.J. Hobbs (eds.) Rural Society: Issues for the 1980s. Boulder, Colorado: Westview Press.
U.S. Department of Commerce, Bureau of the Census
  1926 Statistical Abstract of the United States: 1926. Washington, D.C.
  1962 1959 Census of Agriculture, Vol. II, Chap. 2. Washington, D.C.
  1967 1964 Census of Agriculture, Vol. II, Chap. 5. Washington, D.C.
  1977a 1974 Census of Agriculture, Vol. I, Part 51. Washington, D.C.
  1977b 1974 Census of Agriculture, Vol. II, Part 3. Washington, D.C.
  1979 Statistical Abstract of the United States: 1979. Washington, D.C.
  1980a 1978 Census of Agriculture: Preliminary Report. Washington, D.C.
  1980b Farm Population of the United States: 1979. Current Population Reports. Series P-27, No. 53 Washington, D.C.
  1980c "Number of Farms by State and Value of Sales—1974 and 1978 Censuses of Agriculture." Mimeograph, Table 1. U.S. Census of Agriculture. Washington, D.C.
United States Department of Agriculture
  1979 Research, Extension and Higher Education for Small Farms: Report on Small Farms of the Joint Council on Food and Agricultural Sciences. Washington, D.C.
  1980 Handbook of Agricultural Charts. Agriculture Handbook No. 574. Washington, D.C.

1981 A Time to Choose: Summary Report on the Structure of Agriculture. Washington, D.C.
United States Department of Agriculture, Community Services Administration, and Action
   1978 Regional Small Farms Conferences: National Summary. Washington, D.C.: U.S. Department of Agriculture.
United States Senate
   1979 Status of the Family Farm. Committee on Agriculture, Nutrition, and Forestry. Washington, D.C.
Wimberley, Ronald C., and Michael J. Belyea
   1979 "Measuring County Agricultural Structure." In W. Boykin (ed.), Rural Sociology in the South: 1979. Lorman, Miss.: Alcorn State University.

CHINESE SWEATSHOPS IN THE UNITED STATES:
A LOOK AT THE GARMENT INDUSTRY

Morrison G. Wong

I. INTRODUCTION

Each year thousands of tourists will walk through the streets of Chinatowns in San Francisco, New York, and Los Angeles. They will probably be intrigued by the hundreds of brightly lighted neon lights with "strange" Chinese characters, partake of Chinese cuisine in one of the seemingly endless strings of Chinese restaurants, and buy a souvenir (which was made in Japan) in one of the numerous curio shops as a memento of their visit to this quaint ethnic community. But behind this facade of a model tourist haven is a part of Chinatown which most tourists do not see, let alone know exists. The dependence of Chinatowns throughout the United States upon the tourist industry for their economic survival constrains their residents to suppress any visible manifestation of social unrest, deviance, and/or pathology in order to attract customers. As a consequence, protection of the tourist industry interests conflict with the need of appealing to outside agencies to help alleviate these problems (Light and Wong, 1975:1342-1368). Yet Chinatown is a community which by all objective indicators qualifies as "a ghetto." Yee (1970:57-58) noted that in 1970 (1) two-thirds of the adults in San Francisco's Chinatown had less than a seventh-grade education and the last new school in the area was built in 1925; (2) the unemployment rate in Chinatown was 12.8% versus 6.7% for San Francisco and 3.9% for the country as a whole; (3) the density rate was 885.1 people per acre, ten times the city's average, and the second-highest rate for a given area in the United States next to certain areas of Manhattan; (4) the suicide rate of Chinatown residents was three times the national average; (5) the rate of substandard housing in Chinatown was 67% versus 19% for the rest of San Francisco. Similar conditions are noted in other cities where a sizable Chinese community exists (Chin, 1971:282-295). No doubt the continued immigration of Chinese to the United States exacerbates these problems (Wong and Hirschman, 1983). Though most people are aware that the restaurant business is a major industry in Chinatown, few are cognizant that the garment industry in general, and the sweatshops in particular, are a viable and important industrial structure of the Chinatown economy.

The purpose of this paper is fourfold. It will first briefly describe the changing nature of participation of the Chinese in the garment industry beginning in the early 1860s up to the present. Then it will describe in greater detail the present-day conditions of the Chinatown sweatshop situation, looking at the basic structure of the garment industry (a subcontracting system) and the characteristics and positions of the Chinese worker and shop owner or subcontractor. Third, various relationships within the garment industry will be discussed. These relationships include: (1) seamstress versus subcontractor; (2) subcontractor versus manufacturer; (3) seamstress versus manufacturer; and (4) unions versus seamstress. Last, several alternatives are discussed as possible approaches to help alleviate the exploitation and oppression of the garment workers in Chinatown. It should be emphasized that, although this paper deals only with the sweatshops in Chinatown(s), its general findings and conclusions may be applicable, with some modifications, to other ethnic groups such as the Mexicans, Koreans, Filipinos, and Puerto Ricans who are also involved in the sweatshop economy throughout the United States.

II. BRIEF HISTORY OF THE CHINESE IN THE GARMENT INDUSTRY

In recent years some scholars have suggested a "discovery" of the sweatshop industry in Chinatown. However, the present-day garment shops in Chinatown are but lineal descendants of the Chinese guild that organized apparel factories in California in the 1860s. Arriving in large numbers during the California gold rush, the Chinese were welcomed as they filled occupations previously designated as "women's work" (i.e., laundry work and cooks) in a predominantly male society. By the late 1860s, many Chinese were employed by many clothing manufacturers, working in the sewing trades. "Pantaloons, vests, shirts, drawers, and overalls are made extensively by Chinamen" (Loomis, 1869:231-1240). One source noted that, next to the cigar industry, the clothing industry was the major source of Chinese employment.

> Next, if not superior in importance to the Chinese cigar factories, are the Chinese clothing factories of which there are altogether 28, including 3 shirt factories.... These factories employ from 50 to 100 men each and their employees number in the aggregate about 2000 (San Francisco *Morning Call*, May 27, 1873).

By 1876 a considerable percentage of the workers in the sewing trades were Chinese. Almost all of the embroiderers, 38% of the lacemakers, 46% of the shirtmakers, and 30% of the men's clothing workers were reported to be Chinese. Although the data are not available, it may be speculated that due to the immigration patterns of the early Chinese, all of the Chinese garment workers were male.

Table 1. Number and Proportion of Chinese and Other Workers in the Garment Industry, 1876*

Employment	White Men	Percent	White Women	Percent	Total Chinese	Percent	Total
Embroidering	-	-	-	-	28	100	28
Lacemaking	-	-	32	62	20	38	52
Shirtmaking	30	6	246	48	239	46	515
Men's Clothing	558	27	884	43	620	30	2062
Other Sewing Trades	163	9	1566	91	-	-	1729
	751	17	2728	62	907	21	4386

Note: *The proportion of Chinese involved in these trades was probably higher since those working on a piece-rate wage system outside the factories were not included in the tabulations. Furthermore, the Chinese involved in the garment industry were predominantly males.
Source: George F. Seward, Chinese Immigration, in Its Social and Ecnomic Aspects. San Francisco: Edward Bosqui and Company, pp. 109-110.

However, one should note that the proportions of Chinese involved in these needle trades was probably much higher since Chinese working on a piece-rate wage system outside the factories were not included in the tabulations. Gibson's estimate (1877:59) for the same period was 1,230 Chinese sewing operators, whereas another source gave a figure of 3,250 Chinese engaged in making clothing, overalls, and undershirts. A government study estimated that the total number of Chinese workers ranged between 2,000 to 2,500 in the 1870s (United States Senate, 1877:252). Whatever the numbers, the proportion of Chinese workers in the garment industry was substantial, especially when one considers their population size relative to the rest of the population.

In 1880 the predominance of Chinese workers in the garment industry continued to be maintained. According to the U.S. Census of 1880, approximately 2,000 Chinese males were involved in the garment industry (Chiu, 1967:98). The majority of the ready-made clothing and nearly all the underclothing made in San Francisco, for both sexes, were manufactured by Chinese (Hittell, 1882:453), and approximately 80% of the shirtmakers were Chinese (Chiu, 1967:101).

Table 2. Number of Chinese in the Garment Industry in San Francisco, 1880*

Employment	Number of Chinese
Working for clothing manufacturers	661
Overall makers	156
Underwear makers	67
Shirtmakers	580
Sewing machine operators	114
TOTAL	1578

Note: *If tailors and seamstresses are included, the number would probably be about 2,000 Chinese workers.
Source: Ping Chiu, Chinese Labor in California, 1850-1880. Madison: The State Historical Society of Wisconsin, p. 98.

Owing to the development of improved technologies, newer equipment, and a greater division of labor, the clothing industry on the East Coast began to expand while the West Coast clothing industry began to decline. Nonetheless, the absolute numbers of Chinese employed in the garment industry remained stable. In 1902-1903, the number of Chinese employed in clothing was about 250, in women's underwear, 570, and in shirts, about 300, or a total of about 1,120 Chinese in the garment industry in San Francisco (San Francisco Board of Supervisors, 1903:165).

As in so many other ethnic enterprises, the predominance of members from a

Table 3. Number and Proportion of Chinese Workers in the Garment Industry in San Francisco, 1902 and 1903

Employment	No. of Factories	No. of Chinese	Proportion of Chinese (in percent)	Total
Clothing	30	250	24	1050
Womens' underwear	22	570	74	770
Shirts	32	300	43	700
TOTAL	84	1120	44	2520

Source: San Francisco Board of Supervisors. San Francisco Municipal Report, 1902-1903, p. 165.

particular district in China was observable for the various divisions of work in the sewing trades in Chinatown. In the late nineteenth and early twentieth century, the people from the Sai-Chiu area of the Namhoi district virtually monopolized the male clothing and tailoring sector of this industry, the owners of the shirt, ladies' garment, and undergarment factories were mostly from Heungshan district, and practically all the factory owners of the overalls and work clothes sector were from the Shun-dak district in China (Chinn, 1971:54).

As the number of Chinese involved in the garment industry increased, the Chinese organized themselves into vertical associations or labor guilds. It should be noted that, due to anti-Chinese sentiment, the Chinese were excluded from joining American labor unions. The three major labor guilds, representing the three major branches of the industry, were: (1) Tung Yip Tang, or the "Hall of Common Occupation," formed by workers on male clothing and tailors; (2) the Gwing Yi Hong, or "Guild of Bright Clothing," composed of shirtmakers and producers of ladies' garments and undergarments; and (3) the Gum Yi Hong, or "Guild of Brocaded Clothing," organized by workers on work clothes and overalls (Chinn, 1971:54). The power of the guilds was at one time far-reaching. They enforced the ruling that no nonguild member could work in the same factory as a guild member. They controlled apprenticeship, competition, the number of hours worked, and the conditions of work. They also enforced a uniform rate structure for the same work throughout the industry in Chinatown, apparently securing, in 1910, a higher monthly wage for their members than that which generally prevailed in Chinatown. However, the absorption of community garment factories as subcontractors by the metropolitan industry, the introduction of more-docile women operators into the overalls and work clothes shops as a major element in the Chinese garment-making labor force, and the fact that the Chinese guild rules did not provide for female membership (many of the women operators were not interested in joining anyway) all resulted in the decline of the power of the garment guilds (Lyman, 1974:154-155; Chinn, 1971:54). As male sewing machine operators retired or died, the strength of the guilds was further sapped. The Gwing Yi Hong disappeared by the end of the 1900s, followed by the Tung Yip Tong in the late 1920s. However, the Gum Yi Hong, formed in 1880, maintained its existence as a guild until 1967, though by the 1930s it was relatively powerless.

After World War I, the sex composition of the Chinatown garment industry had changed from predominantly male to predominantly female. With the decline of the Chinese male garment workers' guilds, a new organization, the Unionist Guild, was formed. In 1919, this guild had unified 32 Chinese garment factories in an effort to eliminate the 11- to 12-hour day and protect workers from bad working conditions. Through the efforts of this guild, its members won a 9-hour day, overtime pay, paid holidays, and an increase in pay (Wei Min She, 1974:31).

As noted previously, anti-Chinese sentiment prohibited Chinese membership in American labor unions. By 1932 the garment industry had grown to be one of the principal industries in Chinatown, with most of the 30 Chinese garment factories operating as subcontractors to major downtown apparel manufacturers. However, Chinese female garment workers were unorganized until the late 1930s when the Chinese Ladies Garment Workers, an affiliate of the International Ladies Garment Workers Union (ILGWU), was organized. In 1938 this union struck against the factory of the National Dollar Stores at 720 Washington Street, in San Francisco, the largest garment factory in Chinatown at the time (Chinese Digest, April 1938). These 200 workers protested against the practice of using part-time shifts and demanded a 9-hour full-time work day. When their employer refused their demands, the workers voted in favor of union representation and went on strike for 14 weeks. The Retail Clerks Union of the American Federation of Labor supported the Chinese Ladies Garment Workers and refused to cross the picket lines, closing down the chain's stores until a court injunction was obtained making picketing in front of the store illegal. Though the garment workers' strike was severely weakened due to the intervention of the courts, a contract was eventually signed giving the workers their demands. However, the owner of the National Dollar Store was to have the last word. Rather than give in to the union demands, the owner closed down his factory and moved his operations to Los Angeles.

Attempts at unionization of the Chinese women garment workers have met with relatively little success. In 1968, 12 workers of a Chinatown sweatshop, contracting work from Margaret Rubel Company, rebelled against their severe working conditions. Though they had been working from 50 to 60 hours per week, their employer forced them to show only 40 hours on their time cards. (Many of the time cards were not the automatic time-punch type but were handwritten.) When they demanded a union shop, they were fired. The workers picketed the factory for four weeks with the support of the ILGWU. However, instead of giving in to the demands of the workers, the owner closed down his factory, forcing the women to find other jobs (Win Min She, 1974:57).

Another attempt at unionization was made by 60 Chinese women garment workers at the San Francisco Gold Company (formerly Alvin Duskin Company). Angered by the unfair labor practices of the company, the Chinese workers sparked a unionization drive at the plant on October 1, 1973. Mobilizing the entire plant of 250 Latin, Filipino, Chinese, white, and black workers, they won union recognition. However, their victory was a hollow one. Owing to a lack of understanding by the union bureaucrats about the particular needs of Chinese immigrant workers, coupled with massive layoffs by the employers, much demoralization (particularly about unions) developed among the workers.

In the last analysis it seems that union shops and strikes were not very effective against the garment contractors. Unionization of Chinese garment workers has been limited. Even with unionization, many of the sweatshop conditions and abuses still persist. The peculiar nature of apparel manufacture—its primitive technology, use of small plants, and easy relocation to places tolerant of management interests—sets it apart from most other industries.

III. PRESENT-DAY SITUATION OF THE CHINATOWN SWEATSHOPS

One may now ask: What are the characteristics of the present-day apparel industry? What is the basic structure of the garment industry? What are the demographic characteristics of the Chinese garment workers and some of the abuses which they face? Who are the owners and how do they get into business? What is their profit and how long do they survive?

A. Characteristics

Lan (1976:42) characterizes the sweatshop industry as consisting of small methods of production, establishments of small size, a separation of functions at the manufacturing level, and seasonal variations in amount of business. Because of the variability of fashion styles, large-scale methods of production and the development of equipment for highly specialized processes, characteristic of other industries, are impossible (Lan, 1976:43; Goodman, 1948:18). These characteristics act to maintain oppressive and exploitative conditions for the workers. The mobility of the industry, the contracting system and the resulting sweatshops, and homework are additional characteristics which are advantageous to the manufacturer. It is under these conditions that the sweatshops of Chinatowns operate.

In San Francisco Chinatown, this periphery industry consists of over 150 shops engaged in the manufacture of ladies' garments. The owners of these shops contract with prime clothing manufacturers to produce approximately one-third to one-half of San Francisco's apparel [Lyman, 1974:154; Report of the San Francisco Chinese Community Citizen's Survey and Fact Finding Committee (hereafter referred to as The Report), 1961:54]; the annual wholesale value has been estimated at from $15 million to $18 million (Lyman, 1974:154; Nee and Nee, 1973:317-318); and the annual payroll is approximately $6 million. Of the 9,100 female garment industry employees in the San Francisco-Oakland area in 1970, about 38%, or approximately 3,500, are employed in sewing shops located in Chinatown. Most of these women are immigrants, speak little or no English, and work for low wages. Except for about 700 of them, the Chinese women garment workers are without union representation or protection (Lyman, 1974:154). Seventy percent of them earn less than $3,000 a year for full-time work. Furthermore, they receive no medical or health benefits, no vacations, and no overtime pay or sick pay (Yee, 1970:57-58). It should be noted that almost all of the apparel companies (manufacturers) which do business in Chinatown do so as secondary contractors. The regular, primary contractors of the firms are the downtown factories. Because the Chinatown sweatshops serve as a stable and cheap reserve labor pool for the contractors, orders and excess work, especially during the busy seasons, are sent to Chinatown, where it is contracted at lower rates.

This not-so-pretty picture is replicated in Chinatowns in other parts of the country. In 1969 about 75% of employed women residents in New York Chinatown reported that they worked as seamstresses in the more than 230 garment factories scattered around the fringes of that district (Sung, 1975:252; Chinatown Study Group, 1969:51). Though many of the New York garment workers are unionized and there are union regulations governing hours, wages, and working conditions, the unions have had little impact in alleviating the Chinese sweatshop situation. The operators still work on the piece-rate basis and union rules and regulations go unheeded. Women working behind locked doors on Saturdays and Sundays is still a common occurrence. Extra hours and the taking home of work are not reported because they may be contrary to union rules (Sung, 1975:252-253). In Los Angeles, the situation is the same for the approximately 100 garment factories in the Chinatown area which employ approximately 1,500 workers (not including the number of workers who sew at home and probably never show up at the shops) (Overend, 1978; Li, et al., 1975:12).

In sum, although the working conditions in the sweatshops of Chinatown are far from satisfactory, the garment industry, nonetheless, is of special importance in the employment picture of the Chinese female immigrant. In 1970, 43.7% of all employed Chinese females in New York City were operatives. In Boston the percentage was 39.6%; in Chicago, 23.4%; in San Francisco-Oakland, 26.3%; in Seattle, 29.6%; and in Los Angeles, 25.6% (U.S. Census, 1973). The percentages are probably higher in 1981 due to the continued influx of large numbers of Chinese immigrants.

B. The Structure

The subcontract system under which almost all of the Chinatown sweatshops operate consists of four major components: the retail outlet, the manufacturer, the subcontractor, and the worker. The subcontracting process begins with the manufacturers, who are the real "bosses." The manufacturers are by definition the owners of the means of production. They acquire the materials and control the use of garment fabrics, the types of designs, advertising, shipping, wholesaling and retailing prices, and contract prices paid to each Chinatown shop for its physical production (Li, et al., 1975:37). The manufacturers reap many benefits by subcontracting. First, they have an almost unlimited supply of labor without the expense or responsibility of maintaining a large labor force. Second, they avoid any problems of unemployment during slack periods. Third, they are free from the responsibility of factory management and maintenance (i.e., workers' wages and work conditions).

The subcontractor bids for work from the manufacturers and receives a certain fee or percentage of the value of completed products. The ease of entry in the contracting business results in keen competition among too large a number of competitors for relatively too small a volume of business. This competition forces subcontractors to keep their bids low. The knowledge that, if they bid too high in order to maximize their profits (or increase the wages of their workers), the work will go to someone else prevents the subcontractor from bidding too high. If the subcontractor gets the bid, he does the work at a negotiated price, usually getting a certain amount for every dozen sewn. Out of this come the workers' wages, overhead costs, and his profits. The procurement of labor and the management of the shop are the responsibility of the subcontractor, not the manufacturer. As a consequence, tremendous savings are made by the manufacturer by subcontracting.

Subcontractors are nothing more than middlemen; they keep the flow of garments moving between manufacturers and the sewing ladies. As such, they struggle to survive as marginally secure entrepreneurs on the very fringes of the garment industry. Using blouses as an example, once they are sewn by the women at a piece-rate of $5 per dozen, these finished blouses are returned to the manufacturer who then sells them to retail outlets, like Macy's and Joseph Magnin, for about $10 to $15 each. The retail outlet then sells the product from $20 to $30 retail.

> The structure of the apparel industry is one in which the manufacturer has practically all the power and most of the profits, but very little of the responsibility for maintaining legal standards on wages and working conditions. In addition, the meager prices paid for contract work are forced still downward by pitting one contractor against another (Lan, 1971:50).

1. The Workers

There is no area of the Chinatown community about which it is harder to get information than the garment factory in general and the Chinese garment workers in particular. However, within recent years, certain facts have begun to surface concerning the sweatshop conditions and the plight of the garment workers in Chinatown.

The major conclusions of numerous studies of the Chinatown garment industry are that the Chinese women garment workers are exploited; that they work long hours for well below the minimum wage, usually at piece rate, regardless of whether it is a union shop (Buck, 1979; Li, et al., 1975; Lyman, 1974; Nee and Nee, 1973; Chinn, 1971; Lan, 1971, Lim, 1969). For example, the piece rate for a blouse may be $1.00. If the worker is able to complete three blouses in one hour, then she will be making about minimum wage. However, if she is able to complete only two blouses, then she will be making only $2 an hour, or $1.10 below minimum wage. To a certain degree, it is possible that it may be to the worker's advantage, especially if she is a quick and experienced worker, to work at the piece rate, and hence quite possibly make more than minimum wage. However, there are two disadvantages. First, if one is slow or inexperienced, then one will undoubtedly make less than minimum wage. Second, when wages are paid by piece rates, one is not paid for the additional time expended in correcting mistakes in sewing. By and large, the majority of the garment workers in Chinatown are making below minimum wage.

Hourly paid workers also are exploited. On July 13, 1967, Sharon Chew testified before the California Industrial Welfare Commission that her boss made her falsify her time card. "Every week we work over 70 hours but are paid for 35.... We work every day, get 50 cents per hour, sometimes 35 cents... the average is 75 cents per hour." The commission's findings put the nature of exploitation in more-economic terms. Using one sewing shop as an example, they noted that, based upon the old rates (at the time, the sewing shop owner had just negotiated new piece rates with the prime contractor or manufacturer), for a given week an additional $523.18 would be due to the employees. Under the new negotiated rates, $363.64 would be necessary to bring the wages in Chinatown up to the minimum of $1.65 per hour (Wei Min She, 1974:58; The Report, 1969:66).

In 1969 a San Francisco Human Rights Commission investigation found that 68% of the women interviewed earned below $2,900 annually for the equivalent of a 40-hour week or longer. Only 4% of the workers made more than $4,000 annually. Furthermore, the commission noted that the Chinese women garment workers in Chinatown did not receive pay for overtime work, did not receive any vacation or sick-leave pay, and that 88% of the workers were not covered by any medical or health plan.

Lim (1969) arrived at similar conclusions in his interviews with 45 Chinese garment workers. He found that the Chinese seamstresses in Chinatown were paid on a piece-rate basis and earned an average of $140 bi-weekly during peak seasons and $78 during slack times. Their annual earnings for 1968 averaged $2,000. All the women worked six days a week during peak seasons. Forty percent of them worked from 9 A.M. to 7 P.M. (10 hours) with a 20-minute break for lunch. Another 18% said that they worked from 9 A.M. to 10 P.M. (13 hours) with about 75 minutes for lunch and dinner. Almost half (48%) said that they took garments from the factory to work on at home, a practice prohibited by union regulations.

On May 10, 1972, the U.S. Department of Labor accused 52 garment factories in New York Chinatown of failing to keep accurate wage and hour records of the employees, especially records of overtime work hours. These Chinese sweatshops were accused of having their employees, predominantly women who had recently immigrated from Hong Kong and Taiwan, work as much as 50 hours a week and paying them as little as 65 to 75 cents per hour. The report concluded that the Chinese women garment workers in Chinatown were one of the most exploited groups in the New York metropolitan area. Buck (1979) summarizes these reports, stating:

> For ten, eleven, sometimes even twelve hours a day, they [Chinese women garment workers] work under conditions that range from the tolerable to the squalid, earning wages often so low—bring home in some cases less than $50 a week—they approach the closest thing we have in this country to a slave-labor system... There are even documented cases of sweatshop managers refusing to pay a worker's wages simply because they know that their predominantly alien force had no way of seeking redress for their grievance.

The working conditions of the factories are but another aspect of the oppressive conditions which confront the garment workers. Conant (1969a, 1969b, 1969c) observed that the San Francisco Chinatown sweatshops were located in low-ceilinged basements and that they were poorly ventilated, improperly lighted, and unsanitary. Some factories had no windows for sunlight or fresh air and no heating for the winter. Furthermore, many of these shops were infested by rats and cockroaches (Wei Min She, 1974:52-53). Of 138 Chinatown garment shops inspected by the city's health inspectors, 117, or about 85%, failed to pass. The violations ranged from the presence of rats to faulty wiring (Wong, 1967c). The working conditions for the Chinatown sweatshops of New York were no different.

> Usually they're in grimy walk-up tenements, converted apartments or storefronts, their windows closed to the scrutiny of the outside world by a coat of gray paint or a soiled sheet hung with tacks. Only the signs posted outside... and the lights that sometimes burn all night indicate what's going on within (Buck, 1979).

Numerous studies have dispelled the myth that the Chinese women garment workers work merely to supplement their husbands' income. The San Francisco Human Rights Commission found that 71% of the women had husbands who were service workers (mainly in restaurants) or had retired. Hence, for the majority of the women working in the Chinatown garment shops, the income from their work, as meager as it is, represents a proportion of their families' income equal to or higher than the wages earned by their husbands. More importantly, it was noted that, even with both parents working, many of these families fall into the 41% of Chinatown's population which is below the poverty level by federal standards (Nee and Nee, 969). Another study found that, although about 40% of the Chinese garment workers in Los Angeles looked upon garment work as supplementary income, an equally large number, about 33%, saw sewing as vital to their income (Li, et al., 1975:16). Hence it may be concluded that, for a large proportion of the Chinese women garment workers, work in Chinatown sweatshops is an economic necessity.

With the exploitative nature of the sweatshop, the question which may be asked is: What motivates the Chinese immigrant women to become garment workers? The San Francisco commission found that 48% of the women felt that garment work was the only type they could do. This seems quite realistic when one realizes that the garment workers are predominantly recent immigrants, with about 85% having less than six years of formal education and about 70% stating that they have only "limited" facility with the English language. Six reasons Chinese women garment workers in New York Chinatown gave (in order of importance) for working as garment workers are: (1) ease of getting a job; (2) don't have to ride the bus or subway to get to work; (3) flexible schedule; (4) don't speak English; (5) can learn job proficiently in about a week; and (6) social and informal atmosphere in factory (Sung, 1975:129). The most favorable opinion toward working in Chinatown factories in Los Angeles concerned the flexibility of the shop hours. As opposed to the shops in the downtown area, the shops in Chinatown do not have fixed working hours for the workers, regardless of whether they were unionized. As a consequence, the workers had the freedom to come and go at just about any time of the day (or night) as long as they had previously arranged their hours with the owners so that their absence would not impede production. Hence, the workers could go shopping, fetch their children at school, take care of family errands, and sew at their own pace (since they were paid piece-rate). Furthermore, many workers also did their work at home. Other favorable comments were that it provided work for non-English-speaking immigrants who could not find jobs elsewhere; there was less alienation while working, as many of their friends worked in the shop; one could dress informally and hence save money on clothes and cosmetics; it was a good occupation for elderly women (Li, et al., 1975:25-26).

The Chinatown sweatshop, in spite of its oppressive and exploitative nature, represents more than just an economic institution, but a way of life.

> To the newly arrived immigrant seamstress it is a place where she can go to be with her own kind, where the local gossip is exchanged, and where news regarding the mainland of China is also exchanged. In general, it is a manifestation of her culture, embodying all that she is familiar with. It is a home away from home. As such, it is a social institution, and it is what makes it different from a typical American place of work (The Report, 1969:67-68).

However, though the garment industry is an economic mainstay for the Chinese residing in Chinatowns (Action for Boston, 1970:56; Sung, 1967:188; Kung, 1962:181, 203: Lee, 1960:60), it is less important for other Chinese. As the more educated native-born Chinese move out of the Chinatowns to the surrounding suburbs, the remaining Chinatown residents are disproportionately foreign-born, non-English-speaking, lacking in skills, and generally the most disadvantaged in the general labor market (Light and Wong, 1975:1348). Because of these disadvantages in social background resources, the only jobs which many of these immigrants could find were in the garment factories (or restaurants). No doubt, many of these women had dreams of "making it"—of learning English, saving some money, and then moving out of Chinatown. But for most, it remains a dream. Because of the long hours behind the sewing machine, they have few opportunities to be exposed to or learn English. Because of low wages, they earn only enough money to keep going. They save very little. They are trapped in a sweatshop subeconomy which is dependent upon them for cheap labor and upon which they are dependent in order to survive.

2. The Owners

By and large, the majority of the owners or subcontractors for Chinatown garment factories are immigrant Chinese. They serve as middlemen between the manufacturers and the workers. The initial capital investment by the owners in a Chinatown sewing factory is relatively small, normally requiring $2,000-$3,000, which would include such things as rent, utilities, and rental payments for the sewing machines. Most of the heavy equipment is either rented or purchased through monthly payments. As with other Chinese businesses, it is common that partnerships play a vital role in the initial investment of the Chinatown garment shop. In Los Angeles Chinatown in 1973-1974, although 56% of the garment factories had only one owner, 27% had two owners, 5% had a partnership involving three owners, and 2% had four partnership owners. The remaining 9% either were incorporated or had unknown ownership status (Li, et al., 1975:13, 31-32).

There are some basic differences between the way the owners in Chinatown and those downtown operate their shops. The owners of the Chinatown sweatshops have a personal interest in the shops, not only as owners, but as owner-workers. In other words, being an owner of a Chinatown shop means participating in all the shop's activities. This allows the workers to see owners not merely as owners but also as workers much like themselves, promoting a sense of solidarity, unity, and loyalty among the workers toward their employers. The owners also tend to hire relatives to work at the shops, making the family-run type of sewing shop very common in Chinatown (Li, et al., 1975:13-14, 21-22, 31).

In sum, the owners of the garment shops in Chinatown are small petty bourgeois. Because entry into the contract business is relatively easy, requiring a relatively low initial investment, the competition for business is intense. As a consequence, the position of the owners (subcontractors) is indeed precarious, as indicated by the high number of garment factories which close each year. Furthermore, because all the shops and workers in Chinatown are exploited indiscriminately by the garment manufacturers, the status of the owner-worker has a two-sided character.

> On the one hand, many of the owners had once been workers themselves and as owner-workers at their own shops, their interests are at times similar to the working class; i.e., they can concretely see all small shops are exploited by contractors (manufacturers) as a whole. But on the other hand, because they are owners, their interests are opposed to the workers. This group would take the side of workers if they could also benefit.... But this group can be expected to side with other small shop owners if it comes to settling whether owners or workers should receive more pay and benefits (Li, et al., 1975:36).

IV. RELATIONS

The structure of the garment industry promotes conflictual relations. Four such relations are: (a) seamstresses vs. subcontractors; (b) subcontractors vs. manufacturers; (c) seamstresses vs. manufacturers; and (d) unions vs. seamstresses.

A. Seamstresses vs. Subcontractors

One of the most immediate areas of potential (or actual) conflict occurs between seamstresses and the subcontractors or owners of the sweatshops. The steady influx of new immigrants with only limited facility in English, seeking work and willing to accept extremely low wages rather than no wages at all, puts the Chinatown sweatshop owner in an extremely powerful position. Because these women have no alternative job opportunities (except possibly in other ethnic enterprises such as restaurants), the owners can virtually dictate the terms of employment to those who come in search of work. Hence, they can give low wages, not pay for overtime work, and lay off anyone who is dissatisfied or is considered a troublemaker (e.g., anyone who tries to organize support for the union). Furthermore, workers have claimed that the names of "troublemakers" were put on blacklists so that it was impossible for them to find work in any other Chinatown shop. The major complaints of the Chinese women garment workers have been that owners claim they are paying an hourly wage, when in actuality they are paying piece rates; that no pay is received for overtime work, even in "company union" shops; and that in many cases pay is withheld (Li, et al., 1975:27; Nee and Nee, 1973:304; East West, 1969).

However, the conflict is not as volatile as the above description seems to suggest. As mentioned above, there seems to exist also a shared sense of solidarity and unity among the seamstresses and shopowners in their relation to more powerful forces outside. Despite the unequal terms of the relationship between owner and worker, the small workshop settings of Chinatown shops often encourage the development of personal ties between these two groups which extend beyond the employer-employee relationship. This is expressed in paternalistic feelings of responsibility for workers, which may take the form of gifts on special occasions, the offer of jobs for unemployed relatives of workers, or the running of errands around the city for workers. In turn, many workers feel a strong sense of loyalty and devotion to the owner. It seems that the loose, informal, and unstructured working situation in the Chinatown shop and the status of the owner as worker-owner are conducive to the development of these sorts of relationships, relationships which differ for the downtown garment factories.

B. Subcontractors vs. Manufacturers

Conflict is almost inevitable between the subcontractors and the manufacturers. However, due to the dependence of the subcontractor on business from the manufacturer, this conflict tends to be covert rather than overt. The advantages of this subcontracting system for the manufacturer have already been elaborated on. A major problem of the owners or subcontractors is the constant difficulty in getting fair and steady contracts from the manufacturers. Long, idle periods are commonplace when there is not enough work to open shop. There is also considerable anxiety over the threats of the manufacturers to move away, particularly to the Southwest where undocumented Mexican immigrants' labor is cheaper, if the price of labor becomes too high. These problems are further exacerbated for those Chinatown shops which have become unionized. Unionization has meant that subcontractors must ask for higher piece rates, which results in a greater probability of not getting a contract. Furthermore, many subcontractors believe that there is some collusion among the manufacturers to boycott the Chinatown shops which have become unionized or that there is a conspiracy among the manufacturers to keep the piece rate as low as possible.

> Manufacturers play one contractor against another to obtain the lowest possible bid for a given piece of work....Contractors are told, "If you can't do it, we'll get someone else" (Wong, 1967a).

Furthermore, because the Chinatown subcontractors are dependent on the firms for their livelihood, they have become the manufacturers' scapegoats, taking the blame for all the injustice and malpractice of the Chinatown garment industry, when in fact it is the manufacturers who are the most exploitative. Hence the subcontractors are both dependent on and antagonistic toward the manufacturers: dependent upon them for business and antagonistic toward them in that they feel that the manufacturers are treating them unfairly.

C. Seamstresses vs. Manufacturers

Like the subcontractors the seamstresses realize that the source of low wages and unsteady income in the Chinatown garment shops lies in the contracts negotiated with the downtown firms and the manufacturers, that it is the manufacturers who are the real "bosses" and who are the most exploitative. Like the shopowners, workers complain that the contracts are unreliable, that there are long stretches of little or no work during the off-seasons, or during periods when the manufacturer, hearing about a lower bid from another shop, may take his work elsewhere. They endorse the union's and shop owners' claim that unionized shops are systematically boycotted by these firms and manufacturers.

The garment workers are in a delicate situation. They are both antagonistic and yet dependent upon the garment manufacturers—antagonistic in that they feel that they are not getting a fair price for their work and dependent in the sense that any job, even with its extremely low wages or piece rates, is better than no job at all. As a consequence, some of the hostility and frustration of the seamstresses, instead of being directed against the true source of their exploitation, the manufacturers, is directed against the shop owners.

D. Unions vs. Seamstresses

It was not until recently that there has been a concerted effort by unions to organize the Chinese garment workers. The union's (ILGWU) goals are simple and basic: to raise the living standard, increase the benefits, and improve the working conditions of the Chinese garment workers and hence protect the workers against unfair competition. The union promises such benefits as seven holidays per year with pay, vacation allowance, a health plan, old-age benefits, death benefits, free eyeglasses, a decent minimum wage, and a raise in the piece rate (East West, 1967). This would assure the workers financial stability and job security. With such noble goals and benefits, one may ask why there has been so much resistance to unionization, not only on the part of the owners but also on the part of the Chinese women garment workers for whom unionization would offer many advantages. There are many reasons, which are intertwined with each other, sometimes mutually supporting and sometimes conflicting. Several of these are discussed below.

Many Chinese question the exact motives of the unions. Tan (1971:182-183) points out that the sweatshop working conditions of the Chinatown garment shops have existed for many decades. Yet there was not any major effort by the unions until the late 1960s to try to organize the Chinese women in Chinatown. He notes that the timing of this was action by the unions is directly related to the accelerated increase of Chinese immigration to the United States since 1966. From 1966 on, the number of Chinese immigrating to the United States has increased to about 21,000 new arrivals annually, with a great many of them remaining in San Francisco (Wong and Hirschman, 1983). Hence, it has been speculated that the vision of a seemingly endless source of cheap labor materialized in the eyes of the union leaders, labor which would be in direct competition with their interests. From this point of view, the action to unionize the Chinese women garment workers in Chinatown by the unions stems not from the unions' interest in alleviating the plight of the Chinese working women but from the desire to protect union interests.

The Chinese garment workers are also fearful of the union organizers and the possible consequences unionization will bring about. Of paramount concern to the workers is job security, many fearing that what they have now will be taken away from them. With unionization, many question what will happen to the

Chinese garment workers who are new immigrants, who know no English, have no skills, and who would be regarded as substandard workers according to union standards. When an ILGWU official was asked if a union contract would affect the "slow workers" or the elderly, his reply was, "Provisions will be made for them." When pressed for details, he said, "This is not a union problem. The slow workers may find something else to do or they can go on welfare" (Chow, 1967; Wong, 1967b). There is also considerable anxiety that, if workers unionize, the manufacturers will move away to other regions of the United States where the cost of labor is cheaper, an action which many manufacturers have threatened. As a consequence, unionization would mean lack of jobs. Furthermore, there is a lack of evidence of good faith and performance on the part of the "outside" organizers who come with offers to provide "leadership" (The Report, 1969:68). For example, in one union campaign, the ILGWU attempted to unionize Chinatown's seamstresses and at the same time sought to zone the garment industry out of Chinatown completely. Cornelius Wall of the ILGWU proposed an amendment to the San Francisco zoning ordinance which would declare Chinatown a strictly residential area and "that all garment shops and factories shall close and cease," an act which would have put thousands of Chinatown families on the welfare rolls (Nee and Nee, 1973:295-296). Hence, many Chinese ask: whom is the ILGWU really trying to help? If we don't unionize, will the unions try to deny us an opportunity to make a living? Is this fair? Is this in our best interests? The hesitancy on the part of the Chinese in joining the union rests in part upon the history of exclusion, exploitation, and discrimination in job opportunities in the past, and upon the general distrust of the unions.

The subcontractors or owners of the Chinatown garment shops have mixed feelings concerning unionization. On the one hand, many subcontractors feel that unionization would be beneficial not only to them but also to their workers. They would be able to realize greater profits in the form of more constant work as primary contractors, and the workers would be more secure. Furthermore, this would not cost the contractor an extra cent as it is the manufacturers outside Chinatown who pay the workers' wages. On the other hand, the subcontractors are afraid. They fear that if they cooperate with the union the manufacturers will send their garments elsewhere, to other subcontractors who are not unionized or to other parts of the U.S. where the cost of labor is cheaper, thus forcing them to close shop (East West, 1967).

Fourth, as past efforts at unionization of Chinatown sweatshops have shown, there is the problem that, despite unionization, no dramatic changes occur. A compliance officer in the San Francisco Wages and Hours Enforcement Division of the United States Department of Labor estimated that in 1971 about 70% of Chinatown shops still paid below the state minimum of $1.65 an hour—and this was when about three-fourths of the Chinatown shops were supposedly unionized (Nee and Nee, 1973:303-304). In San Francisco in the late 1960s, the ILGWU did have some 1,200 Chinese members, with approximately 700 working in Chinatown (The Report, 1969:67). The various shops paid union dues in a lump sum taken from the seamstresses' wages in order to maintain formal union membership. However, the piece rate, the unfixed hours, the take-home work still remain after unionization. Furthermore, the Chinese garment workers in Chinatown have no conception of what a union really is or what membership in the union entails. Hence, it is only in name that the garment workers are union members. In fact, one disgruntled garment worker said that the only thing that the union has done was to give her health insurance—which cost her $85. However, there have been several positive effects of unionization. First, in 1970, health insurance was provided for nearly three-fourths of Chinatown shops, in contrast to only 12% in 1969. Second, there was an increase of 12% in the number of workers who earned over $4,000 a year. However, the percentage of women who earned less than $2,900 as garment workers remained nearly half (44%) of the labor force.

Why do problems still persist in union shops in Chinatown? Lan (1971:48) states that the women in the shops have no place to go if they lose their jobs and that they are not likely to retain their jobs in the garment industry in Chinatown if they reveal their true situation. Hence, business and its accompanying sweatshop conditions continue as usual, regardless of whether there is a union or open shop. The Labor Department receives frequent unconfirmed reports of uncompensated overtime and payroll irregularities in union and nonunion shops in Chinatown (East West, 1969). However, when it comes time to investigate, the government cannot breach the walls of silence. As one observer noted, "The shop managers and employees just sit there, smile at us, and say nothing. There isn't a darn thing we can do" (Buck, 1979). This is frustrating to the unions. According to ILGWU's Zimmy, "Chinatown is a clan, a closed, secretive organization. We try our best, but an awful lot goes on down there that we never even hear about" (Buck, 1979:222). It should be noted that he is talking about the Chinese sweatshops that are unionized. If the union is undergoing that kind of resistance in its own shops, one can imagine the barriers to organization elsewhere. As a consequence, the ILGWU has stopped trying to unionize the sweatshops of Chinatown. An official of the ILGWU sums it up by stating:

> We haven't tried to organize any shops in Chinatown because it wouldn't do any good. There aren't any manufacturers there, just contractors. . . . What happens if you go after a contractor and win a union election is that the contractor goes to the manufacturer and says he has labor problems. Then the manufacturer decides to send his work to somebody else. . . . All you end up with is a contractor and a bunch of workers without jobs. . . . If you get a big manufacturer, how much can you hurt him by organizing one shop in Chinatown?. . . When you're hungry you either work for next to nothing or you don't work at all (Overend, 1978).

In sum, the questioning of the motives of the unions, the fear of losing one's job, ignorance of the consequences, benefits, and process of unionization and what it means to be a union member, and the double bind of the subcontractors are all major obstacles which the union faces in organizing the Chinatown sweatshops.

V. DISCUSSION AND CONCLUSIONS

Not known to many, some of the nation's most pervasive poverty exists in Chinatown, particularly among the numerous women garment workers. Being recent immigrants and having little formal education, no occupational skills, and limited ability with the English language, the Chinese women are trapped in the subeconomy of the Chinatown sweatshops. They are exploited and oppressed to a certain degree by the somewhat paternalistic contractors and even more by the manufacturers. These women work extremely long hours for extremely low wages rather than not work at all. The workshop conditions of the Chinatown garment factories are among the most wretched and deplorable in this country, by any standards. And yet, when the unions (ILGWU) tried to organize the Chinese women garment workers, they were met with resistance. Even when the Chinatown garment factories were unionized, only minor changes in the oppressive sweatshop conditions were noted and the exploitation continued. This dismal failure of the unions leads one to ask: what are the alternatives which may help alleviate the sweatshop conditions in Chinatown? Several alternative models presented below are not intended, by themselves, to solve the social ills of the Chinatown sweatshops, but are intended to give some food for thought and possible action.

One possible alternative is the unionization of all the Chinese sweatshops in Chinatown under the ILGWU. This has already been discussed. The advantages of joining the union are numerous (e.g., benefits, minimum wage, increased standard of living), although they are more theoretical than real. At the present time, the same oppressive and exploitative sweatshop conditions exist in union shops as in nonunion shops. The unionization of a few Chinese shops has had relatively little impact on the large downtown manufacturers. The unions have been attacking the symptom instead of the cause. If the unions really have the interests of the Chinese women workers in mind, if they want to unionize all the sweatshops of Chinatown and make the union a viable source of power in negotiations between manufacturer and shops, and if they want to improve the conditions of the workers, their focus of attack should not be on the Chinatown sweatshops, which are but pawns in the garment industry game, but on the source of the exploitation and the major force in the perpetuation of the sweatshop situation, the manufacturers. Unionization of the manufacturer would compel the contractors to organize, a prospect many contractors find agreeable. Furthermore, it has been noted that the unionization of some Chinatown garment shops occurred when their manufacturers, from whom they receive contracts, were unionized. But the manufacturers resist unionization and for good reason. By so doing, they can continue to exploit the cheap labor pool of Chinese labor in Chinatown (East West, 1967). However, it should be noted that an alternative of the manufacturers to unionization is to relocate in regions more tolerant of management interests.

A second possible alternative to the present-day garment situation is the cooperative garment factory, where the workers have a say in decisions concerning all phases of the business, from buying the material to the distribution of the finished product to retail outlets. In this way, there would be less alienation among the workers. By having a collective ownership of the means of production, this would mean an end to exploitation. But however idealistic the cooperative garment factory is, it is plagued with problems which will lead to only limited success. Because of its small size, it cannot compete with other manufacturers in buying fabrics at wholesale prices. It has the additional problem of finding retail outlets for its products. Furthermore, operating under a capitalistic system, it must compete with other contractors and with the entire economic system of the sewing industry. Li, et al. (1975:38-39) conclude:

> Since we live under capitalism, the dominant outlook is not cooperation, but individual competition. Therefore without a sense of class consciousness initially, workers in a cooperative have a tendency to compete with one another just as they would in a small shop.

This is not to say that the establishment of cooperative garment factories should be discouraged. It is important not only for the development of political consciousness among Chinese garment workers but also in providing a model to show that the sweatshops need not necessarily be exploitative.

A third possible alternative model to alleviate the sweatshop conditions of Chinatown may be for the Chinese to organize a union of their own. As history teaches, the Chinese did form guilds when they were excluded from participation in American labor unions, and these guilds were quite successful in promoting equitable returns for their labor and satisfactory working conditions. Furthermore, unlike the present union sweatshop situation, these Chinese unions would be built upon the rank-and-file members as opposed to a union membership drive promoted by "outsiders" and making workers union members in one sweep. The advantages of this situation are that the Chinese women garment workers would have a greater understanding of what union membership means and, hence, make the unions a more viable factor in negotiations; that there would be greater trust and solidarity among the Chinese contractors and workers due to the interaction of class and ethnic factors; and that these unions would be more responsive to the particular need of slow workers or the elderly. However, there are countervailing forces which act against the development or success of Chinese unions. One is that such a development may generate conflict with the ILGWU, which may consider this development to be in conflict with their own interests. Furthermore, the development of Chinese unions might also result in the resurfacing of the anti-Chinese sentiment for which unions have been notorious in the past.

In sum, exactly which of the three alternative models to the present-day sweatshop situation is most feasible and will have the greatest impact in alleviating the plight of the Chinese women garment worker is hard to judge. It may be that none of the alternative models is feasible or that some combination of these and other alternatives is necessary. Whatever the case, as the situation presently stands, the Chinese women garment workers continue to be oppressed and exploited.

One last comment. Though the particular focus of this paper is on the Chinese women garment workers in Chinatown(s) throughout the United States, its implications are far-reaching. With very few modifications this paper on the plight of Chinese garment workers in the sweatshops of Chinatown is also a paper on the sweatshop conditions and plight of the Mexican garment workers in the barrio of East Los Angeles or the Puerto Rican workers in Manhattan's Spanish Harlem, or of any worker involved in the peripheral sweatshop subeconomy. The characters and the places may vary, but the story of oppression and exploitation remains the same.

ACKNOWLEDGMENTS

This research was partially supported by a U.S. Public Health Service Grant (MH-15497-01) and a National Institute for Child Health and Human Development Grant (1-R01-HD-14337-01). I would like to thank Ida Harper Simpson and Richard L. Simpson for their valuable comments and critiques of earlier drafts. I would also like to thank Kei Tin Wong and Edith Jung Wong for their support.

REFERENCES

Action for Boston Community Development, Inc.
   1970   The Chinese in Boston, 1970. Mimeographed. Boston: ABCD.
Buck, Rinker
   1979   "The new sweatshops: a penny for your collar." New York Magazine (January 29).
Chinatown Study Group
   1969   Chinatown Report: 1969. New York: East Asian Institute, Columbia University.
Chinese Digest
   1938   April Issue. Pp. 54 in Thomas Chinn (ed.), History of the Chinese in America. San Francisco: Chinese Historical Society of America.
Chin, Rocky
   1971   "New York Chinatown today: community in crisis." Pp. 282-295 in Amy Tachiki (ed.), Roots: An Asian American Reader. Los Angeles: Continental Graphics.
Chinn, Thomas W.
   1971   A History of the Chinese in California, A Syllabus. San Francisco: Chinese Historical Society of America.
Chiu, Ping
   1967   Chinese Labor in California, 1850-1880. Madison: The State Historical Society of Wisconsin.
Chow, Christopher
   1967   "Still another face to Chinatown." East West (August 23).
Conant, Jane E.
   1969a "Unrest stirs Chinatown sweatshops." San Francisco Examiner (August 16).

1969b "The seaming side of Chinatown." San Francisco Examiner (August 17).
1969c "Coolie labor pours from Hong Kong." San Francisco Examiner (August 18).
East West
    1967 "Union, a dirty word or..." (August 1).
    1969 "Twenty seamstresses unpaid for months." (December 17).
Gibson, Otis
    1877 The Chinese in America. Cincinnati: Hitchcock and Walden.
Goodman, Charles
    1948 The Location of Fashion Industries; With Special Reference to the California Apparel Market. Ann Arbor: University of Michigan Press.
Hittell, John S.
    1882 The Commerce and Industries of the Pacific Coast of North America. San Francisco: A.L. Brancroft.
Kung, S.W.
    1962 Chinese in American Life. Seattle: University of Washington Press.
Lan, Dean
    1971 "Chinatown sweatshops." Amerasia Journal 1(3):40-57.
Lee, Rose Hum
    1960 The Chinese in the United States of America. Hong Kong: Hong Kong University Press.
Li, Peggy, Buck Wong, and Fong Kwan.
    1975 Garment Industry in Los Angeles Chinatown 1973-74. Working paper of the UCLA Asian American Studies Center. Los Angeles: University of California.
Light, Ivan, and Charles Choy Wong
    1975 "Protest of work: dilemmas of the tourist industry in American Chinatowns." American Journal of Sociology 80 (6):1342-1368.
Lim, Stanley
    1969 "Analysis of Chinatown garment workers survey questionnaire." A report submitted to the Employment Committee of the Human Rights Commission, October 23.
Loomis, A.S.
    1869 "How our Chinamen are employed." Overland Monthly March: 231-240.
Lyman, Stanford
    1974 Chinese Americans. New York: Random House.
Nee, Victor G., and Brett de Bary Nee
    1973 Longtime Californ': A Documentary Study of an American Chinatown. New York: Pantheon.
Overend, William
    1978 "The Chinatown tourists don't see." Los Angeles Times (July 30).
San Francisco Board of Supervisors
    1903 San Francisco Municipal Report 1902-1903. San Francisco.
San Francisco Chinese Community Citizens' Survey and Fact Finding Committee
    1969 Report of the San Francisco Chinese Community Citizens' Survey and Fact Finding Committee. San Francisco: H. J. Carle and Sons.
San Francisco Morning Call
    1873 May 27. Pp. 53 in Thomas Chinn (ed.), A History of the Chinese in California. San Francisco: Chinese Historical Society of America.
Seward, George F.
    1881 Chinese Immigration, in Its Social Economic Aspects. San Francisco: Edward Bosqui and Company.
Sung, Betty Lee
    1967 Mountain of Gold. New York: Macmillan.
    1975 Chinese American Manpower and Employment. Report to Manpower Administration. Washington, D.C.: United States Department of Labor.

Tan, Mely Giok-lan
  1971   The Chinese in the United States. Taipei: Oriental Culture.
United States Bureau of the Census
  1973   1970 Census of Population. Subject Reports. Japanese, Chinese, and Filipinos in the United States. PC(2)-1G. Washington, D.C: U.S. Government Printing Office.
United States Senate
  1877   Report of the Joint Special Committee to Investigate Chinese Immigration. 44th Congress, 2nd Session, 1876-1877. Senate Report 689. Washington, D.C.: U.S. Government Printing Office.
Wei Min She Labor Committee
  1974   Chinese Working People in America. San Francisco: United Front Press.
Wong, Ken
  1967a   "City hall Chinatown probe." East West (August 21).
  1967b   "War declared on sweat shops." East West (September 1).
  1967c   "Chinatown pic retouched." East West (September 21).
Wong, Morrison G., and Charles Hirschman
  1983   "The new Asian immigrants." In William C. McReady (ed.), Culture, Ethnicity, and Identity: Current Issues in Research. New York: Academic Press. Forthcoming.
Yee, Min
  1970   "Chinatown in crisis." Newsweek (February 23).

Research Annuals in SOCIOLOGY

Consulting Editor for Sociology

Samuel B. Bacharach
Department of Sociology and School of Industrial and Labor Relations
Cornell University

Advances in Early Education and Day Care
Series Editor: Sally Kilmer, *Bowling Green State University*

Advances in Health Economics and Health Services Research
(Volume 1 published as *Research in Health Economics*)
Series Editor: Richard M. Scheffler, *George Washington University*. Associate Series Editor: Louis F. Rossiter, *National Center for Health Services Research*

Advances in Special Education
Series Editor: Barbara K. Keogh, *University of California, Los Angeles*

Advances in Substance Abuse
Series Editor: Nancy K. Mello, *Harvard Medical School—McLean Hospital*

Comparative Social Research
Series Editor: Richard F. Tomasson, *The University of New Mexico.*

Current Perspectives in Social Theory
Series Editors: Scott G. McNall and Gary N. Howe, *University of Kansas*

Knowledge and Society: Studies in the Sociology of Culture Past and Present
(Volumes 1-2 published as *Research in the Sociology of Knowledge, Sciences and Art*)
Series Editors: Robert Alun Jones, *University of Illinois*
Henrika Kuklick, *University of Pennsylvania*

Perspectives in Organizational Sociology
Series Editor: Samuel B. Bacharach, *Cornell University*

Political Power and Social Theory
Series Editor: Maurice Zeitlin, *University of California, Los Angeles*

Research in Community and Mental Health
Series Editor: Roberta G. Simmons, *University of Minnesota*

Research in Economic Anthropology
Series Editor: George Dalton, *Northwestern University*

Research in Law, Deviance and Social Control
(Volumes 1-3 published as *Research in Law and Sociology*)
Series Editors: Rita J. Simon, *University of Illinois* and Steven Spitzer, *Suffolk University—Boston*

Research in Political Economy
Series Editor: Paul Zarembka, *State University of New York, Buffalo*

Research in Race and Ethnic Relations
Series Editors: Cora B. Marrett, *University of Wisconsin,* and Cheryl Leggon, *University of Chicago*

Research in Social Movements, Conflicts and Change
Series Editor: Louis Kriesberg, *Syracuse University*

Research in Social Problems and Public Policy
Series Editor: Michael Lewis, *University of Massachusetts*

Research in Social Stratification and Mobility
Series Editors: Donald J. Treiman, *National Academy of Sciences,* and Robert V. Robinson, *Indiana University*

Research in Sociology of Education and Socialization
Series Editor: Alan C. Kerckhoff, *Duke University*

Research in the Interweave of Social Roles
Series Editor: Helena Z. Lopata, *Loyola University of Chicago*

Research in the Sociology of Health Care
Series Editor: Julius A. Roth, *University of California, Davis*

Research in the Sociology of Work
Series Editors: Ida Harper Simpson, *Duke University,* and Richard L. Simpson, *University of North Carolina, Chapel Hill*

Studies in Communications
Series Editor: Thelma McCormack, *York University*

Studies in Symbolic Interaction
Series Editor: Norman K. Denzin, *University of Illinois*

Please inquire for detailed brochure on each series.

JAI PRESS INC.